D1555048

Metaphor in Context

Metaphor in Context   Josef Stern

A Bradford Book
The MIT Press
Cambridge, Massachusetts
London, England

This book was set in Times New Roman on '3B2' by Asco Typesetters, Hong Kong, and was printed and bound in the United States of America.

Library of Congress Cataloging-in-Publication Data

Stern, Josef (Josef Judah)
 Metaphor in context / Josef Stern.
    p.   cm.
 "A Bradford book."
 Includes bibliographical references and index.
 ISBN 0-262-19439-2 (alk. paper)
 1. Metaphor. 2. Semantics. I. Title.
P325.5.M47 S74 2000
401'.43—dc21   00-040221

For Cheryl, my Juliet

Contents

Preface

The last twenty-five years have witnessed an explosion of books, anthologies, and journal articles on the subject of metaphor. Exactly what ignited this intellectual outburst is anyone's guess. It has gone off not only among philosophers, whose fascination with metaphor was first sparked by Aristotle, and among literary theorists, metaphor's native consumers, but on every intellectual front: among linguists, psychologists, anthropologists, historians of science, art historians, and theologians. What was once a specialized topic in rhetoric and poetics has now also come to be fertile ground for interdisciplinary research. Yet when we survey the plethora of offspring of all this crossbreeding, it is difficult not to wonder about their species. What about metaphor are all these theories of metaphor theories of? What problem(s) posed by metaphor are they trying to solve?

We might begin by distinguishing two main kinds of interest that have drawn thinkers to metaphor over the course of its long history. (At this point I'll retreat to philosophy, the discipline I know best, but most of what I say also applies elsewhere.) The first of these interests is older and, since the Romantics and Nietzsche, it has also achieved a certain prominence. For thinkers of this persuasion metaphor is an "intrinsically interesting" phenomenon, something on the order of human love or a complex moral problem or the origin of the physical universe, subjects that do, or should, command our direct attention. Some philosophers find this intrinsic interest in metaphor because they take it to be exemplary of human creativity, or the fundamental mode of expression in thought and language, or a window into the imagination. Others view a metaphor as the basic unit, or work, of art or of poetry, and still others as a central tool of scientific explanation or as an essential element of theological discourse. In short, for everyone with this first kind of interest, metaphor belongs up there with The Big Questions. Mark Johnson puts the view well: "the examination of metaphor is one of the more fruitful ways of approaching fundamental logical, epistemological, and ontological issues central to any philosophical understanding of human experience."[1]

Thinkers with the second kind of interest do not find any such intrinsic philosophical value in metaphor, or at least no more than they find in, say, slips of the tongue or hyperbole. These phenomena may raise interesting empirical or descriptive questions but they sound no deep philosophical chords. Nonetheless metaphor *is* interesting for these philosophers (as well as linguists and cognitive scientists) because it bears on other issues or questions that are themselves intrinsically interesting. Metaphor excites these inquirers for the same reason "exotic" phenomena draw physicists: because of their admittedly remote but potentially significant implications for general explanatory principles that are of primary interest to the field.

To draw a comparison closer to home, consider the interest that certain oddly ungrammatical strings hold for contemporary theoretical linguists, strings like 'We try John to win' or 'Himself left'. As phenomena in their own right, these strings should have no intrinsic interest: They are never uttered and, therefore, they need no explanation. However, against a theoretical background they stand out in virtue of the particular ways in which they are ungrammatical. The bizarre ways in which they are deviant have the power to confirm or falsify hypotheses concerning abstract principles of grammar, which, in turn, do explain the grammatical properties of strings that *are* uttered and, therefore, call out for explanation.

In recent years metaphor has assumed an analogous kind of *non-intrinsic* interest for philosophers—as well as linguists and cognitive scientists—developing semantic theories of natural language. As increasing attention has been paid to the nuances, complications, and apparently irregular aspects of natural language, metaphor has been one case that has tested and tried our ability to give precise, systematic characterizations of the ordinary notions we use to describe its ordinary functioning, notions like meaning (or change of meaning), truth, or significance. Suppose, for example, we distinguish between an individual's knowledge of language—including his knowledge of semantic rules that assign interpretations to strings of words—and his ability to *use* that knowledge to make utterances with other meanings and effects. On which side of the divide should metaphor fall? If metaphorical interpretations of strings are not predicted by specific proposed semantic rules, what conclusion should we draw? That the fault lies with the semantic rules? Or that the failure is proof that metaphor does not fall in semantics and language proper? That it is instead just one among many ways of using (or misusing) our knowledge of language? The conclusion we draw will obviously carry serious implications for our background semantic theory. Within such a theoretical context, metaphor acquires important albeit derivative interest.

I do not intend to fall into the trap of trying to classify all philosophers who have written on metaphor into one or the other of these two categories of interest. For one thing, the categories are not mutually exclusive. For another, there is the danger that one might be tempted to identify philosophers with the first kind of intrinsic interest as the "friends" of metaphor and those with a derivative interest as its "enemies." As much as these labels make any sense at all, friends and enemies of metaphor are to be found among thinkers with either kind of interest. Hobbes and Locke, two of the greatest detractors of metaphor in its history, no less than Nietzsche and Coleridge, two of its greatest inflators, share an intrinsic interest in metaphor. And who is to say whether someone who takes metaphor to be a use of language rather than a type of semantic interpretation is a "friend" or "enemy"?[2]

So long as we heed these warnings not to abuse the distinction, it can be helpful to know which kind of interest motivates an author if only because it will put the problems and topics he addresses in perspective. In this essay, for example, I am guided in the first place by a derivative interest of the second kind. Throughout the last two decades' abundant writing on metaphor, one assumption has been typically taken for granted (although it is occasionally given a supportive argument and, less occasionally, challenged): that metaphor lies outside, if not in opposition to, our received conceptions of semantics and grammar, semantics in the classical sense of the Frege-Tarski tradition and grammar as linguists conceive it as a speaker's knowledge of language. Some authors (e.g., Jerry Sadock, Paul Grice, John Searle, Robert Fogelin, Ted Cohen, Daniel Sperber, and Dierde Wilson) think that we must *supplement* semantics with theories of pragmatics, conversation, or speech acts in order to deal with metaphor. Others (e.g., Donald Davidson, Richard Rorty, David Cooper) think that the significance of a metaphor being a use of language is that it resists *any* kind of general theoretical explanation, semantic or pragmatic; at best, they hold, we can tell detailed but ad hoc stories for individual utterances of metaphor. And for yet a third group (George Lakoff and his school, and Paul Ricoeur), the fact that metaphor lies outside the purview of classical semantics is one more example of the poverty of the tradition, one more symptom that what is really needed is nothing less than a radical revision—or wholesale rejection—of classical semantics, which, they charge, was framed on the model of literal language with a built-in bias against "nonscientific" or "nonmathematical" language.[3] Despite the many differences between these views, they all assume (generally without argument) that metaphor cannot be explained by or within semantics. By the same token, it is also taken for granted that metaphor has little if anything to teach us about semantic theory. One aim of this book is to challenge these two assumptions: I hope to show how semantic theory can constructively inform our understanding of metaphor and how metaphor can illuminate semantic theory in general and the role of context in theories of meaning in particular.

To be more specific, I am concerned primarily with one question: Given the (more or less) received conception of the form and goals of semantic theory, does metaphorical interpretation, in whole or part, fall within its scope? Or in more material terms: What (if anything) does a speaker-hearer know as part of his semantic competence when he knows the interpretation of a metaphor? These questions are not entirely new to discussions of metaphor, but using the theoretical apparatus of current semantics we can bring powerful and relatively well-tuned explanatory tools to bear on them. For example, it is often said that a defining characteristic of a metaphor is that its interpretation "depends" on its literal meaning, but what is the nature of that "dependence"? Is it a kind of functionality and, if so, is it semantic or pragmatic? And if the metaphorical interpretation of an expression "depends" on its literal meaning, then the expression must still "have" its literal meaning. In what sense? And how is the literal meaning that the expression has, even while it is interpreted metaphorically, different from its metaphorical interpretation or meaning? As these questions are usually formulated, terms like "meaning," "interpretation," and "dependency" are left in a vague, unexplicated, pretheoretical state, making it almost impossible to give them definite answers. But the pay-off need not be only for metaphor. If we can show that features heretofore thought to be peculiar to metaphor are instances of more general semantic regularities that hold throughout natural language, we can also enrich the explanatory power of our general semantic theories.

In addition to these semantic problems raised by metaphor, I shall also try to throw some light on a spectrum of questions that have heretofore been addressed mainly by writers concerned with metaphor as an intrinsically interesting phenomenon, especially questions concerning the cognitive significance of a metaphor. However, my approach will differ from that of most previous metaphor theorists who have taken these problems to be sui generis to metaphor. Instead I shall try to show how, by employing our semantic theory, these puzzling aspects of the behavior of metaphors can be given a diagnosis, or description, that does not deny their distinctiveness, yet subsumes them under the same rubric as other semantic facts that hold for nonmetaphorical language.

I cannot, of course, simply assume, as if it needs no defense, that metaphor lies within the scope of semantics. But the best defense is sometimes a good offense. Although I shall address various objections to the semantic status of metaphor in chapters 2, 7, and 8, my strongest evidence will consist in the semantic explanations I propose as working hypotheses. Yet, I should emphasize that, despite my sympathetic stance toward classical semantics, I do not mean to suggest that I think that the specific claims of the current semantic theories I employ are the final whole truth. Along with (I would imagine) most contemporary philosophers of language, I readily concede that we are still at the very beginning of our understanding of natural language and that our available semantic theories are far from finished. This is especially true for our theories of demonstratives and the semantic treatment of context—those parts of semantics that will matter most for our account. To the degree to which my account of metaphor rests on these notions, it is also no more than a first approximation to a final answer. It would be better, then, to view this essay not as an attempt to give a *theory* of metaphor but, more modestly, as an attempt to "map out" the semantic topography of metaphor. Even if all I accomplish is to *locate* metaphor relative to some of the other landmarks of current semantics or, a bit better, if I persuade you that the attempt to *situate* metaphor in relation to current semantics is a project worth pursuing, this essay will have succeeded.

The proximate stimulus for this book was the 1974 Linguistics Institute at University of Massachusetts, Amherst where I took a course on pragmatics with Robert Stalnaker who introduced me both to his own seminal essays on presuppositions and to David Kaplan's (then unpublished) "Dthat." My debt to the writings of Stalnaker and Kaplan will be obvious to the reader. Kaplan's work in particular has been a rich source of stimulation for my own philosophical imagination, and I hope this application of his semantics for demonstratives to metaphor will be a small contribution to his own program.

It was around the same time that I noticed the failure of substitutivity of (literally) co-extensive expressions interpreted metaphorically and, when I returned to Columbia from Amherst in the fall of 1974, the basic idea of this book—to treat metaphors as demonstratives—occurred to me. My first sustained attempt to work out the idea was my 1979 Columbia dissertation, written under the direction of Charles Parsons, Sidney Morgenbesser, and James Higginbotham. I am deeply grateful to all three of them, not only for their help with the thesis, but for a superb philosophical education in general. I should also single out Jim Higginbotham who first taught me philosophy of language and linguistics and then lavished endless hours on the dissertation, generously sharing his own ideas as well as criticisms. From that same era, I also want to thank for discussions and comments the late Monroe Beardsley, Merrie Bergmann, Arthur Danto, Robert Fiengo, Richard Kuhns, Isaac Levi, Robert Matthews, Georges Rey, Israel Scheffler, Robert Schwartz, Ted Talbot, and Ellen Winner.

Since arriving at the University of Chicago in 1979, Muhammad Ali Khalidi, Leonard Linsky, the late Jim McCauley, Ian Mueller, Jerry Sadock, Joel Snyder, and Bill Tait have offered valuable feedback and encouragement. A number of conversations with Donald Davidson, who was still at Chicago when I first arrived, also helped me appreciate his position better. I am especially indebted to Ted Cohen for numerous examples and ideas, some of which are even acknowledged in this book. A former teacher of mine at Columbia and then my senior colleague at Chicago, Howard Stein has been a model of intellectual and moral standards I can only attempt to emulate. According to the rabbis, we learn the most from our students; in particular I wish to thank Don Breen, Jesse Prinz, Gabriela Sakamoto, and Lauren Tillinghast for their critical reactions in and beyond the classroom.

Much of the present manuscript was written in Jerusalem, and I have benefited from the comments of many audiences in Israel and from the hospitality of the department of philosophy of the Hebrew University. I am grateful for discussions with Gilead Bar-Elli, Jonathan Berg, the late Yael Cohen, Asa Kasher, Igal Kvart, Malka Rapaport, Susan Rothstein, Ellen Spolsky, and Mark Steiner. Sidney Morgenbesser first told me to seek out Avishai Margalit while I was writing my dissertation, and in addition to everything I have learned from his own papers on metaphor, he has been one of my best critics since then. Another debt I owe Avishai is that he first introduced me to the Library of the Van Leer Institute, a remarkable oasis of philosophical composure in Jerusalem where the penultimate drafts of this book were composed during 1995–1997.

During its last stages of preparation, the manuscript benefited from the criticism of Sam Glucksberg and Boaz Keysar (on ch. 5) and several referees for MIT Press. In particular I want to thank Mark McCullagh for very helpful comments especially on chapters 1 and 3 and Roger White for criticisms of chapters 2, 5, and 6; both significantly improved the manuscript. It wasn't, unfortunately, until very late in the writing that I learned of White's own recent book on metaphor. Nonetheless I have tried to incorporate responses to a number of White's concerns—as well as shamelessly drawing on his impressive knowledge of Shakespeare and literature for examples. My thanks, too, to Amy Brand, Carolyn Gray Anderson, and especially Judy Feldmann of MIT Press for all their help and advice in the final production of this book. Last of all, I have benefited from written and oral exchanges in recent years with Murat Aydede, David Hills, Michael Leezenberg, Patty Nogales, and Francois Recanati.

I am most grateful to various foundations who translated their faith in this project into essential material support: the Giles Whiting Foundation and the Lawrence Chamberlain Fellowship while writing my dissertation in 1977–1979; the Lady Davis Foundation, for a postdoctoral fellowship in 1984–1985; the American Council of Learned Societies, for a fellowship in 1988–1989; the Chicago Humanities Institute of The University of Chicago, for a quarter's fellowship in 1991–1992; and the National Endowment for the Humanities, for a fellowship in 1996–1997. I would also like to thank the Division of the Humanities, The University of Chicago, for its support during my research leaves and especially Stuart Tave, Dean in 1988–1989, for his encouragement.

In Hebrew, *aharon aharon haviv*: Last is dearest. I want to thank my parents, Kurt Stern and the late Florence Sherman Stern, for their continual love and support. David Stern, my unliteral identical other half, constantly mistaken for me just as I am for him, has graciously agreed to accept full responsibility for all blunders in what follows. From Amitai, Rafi, and Yoni, my own Stern Gang, I have learned how many metaphors resist literal expression; my thanks to them also for use of the computer in their spare time. Finally, not only can't literal words express what I owe Cheryl Newman for the love and devotion that made this book possible and continue to make most everything else in my life worthwhile; even metaphor can't say it all.

A final disclaimer: Any resemblance between characters mentioned in examples and actual persons, living or dead, is entirely coincidental.

Sources

I wish to thank the following for permission to reprint revised selections of previously published papers:

"Metaphor as Demonstrative." From *The Journal of Philosophy* 82 (1985): 677–710. Used by permission of the editor of journal.

"Metaphor without Mainsprings: A Rejoinder to Elgin and Scheffler." From *The Journal of Philosophy* 85 (1988): 427–438. Used by permission of the editor of journal.

"What Metaphors Do Not Mean." From *Midwest Studies in Philosophy* (volume XVI): *Philosophy and the Arts*, edited by Peter A. French, Theodore E. Uehling, and Howard K. Wettstein. © 1991 by University of Notre Dame Press. Used by permission of the publisher.

"Metaphors in Pictures." From *Philosophical Topics* 25/1 (1997): 255–293. Used by permission of the editor of journal.

Chapter 1
Metaphorical Competence

I Knowledge *that* Metaphor, Knowledge *of* Metaphor, and Knowledge *by* Metaphor

Suppose that Romeo and Juliet actually existed and did everything Shakespeare says they did.[1] And suppose that Romeo uttered (1)

(1) Juliet is the sun

in a context exactly like that depicted in the respective act and scene of Shakespeare's play. What did Romeo say in uttering (1)? How should we interpret his utterance? And what does one—both Romeo and his audience—know when one knows the interpretation of (1)?

A first stab at describing Romeo's utterance might go like this. Romeo, we safely assume, knows the difference between a human and the sun; hence, he cannot intend to say what his words literally mean: that the human Juliet is the celestial sun. Instead his utterance should be interpreted in some other nonliteral way. What he has said under this alternative mode of interpretation—given what we know about Romeo, Juliet, and the sun in that context—is, say, that Juliet is exemplary and peerless, and/or that she is worthy of worship and adoration, and/or that he cannot live without her nourishing attention. Let's call these "metaphorical interpretations" of the utterance of (1).

Tasks of metaphorical interpretation like this are legion in everyday life as well as in the more sophisticated contexts of literature and poetry. As speakers and interpreters we perform them with the same naturalness, ease, and sense of competent comfortableness with which we interpret other kinds of utterances. Most (though not all) of the time we succeed in interpreting even the most novel and imaginative metaphors without special difficulty (even when they require more effort). Explaining this ordinary achievement, however, is a task of a different order for the theorist of language.

Two comments will help clarify the character of our task. First, let's abstract away from *how* speakers and hearers respectively understand an utterance, the physiological and psychological abilities they employ in their processing, production, and perception of (metaphorical) speech. Instead let's focus on *what* they each know when they understand an utterance and its interpretation. If and when they succeed in communicating, there must be common understanding, an interpretation they both grasp. Our task is to identify that common object of knowledge and its structure.

Second, the word "interpretation" in popular usage is used to refer to a mixed bag of contents; in the case of metaphor, there is additional controversy over the particular contents that belong in the bag. (Indeed this book might be read as an attempt to argue for one particular kind of content to be included among those for metaphor.) For now, I shall simply stipulate what I mean by the term; the proof will follow in the eating. I demarcate my notion of interpretation along three dimensions.

(i) A metaphorical interpretation is propositional: it is *what is said* on an occasion of utterance, its informational content (leaving it open for now whether this consists in truth-conditions or something else).[2] Although many nonpropositional elements—feelings, attitudes, images, and other associations—may also be "conveyed" (to introduce a neutral term) by the utterance of a metaphor, I do not include them within its interpretation.

(ii) Like any utterance, a metaphor typically conveys more information than its interpretation; one knows that the speaker is speaking metaphorically, in English, addressing someone, in a tone expressing a particular emotional attitude, etc. Of these various conveyed pieces of information, the interpretation is the information that is either semantically encoded in or determined by the utterance relative to specified contextual parameters. (I spell out these latter notions in chs. 3–4.) In more familiar philosophical terminology, I am concerned with the proposition *expressed* by the utterance of the metaphor in its context of utterance. This semantic interpretation is not "everything" a metaphor "means"; sometimes it is not even what is most interesting about the metaphor. But whenever we understand an utterance, I assume that a central part of our understanding consists in knowing its propositional content—and the same holds for utterances of metaphors.

(iii) Among the propositional interpretations of the utterance of a metaphor, some but not others may be intended by the speaker. Let's say that an interpretation that meets the first two conditions is a *possible* interpretation of an utterance even when it is not what its speaker intended, had in mind, or occurrently entertained on the occasion. Of course, when we ask for "the" meaning of a metaphor, we are usually asking for the speaker's intended interpretation, the interpretation he meant, not simply a possible interpretation. However, what it is possible for a speaker to intend by a given metaphor depends on what it is possible to express with it. It is with all those possible interpretations that I am concerned, disregarding the additional teleological, intentional condition built into our ordinary usage.

For now, then, let's assume that at least some utterances containing expressions used metaphorically express possible propositional interpretations. The task of this book is to answer the question: What does a speaker-hearer[3] know when he or she knows such an interpretation of a metaphor?

This question should be broken down into two subquestions. But before turning to them, we should distinguish a third question that has been widely discussed in the metaphor literature although I shall pursue it here only briefly. This is the question of how one knows *that* an utterance is a metaphor. What are the conditions, heuristics, clues, cues, trains of reasoning, or steps followed by speaker-hearers by which they identify or recognize particular utterances as metaphors, rather than as literal utterances or as nonliteral utterances of other kinds or as strings of nonsense sounds? Let's call this the "recognition" question.

Once upon a time (and in some quarters still nowadays), many philosophers would have responded to the recognition question with necessary and/or sufficient conditions that signal and even "warrant" the judgment that an utterance is to be interpreted metaphorically.[4] The received story went like this: (i) Every utterance is presumed to be literal until proven otherwise, that is, unless it is "impossible" (in a sense that usually goes unexplained) to interpret it literally. (ii) A class of utterances *M* (for instance, our own example (1)), taken at their literal face value, are either grammatically deviant, semantically anomalous, explicitly or implicitly self-contradictory, conceptually absurd, nonsensical, category mistakes, sortal violations, pragmatically inappropriate, obviously false, or so obviously true that no one would have reason to utter them. Hence, each utterance in *M*, were it interpreted literally, would be "deviant" in one or another of these ways (choose your own favorite). (iii) Presented with one of M, the hearer recognizes that it is "impossible" to interpret it literally and (iv), therefore, identifies it as a metaphor. (v) M, it is also assumed, contains all (and only those) utterances actually identified as metaphors.

Despite the venerable tradition of writers on metaphor who explicitly or tacitly endorse this account, it is subject to fatal descriptive and explanatory problems. Of course, many metaphors happen to be, as a matter of fact, literally "deviant" in one or the other of these ways. But there are also countless counterexamples to the conditions of (ii), counterexamples that are exceptional only insofar as philosophers have ignored (or repressed) them for so long. These counterexamples have perfectly good literal as well as metaphorical interpretations, and some are even "twice-true," that is, true in the very same contexts *both* when they are interpreted metaphorically and when they are interpreted literally.[5] A few examples:

(a) Mao Tse-tung's comment, "A revolution is not a matter of inviting people to dinner."

(b) The caption on a photo of Japanese nuclear reaction plants (in a *Time* article on the pros and cons of nuclear power following Chernobyl): "Japan: the land of Hiroshima and Nagasaki feels it has no alternative."

(c) A description of a radical reinterpretation of "Endgame" for which Beckett sued the director: "Audiences today are accustomed to gospel versions of Sophocles or Paleozoic resettings of Shakespeare. But Sophocles and Shakespeare live on Parnassus. Beckett lives in Paris" (*Time*, Jan. 21, 1985).

(d) "[H]e was esteemed by the whole college of physicians at that time, as more knowing in matters of noses, than anyone who had ever taken them in hand" (Lawrence Sterne).[6]

(e) "Two roads diverged in a wood, and I—
    I took the one less traveled by,
    And that has made all the difference" (Robert Frost).

(f) An article on the merger of the two Wall Street investment houses Morgan Stanley and Dean Witter begins with the simile/metaphor: "If Morgan Stanley is like a buffed pair of calf-skin oxfords, then Dean Witter is a comfortable pair of broken-in loafers." This is clearly figurative (and, as we shall see in ch. 5, a good example of a metaphor schema or family). However, the following (italicized) clauses in the same article are metaphorical (or a mix of metaphor and synecdoche) *and* literal in the same context:

> Those bridges [connecting the two firms] will connect vastly different cultures. Morgan Stanley's senior executives, *in their tasseled Gucci loafers and Armani suits*, make many millions of dollars a year as they jet around the world to do deals with government ministers and business tycoons. Their counterparts at Dean Witter, meanwhile, *favor Brooks Brothers suits and Dexter shoes and shuttle around on suburban highways*, where even the more successful earn at most several hundred thousand dollars a year hawking mostly plain vanilla mutual funds, stocks and bonds to Main Street America. (*International Herald Tribune*, Feb. 10, 1997)

(g) An example where an expression that could be taken either (both) literally or (and) metaphorically is to be taken literally *rather than* metaphorically: The publisher of the *Village Voice*, David Schnidermann, was reported to have said: "I want the *Voice* to be a journalistic player in this town and not a cute little thing from the '60s that amuses everyone from time to time with *its own internal food fights*" (my emphasis). Since we would naturally take the italicized phrase to be a metaphor, the reporter immediately added in parentheses: "He was not speaking metaphorically. An angry *Voice* writer once threw potato salad at the Letters Editor" (*International Herald Tribune*, Feb. 21, 1997, p. 22).

(h) "Man, after all, is not a tree, and humanity is not a forest" (Levinas 1990, 23).[7]

From a simply descriptive perspective, these counterexamples demonstrate that the received account that relies on some kind of deviance condition cannot be the whole story. Furthermore, even if some version of the deviance condition were satisfied, its explanatory significance is not obvious. At most the deviance would explain why the sentence is *not* taken literally, not why it *is* interpreted metaphorically, a point that requires further explanation because a single string frequently admits alternative nonmetaphorical (but nonliteral) as well as metaphorical interpretations.[8]

There is also a deeper difficulty with the received story. The deviance account proceeds on the presumption that every utterance is first interpreted literally. Following a serial or linear model of processing, the speaker-hearer turns to a nonliteral interpretation only after the literal interpretation has been eliminated. However, it is equally possible—and we now possess confirming evidence for this alternative—that both literal and nonliteral interpretations are processed and evaluated in parallel or simultaneously. Among such parallel alternatives, the preferred interpretation is the one that is most *accessible* (where accessibility is itself context relative) rather than the one that is most literal.[9] Such a parallel-processing model is also indirectly supported by the observation that the criteria we use to select a metaphorical (or any other kind of nonliteral) interpretation over a *literal* one cannot be sharply distinguished from the varied criteria we use to select *among* alternative *non*literal interpretations of one utterance. Just as there is no one condition in the latter case, there is no reason to think that there is a single necessary and/or sufficient condition that overrules the literal for the metaphorical. Adherents of the grammatical deviance condition narrowly focus on the limiting case where the metaphorical interpretation is the *only possible* interpretation of the utterance. But their tunnel vision obscures the fact that we may select one over another interpretation because it is the *best* (or better) rather than the *only* candidate. And judgments about the *best X* typically depend on multiple balancing factors rather than necessary and/or sufficient conditions. Moreover, among these factors it is not the actual syntactic and semantic properties of the sentence uttered that matter the most, but the speaker-hearer's beliefs and presuppositions about those properties as well as about the purpose and setting of the utterance. These factors make metaphor identifications more like judgment calls with no single determinate answer than like warranted judgments.

Jonathan Culler gives us a good example of the subtle interplay and unresolved indeterminateness of metaphor recognition on a parallel-processing model. When we read the sentence in *Hamlet*, "Look, the morn in russet mantle clad Walks o'er the dew of yon eastern hill," we face multiple interpretive possibilities: Either we can assume "that in the world of this play (which does, after all, contain ghosts) morn is a figure that walks over hills; we could posit that Horatio is hallucinating (the ghost has been too much for him); or we could assume that the morning here behaves in accordance with our usual models of verisimilitude and that the false assertion that morning 'walks' should lead us to reflect on the qualities of dawn."[10] On the first two alternatives we take the sentence literally, as the description of something either fantastic or illusory; only on the last alternative is any expression in the sentence interpreted metaphorically (and there are obviously further metaphorical alternatives). In "deciding" on one of these interpretations, or in evaluating them, it should be noted that Culler does not appeal to any sentence-internal feature of the utterance (which, as a matter of fact, is deviant); rather, to varying degrees, he presupposes some (partial) understanding of what the interpretations of the sentence on its various literal and nonliteral alternatives *would* be. In any case, he concludes, there is no single unique kind of interpretation that we can confidently assign to the utterance once and for all. Depending on subtle preferences that will vary with the context, one or the other of the interpretations will be more or less appropriate.

Although we undoubtedly do exploit a wide range of contextual cues in this task of identification, it is essential to distinguish this role of the context in selecting among types of interpretations from its other role(s) in determining the content of an interpretation.[11] We can know *that* an utterance is to be interpreted metaphorically—rather than literally or in some other nonliteral way—without knowing *what* its metaphorical interpretation is (or would be), and, inversely, we can know what the metaphorical interpretation of an utterance *would* be even when we do not know whether it should be recognized as a metaphor on that occasion. The competence or abilities involved in the one task should be distinguished from those of the other. And for the remainder of this book, I'll be concerned with metaphorical interpretation rather than recognition.

Bracketing the recognition question, it will be helpful at this juncture to distinguish two subquestions about the interpretation of a metaphor:

1. What kind of knowledge, or ability, enables a speaker-hearer to interpret a metaphor? Is it part of one's general knowledge of language, a species of one's semantic knowledge, the same competence that underlies one's ability to interpret nonmetaphorical, "literal" language? Or is it, in whole or part, extralinguistic? And in the latter case, is it a yet-to-be-identified power that lies *beyond* the ordinary speaker's repertoire—a kind of genius, as Aristotle and perhaps Kant hinted? Or is it simply one among the many ordinary (though no less remarkable) abilities we all possess to *use* ordinary language in an indefinite number of ways?

2. What type of knowledge, cognitive content, or information—if any—does the utterance of a metaphor express or convey? Is it a kind of information or cognitive content that can only be communicated, or expressed, by a metaphor (the same or another)? Or could it be expressed equally well in literal language?

The first of these two subquestions addresses, I shall say, our knowledge *of* metaphor; the second, our knowledge *by* metaphor. Although the two questions are distinct, they are frequently conflated. Suppose a speaker's knowledge of metaphorical interpretation is part of his general linguistic competence, knowledge that includes a stock of concepts that constitute the linguistic or lexical meanings—literal meanings, if you will—both of the simple words in the language and—together with knowledge of their modes of composition—of the complex expressions that can be composed from those simple words. Then at least "in principle"—that is, assuming he possesses the literal vocabulary—any concept or meaning he is able to express with a metaphor should belong to the stock of linguistic, or literal, meanings he knows in virtue of his knowledge of language. Hence he should be able to express any of those concepts using some word(s) literally (even if more awkwardly). Thus the one position on our knowledge *of* metaphor would seem to entail a correlative position on our knowledge *by* metaphor.

On the other hand, if one's ability to interpret a metaphor is something other than, or in addition to, his general linguistic competence, it should at least be possible for the contents of at least some metaphors to be inexpressible by any literal expression. The extralinguistic ability underlying metaphorical interpretation might be common or singular but, in either case, there would be no reason to think—and, in some cases, perhaps good reason not to think—that it must be possible to put the meaning or concept expressed *by* the metaphor into literal words, words that express concepts or meanings the speaker-hearer knows simply in virtue of his knowledge of language. Again, the second position on our knowledge *of* metaphor would seem to entail a corresponding position on our knowledge *by* metaphor.

Following these lines of reasoning, our knowledge *of* metaphor and knowledge *by* metaphor go hand in hand. This, in turn, encourages the view that if our knowledge of metaphor is part of our general semantic competence, and everything the metaphor expresses is (in principle) expressible literally, the metaphorical mode of expression is cognitively dispensable. From which it is next argued that, because no literal paraphrase of a metaphor ever is adequate and the metaphorical mode of expression is manifestly not eliminable, our knowledge of metaphor is *not* part of our semantic competence. In this book I shall argue that this conclusion does not follow.[12] There is an essential component of a speaker's knowledge of metaphor that lies within his general semantic competence—although this knowledge is just a component and is never by itself sufficient to yield knowledge of a metaphorical interpretation (for which knowledge of context is also necessary). Furthermore, this semantic knowledge of metaphor is the same kind of competence that underlies a speaker's knowledge of a significant subclass of so-called literal language, namely, demonstratives and indexicals. Finally, it will turn out that this very same competence enables the speaker to express knowledge, or information, *by* a metaphor that is not expressed in literal paraphrases of the interpretation of the metaphor; indeed it is not expressed except through the metaphorical mode of expression of the metaphor.

The arguments for these complementary claims constitute the bulk of this book. But because it will require some preparatory work to lay out the account, in the next section I'll present an overview of the theory. This sketch will hopefully raise the reader above the trees so she can glimpse our destination despite the winding path through the dense forest that our argument will follow.

II   Metaphor and Context-dependence: A Quick Tour of the Argument

Consider again (!),

(1) Juliet is the sun,

its literal meaning L, and the various things it conveys (again, to use this as a neutral term) metaphorically about Juliet—that she is exemplary and peerless, worthy of worship and adoration, one without whose nourishing attention another cannot live, one who awakens those in her presence from their slumbering, who brings light to darkness. Call these features M.[13] The question at the center of the major disagreements over metaphor among philosophers, linguists, and others in recent years concerns the precise way to characterize the relation between the utterance of a sentence like (1), its literal meaning L, and the various possible metaphorical conveyances in M. Everyone agrees that L is—at least if anything is—a semantic interpretation of (1), something we know in virtue of our semantic competence. Everyone also agrees that somehow, *by* uttering (1), the speaker conveys something metaphorically about Juliet, one or another of the features in M. Where writers disagree is over the nature of the relation R between these three entities: the utterance, L, and M. Is M (or some of its elements) something that the hearer is *caused* to notice or to infer as an *effect* of the utterance of (1) with its literal meaning L? Or is M something the *speaker* means as opposed to the (literal) meaning L of the *sentence*? Or is M, though not literal, nonetheless an *interpretation* determined by the semantics of the language much as is L?

There is no lack of answers to these questions but the vast majority of authors in the metaphor literature have answered the last question— whether R is a semantic relation—with a resounding "No."[14] Since we shall touch on the many reasons for this denial in coming chapters, I shall not review them all here. However, to motivate my own account whose starting place is the "context-dependence" of metaphorical interpretation, let me begin with one deeply held source of resistance to semantic approaches to metaphor.

Suppose our ability to interpret a metaphor were solely a matter of our semantic competence; then all semantically competent speakers ought to be able to interpret all metaphors. But not all speakers can. Therefore, there must be something else to metaphorical competence. Either it is a special power, like the kind of singular genius Aristotle and Kant may have envisioned, or it is an ordinary skill of speech that, for lack of a better word, we can subsume under the umbrella word "use." On either alternative, the idea is that, unlike standard cases of semantic interpretation, the interpretation of a metaphor varies so irregularly, idiosyncratically, and unpredictably that no theory, let alone a semantic theory, could aspire to explain it. In a pejorative sense, this is also what authors sometimes mean by the slogan that metaphor is context-dependent, in contrast to literal interpretation, which is claimed to be context-*in*dependent: invariant, predictable, and regular—hence within the domain of a *theory* and in particular a theory of *meaning*, as opposed to atheoretical (or antitheoretical) use. Thus Richard Rorty:

[S]emantical notions like "meaning" have a role only within the quite narrow ... limits of regular, predictable, linguistic behavior—the limits which mark off (temporarily) the literal use of language. In Quine's image, the realm of meaning is a relatively small "cleared" area within the jungle of use.... To say ... that "metaphor belongs exclusively to the domain of use" is simply to say that ... [it] falls outside the cleared area.[15]

In this sense, its "context-dependence" or status as "use" would seem to render metaphor impregnable to any kind of theoretical explanation and to semantic theory in particular. Donald Davidson gestures toward the same view when he groups metaphors together with works of art and dreamwork, all of which he locates in the realm of the imagination where, we are given to believe, anything goes: "understanding a metaphor is as much a creative endeavor as making a metaphor, and as little guided by rules."[16] This description, which recalls Aristotle's and Kant's discussions of genius, might fit the creations of some *masters* of metaphor, but it is a far cry from the metaphorical competence required for its *mastery* by the ordinary interpreter. Indeed the opposite is the case: much more regularity and predictability characterize metaphorical interpretation than the impression fostered by Rorty and Davidson suggests. First, there is evidence of substantial interpersonal agreement among speakers over the classification of utterances as metaphorical rather than literal and over paraphrases of particular metaphorical interpretations (in contrast to paraphrases of sentences classified as nonsense).[17] This argues against the perception that metaphor is entirely unpredictable and idiosyncratic, although it does not yet support the view that metaphor is *semantically* regular or law-governed. Second, and more relevant for our semantic claim, when we look beyond the individual interpretations of particular utterances of metaphors to reoccurrences of the same expression, each time used metaphorically, in different sentences uttered on different occasions, we find a second kind of interpersonal regularity. For example, contrast the interpretation of 'the sun' in (1) with its interpretation in

(2) Achilles is the sun

where it expresses Achilles' devastating anger or brute force; or in

(3) Before Moses' sun had set, the sun of Joshua had risen (BT *Qedushin* 72b)[18]

where it expresses the uninterrupted continuity of righteousness, which, according to the Talmud (based on Eccl. 1: 5), preserves the world; or in

(4) "The works of great masters are suns which rise and set around us. The time will come for every great work that is now in the descendent to rise again." (Wittgenstein, *Culture and Value*)

in which 'sun' expresses the cyclicity and eternal recurrence of greatness, that things once great will be great again; that descent will be followed by ascent, by descent, and so on. Or consider the different metaphorical interpretations of 'is a bubble' in

(5) Life is a bubble

and

(6) The earth is a bubble[19]

or the two metaphorical uses of 'hill' by John Donne in (7) and (8):

(7) ... On a huge hill,/Cragged, and steep, Truth stands, and he that will/Reach her, about must, and must go ... (Satire 3)

(8) The Church is such a Hill, as may be seen every where. (Sermon 13)

According to the eminent Donne scholar John Carey, the poet's choice of 'hill' in (7) expresses the idea that "it is necessary to take a circuitous route, investigating the claims of different churches, before reaching [the truth]," while in (8) it expresses the contrary thought that the position of the church "allows it to be seen unmistakably from all sides, so there is no need to investigate the claims of different churches."[20] Or, finally, compare these two metaphorical interpretations of 'is (like) a martini':

(9) A great diamond is like a perfect martini—cool and sexy. (Timothy Green, *The World of Diamonds*)

(10) The University of Chicago is like a martini. There are some people who find it an acquired taste. (Charles O'Connell, former Dean of Students, The University of Chicago)

Ignoring details, we should agree first that there is *some* difference between the metaphorical interpretations of the members of each of these sets. Second, we should observe that these differences seem to correspond to some difference related to a feature of their respective contexts. As a first conjecture, we might think the relevant difference in context is linguistic: the different subject noun phrases with which the metaphor, in predicative position, co-occurs (or, in Max Black's well-known terminology, the different frames in which the same metaphorical focus occurs). However, it is easy to see that the same kind of difference of metaphorical interpretation can also arise where different tokens of one sentence occur on different occasions with different beliefs or attitudes associated by the speaker-hearer with the noun phrase (or frame). In contrast to Romeo's utterance of (1) in the context depicted in Shakespeare's play, imagine an utterance of (1) in a context in which Paris's opinion of Juliet is that she is the kind of woman who destroys admirers who try to become too close or intimate with her. In that context, (1) might be used to warn Romeo not to get involved with Juliet. As this example shows, the relevant difference in context must include extralinguistic, and nonverbalized, attitudes (however we work out the details). The moral I draw is this: There may be little systematic or predictable so long as we look just at the particular contents of the different metaphorical interpretations one by one, but at one level of interpretation more abstract—at a level that relates each content of the same expression used metaphorically to a relevant feature of its respective context of use (whatever the relevant feature of context turns out to be)—metaphorical interpretation does seem to follow patterns and to support predictions. Same expression, same context, same interpretation; same expression, different contexts, different interpretations. Thus the degree to which we find metaphorical interpretation to be regular and predictable depends on the level we focus on. As we shift our attention one notch upward, we discover regularities and systematicities that otherwise go unnoticed. The structure of these variations, as we shall see in later chapters, is essential to understand both the productivity of metaphor and speakers' mastery of the mechanism of metaphorical interpretation.

A second group of philosophers who are no less antithetical to a semantics of metaphor rejects this "nihilistic" reading of the slogan that metaphor is context-dependent. Their resistance stems from a second source that holds that our knowledge of metaphorical interpretation is context-dependent or a matter of use in that it is a function not, or not only, of our knowledge of language but (also) of all sorts of extralinguistic—hence, contextual as opposed to linguistic—knowledge, beliefs, and skills. Metaphorical interpretations are either built up out of our extralinguistic beliefs, common knowledge, and presuppositions—about extralinguistic entities such as Juliet, martinis, the Church, and the University of Chicago—or they are a function of psychological abilities such as the perception of similarity or analogy, abilities or skills that are not language-specific and that are employed in all sorts of nonlinguistic modes of communication or symbolization. These abilities and the faculties responsible for the relevant presuppositions fall beyond a speaker's semantic competence proper; hence, metaphorical interpretation also falls outside the scope of semantics—and instead in either pragmatics, theories of language-use or speaker's meaning, or general accounts of cognitive or symbolic activity.[21]

This inference from use or context-dependence to the nonsemantic status of metaphor cuts to the heart of my own position. I also begin from the observation that metaphorical interpretations are composed out of presuppositions and beliefs that are not part of our knowledge of language proper, that are instead acquired through general symbolic skills. What is right about the second view is that metaphorical interpretation is not *exclusively* a function of linguistic competence. However, in contrast to the second view, I shall argue that the extralinguistic context-dependence of a metaphor is nonetheless compatible with and, indeed, requires semantic knowledge in order to *constrain* the kinds of interpretations it is possible to assign an expression used metaphorically. Indeed the greater the role of its extralinguistic context in determining the content of a metaphor, the more we need to explain why only some and not other interpretations can be expressed by the given expression. A primary function of the notion of meaning is to furnish such constraints on interpretations that draw on extralinguistic resources. So, rather than exclude a semantics of metaphor, its context-dependence exposes the proper role of semantic knowledge—as knowledge of constraints—in metaphorical interpretation. Furthermore, although semantic competence by itself is not sufficient for metaphorical interpretation and contextual input is absolutely necessary, semantics plus context are *all* that are necessary. There is no other special power or skill needed for a mastery of metaphor, even while some of us are more accomplished masters of metaphorical use than others.

This marriage between context-dependence and semantic knowledge may appear to create an odd couple, but in fact metaphor is hardly unique. There are many topics concerning the interaction between context and language—for example, speech-acts and conversation—that fall outside the scope of semantics, but one set of questions concerned with the role of context in determining the interpretation of an expression on an occasion is squarely semantic. Following David Kaplan (1989a, 522, 546), let's distinguish between the study of *sentences-in-contexts* and the study of *utterances* and *speech-acts*. An utterance is a spatiotemporal event that requires a speaker who uses a sentence to make a statement (or perform some other act). An utterance is also subject to nonlinguistic constraints, for example, the physical/biological fact that no human can typically make more than one utterance at any one time and (if contexts are individuated by their times) that no more than one utterance can occur in any one context. A sentence, on the other hand, can *occur* in a context even if the speaker of the context does not *utter* it; likewise, an indefinite number of sentences can simultaneously occur in one context (in order to render it possible to evaluate them as the premises and conclusion of a single argument). Given this distinction, we can then take the job of semantics as the characterization of a *sentence being true-in-a-context* rather than either the narrower study of sentences in isolation from all context (or in the null context) or the much broader study of utterances and speech acts. Semantics with this contextual edge is not new. The analysis of a whole class of expressions of exactly this kind—namely, the demonstratives (e.g., 'this' and 'that') and indexical expressions (e.g., 'I', 'now', and 'here')—has long been assumed to fall within semantics. But now, with David Kaplan's seminal work on demonstratives (a term I'll use generically to include indexicals), we finally have the beginnings of a rigorous formal theory that also does philosophical justice to the subtleties of these context-dependent expressions.

To return now to metaphor: instead of allowing its context-dependence to be an *obstacle* to its semantic candidacy, I'll argue that the *key* to its satisfactory semantic analysis is to embrace its context-dependence. To go one step further, I shall treat a metaphor as a type of context-dependent expression of the same general kind as the demonstratives. What is needed for such an account is to show that metaphors and demonstratives share the same formal structure, to isolate the contextual parameter (like the speaker for 'I' and time for 'now') that determines a metaphorical interpretation, and to specify the rules that determine the contents of metaphors in each of their contexts of utterance.[22]

To motivate the parallel between demonstratives and metaphors, I might also mention that the same argument from context-dependence that locates metaphors entirely outside semantics can be made for demonstratives—and deserves the same kind of reply. Suppose (as Russell once did) that a speaker's context-dependent knowledge of demonstrative reference is simply knowledge of the entity to which one actually refers on each occasion with a demonstrative token, like one's knowledge of the referent of a proper name. In that case, one's knowledge of demonstrative reference would be entirely extralinguistic; there would be no isolable language-specific knowledge the speaker would possess. What, if anything, would be missing from such an extralinguistic account of demonstrative reference?

Knowledge of the *propositional content*, or truth-conditions, of an utterance containing a demonstrative, say, of 'this is red', requires, of course, extralinguistic knowledge of the thing demonstrated on the occasion, the actual referent of the token of 'this'. But when we *understand* this utterance we also know the *kind* (however general it may be, such as an object rather than property) of the extralinguistic entity that is admissible as the referent of the demonstrative. We might, therefore, factor our knowledge of demonstrative reference into two parts: (i) knowledge of the *kind* (or range) of values that (any token of) the demonstrative (type) can be assigned on any occasion of use; and (ii) knowledge of the *actual value* of the demonstrative (token) on a particular occasion of utterance. These pieces of information are clearly distinguishable. A speaker-hearer can know the first without knowing the second, and a theory of the first is independent of the particular form we adopt for an account of the second. But knowledge of the first type is exactly what we would predict an object of linguistic, or semantic, competence to be. Any account of demonstrative reference that failed to distinguish it would fail to capture a significant dimension of the speaker's knowledge.

For the same reason, the speaker's knowledge of the *type* of parameter on which a metaphorical interpretation depends should be distinguished from his knowledge of the *value* of the parameter in particular contexts for particular utterances of metaphors. Knowledge of the first kind, as we would expect of linguistic knowledge, remains invariant from one to another utterance of the metaphor despite the fact that the extralinguistic factors that constitute the parameter will vary over contexts, yielding different interpretations for the metaphor on the different occasions. Here, for metaphors as for demonstratives, the speaker's knowledge should therefore be divided into two distinct components, (only) the first of which will fall in his semantic competence proper.

To articulate the difference between these two types of knowledge involved in metaphorical interpretation, I'll adopt David Kaplan's distinction for demonstratives between two semantic "levels" that were originally conflated in Frege's notion of sense. Kaplan calls the first level *content*, the second *character*. Content is (roughly) what we have been calling the interpretation of a metaphor: what the metaphor says, its propositional component, or truth-condition(al factor). So, just as the content of a (singular) demonstrative is an object or individual, the content of a (predicative) metaphor is (something like) a property. Character roughly corresponds to the (linguistic) meaning of an expression: a rule known by speakers as part of their linguistic competence that determines the content of the expression in each context of utterance (like the rule for 'I' that each of its utterances has its individual utterer as its content). Both demonstratives and metaphors have *nonconstant* characters: characters that determine different contents in different contexts.[23] This is obvious in the case of demonstratives but, as our earlier examples (1)–(10) make clear, the same is true for metaphor. One expression type, say, 'is the sun', is interpreted metaphorically in (1)–(4), hence with one metaphorical character; yet the one character yields different interpretations, or contents, in different contexts (where, as I'll argue, the relevant difference in context is due to different contextual presuppositions).

An expression interpreted metaphorically has, then, a "metaphorical meaning" in addition to a literal meaning. But this notion of meaning, it should be noted, is rather different in kind from what previous writers—especially its detractors—have assumed a metaphorical meaning would be. Its critics take the "meaning" of a metaphor to be something like the property it expresses in a context. But that is what I take to be the content of the metaphor in a context. On my account, the meaning of a metaphor is the rule that determines its content for each context, that is, its character. If we carefully bear in mind the character-content distinction, we can answer a slew of questions that have standardly been raised to challenge the legitimacy of a notion of metaphorical meaning and the possibility of constructing a semantics for metaphor. For example:

1. If sentences (containing an expression) interpreted metaphorically are semantically significant, then, like other compound semantically valued expressions, they must be compositional in structure. What kind of metaphorically relevant semantic structure can we articulate within them in order that their truth-value be a function of the semantic values of their parts?

2. It is a truism that the interpretation of a metaphor "depends on its literal meaning." Is that "dependence" semantic functionality? If so, what is the function?

3. If the metaphorical interpretation of an expression Φ depends on its literal meaning, then Φ must still "have" (in some sense) its literal meaning, even while it is interpreted metaphorically. How? In what sense of 'have'?

4. If an utterance of a sentence interpreted metaphorically has a truth-value that is (or might be) different from what its truth-value would be were it interpreted literally, then we would also reasonably think that it differs in meaning from its literal interpretation. What kind of meaning might that be and how is it related to our notion of literal meaning? Does metaphorical interpretation render an expression ambiguous or polysemous? Does the expression *change* its meaning when it is interpreted metaphorically? How does this kind of change of meaning relate to other changes of meaning?

Two additional consequences of the character-content distinction for metaphor deserve mention. First, the "received" conception of semantics "gives the meaning" of sentences in the form of an account of the speaker's knowledge of the full-blooded truth-conditions or propositional contents directly assigned to the sentences. But semantics can maintain this aim only as long as it innocently directs its attention at eternal, or context-independent, expressions. When we focus on context-dependent expressions like demonstratives, a direct assignment of truth-conditions to expressions is ruled out. For these expressions, where context intervenes, either we conclude that there is no semantic assignment at work, that their "meaning" lies outside the scope of semantics, or we must revise our conception of semantics. Rather than concern itself with truth-conditions or contents directly assigned to sentences, semantics now becomes a theory of a speaker's knowledge of the *form* of truth-conditional or propositional interpretations of sentences, that is, of the form or structure of sentences that displays the contextual conditions or parameters with respect to which their interpretations vary. In a word, semantics is now the study of our knowledge of character rather than content—and similarly for a semantics of metaphor.

Second, the nonconstant character of a demonstrative (e.g., the rule for 'I' that each of its tokens refers to its utterer) *underdetermines* its content or interpretation, namely, an actual individual. For the same character (e.g., of 'I') yields different contents in different extralinguistic contexts (namely, those containing different speakers). Hence any theory of a speaker's *semantic* competence in demonstratives—a theory of her knowledge of their character—will be, in one sense, "incomplete" as an account of her knowledge of their interpretation. Analogously for metaphors: Their interpretations, or contents, which also depend on all sorts of extralinguistic abilities, beliefs, and associations, are underdetermined by their respective characters, or meanings.[24] As we saw when we contrasted (1) first uttered by Romeo in Shakespeare's context and then uttered by Paris as a warning to Romeo, the same sentence, with the same metaphorical character, or meaning, can yield entirely different, even incompatible interpretations, given different presuppositions and attitudes. Thus a *semantic* theory of metaphorical interpretation—a theory of the speaker's knowledge of the character of the metaphor—will also be "incomplete" as an account of her knowledge of the full interpretation. This kind of incompleteness does not, however, signal a deficiency in the approach. Just the opposite. The virtue of the incompleteness is that it enables us to discern the substantive contribution our semantic knowledge specific to metaphor, our knowledge of its character, makes to our understanding of metaphorical interpretation.

In sum, I shall argue that by exploiting the parallel between demonstratives and metaphors, we can identify a type of knowledge underlying a speaker's ability to interpret a metaphor that belongs to his semantic competence. Yet many readers may still not be persuaded that metaphor *should* be explained by semantics, rather than by pragmatics or by a theory of use. For the costs, one might object, especially the complications that accrue to our overall linguistic theory as a result of incorporating metaphor in semantics, outweigh the benefits. In reply, I will argue, the actual costs are negligible. We complicate our overall semantic theory by including metaphor only if that requires us to introduce apparatus not *already* and not *independently* necessary for the semantics. But if our parallel between demonstratives and metaphors holds, the *semantic* rules underlying our ability to interpret metaphors are of the very same kind as those that underlie our ability to interpret demonstratives. Those rules (or something like them) *already* constitute part of our semantic competence in *non*metaphorical language, our competence in demonstratives. (All that is additionally necessary, I will propose, is one general operator added to the lexicon and one rule governing its operation.) So, if knowledge of demonstratives belongs to linguistic competence, so should the corresponding knowledge governing metaphorical interpretation. Given a semantics for demonstratives, metaphor can be had (virtually) for free.

With this overview of the argument in hand, let me conclude this section with an outline of the chapters to follow.

Given my focus on context-dependence, the obvious, natural place to locate metaphor within an all-inclusive linguistic theory is in pragmatics or a use-oriented account; and this is, as we have said, the datum from which many writers in fact conclude that metaphor should be explained as a type of use or speech performance. To motivate my turn instead to a semantic account of metaphor, I therefore begin, in chapter 2, with a closer look at pragmatic or use theories. Concentrating on the influential essays of Donald Davidson, I argue that use theories *need* semantics precisely in order to constrain their too-powerful resources—to explain why specific expressions can be used to express only specific metaphorical contents. A close critical look at Davidson's truth-theoretic semantic treatment of context-dependence (e.g., demonstratives) within his use theory also serves a second purpose: to motivate my own use of David Kaplan's semantic framework that focuses on character rather than content for my account of metaphor.

With this motivation in hand, chapter 3 lays out the necessary semantic background adopted from David Kaplan's seminal work on the logic of demonstratives. I concentrate on two themes that play central roles in my story: Kaplan's distinction between character and content and his invention of the operator 'Dthat' to lexically represent demonstrative interpretations (or uses) of (arbitrary, eternal) definite descriptions.

In chapter 4, I begin to lay out my semantic theory of metaphor as a kind of context-dependent interpretation of an expression on the model of demonstratives. I spell out the relevant feature of the context on which the interpretation of a metaphor depends, a contextually given (sub)set of presuppositions, and the semantic rule of character that constitutes the meaning of the metaphor, the rule that determines its content or interpretation in each context. In our earlier terminology, this is an account of our semantic knowledge *of* metaphor.

In chapter 5 I turn to the first brand of our knowledge *by* metaphor, concentrating on information conveyed as the *content* of the metaphor in a particular context. This discussion helps my argument along in a number of ways, apart from offering a first explanation of how our semantic knowledge of metaphor enables us to express contents not expressible by nonmetaphorical language. It also offers the first detailed illustrations of applications of our semantic knowledge to contextual presuppositions, which in turn give a sharper view of the different kinds of knowledge involved in the pragmatics of metaphorical interpretation and the not-language-specific symbolic skills (such as the perception of similarity or exemplification) that enter at this juncture. Finally, as part of my explanation of these skills, I introduce the role of networks of expressions in metaphorical interpretation; these networks also play an important role in capturing the knowledge by metaphor conveyed at the level of metaphorical character, the topic of chapter 7.

Before turning to this last topic, however, I return in chapter 6 to the relation between metaphorical character and meaning, and I use my account to solve some outstanding problems about the pretheoretical notion of metaphorical meaning and the formal problems raised by the semantic data introduced at the end of chapter 2. Finally, I turn to the relation of metaphor to other figurative and nonliteral uses of language, contrast my account with three other semantic theories in the literature, and conclude the chapter with replies to a number of anticipated objections.

I finally turn, in chapter 7, to the "character-istic" information or significance metaphors carry. This information is manifest in a variety of ways—in the explanatory power of beliefs containing metaphors, in the sense of surprise associated with metaphor, and in the often repeated claim that metaphors make us *see* one thing *as* another. Furthermore, since this "character-istic" information is not expressed in the content of the metaphor in a particular context, it is also not contained in paraphrases of those contents. Through this variety of ways, our semantic knowledge of a metaphor—our knowledge of its character—enables us to acquire information by the metaphor that we cannot grasp except through knowledge of its character. On the one hand, then, the significance of a metaphor is not exhausted by its content in a context; on the other, there is nothing about that significance that is antithetical to a semantics of metaphorical interpretation.

Finally, chapter 8 briefly demarcates the boundaries of metaphor—linguistic versus pictorial metaphors, dead versus live metaphors, and the literal versus the metaphorical.

III Methodological Preliminaries

Before beginning I want to raise several methodological and terminological issues concerning (i) the unit of metaphorical interpretation, (ii)
the literal, (iii) the truth of metaphors, and (iv) the use of examples and
evidence. The first three discussions will be brief, the fourth more detailed.

(i) The Unit of Metaphorical Interpretation

We should all agree both that the proper name 'Juliet' has the same interpretation (take your pick: extension, referent, content, intension, etc.)
in Romeo's utterance of

(1)   Juliet is the sun

in Shakespeare's context as it has in

(11)   Juliet is Romeo's beloved

and that 'is the sun' (or 'the sun') has a different interpretation in (1) than
it has in

(12)   An especially bright star in our solar system is the sun.

We typically, and innocently, describe the different interpretation of 'is
the sun' in (1) as "metaphorical" in contrast both to its interpretation in
(12), which we call "literal," and to the interpretation of 'Juliet' that
undergoes no change from (1) to (11). And based on this kind of familiar
data, we should say that the basic unit of metaphorical interpretation is
the specific subsentential constituent whose interpretation (whatever you
take that to be) undergoes change, namely, 'is the sun', not the whole
sentence (1) and not even the pair of constituent expressions ⟨'Juliet', 'is
the sun'⟩.

Despite this seemingly straightforward way of identifying 'the (a)'
metaphor, say, in (1), several philosophers and linguists have other candidates. Max Black (1993, 24) says that "metaphor" is always short for
"metaphorical statement" and that "statement-ingredients (words and
phrases used metaphorically)" are only derivatively metaphorical.[25]
George Lakoff (1993) says that in "contemporary research" a metaphor is
really "a cross-domain mapping in the conceptual system" and that the
so-called metaphorical expression is nothing more than a linguistic item
that "is a surface realization of such a cross-domain mapping" (203).[26]
Eva Kittay (1987), who assumes a version of the deviance condition,
says that "a unit of metaphor is any unit of discourse in which some
conceptual or conversational incongruity emerges" (24), and within the

metaphor she distinguishes a focus and frame. And, most recently, Roger White (1996) has challenged "the widespread assumption" that "in every metaphor there is an isolable word or phrase which is the word or phrase being used metaphorically" (57).

What is at issue is not terminological but a matter of distinguishing between the unit whose interpretation is being determined and the units that determine the interpretation. Black is right to focus on the whole statement insofar as its utterance is the minimal speech unit and all constituents of an utterance can play a role in determining the metaphorical interpretation of any single constituent.[27] Lakoff is right insofar as it is only generally as part of much larger linguistic (or, as he calls them, conceptual) networks that individual expressions acquire their metaphorical interpretations. Indeed I'll argue that the context in which an expression is interpreted metaphorically must be broadened to include not only its immediate linguistic environment, but also its extralinguistic situation (including nonverbalized presuppositions and attitudes). But none of this changes the fact that *what* is interpreted metaphorically in a context may be a proper constituent within the sentence. Of course, the metaphorical constituent is not always a simple expression rather than a phrase; more than one expression can be interpreted metaphorically in a given utterance; and we cannot always individuate or identify the metaphorical constituent by looking merely at the (phonologically interpreted) surface structure of the sentence uttered. It is also possible for an expression interpreted metaphorically to be concurrently interpreted literally in the same utterance in the same context, in which case it will be lexically ambiguous, and it is possible for an utterance to admit multiple syntactic analyses, each of which yields not only a metaphorical interpretation but a different one. By saying that the metaphor can be a constituent expression, I should also not be taken to imply that its change in interpretation (extension, referent, content, intension, etc.) "exhausts its metaphorical significance."[28] As I'll argue at length in chapter 7, the character of a metaphor carries information beyond that of its content (in its context), part of which is also a function of the networks to which it belongs.

The question of the proper unit of metaphorical interpretation is bound up with many issues we will take up in later chapters. For now, simply as a matter of terminology, I shall mean by *metaphor*: '(a token of an) expression (type, simple or complex) that is interpreted metaphorically in its context of utterance', and by *sentence interpreted metaphorically* or *metaphorical sentence*: 'a sentence containing at least one expression that is interpreted metaphorically in its context of utterance'. For brevity, I shall also say that a metaphor is true or false, meaning that an utterance of the (containing) sentence in which the given expression is interpreted metaphorically is true or false. Finally, a metaphorical sentence (statement, utterance) is not something that is only metaphorically a sentence (etc.), but a sentence (etc.) interpreted metaphorically.

(ii) The Literal

The term "metaphor" is often said to have two senses, one wide, one narrow. In the wide sense, the metaphorical is contrasted with the literal and includes the full range of nonliteral or figurative interpretations of language—irony, metonymy, synecdoche, hyperbole, and so on. In the narrow sense, the metaphorical is contrasted not only with the literal, but also with these other figures or tropes. I shall use the expression (unless noted otherwise) in the narrow sense—metaphor as distinguished from both the literal *and* the other tropes. But (to anticipate my discussion in ch. 6) I shall argue that our *semantics* for metaphor (in the narrow sense) could be extended to certain of the other figures though not to others: to metonymy and synecdoche, for example, but not to irony or hyperbole. The notion of metaphor that will emerge from our analysis will be both narrower and more variegated than the one in common circulation.

I rely on *some* distinction between the metaphorical and the literal and I accept the truism (in a sense yet to be explicated) that the metaphorical depends on the literal. But I shall not defend either of these assumptions at this stage. For one thing, critics who baldly deny the distinction owe us, in my view, a clear statement of what they think they are denying; for another, I cannot yet clearly articulate the distinction I wish to draw without much more groundwork. Indeed, different notions of the literal will emerge in the coming chapters and, as I'll argue in chapter 8, the notion of the literal is in worse theoretical shape than the metaphorical. As a working hypothesis, I shall assume that the literal meaning of a *simple* expression is whatever, according to our best linguistic theory, turns out to be its semantic interpretation, and that the literal meaning of a sentence is the rule-by-rule composition of the literal meanings of its simple constituents.[29] As a matter of fact, current semantic theory is not yet in a position to state with any authority *what* the semantic interpretation of a simple expression is, but it should also be noted that we do know it is nothing like a set of necessary and sufficient descriptive conditions. Minimally, it contains the extension or referent of the expression and the constraints and conditions that govern both its interaction with the syntax and with the extralinguistic context.

Finally, to explain how the metaphorical interpretation of a token of (a type) Φ depends on its literal meaning, I'll need the vocabulary to say that the token (in one sense) "has" its literal meaning and (in a second sense) does not "have" it. For that purpose, I'll use the term of art *literal vehicle* to refer to the expression type Φ *with its literal meaning* when the token of Φ is interpreted, or used, metaphorically.

(iii) Metaphors and Truth

In proposing a semantic theory of metaphor, I have assumed (without argument) that metaphors—or declarative sentences in which at least one expression is a metaphor—are truth-bearing entities; that they are true or false no different from literal sentences like 'snow is white'; equivalently, that they express propositions. This assumption is far from uncontroversial, so it might be objected that I am assuming the crux of what I claim to demonstrate in this book.

For a start, the best defense is a good offense. It certainly *looks like* metaphorical (declarative) sentences are true or false. Many of our innocent assertions employ metaphors. To the man on the street unversed in philosophical semantics, the assumption that utterances containing metaphors are true or false (as the case may be) would be beyond reproach. When Romeo utters (1), he not only wants to "call our attention" to a (particular) similarity between Juliet and the sun; he also intends to say something true about Juliet, to assert that she has a certain property (or set of properties) "corresponding" to the predicate 'is the sun'. Now, whatever it is that he is asserting, and thereby representing himself as believing to be true, it is *not* what is expressed by (1) interpreted literally. What, then, would be simpler than claiming that the property he believes to be *true of* Juliet is a property metaphorically expressed by the predicate 'is the sun'? That he is asserting a proposition metaphorically expressed by (1) that he believes to be true?

Suppose that Count Paris disagrees with Romeo's utterance of (1). He is surely not denying the proposition expressed by (1) interpreted literally. Romeo and Paris agree about *that* proposition that it is false. So what is the common thing Romeo asserts and Paris denies? Isn't it the proposition asserted by (1) when it is interpreted metaphorically? Indeed why not?

In short, the ordinary appearance is that utterances of sentences that contain metaphors are truth-valued, express propositions, and can be used to make assertions (or other speech acts that presuppose assertion). The burden of argument, therefore, falls on those who deny that this appearance is reality. To be sure, there is no lack of arguments for the other side. These range from observations based on our ordinary use of metaphors (to "call our attention to a certain likeness," or "invite" us to "appreciate" a resemblance, or "inspire" a certain vision, or "propose" that things be viewed a certain way) to theoretical considerations about compositionality and the formal structure of a semantic theory. I shall address these objections in the course of the book, but I defer them until I can first set out my own alternative theory.

One last methodological remark on this issue: Despite the ordinary presumption to which I have appealed, the thesis that metaphorical interpretation falls within the scope of semantics cannot be settled simply by appeal to "facts" like our practices to use metaphors in assertions. On the one hand, actual practice can always be interpreted and explained in a variety of ways consistent both with the assumption that metaphors are truth-valued and with the assumption that they aren't. On the other hand, even if ordinary practice were different, the decision to treat metaphors as truth-bearers could be justified on theoretical grounds. Truth-values are theoretical entities. They serve as the semantic values or roles of sentences in a complex, systematic, powerful theoretical framework that aims to account for our understanding of language. If this same framework provides an illuminating account of metaphor, the assumption that metaphors are truth-bearers will be warranted—like any theoretical posit that is justified by the evidence for its containing theory and by its explanatory success.

(iv)   Examples and Evidence: Living vs. Dead Metaphors

Theories of metaphor are often a function of their authors' examples.[30] Philosophers and linguists focus on metaphors heard in "ordinary speech"; no wonder, it is charged, that their theories best, or only, fit "conventional," "frozen," or "dead" metaphors. Literary critics and rhetoricians analyze the "novel," "imaginative," and "creative" metaphors of poetry and literature—whose complexity and subtlety tend to make them suspicious of the possibility of any linguistic theory of metaphor, period. As a description of current practice, this observation contains a grain of truth. However, some theorists go further, claiming that there are also good *reasons* to take one or the other kind of example as the paradigm of a metaphor. Others, typically in the course of polemically defending their own theory, charge that counterexamples of the other kind are not "real" metaphors—hence are not counterexamples.[31] A familiar complaint of this sort is that philosophers' and linguists' theories are inadequate to deal with the subtleties of poetic metaphors because they are based on simple (or is it simplistic?), tired, and sometimes dead examples (e.g., 'Man is a wolf').[32] On the other hand, certain linguists have recently claimed that theories that focus on poetic metaphors miss the systematicity and conventionality exemplified by the ubiquitous metaphors of ordinary, normal speech, properties that these authors further argue are essential characteristics of metaphor (and, once identified in ordinary speech, can also be found to underlie poetic metaphors).[33]

These debates frequently appeal to the distinction between live (or, better, living) and dead metaphors. This is a time-worn distinction calling out for reconsideration, to which I shall return in chapter 8. Here I want to address a prior, methodological question: Are there principles that ought to govern our selection of examples? Are some types of metaphors to be preferred over others? What of the charge that a theory ignores a whole sample space of metaphors?

To begin with, I want to distance myself both from the populism advocated by the spokesmen for metaphors of ordinary speech and from the elitism fostered by the cognoscenti of poetry. From a semantic point of view, there is one metaphorical competence that underlies our ability to produce and comprehend all metaphors regardless of their context of use, be it poetry or ordinary speech. All that distinguishes these different metaphors are the different skills and sensibilities recruited in addition to our semantic competence to complete their actual interpretations in their respective contexts. At the level of semantic explanation, the linguistic phenomenon of metaphor should not be identified exclusively, or even too closely, with any one particular brand, or use, of metaphors.

On the other hand, the evaluation of a semantic theory of metaphor need not depend, first and foremost, on whether it "covers all the data" equally well. As evidence for or against a particular theory, it does not follow that one metaphor is never more relevant than another. Not that there are "don't cares." Every theory must account for some class—some interesting class—of data, but no theory must (or can) account for "all" the data. A theory need only account for the relevant data and, most important, it is the theory itself that provides the criterion of relevance.[34] Examples, to be examples, should be representative of the explanandum, but what counts as representative of a phenomenon X cannot be determined independently of, or prior to, a particular theory of X.

These general lessons apply equally to metaphor. Our concern is with the semantic competence underlying metaphorical interpretation that consists in knowledge of context-sensitive rules that determine the structure of metaphorical interpretations; it is not with the interpretations themselves or with their effects. Our examples should accordingly be ones that bear on the context-dependent structure of those rules and, not surprisingly, these will be metaphors whose interpretations maximally depend on their context—"living" metaphors in one sense of the term. Interpretations that are dead to their context of utterance—that are called "metaphorical" only because of their historical origin—simply do not tell us much, pro or con, about the claims of our theory. And the more borderline—the less context-sensitive—the example, the less desirable it will therefore be for our purposes. But matters could be otherwise. For another purpose, say, to explain why some but not other metaphors endure, or to explain what makes a metaphor rhetorically or aesthetically effective, it may well turn out that (certain) dead metaphors are better examples than live ones. As Borges reminds us:

> When I was a young man I was always hunting for new metaphors. Then I found out that really good metaphors are always the same. I mean you compare time to a road, death to sleeping, life to dreaming, and those are the great metaphors in literature because they correspond to something essential. If you invent metaphors, they are apt to be surprising during the fraction of a second, but they strike no deep emotion.[35]

Apart from metaphors whose interpretations are relatively dead to their contexts, I should also mention here a second class of metaphors that are not maximally germane to my theory. These are metaphorical interpretations that *extend* the (literal) meaning of an expression, say, by dropping at least one condition in the (literal) meaning, in contrast to interpretations that involve changes (say, of extension) of the type Aristotle called *transfer*. When we say, for example, that Quine *demolished* Carnap's argument, we drop, as it were, one or another condition of application associated with the (italicized) term under its literal interpretation, so that the resulting metaphorical interpretation extends, and properly contains, the original one. Such extensions might be context-dependent in that the context determines the conditions to be dropped on the occasion, and different conditions might be dropped in different contexts. However, these extended interpretations are context-*independent* insofar as they do not draw upon extralinguistic presuppositions for the content of the metaphorical interpretation.[36] In the case of transfer, we interpret the expression to express a particular content depending on contextual presuppositions somehow associated with the term, such that the resulting interpretation is applicable to a domain disjoint from its original one (or sufficiently disjoint for the change to count as one of transfer). For example, what is metaphorically expressed by 'the sun' in 'Juliet is the sun' is transferred from, rather than an extension of, its literal meaning. For the purposes of my theory, we will be primarily concerned, then, with transferred rather than merely extended interpretations—even though my account can be broadened to cover extended interpretations.

In sum, a theory (like mine) that claims to apply to all metaphorical interpretations need not, and typically will not, be equally confirmed by all metaphors (or disconfirmed by just any). Furthermore, *which* metaphors are germane to the evaluation of the theory will be determined, at least in part, by the very theory. Finally, the kind of metaphor that *is* germane evidence for my semantic theory, I now want to argue, is not appropriately described either as the conventional, dead metaphor of ordinary speech or as the novel, creative, living metaphor of poetry.

Let me return for a minute to the distinction between dead and living metaphors. Although I will defer a full discussion of what makes a metaphorical interpretation living or dead until chapter 8, I have already suggested that the liveliness (in one sense) of a metaphor is at least in part a function of its degree of dependence on its context. Notice, however, that this distinction between the living and the dead is not between kinds of *expressions* but between *interpretations* in contexts. Obviously some metaphorical interpretations of some expressions are dead in some contexts, but even the received interpretation of a time-honored dead metaphor like 'leg of a chair' only happens to be dead most of the time in most contexts. The same expression might yet be given a different living metaphorical interpretation; indeed even its dead metaphorical interpretation might be brought back to life or resuscitated in another context. Someone might tell us to look at the sexy legs of a couch; 'hot as hell' gets new life as 'hot as the hinges of hell', and 'full of wind' becomes, in a poem of Yeats, 'an old bellows full of angry wind'. Sometimes, too, we can verbally resuscitate a dead metaphor by extending it, that is, by making explicit the family of metaphors to which it belongs. Thus each metaphor in the following passage would be more or less dead standing alone in an isolated context. But juxtapose them and they start breathing with life:

Although George's own claims were *indefensible*, he *attacked* every *weak* point in my argument. I *won* the argument with him—despite his criticisms which were often *right on target* and despite his attempts to *shoot down* all my own claims—only because I managed to *demolish* him.[37]

Furthermore, whether a metaphor is dead or living can never be determined simply by "looking" at it, either at the concrete expression itself or at its metaphorical interpretation.[38] We must also know how that metaphorical interpretation was arrived at in its respective context, which depends both on its logical form (or character) and on the role of the context in the assignment. And this way of distinguishing living and dead metaphors cuts across the distinction between poetry and ordinary speech. Living, creative, or novel metaphorical interpretations can be found in ordinary exchanges as well as in poetry or literature, and dead metaphors might equally well turn up, and be used effectively, in poetry (or literature, as Borges said). *Time Magazine*, one of my own favorite sources of metaphors, is a publication whose understanding surely requires no special literary sensibility; yet its metaphors are frequently novel, imaginative, witty, and full of life. Here is one example:

At Checkpoint Charlie, the hideous maw of the Berlin Wall gapes briefly, affording a narrow passage into the divided German soul. On its Western side, a sea of sensuous color rushes down the Kurdamm, past the ruins of the Kaiser Wilhelm Memorial Church, and spends itself violently but impotently in a scatological orgy of graffiti against the cold barrier.... Propelled by the engine of the postwar Wirtschaftswunder, the capitalist Federal Republic of Germany is a sporty blond racing along the autobahns in a glittering Mercedes-Benz. The Communist German Democratic Republic, bumping down potholed roads in proletarian Wartburgs and Russian-built Ladas, is her homely sister, a war bride locked in a loveless marriage with a former neighbor. (*Time*, March 25, 1985)

In sum, living metaphors should not be identified with poetic metaphors. Although we have good reason to prefer examples that are living (i.e., maximally context-sensitive) metaphors, we need not look specifically to poetry to find them.

Nonetheless, despite the reasons I have given—and indeed, one suspects, despite *any* reasons *anyone* might give—many, especially literary, theorists will be unmoved by what I have said. They will insist that we misrepresent the nature of metaphor if we really think that "ordinary" metaphors are as vital and as representative of the phenomenon as poetic metaphors. What more can we respond to this point of view?

Resistance of this kind runs very deep, resting on deeply ingrained attitudes rather than on reasoned arguments, on attitudes for which there are undoubtedly a number of sources, however difficult it is to pinpoint them.[39] One source might be Aristotle's well-known claim that "true" metaphors are a "sign of genius" (*Poetics* 1458b), though he does not single out poetic metaphors in this passage. Yet, insofar as the ordinary speaker's understanding of his metaphors does not involve genius, it might be thought that Aristotle is describing one special class of metaphors, namely, those of poetry.[40]

A second source is a complex of motifs. One of these is the *identification* of metaphor and poetry. Each live, novel, or creative metaphor is treated as if it were itself a work of art or poetry; alternatively, the most basic form of literary art, or poetry, is claimed to be the individual metaphor.[41] A second motif holds that there is a subject-specific "proper" mode of inquiry to study, or understand, works of art or poetry, and hence, to study or understand metaphor. It is almost impossible to spell out this "method" but the idea rests on an opposition between the humanistic disciplines, exemplified by poetry and art, and the methods of physical science. Underlying this second motif we can already detect a slew of familiar dichotomies: science versus art, reason versus feeling, poetic versus nonpoetic language.[42] A third motif is that metaphor is claimed to be *the* essential kind of language in general, "the most vital principle of language and perhaps of all symbolism."[43] In this last step, the attitude that at first was specific to metaphor is now generalized to embrace all language: It opposes any attempt to subject language to naturalistic methods of study and instead views it as if it were "something 'higher,' mysterious, 'spiritual,'" something that cannot be studied on a par with natural phenomena.[44]

Like many attitudes, this stance toward metaphor is not one against which one can argue directly. We can change peoples' attitudes of this sort only by addressing their underlying fears and concerns, by showing them how to do what they fear cannot be done by a theory. We must subject metaphor to rigorous analysis and prove by example that to do so is not to do injustice to its subtleties.

One final methodological point about the opposition between the poetic and nonpoetic: Those who insist on this dichotomy only emphasize the difference between metaphors *in* and *out* of poetry; they indiscriminately lump together all (living) metaphors *within* poetry without acknowledging *their* significant differences. Among living poetic metaphors, I would also argue, there are some our theory should not attempt to explain, at least not directly.

To borrow some terminology from Chomsky, let's distinguish *core* as opposed to *peripheral* metaphors. This is not a distinction of kind but of degree and it is highly theory relative. If the aim of our semantic theory of metaphor is to discover the general (and presumably universal) semantic principles governing metaphorical interpretation, *core* metaphors are those whose properties most directly bear on those principles; peripheral metaphors are those whose exceptional properties require significant additions to our general theory. There is also a second way to draw this distinction: To the extent to which the general principles of metaphorical interpretation are semantic universals (or are determined by such universals), core metaphors whose properties are explained by those semantic principles involve no true learning. Peripheral metaphors, on the other hand, are marked; to the degree to which they involve exceptional properties, that is, properties not explained by universal semantic principles, their *rules* of interpretation must be explicitly learned. Both core and peripheral metaphors may, then, be dependent on context-specific presuppositions (the content of which, if extralinguistic, must be learned for both) and be dependent in one, specifically metaphorical way. But they differ in that peripheral metaphors require, *in addition*, training or learning in order for one to fully grasp their *technique* of interpretation, a technique that still presupposes the semantic competence to interpret metaphors.[45] Now, there are very specific, different kinds of poetic metaphors that are peripheral in this sense, but they are highly prominent in the work of modernist, surrealist, symbolist poets, such as Rilke, Celan, Mayikovsky, or Pound. These metaphors require a theory of interpretation, but it will not consist *solely* of our semantic theory (supplemented by our knowledge of the extralinguistic context).[46] By distinguishing them from the core metaphors, my point is not that we should disregard them. Rather, if we give them undue emphasis, we obscure the general principles of metaphorical competence they presuppose. And it is these general principles that are our primary focus in this book.

Chapter 2

From Metaphorical Use to Metaphorical Meaning

Few distinctions are more basic to twentieth-century philosophy of language than that between "what words mean and what they are used to do."[1] And if a philosopher of language trained in this century were asked to explain the phenomenon of metaphor, your best bet is that his gut reaction would be to treat it as a use of language rather than as a type of meaning, by a pragmatic rather than semantic theory. Now, a theory of use *is* the natural starting place for an explanation of metaphor—and especially if one focuses, as I do, on its context-dependence. My aim in this chapter is to show why we nonetheless *need* a semantics of metaphor. That is, I shall argue for a theory of metaphorical meaning by demonstrating, given the assumption that use in a context is essential to their interpretation, that it is necessary to posit meanings for metaphors in order to *constrain* their use.

There are any number of use, pragmatic, speech-act, or conversational theories of metaphor in circulation, but among them we can distinguish two camps. The first holds that just as there are semantic theories, so there are pragmatic theories, including pragmatic theories of metaphor. Some of these theories treat metaphor as an instance of speaker's meaning like an indirect speech act (Searle 1993), some as a type of figurative speech act (Cohen 1975; Loewenberg 1975), others as a brand of calculated conversational implicature (Grice 1975; Sperber and Wilson 1985/6), and yet others as a form of Gricean interpretation of speech that depends on mutual recognition of intentions (Fogelin 1994). The second camp takes metaphor to be a matter of use in the Wittgensteinian sense, according to which it eludes explanation in terms of regularities or rules, including those captured by notions like speaker's meaning, illocutions, perlocutions, or (violations of) maxims of conversation. The best-known representative of this second camp, Donald Davidson, denies both the possibility of a *theory* of metaphor—by which he means a finitistic rule-like account of metaphorical interpretation—and of any nonvacuous explanatory notion of metaphorical *meaning*.[2] What a metaphor conveys is largely nonpropositional, the product of a non-rule-governed creative skill, an unpredictable causal effect of its utterance-event understood exclusively according to the literal meaning of its words.

The difference between these two approaches to metaphor reflects a deeper division over the status of pragmatics or use. For philosophers like Searle semantics and pragmatics are each *theories*, with their own respective principles of meaning, corresponding to different domains of phenomena. For Davidson the very idea of pragmatics as a *theory* of a domain marked off as *use* of language is a misnomer. Instead, as he sees it, in the beginning was the utterance, which we identify as intentional and linguistic and go on to interpret. Where we can identify regularities across utterances, and across our interpretive practices, we abstract, with the usual degree of idealization, a theory of meaning or semantics. To the extent to which utterances, or language use, submit to any sort of theory of interpretation, that theory is semantics. Language use like metaphor that does not submit to semantic theory does not submit to another kind of theory; instead it is use of language that resists all theoretical explanation of the type provided by principles of meaning. *If* it can be "explained," it will only be causally.

I'll begin this chapter with a quick look at two theories representative of the first camp, Grice's and Searle's. (I'll return to other pragmatic accounts, such Fogelin's, in later chapters.) However, I shall mainly focus on Davidson, whose influential paper articulates a widespread attitude among philosophers and poses the most serious challenge in the literature to my position.

Davidson explicitly makes two negative claims ((1) and (2)), the first of which comes in two versions, and one positive proposal (3). In addition, his account makes an implied third negative claim (4):

(1a) Individual words in a metaphorical utterance do not have a "metaphorical meaning" in addition to or in place of their literal meaning; instead they exclusively retain their literal meaning.

(1b) The sentence used in a metaphorical utterance does not have a "metaphorical meaning" in addition to or in place of its literal meaning; instead it exclusively retains its literal meaning.

(2) Apart from the errors of "meaning-ification" in (1a,b), a metaphor does not have "a definite cognitive content that its author wishes to

convey and that the interpreter must grasp if he is to get the message"
(WMM 262).

(3) A metaphor is an imaginative *use* of a sentence, exclusively with its
ordinary literal meaning, whose intended *effect* is to make us notice a
likeness.

(4) There can be no (finitistic) theory that would show how the
metaphorical meaning (or metaphorical propositional content), if there
were one, of every metaphor expressible in a language is a function of a
finite number of features (or a finite number of meaning-axioms for a
finite number of simple expressions in the language) and a finite number
of rules of composition. That is: there can be no semantic theory of
metaphor.

In this chapter I shall bracket Davidson's arguments for (2) and return
to them in chapter 7 when I take up "knowledge *by* metaphor." The
fourth claim, Davidson's denial of the possibility of a semantic theory of
metaphor, is the thesis most directly opposed to my position, but he does
not explicitly defend it. I'll return to some possible considerations in its
support in the last section of this chapter. However, a satisfying (or, at
least, satisfactory) reply will come only when we sit down together to eat
the pudding I shall begin concocting in the next chapter. What Davidson
states in WMM are necessary conditions that any notion of metaphorical
meaning—hence any notion to be explained by a semantic theory of metaphor—must satisfy, and, throughout the essay, he directs us to a number
of prima facie obstacles that stand in the way of straightforwardly meeting those conditions for metaphor. In this chapter I shall concentrate on
these conditions for meaning and Davidson's reasons for thinking that
purported metaphorical meanings cannot satisfy them. At the same time,
I shall assess his complementary proposal that "how metaphor works"
can be adequately explained in terms of the use of sentences with nothing
but their literal meaning. By pinpointing the inadequacies in Davidson's
story, I hope to show why a use "theory" *needs* a notion of metaphorical
meaning. Finally, I shall try to show why such a notion of meaning cannot be adequately captured in Davidson's own general theory of meaning
(as a theory of truth-conditions). The problem, I shall argue, reflects a
more general difficulty in Davidson's treatment of context-dependent expressions, and this problem will motivate my shift (in ch. 3) to Kaplan's
conception of semantic theory based on the character-content distinction.[3]

In WMM Davidson explicitly presents both his critique and positive
proposal only in a few lean sentences. But his argument can be recon-

structed in light of his other writings on radical interpretation and, in particular, one of his most recent papers, "A Nice Derangement of Epitaphs."[4] Although my aim is not Davidsonian exegesis, I will freely weave among these papers to construct as strong a case as I can.

I Meaning vs. Use

According to Davidson, "metaphors mean what the words, in their most literal interpretation, mean *and nothing more*" (WMM 246, my italics). "Nothing more" excludes "*semantic* resources beyond ... the ordinary" (WMM 245, my italics), special metaphorical word- or sentence-meanings, and also anything a metaphor might be thought to convey as utterance- or speaker's meaning a la Grice and Searle. As Davidson adds parenthetically: "nor does [the] maker [of a metaphor] say anything, in using the metaphor, beyond the literal" (WMM 247). Davidson's remark is not specific to his view of metaphor. He is skeptical in general about the possibility of codifying the abilities and skills involved in so-called speaker's or utterance-meaning in the form of "principles" (a la Searle) or "maxims" (a la Grice); the kinds of inferences and reasoning these activities employ require only the "cleverness," "intuition, luck, and skill" that are necessary for any rational activity or for "devising a new theory in any field."[5] What words are *used to do* should never be considered *meaning*, even when qualified by the terms "speaker" or "utterance."

Here is not the place for a full evaluation of conversational implicatures and speaker's meaning as candidates for meaning. However, I agree with Davidson that metaphor, insofar as it is a matter of use, should not be subsumed under speaker's or utterance-meaning. A quick glance at Grice's and Searle's treatments should make clear why.[6]

Grice takes up metaphor—for example, 'you are the cream in my coffee'—in order to illustrate how the flouting of a maxim (e.g., Quality) leads to a conversational implicature. The reasoning underlying the implicature consists in two steps. First, because metaphors "characteristically involve categorial falsity" when they are taken literally (according to "what the speaker has made as if to say"), we infer that the speaker could not have meant *that*. But neither could he have meant its contradictory (as in irony) because that interpretation in turn would be a truism. Therefore, at the second step, we infer as "the most likely supposition ... that the speaker is attributing to his audience some feature or features in respect of which the audience resembles (more or less fancifully) the mentioned substance."[7]

Notice that the maxim of Quality functions in this calculation to conversationally implicate only *that* the utterance is *not* to be taken literally (or, for that matter, ironically) and *that* it is to be interpreted metaphorically.[8] That is, the stage of Grice's explanation that actually employs a violation of a conversational maxim only bears on our knowledge *that* the utterance is a metaphor, the recognition task, *not* the task of interpretation, our determination of *what* the metaphor means. When Grice turns to the latter task, he appeals to a probable ("the most likely") supposition involving resemblance, that is, an ad hoc though traditional principle added to the conversational maxims that involves no calculation or implicature. Hence even if we were to count calculated implicatures that result from floutings of maxims as "meanings," the *content* of the metaphorical interpretation would still not be such a product. On Grice's own grounds, we have been given no reason to consider the feature of resemblance that constitutes the content of the metaphor as a kind of implicationally derived *meaning*.[9]

Searle, too, counts metaphorical interpretation as a kind of "speaker's utterance meaning" as opposed to sentence meaning. He begins from the premise that our ability to understand a metaphor, although not part of our semantic competence (which governs sentence meaning), is nonetheless "systematic rather than random or ad hoc." Hence, there must be "principles" that explain how speakers "can say metaphorically 'S is P' and mean 'S is R,' where P plainly does not mean R" (Searle 1993, 113). Searle emphasizes that there is no single principle that explains how this is achieved for all metaphors; instead he proposes eight different principles, adding the "confident" proviso that they are not exhaustive. However, all the principles, he adds, "call R to mind" given an utterance of P.

Let's grant for now that the various principles indeed call R to mind. Does the effectiveness of the "principles" justify Searle's claim that R is the *meaning* of the metaphorical use of P?

Two points emerge when we examine Searle's eight principles. First, they demonstrate that the contents or features R that serve as metaphorical interpretations of expressions P are as heterogeneous as can be. The Rs can range over features that are either definitionally (Principle 1) or accidentally (Principle 2) true of the Ps but *in general* they need not *be* true or even be *believed* to be true of the Ps. An R feature may only be culturally or naturally "associated with P in our minds" (Principle 4), or R may simply hold under a condition somehow "like" that of P (Principle 5). There is, in other words, no single principle (e.g., resemblance) that would describe the contents of all metaphorical interpretations; the best we can do is say that *P* "calls [*R*] to mind," describing the range of *R*s case by case. For this last descriptive function, Searle's eight principles provide us with a helpful, if rough, catalog of *what* can serve as an interpretation of a metaphorically used expression, the range of possible values of *R* for different *P*s.

But this descriptive strength of Searle's principles is also their explanatory weakness. Because of their descriptive ecumenicalism, the principles place no restrictions on the class of possible features that can enter into a given metaphorical interpretation. What one principle rules out, another rules back in. Furthermore, it is completely obscure what it is for *one thing to call another to mind*. No one knows what kind of psychological ability or complex of abilities this is; at the very least, it is no better understood than the phenomenon of metaphor it is meant to explain. Searle himself comes close to acknowledging the explanatory poverty of his account when he says that the "question, 'How do metaphors work?' is a bit like the question 'How does one thing remind us of another thing?'" However, he thinks that the two questions are alike because "there is no *single* answer to either" (my italics). One might rather say, as philosophers since Hume have recognized, that what they have in common is that we know *no* answer to either of them. More important, even with an explanation of this psychological phenomenon, it should be obvious that not everything that something calls to mind, or reminds us of, is something it *means*. That a metaphor calls a feature *R* to mind is hardly sufficient to count *R* as part of its meaning. What would be necessary for something to count as metaphorical meaning is not only that it achieves an end but that it does so by providing a distinctive means—"the metaphorical way of using or interpreting words," whatever that turns out to be. "Reminding" or "calling to mind" simpliciter can't do that job. In sum, Searle's eight principles, however valuable *descriptively*, provide no *explanation* of how *P* imparts *R* or why such a means should count as meaning.

If these brief remarks are on the right track, then, as Davidson also thinks, we gain little explanatory value by thinking of the features communicated by a metaphor as its utterance- or speaker's meaning. Better not to use "meaning" when all we mean is use. However, Davidson's own thin remarks criticizing metaphorical meaning suggest another direction to explore in search of a candidate. What is wrong in "posit[ing] metaphorical or figurative meanings, or special kinds of poetic or metaphorical truth," in order to explain how "words work in metaphor" is, Davidson says, that this is like explaining why a pill puts you to sleep by saying it has a dormative power. Literal meaning and literal truth conditions can be assigned to words and sentences apart from particular contexts of use. This is why adverting to them has genuine explanatory power. (WMM 247)

Here Davidson says that appeal to metaphorical meaning is explanatorily vacuous for a reason connected somehow to its context-dependence. Thus a feature like one of Searle's Rs can't be a metaphorical "meaning" because (i) it "is not a feature of the word that the word has prior to and independent of the context of use," and (ii) unlike literal meaning that explains why all utterances of one sentence have the same truth-conditions, there are no analogous cross-contextual regularities to explain for metaphor: Each metaphorical utterance in its context appears to express a different feature from every other one.[10] Now, this criticism can be turned on its head: If we could find some *other* candidate (different from one of Searle's features R) that did meet these conditions, we would be well on our way toward a notion of metaphorical meaning. Rather than refuting the possibility of metaphorical meaning, we can read Davidson as stipulating two adequacy-conditions to be met by a kosher notion of metaphorical meaning. In the coming sections we shall try to get a better grip both on these conditions and on the kind of candidate for metaphorical meaning that might satisfy them.

II If Literal Meaning, Why Not Metaphorical Meaning?

To understand better why a (metaphorical) meaning must be "prior to and independent" of its context of use, let me turn first to Davidson's conception of literal meaning and its place in a theory of use.[11]

Following Davidson, a theory of language is at bottom a theory of linguistic use, that is, a theory of utterances to be explained as a species of rational acts ultimately performed for the purpose of communication.[12] Communication succeeds when a speaker S's utterance is interpreted as he intends, that is, when the hearer or, as Davidson prefers, interpreter I understands S's utterance just as S intended it to be understood. In that case, Davidson argues, we can shift the explicit object of our theorizing away from S to I's knowledge that enables him to interpret S. Furthermore, since we often communicate with utterances of ungrammatical as well as grammatical strings, Davidson assumes that a theory of interpretation must account for them all, including (as we discover in NDE) malapropisms, slips of the tongue, and half-finished sentence fragments. Finally, because communication occurs when I understands what S

intends to say, a theory of interpretation should be "adequate" (NDE 444) to the requirements of shared (linguistic) *understanding*.

It is this focus on understanding that yields Davidson's well-known proposal that a theory of interpretation takes the form of a Tarskian theory of truth. However, it is helpful to distinguish two distinct routes by which understanding leads to this conclusion. The first route attempts to negotiate its way between one claim that given the holistic nature of (linguistic) understanding, any theory of interpretation of a single utterance must provide interpretations for *all* of its speaker's potentially infinite number of novel utterances, and a second claim that the theory must represent this interpretive ability in a form that respects our finite human capacities. The theory accomplishes this by showing how the interpretation of each utterance is a function of the interpretations of its components: elements drawn from a finite stock of basic vocabulary composed into more complex interpretations by a finite stock of rules of composition. At this point Davidson brings on stage Tarski's theory of truth as an "adequate" theory of interpretation with exactly this formal structure. But technical matters aside, there is also a second route by which understanding leads to the same destination. Recall that the fundamental notion in Davidson's communication-oriented theory of interpretation is shared understanding, and it is joint knowledge of the truth-conditions of the utterance that S and I share when communication succeeds at achieving this kind of understanding. Hence a theory of truth, or truth-conditions, must occupy a central explanatory role in Davidson's theory of interpretation.[13] A theory of truth not only has the right structure for a theory of meaning; truth-conditions cash out the kind of understanding that is appropriate to the notion of meaning, or interpretation, that is involved in communication.

Given this conception of a theory of linguistic communication, Davidson next argues that the one notion a theory of interpretation should *not* employ is the idea of a *language* common to the interpreter and speaker— if "a language is anything like what many philosophers and linguists have supposed," namely, a system of "learned conventions or regularities" available in advance and independently of the occasion of utterance. In its place, Davidson proposes a complex account of communication in terms of speakers' and interpreters' mutual intentions and beliefs. Each S and I initially brings to each occasion of utterance his own "prior" theory of interpretation. S brings a theory of how he intends his words to be interpreted, I brings a theory of how he believes S (most likely) intends his (S's) words to be interpreted.[14] Unsurprisingly, S's and I's prior theories do not typically match perfectly as they initially stand. S and I therefore adapt, or mutually adjust, their respective prior theories in order to achieve the fully shared understanding, or interpretation, of the utterance that constitutes communication. The resulting theories that evolve in the course of successful communication Davidson calls "passing" theories. But passing theories, Davidson emphasizes, are too utterance-, occasion-, interpreter-, and speaker-specific to count as *languages*. So, if previous philosophers have posited language only in order to explain how communication by speech is possible, it follows, Davidson concludes, that "there is no such thing as a language, not if a language is anything like what many philosophers and linguists have supposed" (NDE 446).[15] This, I would add, is the full force of Davidson's conception of a theory of interpretation as a theory of use or utterances. Not only the explanandum is use or utterances; the explanans also need not appeal to anything that cannot be extracted or abstracted from use.

With this background, let's return to Davidson's notion of literal meaning, the meanings of words as opposed to what they are used to do. What work does this notion do in Davidson's language-liberated theory of interpretation? Indeed *how* is Davidson able to hold onto the very notion of literal meaning without falling back on explanatory notions like language, a notion he considers bogus?

If we think of an utterance as a rational action whose interpretations are its speaker's communicative and noncommunicative intentions, Davidson proposes to identify the literal meanings of the words in the utterance by ordering its interpretations, or intentional descriptions, in terms of their means-ends relations to each other.[16] For example, my utterance of '*yoreid geshem*' (in Hebrew) addressed to my son is a means to saying that it is raining, the saying of which is a means to asking him to take the laundry off the line, which is a means to reminding him of his house chores, which is a means to demonstrating my parental authority. The first intention in order in this series—to say such-and-such—Davidson labels the *first meaning* of the utterance, which is used in turn to achieve the second and later intentions in the ordering (all of which I'll call *secondary intentions*). This notion of first meaning, Davidson proposes, can serve as a "preliminary stab at characterizing" (NDE 434) the ordinary notion of literal meaning, "what words mean" as opposed to "what they are used to do."[17]

Note that Davidson singles out first meaning as literal meaning only because it is first in the speaker's order of *means* to achieve his ultimate end. Davidson cannot privilege it as *linguistic* meaning, because he denies an explanatory role to language in communication. Nor can he identify first meaning with literal meaning—as the etymology of 'literal' might suggest—on the grounds that it is directly *encoded* in the words as determined by rules of language (and not merely conveyed by their use). Davidson denies that there are any such rules of language.

Yet, even on Davidson's deflationary conception of the literal, there would appear to be another problem in identifying it with first meaning. The explanatory power of literal meaning is owing to the fact that it "can be assigned to words and sentences apart from particular contexts of use ..." (WMM 247). But first meaning—the understanding of an utterance that consists in knowledge of its truth-conditions—is context-dependent to an extreme: It is a feature of "words and sentences as uttered by a particular speaker on a particular occasion." How can we reconcile these two claims?

Davidsonian exegesis aside, two kinds of context-dependence should be distinguished. The first kind is *presemantic*: It registers the fact that our assignments of meanings or interpretations to sounds or inscriptions (including words as purely syntactic entities) depends on various features of the context. Consider the familiar task, on hearing some concrete sound pattern, of determining the semantic description it should be assigned or by which it should be "typed." I hear the sound pattern 'ī'. Even knowing that the speaker is speaking English, I must decide whether what I heard was the first person indexical 'I' or the common noun 'eye' or the affirmative 'aye' or the groan 'ai'. In making this judgment, we rely on all sorts of contextual cues—the appropriateness of the alternative types within the immediate string and then within the larger discourse, our beliefs about the speaker and his intentions, and so on. Now, on Davidson's picture of interpretation, this task is more general and more radical. On *every* occasion of utterance, the interpreter is faced with this task, and not only with the assignment of one among an alternative number of types *within* a language but with the assignment of a "language," or a theory of first meaning, *as a whole*. To be sure, the interpreter brings his prior theory of the speaker to the task, so he need not start from scratch. However, it would be pure chance, or divine providence, if his prior theory turned out to match the speaker's own theory perfectly. Each new, previously unknown proper or common name, as well as deviations from previous word patterns and malapropisms, is a potential source of misfit calling for revision, leading to a different passing theory. And at each turn of discourse, the task begins anew. Therefore, the interpreter utilizes every available contextual cue or piece of information in adapting his prior theory to the interpretation of the ongoing utterance. So, at this presemantic stage, each assignment of a first meaning to an utterance in the resulting passing theory is highly context-sensitive and utterance-specific.

Presemantic context dependence should be distinguished from a second sort of *postsemantic* context-dependence. Having assigned an utterance a first meaning, that utterance may then be used for an indefinite number of extralinguistic ulterior purposes or intentions: to warn, promise, deceive, or threaten. Which of these secondary intentions is realized also depends on the context—the speaker's and interpreter's mutual beliefs, intentions, and expectations. Yet, whichever further intention is attributed to the speaker, and however the utterance is used, its first meaning remains, *indifferently*, as the first of the means to all these ends. Hence the first meaning of an utterance is the meaning it has on *all* its uses or, more accurately, *regardless* of how it is so used.[18]

Given these two ways in which context can bear on the interpretation of an utterance, it should now be clear that first meaning is *presemantically* context-dependent but *postsemantically* context-independent. Context assigns a first meaning to a given utterance but, once assigned, that first meaning remains *invariant* regardless of the further context-dependent purposes or intentions for which it is used. In a word, the first meaning of an utterance is *autonomous* of its extralinguistic purposes or uses.[19] And for the same reason (though, as we'll see in ch. 8, it can't be the whole reason), first meaning *is* an interesting candidate for literal meaning: that is, the meaning of *words*, words regardless of their use. Here, then, the criterion of literal meaning is postsemantic context-independence.

With this account of literal meaning in mind, let's return to metaphor. Davidson's objection to metaphorical meaning cannot be that it is presemantically context dependent—because *all* first or literal meaning is presemantically context dependent. The objection must be that metaphorical interpretation is also *post*semantically context dependent: What the utterance communicates qua metaphor is not autonomous of its extralinguistic secondary intention and, therefore, cannot be meaning.

But what is the ulterior purpose, or secondary intention, of a metaphor? Davidson charges that other metaphor theorists start from the "trite and true observation" that "a metaphor makes us attend to some likeness" (WMM 247) and then falsely read the likeness into the utterance as its meaning. For Davidson this *effect*—our being made to notice a resemblance or some other salient feature—is rather the ulterior purpose distinctive of metaphor. And like other uses of language to obtain special effects—"assertion, hinting, lying, promising or criticizing" (WMM 259), uses that do not introduce special meanings in addition to or in place of their ordinary literal/first meanings—no special meaning should be associated with the metaphorical utterance beyond its literal/first meaning. No explanatory work would be done by such a metaphorical meaning that is not *already* done by the combination of literal meanings of the words uttered and their extralinguistic secondary intention as metaphor to make us notice a likeness.[20]

Take, for example, Romeo's utterance of 'Juliet is the sun'. Romeo wants to tell us that and why he loves, even worships, Juliet. He does this by telling us how she nourishes him with her caring attention, how he cannot live without her. This he does, not by expressing those thoughts literally (for whatever reason, e.g., because he doesn't have or know the right words or because he thinks it will be more effective another way) but by making us notice them, or by inviting us to discover them, by likening Juliet to the sun. And this he does, not by literally comparing Juliet to the sun or by visually displaying Juliet and the actual sun, but by uttering the (false) sentence 'Juliet is the sun'. Of course, for this utterance to make us consider features that Juliet and the sun share, 'Juliet' must mean Juliet and 'the sun' must mean the sun—that is, the words in the utterance must have their literal/first meaning. Q.E.D., Davidson argues, we have fully explained Romeo's utterance by taking into account only the literal/first meanings of the words uttered and the special metaphorical ulterior purpose or intention of the speaker in performing the utterance, namely, to bring features of likeness to our attention. With this explanation in hand, it would be gratuitous to posit a special metaphorical meaning.

As we saw earlier with Searle's features, this is a cogent argument against taking the likeness we are made to notice as the meaning of the metaphor. But the argument leaves untouched the possibility that a metaphorical meaning might be something else. Let me restate the argument, in words Davidson himself would never have put it: Suppose metaphors are truth-valued, or express propositions or content, and, in particular, that Romeo's utterance u of 'Juliet is the sun' is true iff Juliet is P, where P is a feature u makes us notice in virtue of which Juliet resembles the sun. Davidson's argument shows that P cannot be the meaning of u—even though it is a constituent of its truth-condition or propositional content. More generally, the argument shows that, if there is a metaphorical meaning, it cannot be its truth-condition or propositional content. However, the argument does not exclude the very idea of a metaphorical meaning.

If there is some other candidate for metaphorical meaning, it must satisfy the two conditions I mentioned (pace Davidson) at the end of section I. (i) It must be a feature we can specify independently both of the particular utterance in which it occurs and of its context, and (ii) it must be a feature that explains some regular, systematic feature of metaphorical utterances. Re (ii): In chapter 1, section II, I presented a number of examples [(1)–(10)] of apparent systematic variations in metaphorical interpretation; later in this chapter I shall offer additional data. Re (i): Recall that demonstratives are also expressions whose meanings and truth-conditions (in a context) must be distinguished and whose meanings, although sensitive to their contexts, can be specified independently of any particular utterance in a particular context.[21] The trick, then, is to show that there is a rule similar to those that govern the context-dependence of demonstratives that explains regular and systematic variations in metaphorical interpretations. Such a rule would constitute a kind of metaphorical meaning that belongs to our knowledge of semantics rather than pragmatics.

To get a better grasp of this alternative notion of metaphorical meaning, I want to turn now to the least explicit part of Davidson's story: his explanation of how a metaphor works simply in terms of its first/literal meaning and its metaphorical secondary intention. In particular, I'll focus on his claim that the utterance of, say, the sentence 'Juliet is the sun', exclusively with its literal meaning, "makes us notice" a feature whereby Juliet resembles the sun in virtue of which (or of the recognition of which) the metaphor "works." In the standard vocabulary of the metaphor literature, this part of Davidson's account corresponds to the point at which "the metaphorical depends on the literal." For Davidson this formula should be understood to say that the metaphorical use of a sentence depends (exclusively, to the extent to which it depends on meaning) on its literal meaning. In his writings, Davidson suggests two models for this dependence. In WMM the model is causal; in NDE it is inspired by Donnellan's account of the referential definite description. In the next two sections I'll discuss the inadequacies of these two models to motivate why we need metaphorical meaning and explain what it must be.

III Metaphorical/literal Dependence I: Davidson's Causal Explanation

Davidson introduces his "causal account" of metaphors by comparing them to jokes, dreams, pictures, and bumps on the head.[22] Jokes, for example, make us laugh; metaphors make us see likenesses. But no one would posit a "joker meaning" in jokes (in addition to or in place of their literal meaning) to explain why they make us laugh. For the same reason, we shouldn't posit a metaphorical meaning in metaphors to explain their effect. Instead, "joke or dream or metaphor can, like a picture or a bump on the head, make us appreciate some fact—but not by standing for, or expressing, the fact" (WMM 262). Just as the apple that dropped on his head reputedly *caused* Newton to think of the First Law of Gravity, so Romeo's (literally interpreted) utterance of 'Juliet is the sun'—a spatio-temporal event—causes him and us to see (or recognize or notice or think) that Juliet is like the sun in, say, that we cannot live without either of them.[23] And just as the apple itself neither meant nor served as a reason for believing the First Law of Gravity, neither does Romeo's utterance express that resemblance as its meaning nor furnish a reason for the belief that Juliet resembles the sun in some respect.

There is also a second parallel between metaphors, pictures, and jokes. The effect of a joke is a function of its telling in its entirety. A joke cannot be reduced to, or identified with, any of its isolable parts; just try to pack a whole joke into its one punch line. Similarly, pictures have no internal syntax; what the picture as a whole represents is not a function of what its parts individually represent independently of the context of the picture as a whole. In whatever way pictures do represent or mean, it is as basic wholes, not (like language) as composites of separable stand-alone values of their parts. To some extent the same is true of metaphor, at least on Davidson's account. Because he acknowledges no metaphorical meaning that is added to or replaces the literal meaning of one rather than another constituent expression in a metaphorical utterance, he cannot draw any distinction between the constituents that would make one or another subsentential expression "the" metaphor. The metaphor is whatever causes the appropriate effect, whatever makes us notice the "metaphorical" feature or resemblance, and this must be the utterance in its totality. Neither 'Juliet' nor '(is) the sun' individually and in isolation would cause us to see a resemblance between the two of them; hence, the minimal linguistic unit constituting "the" metaphor—*what* does the alerting, inspiring, prompting—must always be the full utterance in its context. On this score, metaphors, pictures, and jokes are all alike.

On the other hand, Davidson also claims—indeed this is his primary positive thesis—that what metaphors achieve "depends entirely on the ordinary meanings of those *words* and *hence* on the ordinary meanings of the *sentences* they comprise" (WMM 247, my emphasis). "As much as metaphor as can be explained in terms of meaning may, and indeed must, be explained by appeal to the literal meanings of the words" (WMM 256–257). But if ordinary literal meanings of words are combined into complex literal meanings using principles of semantic compositionality, and ordinary literal meanings of sentences are a compositional function of the meanings of their parts, then if the metaphorical significance or effect of an utterance "depends entirely" on its literal meaning, we would think that it should also be explicable compositionally in terms of the words and sentences so used. To the extent to which this holds, the analogy with pictures and jokes breaks down.

To complicate matters even more, note that Davidson shifts from talking of the ordinary literal meaning of the *words* that occur in a metaphor to that of the *sentences* that comprise those words. It is clear, as I'll show, that a metaphorical use depends on the literal meaning of the *word*(s) so used, but it is not nearly as clear that it depends on the literal meaning of the *sentence* comprised by those words. That depends, I'll argue, on what in particular we take literal meaning, or literal understanding, to be. To begin with, there is the argument that has recently been put forth (independently) by Avishai Margalit and Naomi Goldblum (1994) and by Roger White (1996) who have urged that each of the individual words in the metaphor 'Juliet is the sun' may have, and retain, its literal meaning, but that the whole sentence does not. For if we identify the literal meaning of a sentence with its truth-conditions, as does Davidson, they argue, we do not even *understand* what must be the case for that sentence to *be* true (not just *confirmed* or *known* or *verified* to be true), namely, the conditions in which Juliet, a human being, is the sun, a star. Of course, we know that and why the sentence is *false*, but knowledge of truth-conditions requires that we also know what the world would have to be like for the sentence to *obtain*—which, in this case, we do not. But if the *sentence* used metaphorically does not have its ordinary literal meaning, its metaphorical effect or significance obviously cannot depend on or be explained in terms of that meaning.

Davidson might reply at this point that the objection assumes a distinction between the literally meaningless and the false which, in turn, presupposes something like the analytic-synthetic distinction.[24] To avoid that controversy, let's therefore allow that 'Juliet is the sun' is literally meaningful and merely false. Yet, in point of fact, Davidson's own explanation of how metaphor works does not appeal to more than the separate literal meanings of the individual *words* in the sentence, ignoring any contribution made by the string syntactically or semantically structured *as* a sentence. For Davidson there is no difference between a metaphor and a poem like T. S. Eliot's "The Hippopotamus": both are "devices that alert us to aspects of the world by inviting us to make comparisons." But Eliot's poem works simply by the alternating presentation or display—the brute juxtaposition, as it were—of stanzas or clauses referring to hippopotami and the Church. Likewise, Davidson would have us believe that metaphor works simply by way of the linear sequence of literal meanings of the individual words of the utterance, regardless of its sentential syntax. Although the metaphorical depends on the literal, there is nothing specific to the literal meaning of the *sentence*, beyond that of its component words, that does any work in Davidson's account of the dependence of a metaphor on the literal.

Our knowledge of the separate and separable literal meanings of the individual *words* that make up a string cannot, however, be sufficient to explain how that string works as a metaphor. If the co-occurrence (as in Eliot's poem) of the words in the utterance with their literal meanings is enough to account for the metaphorical effect, then sentences that differ only, say, in their respective subject-predicate structures—for example, 'a man is a wolf' and 'a wolf is a man'—should not have *systematically* different effects. If we can ignore their (literal) sentential syntactic differences because they both invite us to make comparisons *between* the same *things* or *words*, the two sentences should not differ *predictably* in their metaphorical uses.[25] It should also be emphasized that the difference between 'a man is a wolf' and 'a wolf is a man' is not only a difference in linear surface word *order*, but a difference between their respective syntactic structures, and this difference lies at a deeper, more abstract level of representation of the *sentence*. If we include an account of these representational differences in the explanation of the metaphorical effect, it follows that the effect will depend not just on the literal meanings of the constituent words but also on *some* aspect of the literal meaning of the *sentence* used, in particular, the relevant kind of meaning, or logical form, determined by or corresponding to its syntax. This will not be captured simply by truth-conditions; it requires an additional notion of sentential meaning.

Let's take stock. I have argued that if we understand the formula "the metaphorical depends on the literal" to mean, following Davidson, that the metaphorical use of a sentence depends (exclusively) on its literal meaning, then: (i) the literal meanings of the individual words so used do carry part of the explanatory burden; (ii) (pace Margalit/Goldblum and White) the literal truth-conditions of the sentence uttered play no explanatory role; but (iii) certain syntactic or logical-formal properties of the sentence do contribute to or constrain the metaphorical use. For reasons that will emerge in the next two sections, I also think that (ii) holds, not only for the literally false or anomalous metaphors Margalit/Goldblum and White discuss, but also for metaphors that are literally true and acceptable. Now, the shape of the kind of literal meaning structure that meets (i)–(iii) is not easy to discern (although we shall see in ch. 4 that our metaphorical characters fit it). One tentative conclusion we can draw is that literal (sentential) meaning is not identical with truth-conditions. However, the more important lesson for our immediate purposes is that the combination of (i)–(iii) is, in any case, *not* what we would expect on Davidson's causal model based on his conception of interpretation as on-the-spot construction of passing theories of utterances in their contexts, as opposed to fixed theories of language or grammar that are endowed or learned prior to and independently of the utterance. If causes are singular events, one would expect the kind of literal meaning on which the metaphorical effect depends to be something to be read off, as closely as possible, of the actual concrete utterance. The two natural candidates would be either the literal truth-conditions of the utterance or the literal meanings of its individual words. The *least* natural candidate for Davidson's needs would be the more abstract representation delineated by (i)–(iii), a structure that requires knowledge not just of the literal meanings of the constituent words but also of deeper logical form abstracted away from the truth-conditions of the utterance. So, if (as Davidson holds) metaphorical use depends on literal meaning, the kind of literal meaning that must be taken into account does not square with Davidson's picture of occasion-specific interpretation and use.

Before going on, and in part to prepare the way for my own account, it is worth pausing to consider the "literal meanings" (of words) to which Davidson repeatedly refers. What are they? More specifically, what must literal meanings be in order to do the explanatory work Davidson wants them to do for metaphor?[26] I have no positive answer to the question, but two candidates can be excluded.

Recall that Davidson makes the metaphorical use of a sentence "depend entirely on the ordinary [literal] meanings of those words and *hence* on the ordinary [literal] meanings of the sentences they comprise" (my emphasis). That is, litcral meaning is compositional: if two expressions Φ and Ψ have the same literal meaning, then ... Ψ/Φ ... (the sentence that results from substituting Ψ for all occurrences of Φ in ... Φ ...) has the same literal meaning as ... Φ .... Now,

(1) Juliet is the sun

interpreted literally is an extensional sentence that is true if and only if Juliet is the sun. Furthermore, any sentence (1′) that would result by replacing, say, 'the sun' by another expression with the same literal meaning ought to have the same literal meaning as (1). Therefore, if the metaphorical use or effect of an utterance of (1) depends entirely on its literal meaning, and (1′) has the same literal meaning as (1), its metaphorical use ought to be preserved.

What could be such a literal meaning of a word on which its metaphorical effect, or interpretation, depends? What kind of literal meaning would preserve the metaphorical interpretation of its literal vehicle under substitution of a literally synonymous vehicle? A first candidate would be its extension or referent. However, consider Romeo's utterance of (1) in the context c in which 'is the sun' is used metaphorically to express the property of being worthy of worship (or, equivalently, makes us notice that Juliet, like the sun, is worthy of worship). Suppose also that (1), so used, is true in the circumstance of that context c: Juliet *is* worthy of worship. And suppose that

(2) The sun = the largest gaseous blob in the solar system

interpreted literally, is also true. Hence the two flanking terms (literally) co-refer and, by hypothesis, have the same literal meaning. Yet, from (1) and (2) it does not follow that

(3) Juliet is the largest gaseous blob in the solar system

is true *even* where 'the largest gaseous blob in the solar system' is *also used metaphorically* in the same context c; for the two literally coextensive terms, each used metaphorically in the same context, may none the less express metaphorical interpretations or make us notice metaphorical effects that are not themselves coextensive in any worlds in which they are simultaneously evaluated. Hence, the two (metaphorically used) sentences will not necessarily both be true even when they are both evaluated in the world in which they are both uttered. It follows that the metaphorical use/ interpretation of an utterance cannot depend entirely, or solely, on the literal meanings of its words so long as a literal meaning is an extension and we individuate uses, effects, or interpretations (minimally) by material equivalence.

A second natural candidate for the literal meaning of a word would be (despite Davidson's extensionalism) its intension (or some extensionalistically acceptable surrogate).[27] But by the same reasoning, if metaphor depends on literal meaning, any two expressions with the same intension, or one expression with a constant intension, should have the same metaphorical effect or interpretation on all occasions and in every context. This is not generally true. Metaphors, as we saw in examples (1)–(10) of chapter 1, vary systematically with their contexts. In some cases, the interpretation of the metaphor seems to vary with linguistic features of its context, and in other cases, with nonlinguistic features. For example, 'sweet' metaphorically applied to words (as in 'sweet words') expresses the property of being pleasant for speakers of English, Hebrew, and many other languages, but for speakers of Chinese the corresponding translation expresses the property of being specious. Calling one's lover 'a bedbug' in American English is calling him or her a nuisance or pain, but in Nigeria the term is one of affection—apparently because bedbugs there (as opposed to everywhere else) are thought to be cute.[28] This difference in metaphorical interpretation or effect is due to cultural differences between the respective speech communities—differences in (socially shared) presuppositions and beliefs. But there seems to be no way of incorporating such factors into an account framed only in terms of intensionality. Intensions (or some feature finer than extensions) may indeed turn out to be necessary but a purely intensional account of metaphor neglects another factor essential to its interpretation: the role of its context. So, if we take "literal meaning" to mean either an intension or some extensionalistically acceptable surrogate, Davidson's claim that metaphorical use "depends entirely" on literal meaning should still not be taken literally: Somehow the account must incorporate the role of context.[29]

My last point concerns Davidson's claim that there is a *causal explanation* of how the metaphorical effect of an utterance, the feature we subsequently notice or, more accurately, the noticing of the feature, "depends on its literal meaning." Davidson insists (WMM 249) and I agree (cf. ch. 1, sec. III (ii)) that any account that fails to explain this metaphorical-literal dependence is inadequate as an explanation of metaphor. But it is also Davidson's view of causation and explanation (and I'll grant this for the sake of argument) that a singular causal statement like

(4) Romeo's utterance of 'Juliet is the sun' caused his and his audience's noticing that Juliet, like the sun, is worthy of worship

is explanatory only because, and insofar as, it implies the existence of a law that covers the case. I shall argue now that, from the little Davidson says about the causal explanation of the metaphorical effect, there is no reason to think that such a law would (and perhaps good reason to think that it would not) include the required condition that the metaphorical effect or use depends on the literal meaning of the words or sentence. In that case, Davidson does not offer an *explanation* of metaphor that would be sufficient on his own grounds. Hence his own use account does not thereby render unnecessary the rival account offered by a semantic theory of metaphor that does explain metaphorical-literal dependence. At most Davidson has given us singular causal *descriptions* of our metaphorical utterances and their effects. But those descriptions of use are compatible with a semantic *explanation* of metaphor.

Before spelling out the problem for Davidson, I want to show how the same difficulty arises on a more radical version of his position presented by Richard Rorty (1987). Rorty enthusiastically endorses Davidson's offering of a fully naturalistic but noncognitivist alternative to the received view of "the tradition" that explains why metaphors are "indispensable" by forcing them into a cognitivist mold in which they express a sui generis kind of meaning. Davidson "lets us see metaphors on the model of unfamiliar events in the natural world—*causes* of changing beliefs and desires—rather than on the model of *representations* of unfamiliar worlds."[30] However, in order to expose metaphors as nothing more than noncognitivist causes—"mere stimuli, mere evocations" (ibid., 291)—Rorty goes considerably further than Davidson. He divests them of their status, not only as bearers of special metaphorical meaning, but also as uses of language and even as intentional, rational actions.

Adopting a figure from Quine (1978), Rorty characterizes the "realm of meaning," the domain of semantics, as "a relatively small 'cleared' area within the jungle of use." In this clearing there flourishes the "regular, predictable, linguistic behavior" that constitutes the literal use of language. Metaphor—which, according to Rorty, is unpredictable and irregular by its very nature—falls outside the scope of meaning, in the surrounding "jungle of use" (Rorty 1987, 285), a jungle populated by unfamiliar birdcalls, thunderclaps, and the whole spectrum of exotic sounds found in nature as well as by (some) speech utterances. What all these sounds have in common—and what apparently makes them a jungle—is that they are all just *noise*. They are sounds for which we have no (Davidsonian) prior theory to make sense of them; instead, by their very strangeness and anomalousness, they simply cause *effects* that impinge on us. Metaphors are also such more or less exotic noise. They may stand a tat closer than birdcalls to the cleared space of literal meaning because diachronically they can die—or, as Rorty puts it, be "killed off"—and live on in the afterlife of "stale, familiar, unparadoxical, and platitudinous" literal language (ibid., 295). But as long as they are genuinely alive, metaphors are nothing more (nor less) than noise. Given their irregularity and unpredictability, they cannot be "understood" or "interpreted"— except in "the way that we come to understand anomalous natural phenomena" (ibid., 290), namely, by revising our antecedent (scientific) theories. So, while metaphors may be "responsible for a lot of cognition," Rorty says that this is only in the nonintentional causal sense of "responsible" in which "the same can be said about anomalous nonlinguistic phenomena like platypuses and pulsars" (ibid.). Our ability to "understand" a metaphor does not, in short, fall under the rubric of mastery of language. Indeed the causal power of a metaphor also does not depend on any of its properties *as language* or even as a species of *intentional action*. Like a thunderclap or birdsong, the utterance of a metaphor is nothing but a nonintentional event, despite all its causal functioning.

Davidson might also locate metaphor in a "jungle of use," but the jungle would not be Rorty's. Davidson begins, as I noted earlier, with actual utterances or linguistic acts. The pretheoretical state of their "meaning" might be described as a "jungle" because it is dense, undifferentiated, and only after considerable theory-laden pruning and trimming, systematically differentiable into the meanings of its words (their literal or first meaning) and the various secondary meanings that constitute all the other things words can be used to do. However, even the unruly jungle that remains after we have cleared away the space of literal meaning is populated only by the meanings of intentional, rational linguistic actions. Some of the secondary extralinguistic ends may be causal effects of the utterances—as with metaphors—but the utterances are no less rational and intentional because they also have causal effects. For Davidson, unlike Rorty, it is never noises—nonlinguistic, nonintentional events—that fall in our domain of investigation, only intentional human actions, of which linguistic actions are one subclass. Within that corpus we distinguish what words mean, the subject of semantics, and the many other things they are used to do or mean, including (as in metaphor) those things that their use causes us to recognize or see.

Not all jungles, then, are created equally wild. But despite their differences, Rorty's picture drives home more perspicuously than Davidson's one important consequence of a "causal" explanation of metaphor. The fact that the utterance of a metaphor does (some) causal work is not incompatible with its being an intentional linguistic action, but there is little if any reason to expect that a *causal explanation* of metaphor, using (strict) laws, will make reference to its character as an intentional act or as a use of language. To the extent to which a metaphor's causal explanation and underlying laws all treat it as a physical event, Rorty is correct to view metaphors as just *noise*, that is, nonintentional, nonlinguistic events. But this consequence amounts to a reductio argument against Davidson's position—because metaphors are *not* just noise. As everyone (including Davidson) agrees, a metaphorical interpretation, or effect, depends on its literal meaning. But noise, being nonlinguistic, has no literal meaning. So, Rorty is wrong to describe metaphors *solely* as noise because it is not possible to explain them *fully* as noise. What his story enables us to see sharply is that a Davidsonian causal account cannot claim *both* to give a causal explanation of metaphor and to explain how the metaphorical effect "depends entirely on the ordinary [i.e., literal] meanings of those words." For the causal explanation of a metaphor will treat it as a nonintentional, nonlinguistic event—as meaningless noise—without mentioning features like its literal meaning. Or, to be a bit more cautious, there is no reason to think that a causal explanation of the metaphorical effect employing (strict) laws will employ concepts like that of literal meaning.

Let me recast this argument from a different angle. Recall that on Davidson's own account of causal explanation, for one event to be said to cause another it is only necessary that the events be nomologically related under *some* description of each.[31] Furthermore, a singular causal statement need not itself instantiate the causal explanatory law that it presupposes or refer to the events in question under their nomologically appropriate description.[32] Hence we can agree with Davidson that the metaphor-utterance event causes the resemblance-noticing event (even allowing for the anomalism of the mental) insofar as there are grounds to believe that there exists some nomological relation between the two under some description of each. But this is not enough for Davidson's account of metaphor. His claim is not simply that there is *some* causal relation between the metaphorical utterance and what it makes us notice—under some appropriate description of each. Davidson's thesis is that we can explain how the causal "effect" of the metaphor "is brought off by the imaginative employment of words and sentences [and *depends*] *entirely* on the ordinary meanings of those words and hence on the ordinary meanings of the sentences they comprise" (WMM 247, my italics). The vocabulary of the explanation must itself, then, make reference to words, use, and literal (or first) meaning. But it remains to be shown that any such explanation can plausibly be given. Davidson, for one, gives no evidence that such an explanation is in the offing.

Let me emphasize that I am not objecting to the ultimate possibility of causal explanations of metaphor or, for that matter, of any linguistic phenomenon in terms of the physical or neurophysiological properties of utterances and their effects. Such an explanation would, in principle, treat the utterance of a metaphor and its effect no differently than the auditory perception of a thunderclap or a birdsong and their effects on us. I am objecting instead to the claim that we can *explain* how a metaphor works *both* as a use of language that depends entirely on the literal meanings of its words *and* in terms of a causal relation to the effect of its utterance. We may be able to make the singular *judgment* that Romeo's utterance caused us to see that we can't live without Juliet (just as we can't live without the sun), but as soon as we try to provide an explicit causal *explanation* of that effect, we lose the substance of Davidson's claim that it is *as a use of language exclusively with its literal meaning* that metaphor does its work. On the other hand, a singular causal judgment is not itself incompatible with a semantic explanation employing a notion of metaphorical meaning. To rule out the latter, Davidson would have to provide a causal explanation that renders the notion of metaphorical meaning unnecessary. However, such an account would require a lawlike explanation of metaphor *as* a kind of use of the sentence with its literal meaning in which the explanans itself employs literal meanings, words, and so on. But then metaphors would not only be noises or bumps on the head— unless those also bear meanings *in* the head.

IV   Metaphorical/literal Dependence II: Davidson on Referential Definite Descriptions, Malapropisms, and Metaphor

While contrasting malapropisms with Keith Donnellan's (1966) well-known idea of a referential definite description, Davidson writes:

Jones has said something true by using a sentence that is false. This is done intentionally all the time, for example in irony or metaphor. A coherent theory could not allow that under the circumstances Jones' sentence was true; nor would Jones think so if he knew the facts. Jones' belief about who murdered Smith cannot change the truth of the sentence he uses (and for the same reason cannot change the reference of the words in the sentence). (NDE 440)

Here Davidson claims that when a speaker uses a definite description referentially— as opposed to attributively—he succeeds in communicating his intended meaning (or reference) despite the fact that it differs from the literal/first meaning (or reference) of the words. Yet the words have their literal/first meaning on that use. Hence the referential-attributive distinction marks a distinction between two uses of language that differ in "what they say"—that is, in their truth-conditions and, therefore, in truth-value—without differing in their literal/first meanings. Davidson contrasts this case with malapropisms (and the introduction of new proper and common names) where the literal/first meaning of the word used itself changes in its context of utterance. Metaphor, Davidson adds almost as an aside, is like the use of the referential definite description. The sentence is used metaphorically to say something true, although the sentence used is nonetheless (literally) false; hence the sentence retains its literal/first meaning. Thus metaphor, like the referential description, differs from malapropism, whose literal/first meaning undergoes a change on that use from its prior literal/first meaning.[33]

To support his account of the referential use of a definite description, Davidson recounts Donnellan's well-known example of Jones who believes, though (unbeknownst to himself) falsely, that Max murdered Smith. Seeing Max's behavior in the courtroom dock, Jones exclaims: 'Smith's murderer is insane'. Where Jones uses the description 'Smith's murderer' referentially—as a tool to refer to Max but not to describe him —Donnellan argues, and Davidson agrees, that Jones says "something true" provided Max is insane.

In this example there is no reason to say that the referential definite description has undergone a change of meaning just because Jones is able to "say something true" about Max by uttering 'Smith's murderer is insane' even though Max does not satisfy the content of the description. On the contrary: Jones is able to use the description 'Smith's murderer' to refer successfully to Max because he (falsely, as it turns out) believes, or represents himself as believing, that Max is Smith's murderer *in the prior, literal meaning of those words*. And it is either because his interpreter also (falsely) shares that belief or because he recognizes that Jones (falsely) holds that belief of Max (in the prior, literal meaning of the words) that he interprets Jones' utterance of 'Smith's murderer is insane' to be saying something true about Max. Were we to inform Jones that Max is not in fact Smith's murderer (in the prior, literal meaning of the words), he would *not* respond that we had failed to understand the meaning of his use of that description on that occasion, or that he had intended the words to have a new passing first meaning in that context, a meaning according to which they did uniquely designate Max. Instead he would say—given his intention to use the description referentially—that he had meant to say something true about Max even though he was wrong in believing that he was Smith's murderer (in its passing literal meaning), hence wrong (or misleading) in using that description. So, as Davidson concludes, "the reference is nonetheless achieved by way of the normal meanings of the words. The words therefore must have their usual reference" (NDE 439).

With a malapropism, in contrast, Davidson claims that the word itself acquires as its (passing first) meaning what the speaker intends to say in its context of utterance. For example, when Yogi Berra reputedly thanked the crowd in Yankee Stadium on "Yogi Berra Day" for "making this day necessary," *possible* is what the *word* 'necessary' *meant* on that occasion, and not merely what Yogi meant by *using* that word (in its ordinary, literal meaning).[34] Here is how Davidson would describe this situation. Yogi's interpreter brings a prior theory of Yogi's linguistic behavior to the occasion of utterance, a theory in which 'necessary' means *necessary*. Hearing the absurdity or inappropriateness of Yogi's utterance with that prior first meaning, he knows that Yogi must have intended to say something else. At this point the interpreter has at least two options. Either he can keep its prior first meaning as its passing first meaning *and* add an ulterior purpose for the utterance, say, take Yogi to be speaking ironically or comically; or he can adjust his prior theory of Yogi's first meaning in order to give the word 'necessary' as its passing first meaning what he believes Yogi intends to be saying on that occasion, namely, *possible*. Davidson does not tell us how Yogi's interpreter decides to interpret the utterance one way rather than another. However, if he decides that Yogi intends to be saying that he wants to thank everyone for making this day *possible*, then it is arguable that there is at least as good a (if not a better) reason to take *possible* as the passing first meaning of 'necessary' as there is to take it as something imparted secondarily by Yogi's use of 'necessary' in its prior first meaning. Unlike the case of a referential description, where there are grounds for saying that Jones understands his words in their prior first meaning (namely, the fact that he *believes*, albeit falsely, that Max is Smith's murderer, in the prior first meaning of these words), here there is no such reason to think that Yogi understands by 'necessary' *necessary*, that he intends to say that he wants to thank everyone for making the day *necessary* in its prior first meaning. On the contrary, we would explain why he said what he did by saying that he intended to thank everyone for making the day *possible*—and he believed, or represented himself as believing, that on this occasion 'necessary' just (first) means *possible*. To be sure, Yogi's interpreter can figure this out only because he knows that in Yogi's *prior* theory 'necessary' means *necessary* and 'possible' means *possible*, and he conjectures that Yogi is "confusing" the two (or that they get confused in his mental lexicon because of their semantic proximity). However, that the interpreter knows one interpretation "by way of" the other does not show that the latter belongs to his passing theory and should be prior to Yogi's intended interpretation of the word in the passing theory itself. For the passing theory is a theory of what the speaker intends on the occasion of utterance. And Yogi had no such intention—to mean *necessary* by 'necessary'—on that occasion.

For the sake of argument, let's grant Davidson these characterizations of referential definite descriptions as uses of words to mean something other than what the words themselves literally/first mean and of malapropisms as words that acquire a new passing literal/first meaning on their occasion of utterance. How should we then describe metaphor?

Davidson gives no explicit argument for his classification of metaphors with referential definite descriptions in the realm of use, rather than with malapropisms in the realm of meaning. But his reasoning would presumably go like this: What a metaphor makes us notice "depends on its ordinary [= literal] meanings" (WMM 247); therefore, "an adequate account of metaphor must allow that the primary or original [= literal] meanings of words remain active in their metaphorical setting" (WMM 249). Hence a metaphor like 'Juliet is the sun' must "have" its ordinary, primary, or original meaning—that is, its prior literal/first meaning—as its passing literal/first meaning on its occasion of utterance. In this respect, metaphor is like a referential definite description and unlike a malapropism. The speaker uses a literal/first meaning in order to make us notice hitherto unnoticed resemblances or features, his ulterior purpose for his metaphorical utterance.

But is the way in which a metaphor "depends" on its literal/first meaning really like the way in which a referential definite description "depends" on its prior literal/first meaning? How do we know that "the primary or original meanings of words remain active in their metaphorical setting" *within* the passing theory of the utterance? Perhaps the metaphorical-literal dependence holds *between* a first meaning that the metaphorical utterance acquires in its passing theory and the previous first meaning the word held in its prior theory?

The answer to these questions is, I think, that we have no satisfactory answer using just the conceptual resources of Davidson's theory. We lack for metaphorical utterances the motivation we had for referential definite descriptions to maintain that their prior literal/first meaning remains their passing literal/first meaning. Recall that Jones must intend his words

'Smith's murderer' to be understood according to their prior literal/first meaning because he *believes* that Max is Smith's murderer in their prior literal/first meaning, a belief we must ascribe to him to explain why he uses the (improper) description 'Smith's murderer' to refer to Max. There is no analogous reason to claim that the speaker of a metaphor intends his words to be *understood*, and hence interpreted, according to their prior literal/first meaning. To reinforce this point, recall our distinction between the literal meanings of the individual words in the metaphorical utterance and the literal meaning, or truth-conditions, of the sentence so used. Focus first on the sentence. Romeo surely does not intend to communicate the absurd or patently false proposition that Juliet is the sun—expressed by the literal meaning of the sentence—when he utters 'Juliet is the sun'. As we said, following the argument of Margalit and Goldblum (1994) and White (1996), a literally deviant string like this may not even *have* a literal meaning or literally express a proposition, where either of these is a set of truth-conditions. Even where the sentence used metaphorically is not absurd or false taken literally—for example, Cohen's twice-true 'no man is an island'—there is also no evidence that the literal meaning of the *sentence* does any work in explaining the metaphorical use in the passing theory. Therefore, we have no reason to hold that the speaker believes (or holds some other attitude toward) *that* proposition, hence, that he *understands* the metaphorical utterance by way of taking the *sentence* according to its prior literal/first meaning *in* the passing theory. And in that case, there is also no reason to say that the prior literal/first meaning of the sentence—its prior literal truth-conditions—should also be considered its passing first meaning on occasions when it is used, or interpreted, metaphorically.[35]

On the other hand, there is also good reason not to consign the literal meaning of the *words* used metaphorically entirely to the prior theory of the utterance. The literal/first meaning of the words must "remain active in the metaphorical setting." Whatever turns out to be the exact nature of the dependence of the metaphorical on the literal, knowledge of the literal/first meaning of words is necessary on the occasion of utterance itself in order to determine what they metaphorically make us notice, that is, their metaphorical interpretation. And the relevant literal meaning is not what the literal meaning of the word *was* but what it *is*—on the very occasion on which it is interpreted metaphorically. Therefore, we shouldn't explicate metaphorical/literal dependence diachronically, holding between passing and prior theories. *Within* the passing theory there must also be room for the literal/first meaning of the words of the utterance. The problem for Davidson's account is how to make room for this in the passing theory itself.

Suppose the metaphorical use depends on the literal/first meanings of the *words* used in the passing theory. Since it is the very nature of literal meaning to be compositional, those literal word-meanings should be composible into literal sentence-meanings. But the literal meaning of a sentence is its truth-conditions, the content of our *understanding* of the utterance. Therefore, where the literal meanings of the words are the first meaning of the passing theory of the metaphorical utterance, we are also forced to say that the interpreter takes the speaker to *understand* his utterance according to that literal meaning. But that conclusion, we have argued, is either false, if metaphorical utterances do not have literal meanings qua truth-conditions, or it lacks motivation, insofar as meta-phors are not explained in terms of their literal *sentence*-meanings, how they would be literally understood.

To put it a bit differently, I am arguing that the *words* as used, or interpreted, metaphorically must "have" their literal/first meaning as part of their passing theory of interpretation—because knowledge of their lit-eral meaning is necessary for knowledge of their metaphorical use or in-terpretation. But the appropriate sense of "having their literal meaning" is not one that can be articulated with the conceptual apparatus of Davidson's theory. For the *words* do not "have" their literal meaning in the sense that the *sentences* they comprise are, or are intended to be, *understood* according to their literal/first meaning, that is, their truth-conditions. What we therefore need is a way to make sense of how indi-vidual *words* can "have" their literal meaning without thereby claiming that the *sentence* composed of those words used, or interpreted, meta-phorically must also be *understood* according to its literal meaning or truth-conditions.

V   The Autonomy of Meaning and Metaphor

I suggested in chapter 1 that demonstratives (including indexicals) should serve as a model for our semantic theory of metaphor as a type of context-dependent interpretation of language. As a case in point, I now want to suggest that demonstratives can also point us toward a way out of the impasse to which the argument has led in the last two sections: a way to make sense of the idea that a metaphor may "depend" on the literal meaning of its words but not on the literal meaning (i.e., truth-conditions) of the sentence those words comprise. This way out of the impasse will also direct us away from Davidson's conception of meaning in terms of interpretation in the form of truth-conditions whose shared understanding constitutes communication, and toward the notion of meaning as character, which will feature in Kaplan's semantics in chapter 3.

As we have already had occasion to note, in his less cautious moments Davidson writes as if "literal meaning" and "literal truth-conditions" are equivalent and that what gives both of them "genuine explanatory power" is that they "can be assigned to words and sentences apart from particular contexts of use" (WMM 247). This, of course, is not always the case, as demonstratives amply show; and Davidson knows this. The indexical (type) 'I' and pure demonstrative (type) 'that' have "literal meanings" assigned to all of their utterances (tokens) "apart from particular contexts of use," but their contributions to the truth-conditions of the sentences in which they occur vary with, and depend on, their particular contexts. For example, my, JS's, utterance of 'I love Jerusalem' is true iff JS loves Jerusalem, while DD's utterance of the same sentence is true iff DD loves Jerusalem. Yet our two utterances of 'I' have the same literal linguistic meaning, namely, the rule

(I) Each utterance of 'I' directly refers to its speaker[36]

and it is assigned to the utterances "apart from [their] particular contexts of use."

From the beginnings of his program, Davidson has acknowledged the difficulties posed by demonstratives for a Tarski-style theory of truth that treats sentences simpliciter as the truth-vehicles. To remedy the difficulties he has proposed to make utterances the truth-bearers and to characterize truth for a language relative to a speaker and time (and possibly other contextual devices corresponding to other demonstratives).[37] Thus in place of the Tarskian T-sentence (for sentences s containing no demonstrative expressions)

(T) s is true iff p,

which, according to Davidson, captures what a speaker knows when he knows the meaning of s, he has proposed for the sentence s^* (containing demonstratives, such as '... I ...') a relativized T-sentence of the form

(T_d) s^* is true as spoken by a speaker S at a time t iff p^*

where p^* is a translation of s^* into the metalanguage and contains the corresponding contextual value for each occurrence of a demonstrative in s^*. For example:

'... I ... now ...' is true as spoken by JS on 7/20/98 iff ____JS____
7/20/98____.

This treatment of demonstratives raises a number of technical questions
I shall not pursue here.[38] What is more critical for our purposes is how
to describe the context-dependence of demonstratives like 'I' in a way
compatible with Davidson's criterion that explanatory power requires
context-independence.

Earlier I distinguished presemantic and postsemantic brands of
context-dependence. The context-dependence of 'I' is neither. It is not
postsemantic because what varies with context in its case is not an
extralinguistic intention or ulterior purpose performed by the utterance,
but its communicative intention, its truth-condition, the shared understanding necessary for communication. The context-dependence of 'I' is
also not presemantic. What varies with context in its case is not the lexical
description or type of a (semantically uninterpreted) sound, shape, or
word. The sound 'ī' has *already* been assigned the lexical type of the first
person demonstrative 'I'; indeed it is only *because* it has already been
assigned that type that it is context-dependent in this further way. Therefore, in addition to pre- and postsemantic context-dependence, let's distinguish a third kind of context-dependence for demonstratives: *semantic*
context-dependence. Here the context functions not to pair a type with an
uninterpreted sound or shape, but rather, given a meaningful type *already*
assigned to the sound or shape, to determine a truth-conditional factor on
a particular occasion of utterance.

To accommodate demonstratives within his theory of meaning,
Davidson must allow for this type of semantic context-dependence. His
theory of literal meaning, that is, that meanings are truth-conditions,
must be extended to acknowledge that different tokens of one sentence
type with one literal meaning (e.g., a sentence containing demonstratives)
can have different truth-conditions in different contexts; hence not all
truth-conditions can be "assigned apart from particular contexts of use."
Yet, the *point* of context-*in*dependence for meaning is satisfied no less by
the context-sensitive meaning of demonstratives than it is by the meanings
of eternal expressions. A rule like (I) enables us to capture what is regular
and systematic about different utterances of the word 'I' and we can
specify (I) apart from any particular utterance in which 'I' occurs. This
much Davidson himself ought to readily acknowledge. However, having
taken this (small) step, Davidson *also* ought to be more sympathetic to a
semantics for metaphor *if* (and, I admit, this is no small "if") it could
also be shown that there is a strong parallel between the systematic way

sentences containing demonstratives vary across contexts in their truth-conditions and the way metaphors likewise depend for what they say, for their content or truth-conditions, on their contexts. The same semantic theory should cover metaphors no less than demonstratives. Davidson's charge that metaphorical meaning is "not a feature of the word that the word has prior to and independent of the context of use" would, then, carry no more weight against metaphor than against semantically context-dependent expressions like demonstratives.[39]

The relation between the meaning of a demonstrative, such as (I) for 'I', and its truth-condition(-al factor) also suggests a way to explain how the metaphorical use of an expression Φ "depends" on its literal meaning—though this explanation will now force us to rethink the notion of meaning in non-Davidsonian terms. The rule (I) plays a number of roles. First, it makes it possible to generate an interpretation for the indexical, the individual referent that is its truth-conditional constituent. However, that interpretation is *underdetermined* by the rule of meaning. In different contexts, depending on who is speaking, the same rule of meaning will yield different referents as interpretations. So, the sense in which the interpretation of 'I' "depends" on its meaning cannot be that the latter (fully) *determines* the former. Second, the rule of meaning (I) *constrains* the possible interpretations of 'I'. No matter who a speaker believes himself to be, no matter whom he intends to refer to by his utterance of 'I', no matter how many cues he gives his interpreter about his referential intentions, his utterance of 'I' will refer to himself, the actual speaker, and to no one else. Thus, what one knows by the meaning of 'I' is, in part, an instance of the *autonomy* of meaning: the fact that what expressions (literally) mean is independent, or autonomous, of what individual speakers intend to communicate on given occasions.[40] (I) thereby excludes *impossible* interpretations of 'I' rather than determines what *is* communicated or expressed by it. In this sense, the interpretation of 'I' does depend on its meaning; the one is constrained by the other.

Knowledge of this kind of meaning, exemplified by (I), is not unrelated to the knowledge of meaning—actual truth-conditions—on which Davidson focuses, but it is different in function. For Davidson, meaning is what is understood, and it is shared understanding that makes for informative communication. Hence meaning is cashed out by truth-conditions, for what one must know to understand an utterance is (at least) to know the conditions under which it would be true. But the kind of meaning expressed in rules like (I) is not itself a truth-condition. The descriptive condition in (I) is never itself a component in the truth-conditions for its utterances. Instead the individual referent is the truth-conditional constituent, though (I) and not the individual referent is what the interpreter knows as the literal meaning of each utterance of 'I'. Rather than belonging to *what* is communicated or understood or intended by the utterance, the (I) kind of meaning *constrains* the possible truth-conditional factors for its utterances. But for this reason it also does not fit neatly into Davidson's means-ends ordering of first and secondary intentions. If first meaning is how the utterance is primarily understood, and intended to be understood, (I) is not first meaning; it is "zero" meaning.

The same conception of meaning applies to metaphor, and we should understand how metaphorical use "depends" on literal meaning in exactly the same way. The dependence should not be taken to mean that the literal meaning of the words *determines* their metaphorical use. As we saw in examples (1)–(10) in chapter 1, one expression with one literal meaning (e.g., 'is the sun') can be used metaphorically to different effects, or to express different interpretations, in different contexts. But the literal meaning of the word constrains its metaphorical effects or interpretations, as I shall illustrate immediately.[41] This role of the meanings of the words used metaphorically is not their role insofar as they contribute constituents to an object of (literal) understanding of the utterance, to its literal truth-conditions (where it has them). We don't need to *understand* how the sentence uttered metaphorically would have been understood literally in order to grasp the metaphorical use or interpretation of the sentence. For the same reason, we do not need to know the literal truth-conditions of the sentence interpreted metaphorically, knowledge of which, according to Davidson, constitutes the understanding that, when shared, makes for communication. Yet, the metaphorical use or interpretation of an expression Φ in a sentence ... Φ ... does depend on the literal meaning of Φ (and, for that matter, of other individual words in the sentence) insofar as our knowledge of the latter constrains our knowledge of the former. Thus, as we shift our attention away from truth-conditions to constraints, both for demonstratives and metaphors, we also shift away from Davidson's conception of the domain for a theory of meaning. To illustrate the other conception that focuses on the autonomy of meaning, another theme that it is difficult to mesh with Davidson's conception, let me give one more example of a meaning constraint.

Consider the meaning carried by a grammatical configuration, for example,

(5) He saw John in the mirror,

which *cannot* be understood as meaning

(6) John saw himself in the mirror.

The explanation of this fact appeals to a structural condition that prevents the anaphoric pronoun in (5) from taking the noun ('John') as its antecedent.[42] The condition can be defined (among other equivalent ways) in terms of an abstract "tree" structure that displays the grammatical categories and dominance-relations among the elements in the concrete string. Given a tree structure for the string, let the *scope* of an element be the least subtree to which it belongs. In simple subject-predicate sentences, then, predicates are within the scope of subjects (since the least subtree to which the subject belongs is dominated by a Sentence node that also dominates the predicate and its arguments), but subjects are not within the scope of arguments of predicates (since the least subtree to which predicate arguments belong is [usually] dominated by a Verb Phrase node that does not dominate the sentence subject). Given this abstract notion of scope, we can then state the relevant condition on pronomial anaphora:

(A) No element can seek its antecedent within its own scope.

Therefore, in (5), where the antecedent noun (a predicate argument) lies within the scope of the pronoun (the subject), (A) is violated, ruling out the possible interpretation. In (6), the subject noun lies outside the scope of the reflexive pronoun 'himself', allowing the interpretation that links it to 'John' as its antecedent.

Two features of this explanation are relevant to our present concerns. First, what (A) codifies is a kind of meaning carried by the configuration or syntax of the sentence because it carries definite implications for its truth-value. Second, as with demonstratives, this kind of meaning constrains the interpretation of the anaphoric construction without determining it. The condition does not state what the anaphoric interpretation *is* or *must* be but what it *cannot* be; it *excludes* interpretations. Thus this notion of meaning, like that of demonstratives, does not enter into the content of what speakers understand by an utterance, but at most circumscribes the bounds of that understanding by ruling out impossible interpretations.

Now, how, we might ask, would Davidson explain the *impossibility* of understanding (5) as (6)? Recall his argument that because a theory of meaning (even when formally reconstructed as a Tarski-style theory of truth) is a highly context-specific theory of interpretation of utterances as rational communicative acts, it is nothing like a language (or grammar) "if a language is anything like what many philosophers and linguists have supposed" (NDE 446), that is, a system of "learned conventions or regularities" (or an innate or innately fixed body of principles or rules) available in advance and independently of the occasion of utterance. Instead Davidson puts forth his picture of passing theories of interpretation, which evolve from prior theories yet constantly undergo revision in the course of language use in context. On this picture, one explanation of why it is impossible to understand (5) as (6) might follow the principle that just as we usually do not intend or try to do things we believe nature will prevent us from doing, so we intend to say only what we believe our interpreters will understand or only what we expect others will reasonably be able to interpret us as saying.[43] Hence, given our previous experience and prior theory of our interpreters, we never would intend to mean (6) by (5).

The difficulty in applying this kind of Davidsonian explanation to our data (such as (5)–(6)) is that rules like (A) that exemplify the "autonomy" of meaning are, only very implausibly, the kinds of rules we would expect to find in passing theories. (A) applies to *all* anaphoric configurations and can be formulated only by using syntactic categories and notions like scope and dominance that go far beyond the properties of concrete utterances. Likewise, (I) is an instance of a schema that holds for *all* indexicals in every context in which they are used and rests on the abstract relation of scope. For its notion of direct reference marks the fact that the interpretation (or content) of the indexical is always fixed relative to its context of utterance, regardless of its scope in the sentence and regardless of whether the matrix sentence also contains another expression, or operator, that makes its truth-value (as opposed to content) dependent on circumstances other than that of its context of utterance. For example, my utterance of

(7) I might be assassinated

is true in my context of utterance if and only if there is some possible circumstance in which I, JS, am assassinated; it is not enough for (7) to be true that there be some possible circumstance in which whoever might be speaking in that circumstance is assassinated. Thus (I) also expresses a condition that applies not to the concrete utterance but to a significantly more abstract representation. Both (I) and (A), then, are more general, fixed, and abstract than the sort of context-specific expectations and beliefs that prima facie govern the assignment of first meanings according to Davidson's picture of prior and passing theories. This is not to say that it would be impossible to formulate these conditions in Davidson's use-oriented theory of interpretation. But any Davidson-style explanation of the process whereby speakers come to learn these kinds of conditions, appealing to mutual beliefs and expectations, would necessarily require the attribution of rules of corresponding generality, systematicity, and abstractness. And the more general, abstract, and fixed these rules are, the less will Davidson's account of passing theories be distinguishable from the knowledge of language he rejects.

Furthermore, T-sentences (and the axioms of the truth-theory that entail the T-sentences) known by an interpreter that give the meaning in the form of truth-conditions for utterances that occur in actual use are plausible constituents in prior and passing theories. But rules like (A) and (I), as we've seen, do not themselves determine the content, or truth-condition, of any utterance in any particular context; they only constrain the possible interpretations. Hence it is not clear why they should be included in a prior or passing theory keyed to the actual interpretations of utterances in context.[44]

What lesson should we draw from this story? Davidson argues from the premise that a theory of meaning is a theory of speakers' and interpreters' shared understanding of communicative utterances to the conclusion that our knowledge of such a theory cannot be knowledge of a language or a grammar. But one philosopher's modus ponens is another's modus tollens. The same argument could equally well be taken to show that if a speaker's linguistic competence does consist in knowledge of a language, or grammar, then a theory of that competence will not be a theory of understanding, that is, a theory of interpretation (like Davidson's passing theories) that yields truth-conditions of utterances in their respective contexts. This is not to deny that understanding an utterance (in one of its senses) is knowing its truth-conditions. What is at issue is the assumption that a theory of linguistic, and specifically semantic, competence should directly and fully explain the understanding of utterances. Linguistic competence proper may instead be only one factor that contributes to such understanding, and a theory of a speaker's knowledge of language may be a theory of only one kind of knowledge specific to the linguistic properties of utterances that contributes to understanding.[45]

The same argument applies to metaphor. A theory of a speaker's *semantic* competence in metaphor, a theory of metaphorical *meaning*, should not be assumed to be a theory of the complex ability to use or communicate with metaphors, or a theory that directly explains what an interpreter *understands* by a metaphor—a theory that would determine for each utterance of a metaphor which feature or resemblance it expresses on that occasion. Rather, from among the various competencies, skills, and faculties that conjointly account for this complex ability (including the interpreter's extralinguistic knowledge of the relevant contextual parameter), a *semantic* theory of metaphorical interpretation should address only the interpreter's *knowledge of meaning specific to metaphorical interpretation.* The *evidence* for such a theory, to be sure, will largely consist in actual utterances with their "full" metaphorical interpretations in their respective contexts, but the semantic theory should not account for that evidence per se—the interpreted utterances in their respective contexts. The semantics should account only for the knowledge that underlies the speaker's ability to assign interpretations that is specific to their linguistic, or semantic, properties. The semantic theory of metaphor will consequently leave untouched a variety of aspects of metaphor that depend on a larger model of speech performance or use: criteria of appropriateness, the psychological processing of metaphors, and rhetorical and noncognitive effects of metaphors that bear on their success.[46] All this and more: for if the ability to interpret a metaphor even in the limited sense of assigning it a propositional content, or truth-condition, in a context involves the contributions of multiple extralinguistic abilities, skills, and presuppositions—including the ability to judge similarities or recognize salient features—then the *semantic* theory will never suffice to determine even the *interpretation*, truth-condition or propositional content, of a single metaphorical utterance. An actual metaphorical interpretation of an utterance in a context is underdetermined not only by the literal meaning of the utterance but also by its metaphorical meaning.[47]

What work, then, does *metaphorical meaning* perform? And with what aspects of metaphorical interpretation should a theory of a speaker's specifically semantic competence in metaphor be concerned? To factor out this component, we should begin with those facts about the interpretation of a metaphor that would prima facie be a function specifically of the general idea of meaning. Meaning, we have proposed, provides *constraints* on what it is possible for speakers to intend to say with particular types of expression. For evidence of metaphorical meaning, we should therefore look for evidence of formal constraints on possible metaphorical interpretations. As with demonstratives and our earlier example of anaphora, such a notion of metaphorical meaning is also *autonomous* of the speaker's intentions; it rather serves to constrain how those intentions— say, the features of likeness we are "made" to see by the utterance—enter into the content of the interpretation. These autonomous aspects of metaphorical interpretation are the kind of data for which we should posit metaphorical meaning as an explanation.

I'll conclude this section with two examples of constraints on the potentially unlimited number of possible interpretations that one metaphorical expression (type) can be assigned in different contexts. These constraints call out for metaphorical meaning.

The first example involves a configurational constraint on anaphora like our earlier data explained by (A). Let me begin with a nonmetaphorical illustration. It has frequently been observed that in cases of verb phrase anaphora in which the antecedent allows multiple interpretations, the anaphor must always be given the same interpretation as the antecedent. For example, 'may' can be given the sense either of permission or possibility in

(8) John may leave tomorrow.

But in (9) and (10)

(9) John *may* leave tomorrow, and the *same* is true of Harry

(10) John *may* leave tomorrow, and Harry, *too*

the (italicized) pair of antecedent and anaphor in each string must be given the same interpretation, either possibility or permission. This seems to be a clear instance of the autonomy of meaning: The speaker's communicative intentions are constrained by a structural condition on the "copying" of the interpretation of the antecedent verb phrase onto the anaphor.[48] And because this constraint has obvious consequences for the truth-value of the sentence, it is not simply syntactic but rather a matter of semantic significance, or meaning. Following the same kind of reasoning I rehearsed earlier, it is also implausible to explain this condition on verb phrase anaphora as a condition on use, or in terms of an interpreter's intentions or expectations à la Davidson. Despite my intentions, I simply cannot mean by (9) or (10) that John *has permission* to leave tomorrow, and it is *possible* for Harry to leave then. Sentences (9)–(10) are each only two-ways ambiguous rather than the four-ways we would expect if it were only a matter of intentions and mutual expectations. Hence this is a constraint on interpretation that would appear to call for semantic structure, that is, meaning.

Similar facts obtain for metaphor. Contrast the literal interpretation (i.e., content or truth-condition) of 'is the sun' in the sentence (repeated here)

(11) The largest blob of gases in the solar system is the sun

with its different metaphorical interpretations in

(12) Achilles is the sun

and

(13) Juliet is the sun.

As I said in chapter 1, 'is the sun' varies in its metaphorical interpretations in these strings, and with some systematicity, as a function of some difference in its respective context, either linguistic or extralinguistic (or both). Consider now the following (semantically) ill-formed sentences, which are examples, again, of verb phrase anaphora:

(14) *The largest blob of gases in the solar system *is the sun*, and Juliet/ Achilles *is, too*,

in which the first conjunct has the same interpretation as (11) and the second, the interpretation of (13)/(12); and

(15) *\/?Juliet *is the sun*, and Achilles *is, too*,

in which the first conjunct has the same interpretation as (13) and the second, the interpretation of (12).

Each of these ill-formed strings would seem to be the result of violating the same kind of interpretive constraint at work in (9)–(10). That is, if the interpretation of the antecedent is copied onto the anaphor, both the antecedent and the anaphor must have the same interpretation (whatever it is). Hence in (14) where the interpretation of the antecedent is the literal meaning of 'is the sun' and the interpretation of the anaphor would seem to be metaphorical (on pain of absurdity), we have one violation. In (15) (which is somewhat more acceptable to informants), we have two different *metaphorical* interpretations of 'is the sun', also violating the constraint.[49] Both interpretations are ill formed—although, as is often the case with such figures, we try to *impose* an interpretation on the strings despite the violation. However, it is precisely the feeling of play or pun that accompanies such imposed interpretations that gives away the underlying semantical ill-formedness of the strings.

These are examples in which certain aspects of metaphorical interpretation show themselves to be autonomous of—precisely because they serve as constraints on—interpreters' intentions. As with the earlier examples, it is difficult to see how we might account for these constraints in terms of use or mutual beliefs and expectations. What is needed is a structural condition—the same condition that applies to verb phrase anaphora in general—in which case we must attribute to metaphor the semantic structure, or meaning, necessary for the requisite condition to apply. Hence metaphorical meaning.

A second example of a constraint on metaphorical interpretation is analogous to the constraint on demonstrative content specified in (I) and exemplified by our earlier discussion of (7). Even when a demonstrative occurs within the surface scope of a modal operator, its *interpretation* is determined with respect to its context of utterance and never with respect to the circumstance with respect to which the truth-value of the sentence is determined. Similarly, the interpretation, that is, the truth-condition or content, of a metaphor, which systematically varies with its context (as we saw in ch. 1), is always fixed relative to its actual context of utterance, never relative to any other context or circumstance. Even if the metaphor occurs within the scope of a modal operator, it is never interpreted relative to the counterfactual (or alternative possible) circumstance(s) in which we evaluate whether it is true. Suppose that Paris disagrees with Romeo's utterance of 'Juliet is the sun' but concedes that

(16) Juliet might have been the sun.

(16) will be true in (the circumstance of) its context (call that $w(c)$) just in case there is some possible circumstance w^* in which Juliet has the particular set of properties P which is the content of 'is the sun' interpreted metaphorically in its context c. That is, Juliet must fall in the extension at w^* of the relevant property P, but the relevant property P is fixed relative to the context of utterance c, not relative to the counterfactual circumstance w^*. It is not sufficient for (or relevant to) the truth of (16) that Juliet possesses whatever property would be the content of 'is the sun' were it interpreted metaphorically in w^*. Now, as in the case of (I) for 'I', the kind of condition that accounts for this fact does not *determine* the interpretation of the metaphor; it only specifies what the interpretation cannot be. That is, it only constrains the interpretation. And again, it is difficult to see how to explain the presence of this constraint in terms of use, intentions, or mutual expectations. The constraint calls for metaphorical meaning.[50]

VI Is a Semantic Theory of Metaphor Possible?

Thus far I have argued that if we try to explain metaphor as a use of language—starting from its high degree of context-dependence—we nonetheless *need* a notion of metaphorical meaning. But not just any notion. Davidson is right to criticize previous theorists of metaphor for playing fast and loose in their talk of meaning. If a notion of metaphorical meaning must meet the same conditions of explanatory adequacy we require for nonmetaphorical meanings, the particular feature the metaphor makes us see on an occasion—a novel aspect or similarity—cannot be a *meaning* of the metaphor. On the other hand, if we require (as Davidson also does) that any account of metaphor must explain how the metaphorical depends on the literal, Davidson's own explanation—the causal dependence of metaphorical *use* on literal *meaning*—falls short at crucial moments, leaving gaps that can be filled only by semantic notions like meaning that spell out *constraints* on what we can metaphorically use words to express. The same kinds of constraints, I have also argued, constitute the meanings (as distinct from truth-conditional content) of classic context-dependent expressions such as demonstratives. But once Davidson opens his own semantic theory to admit demonstratives (as he must), if we can show the context-dependence of metaphors to be no different in kind from that of demonstratives, he should welcome metaphors as well.

It is one thing, however, to show that objections do not rule out all possible notions of metaphorical meaning or that there exists a domain of phenomena—that is, the kinds of constraints that call for meaning—that ought to fall under a semantic theory. It is another matter to show that, and how, we can actually construct a theory for metaphor that would satisfy the requirements for a finitistic semantics of the same kind that we have successfully begun to construct for significant fragments of natural language. Davidson denies this possibility (thesis 4 above), and prima facie he has good reason to do so. A finitistic semantic theory explains how the finite speaker knows the interpretations of an infinite set of sentences (or complex expressions) by showing how, in virtue of their structure, each sentential (or complex) interpretation is the product of a finite number of applications of a finite number of recursive rules operating on a finite number of semantic primitives (e.g., the truth or satisfaction conditions of a finite lexical vocabulary). If metaphorical interpretations could be explained by a finitistic theory, they would have to be either interpretations of the finite number of semantic primitives or the products of rules of composition. But we run into major obstacles when we try to pursue either of these routes.

In section III, we reviewed various difficulties that arise if we take a metaphorical use or interpretation to depend on, or be a function of, either its literal extension or its literal intension; the same arguments leave the compositionality of metaphor at best an open question. Furthermore, we noted in chapter 1 (examples (1)–(10)) how the metaphorical content of any individual expression apparently depends on features of its larger configuration—of at least its containing sentence but, as we shall see, also its wider extralinguistic context. This reverses the standard "bottom-up" order of compositional interpretation that constructs the meanings of compound expressions from the isolable meanings of their parts by strict rule-by-rule combination. These considerations make it doubtful that metaphor falls on the compositional side of semantics.

Nor do the phenomena of metaphor constitute a case of meaning of the type that we would identify with a semantic primitive to be explained by the lexical branch of semantics. Despite some important advocates such as Monroe Beardsley (1978), who claims that "there are indeed metaphorical senses" that "behave in many of the same ways as literal senses" (11)—and his evidence includes fallacious inferences like our earlier example (1)–(3)—the idea that a metaphorical interpretation is just another primitive word-sense cannot be the whole story.

First, as we have observed, metaphorical interpretations of one expression (type) vary with the contexts in which it is tokened. But there is no antecedently fixed upper bound on the number of different contexts in which a given metaphorical expression (type) can be tokened; hence there is no antecedently fixed upper bound on the number of distinct metaphorical interpretations of the same expression (type) that speakers are able to produce and comprehend. This leads to a familiar predicament. If each of its metaphorical interpretations is simply a distinct, primitive sense, the ability to interpret a metaphor requires the mastery of an unbounded number of senses for each expression. No matter how many metaphorical interpretations of a given expression a speaker has mastered at a time, each new metaphorical interpretation in a significantly different context is another sense to be learned anew—or miraculously intuited. An account in terms of ambiguity simpliciter that does not spell out how the different interpretations of one expression are systematically related hardly describes this feat.[51]

Second, if metaphorical interpretations are just additional senses, then expressions with metaphorical and literal interpretations are simply ambiguous. But metaphor does not fit neatly into the standard classification of ambiguities, which suggests that a metaphorical interpretation is not *simply* an additional sense of an ambiguous expression. Consider the *idiosyncratic* ambiguity exemplified by words like 'ear' (used of corn and of the bodily organ) or 'corn' (used of the vegetable and the growth on the foot).[52] Their different senses are mutually independent in that knowledge of one does not require knowledge of the other, whereas knowledge of the metaphorical interpretation(s) of an expression does require knowledge of its literal interpretation (in whatever exact way). As Davidson also notes, if we leave out all such "appeal to the original [or literal] meanings of the words ... all sense of metaphor evaporates" (WMM, 248–249). But if we fully assimilate metaphor to idiosyncratic lexical ambiguity, we lose this dependence.

On the other hand, expressions with metaphorical and literal interpretations are also unlike examples of the standard type of *systematic* lexical ambiguity, for example, 'book', which has abstract and concrete senses in (17) and (18), respectively:

(17) John wrote a book.

(18) The book weighs five pounds.

One difference between the metaphorical/literal case and systematic lexical ambiguity emerges in that gray area where syntax and semantics interact: although the explanations for their different types of behavior are not well understood, the systematically lexically ambiguous expressions appear to undergo syntactic transformations that expressions with metaphorical and literal senses do not. The two different senses of 'book', for example, can form a relative clause, as in

(19) John wrote a book that (which) weighs five pounds[53]

—unlike the expression 'is the sun' in

(20) *Juliet is the sun, which (that) has a diameter of roughly 865,000 miles

—which is metaphorical as the verb phrase of the main clause and literal as the antecedent of the relative pronoun. Similar resistance to relativization is found where the expression has two *different* metaphorical interpretations, as in

(21) *Juliet is the sun, whose burning fury consumes the life of Troy.

Differences of this kind, little understood as they are, indicate that, if metaphor is an instance of systematic ambiguity, it is not of the standard lexical type.

In sum, metaphor falls neatly under neither compositional (sentence) nor lexical (word) semantics. Since these two exemplify the main branches of contemporary semantics, one conclusion one might draw is that metaphor lies entirely outside semantics. Add to this the context-sensitivity of metaphorical interpretation—together with the assumption that semantics is task-specific and metaphor depends on all sorts of non-language-specific skills—and it is easy to appreciate why many philosophers and linguists conclude that metaphor belongs under theories of use, speech-acts, or pragmatics.

In response, our main task is to show how a finitistic, compositional semantic theory of metaphor is nonetheless possible. In chapter 3 I embark on this positive project by filling in the necessary background adapted from the semantics of demonstratives; in chapter 4 I begin to apply the apparatus to metaphor.

Chapter 3

Themes from Demonstratives

Two themes from the theory of demonstratives feature in my account of metaphor. The first is the distinction between the *propositional content* (for short, *content*) and the *character* of an expression. The second is a generalization of the idea of a demonstrative from a handful of *expressions*—the pure demonstratives ('This', 'that', 'she', 'then', 'thus', etc.) and proper indexicals ('I', 'here', 'now', 'actual', today', etc.)—to a much broader class of *expressions whose interpretation in a context* (or use on an occasion) is demonstrative. (As noted in ch. 2, I use the unqualified 'demonstratives' as a generic term for all of these expressions.) Both of these themes are directly adopted from David Kaplan's seminal work on demonstratives. But my aim here is not Kaplan exegesis, and so my exposition will anticipate the application of his work to metaphor.[1]

Two preliminary terminological remarks: One obvious difference between demonstratives and indexicals is that they depend on different features of their respective extralinguistic contexts for their referents. However, Kaplan has also noted a deeper difference. Knowledge of the linguistic meaning of an indexical (type) is both necessary and sufficient to determine the direct referent of a token; any accompanying nonlinguistic act like a pointing is either redundant or overruled. In contrast, knowledge of the linguistic meaning of a demonstrative (type) is never sufficient to determine its referent (on a tokening or utterance). Its linguistic meaning must be *completed* by an additional nonlinguistic factor, a demonstration. That is, a demonstrative (type) without a demonstration (that completes a tokening) falls short of being a semantically significant unit; it is an *incomplete* expression. To be sure, there are nondemonstrative uses of the word 'that' that lack demonstrations—for example, 'there was that book by Kant on pure reason'—but for a use of 'that' to count as demonstrative I shall assume, following Kaplan, that it is necessary that (a tokening of) it be completed by an extralinguistic demonstration.

Furthermore, the completing demonstration is necessary both where the demonstrative is simple and where it is linguistically modified, either as a complex demonstrative such as 'that balding philosopher with the limp' or when it contains a lexically built-in sortal like 'she' (= 'that female').[2] When completed by its respective extralinguistic demonstration, I refer to the mixed linguistic-extralinguistic entity, that is, the type of the token, as a *complete demonstrative*.

Second, to anticipate our discussion in chapter 4, note that metaphors are a hybrid: In some respects, they are like the pure indexicals and in others, like Kaplan's dthat-descriptions, that is, descriptions interpreted (or used) demonstratively. The expressions they are *least* like semantically are the complete demonstratives, although the idea of a dthat-description is derived from Kaplan's analysis of complete demonstratives. My discussion will reflect this unbalanced set of similarities and differences, giving the most attention to indexicals and dthat-descriptions.

I Some Prehistory

Kaplan's distinction between character and content emerged in the 1970s as part of a critique by proponents of the "New" theory of reference of the then-reigning doctrine of reference: "Frege's theory," "Fregeanism," the "Frege-Russell theory," "Descriptionalism," or, as I'll simply call it, the "Old" theory of reference.[3] The basic idea of the Old theory was that associated with each expression in the language, there is a fully conceptualized, purely qualitative representation that individuates the object that is its referent or extension. This representation plays at least five roles in the theory: (1) It furnishes the conditions to be satisfied in an (idealized) mechanism or procedure by which the extension or referent of the expression is fixed, that is, the factor contributed by the expression to the truth-value of its containing sentence. (2) It is what a speaker knows when he understands the expression. (3) It is, or expresses, the linguistic meaning of the expression. (4) It contains a *mode of presentation,* or way of thinking, of the referent that accounts for the "cognitive significance" or "information value" of the expression; as such, it is employed to solve problems like Frege's puzzle of identity. (5) It is the object of psychological attitudes and indirect discourse: *what* is believed, said, or asserted. Finally, on the Old theory, one and only one thing performs all five of these functions.

The paradigmatic type of expression according to the Old theory is the singular term and, among singular terms, the complete definite description 'The F_1 & ... & F_n'. Since its conjunction of predicates

F_1 & ... & F_n explicitly states the set of descriptive conditions the unique satisfaction of which is the mechanism by which its referent is fixed, the complete definite description transparently carries its associated representation on its sleeve. Let's say that a singular term (or an occurrence of) β *denotes* an object b if and only if there is a conceptual complex C of individuating descriptive or qualitative conditions associated with β (either relative to or independent of a context), and b uniquely satisfies C. (If nothing satisfies the conditions, then the term denotes, and thereby refers to, nothing.) This mechanism makes reference a matter of "fit," and determination of the referent (at a circumstance) is conditional on, or mediated by, the complex C. The reference relation itself is, then, *indirect*. What the singular term directly contributes to the (truth) evaluation of its sentences is C, and the referent is whatever turns out to satisfy C. Hence one apparent implication of the Old theory is that in different circumstances of evaluation the same singular term, with the same associated representation C, might denote, and refer to, different individuals or extensions, namely, whatever happens to satisfy C in that circumstance. That is, the Old theory seems to imply that, if we take the complete definite description as the standard from which we generalize, singular terms are, in now familiar terminology, *nonrigid* designators.

Since the 1970s, the Old theory has been subjected to a barrage of well-known criticisms by New theorists for its conception of the first role of the associated representation. I shall not review all the objections, but the New theorists have drawn two general morals.[4] First, although it may be the case that complete definite descriptions are nonrigid, New theorists argue that this is not so for all singular terms. In particular, paradigmatic singular terms, proper names and demonstratives (as used in a given context), refer to the same individual or extension in all possible circumstances of evaluation; that is, they designate *rigidly*.[5] Second, New theorists challenge the Old theory's account of how we determine the referents or extensions of proper names, demonstratives, and even some definite descriptions. In place of satisfaction, they argue that a speaker is able to refer successfully with many of her singular terms without possessing the rich, fully conceptual, purely qualitative knowledge required for denotation. For in addition to the (limited) conceptual resources she possesses, she also employs contextual relations, extralinguistic heuristics, and her connections to other members of the linguistic community from whom she acquires her language. In sum: Not by concepts alone do we refer.

The Old theory has fared better with respect to some of the other roles for its associated representation, especially the fourth and fifth roles that capture its epistemology. According to this general doctrine, which I'll call *perspectivalism*, all attitudes, knowledge, and reference—namely, all thought and speech about objects—are from a particular perspective. Just as we always perceive some thing from some definite angle or direction, whenever we think about (refer to, talk about) a public object it is from some specific point of view.[6] Since nothing is ever seen in its "totality," that is, simultaneously from all perspectives, each perspective might be said to furnish a "partial" view of the referent. This partiality of a perspective is what enables the associated representation to do its cognitive work: to solve Frege's identity puzzle and account for belief reports. Each such partial perspective also corresponds to a (Fregean) mode of presentation, or way of thinking of a thing that is (conventionally or contextually) associated with a term. Just as we often fail to realize that an object perceived from one perspective is the same object perceived from a second perspective, so we fail to identify one object represented in two ways, corresponding to two terms. Hence it is informative to learn the truth of an identity statement flanked by different terms (types), associated with different representations, unlike one flanked by the same term (type) with one representation.

Kaplan's theory of demonstratives shares this perspectivalist epistemology, although unlike the classical Fregeans who account for it in terms of sense (their associated multipurpose representation), he explains it with his notion of character. In chapter 7, I'll also employ the idea of metaphorical character to explain how metaphors contribute a distinctive cognitive perspective on their contents. So, insofar as Kaplan and I take the cognitive phenomena as "data" to be explained by a semantic theory, there remains a deep Fregean current running through our accounts.[7] However, the Old theory goes beyond this general form of perspectivalism in two ways. First, it holds not only that we refer *from* a perspective or think of things *in* a particular way but also that these perspectives or ways of thinking of things are always expressed, contained, or encoded in purely conceptual or qualitative, context-transcendent representations.[8] Second, it holds not only that all thought or speech about an object is from a perspective but that the perspective determines the object we are speaking or thinking about. Therefore, the conceptualized representation of the object must be as specific and complete as denotation requires. Kaplan and I reject these two further theses together with the thesis that denotation is the mechanism that fixes reference. To account for the cognitive phenomena, it is enough if there is *some* difference between the conceptual perspectives "contained" in the representations (or characters) associated with different co-referring singular terms—even if neither perspective is complete or purely conceptual. This, I will argue, suffices both for demonstratives and metaphors.

II Character and Content

Much of the critique of the Old theory has centered on proper names. But demonstratives and indexicals also play a prominent part—with slightly different morals. Consider, again, the first person indexical 'I'. Any account of this expression must explain, to begin with, (i) how its linguistic meaning, the rule (I) (repeated here, with slight modification)

(I) Each occurrence of 'I' directly refers to the agent of the context, e.g., its speaker

remains the same for all speakers and across all utterances, while (ii) the referent of each utterance of 'I' varies with its speaker. If (I) is (roughly) the Old theory's associated representation for 'I', these two data are already in conflict—the same representation should determine the same referent on all utterances. But this is not all. The Old theory identifies the meaning of a term (the third role of the associated representation) with its propositional or truth-conditional content (the first and second roles). But if you (Max) and I (JS) each utter

(1) I am laughing,

not only do the referents of our two utterances of 'I' differ; because my utterance might be true and yours false, *what is said* by our utterances, their propositional contents or truth-conditions, must also differ. My utterance of (1) generates the proposition represented as

(1a) ⟨JS, *Is-laughing*⟩.

Yours:

(1b) ⟨Max, *Is-laughing*⟩.

So, while its linguistic meaning remains constant, the propositional content or truth-condition of (1), and not only the referent of the indexical, also varies from utterance to utterance. Meaning and propositional or truth-conditional content also, then, cannot be identical, and at least two substrata must be distinguished within the Old theory's multipurpose associated representation. Following Kaplan, we shall call these its *character* and (propositional) *content*.

The *content* of a sentence (uttered in a context), namely, a proposition, is what is evaluated at a circumstance to determine its truth-value (at that circumstance). The contents of terms, predicates, etc. are their contributions (whatever they turn out to be) to their containing propositions. Circumstances of evaluation can include any feature with respect to which we may evaluate the truth-value of a sentence (or, more generally, the extension of an expression), but I shall generally take them to be simply worlds. In a possible worlds semantics, contents can be represented as intensions: functions from the set of possible circumstances to the appropriate type of extension. But for our purposes, no particular formal analysis of content is necessary. I'll return in the next section to the sentence-like structure of (1a–b).

This notion of content is more or less familiar; the novel element in Kaplan's proposal is character, the general notion he proposes to correspond to the constant knowledge of speakers across utterances such as (I) for 'I'. Technically, *character* is the semantic property (or value) of an expression (type) that determines, for each context of utterance, the content of (a token of) the expression in that context. As in (I), characters can be stated informally as rules that specify the features of the context on which their content depends. But like contents, Kaplan also proposes that we represent characters as functions—from the set of possible contexts to the appropriate type of content.[9] All expressions in the language, it should be emphasized, are assigned characters, but only those expressions that are context-sensitive have *nonconstant* characters: characters that determine different contents in different contexts. Eternal expressions have *constant* characters: They determine the same content in every context.[10]

Unlike the Old theory, which assigns two semantic values to each expression (sense/meaning/content and reference), we now assign three: reference, content, and character. Analogously, we can distinguish three stages, at each of which we raise a different question about an utterance and at each of which context functions in one of the three roles we distinguished in chapter 2.

Suppose a sound event occurs. The first question is whether the event is an utterance of a well-formed expression (a word with a particular meaning) in a language and, if so, which one. In answer to this question we assign the event a linguistic description that includes a rule of character that determines how the event, identified as a token of a certain type in a certain language, should be linguistically understood on that occasion. For example, to the sound 'ī' we assign the character of the first person indexical 'I'. Call this the *character-assignment stage*; as I said in chapter 2, context informs this assignment, but its role here is presemantic.

With the utterance assigned a character, its occurrence in some context *generates* a content for the expression in that context. Call this the *content-generation stage* in the interpretation of the utterance.[11] At this stage, we ask: Given the expression type assigned to the utterance, what is being said? What factor does the utterance of 'I' contribute to those that must be taken into account in evaluating (at the next stage) whether the sentence in which it occurs is true or false? At this stage, context again plays a central role. Thus, for 'I', corresponding to the character (I) it was assigned, the context furnishes an individual, namely, the agent of the context or speaker. This role of the context is semantic: Part of a speaker's semantic competence consists in his knowing, for every expression, the appropriate extralinguistic parameter (if any) in any context that determines what its content would be (or what the utterance would say) in that context.

Finally, given the content of the utterance that was determined at the previous stage, its evaluation at a circumstance yields a truth-value for the sentence uttered. Call this the truth-*evaluation stage*. Here we ask: Is what is said, the content of the utterance, true or false? Again context comes into play because we are typically concerned with the *actual* truth-value of the utterance, that is, its truth-value in its actual circumstances—the circumstances of its context. But this role of the context is postsemantic, for the truth-value of the utterance is significant only insofar as the utterance is used to make a particular kind of speech act, an assertion (or some other act or use that presupposes assertion). If the sentence were to be uttered (also) for some nonassertoric purpose, context would, most likely, again enter—but for an evaluation of a different kind of appropriateness. In either case, the context is functioning postsemantically.

III Direct Reference: Singular and Predicative

I said in section I that the New theory critics of the Old theory of reference challenge both its implication that all singular terms (hence demonstratives) are nonrigid designators and its denotational model of the fixation of reference. In contrast, Kaplan claims that demonstratives (along with proper names and certain common nouns such as names of natural kinds) are not only rigid but also *directly referential terms*. Again, I won't rehearse his arguments for this thesis. However, I do want to emphasize what the claim means, first for singular demonstratives— which have been Kaplan's almost exclusive focus—and then predicate demonstratives. This is important for our project because metaphors, as

I'll argue in chapters 4 and 6, are primarily predicative but are also directly referential.

First, the thesis that a demonstrative is directly referential is—beyond the claim that it is rigid, which is a thesis about its referent or extension— a thesis about *how* its referent or extension (at a circumstance) is determined.[12] And since content is what determines reference (at a circumstance), it is a thesis about, and exclusively about, the *content* of the demonstrative. Second, the thesis is best understood by the *via negativa*: What makes a term directly referential is that it is *not in*directly referential and, in particular, that it is not denotational. The content, or propositional contribution, of a directly referential term is not a qualitative, conceptual individuating condition by which it denotes its referent (at a circumstance). It is not even a concept or qualitative condition that turns out to denote the same individual at all circumstances, a consequence that would be compatible with the term's being rigid. Kaplan depicts this nondenotational nature of direct reference by incorporating the very individual who is the (rigidly designated) referent into its respective proposition. This depiction, as we'll see next, is also potentially misleading— but the force of the image is its exclusion from the propositional content of a conceptual complex in virtue of which the term could be said to denote its (constant) referent.

In saying that the direct reference thesis is a claim *only* about the content of the demonstrative, I also intend to emphasize that the thesis says nothing, pro or con, about additional kinds of "meaning" or "linguistic significance" other than content that the expression might possess. This should be underlined for two reasons: (1) Kaplan's image of an individual as propositional content may reinforce the opposite impression; and (2) Kaplan's own paradigm of a directly referential term, the free variable under an assignment, in fact has no additional meaning or significance. Everything that might be said about the way in which its value (which is its content) is assigned, or generated, is presemantic: prior to the assignment of *any* semantic value or significance to the expression. Similarly for logical constants, that is, variables with a constant assignment relative to a language, and ordinary proper names whose referents are "assigned" through a historical (or causal) chain originating with a baptism or dubbing, a story that is, most plausibly, also presemantic.[13] For these expressions, denotation plays no role at any stage, either when their content is evaluated at a circumstance or when the content is itself generated. The only *semantic* value or significance these expressions possess is their referent, the element they contribute to the truth-valuation of their sentences. These expressions, I shall therefore say, are not only directly referential (in content) but also *thoroughly nondenotational*—to exclude denotation from any stage.

Kaplan formally represents the contents of sentences containing directly referential terms as sequences containing individuals, times, and other (direct) referents—what are now called *Russellian* or *singular* propositions; examples are (1a–b). These quasi-sentential Russellian propositions are meant to capture aspects of logical syntax and semantic structure that are lost in set-theoretic conceptions of a proposition, such as the possible worlds model of a proposition as a function or (characteristic) set of possible worlds.[14] However, there are still other aspects of logical structure not captured in representations like (1a–b); for example, complex singular demonstratives have complex logical structure, represented in their character, but simple content, an individual. To capture this kind of logical but nonpropositional structure without abandoning Russellian propositions, we can borrow some formal machinery from Kaplan. If Φ in an expression, let $\{\Phi\}$ stand for its character. (I suppress reference here to the model for our interpretation and an assignment function for any free variables that occur in Φ.) We can then represent the content of Φ in a context c as $\{\Phi\}(c)$. Thus my utterance of (1) in c can be represented not only as the Russellian proposition shown in (1a) but also as the Russellian proposition (1a′):

(1a′) $\langle\{\mathrm{I}\}(c), \textit{Is-laughing}\rangle$.

Note that the propositional constituent represented in (1a′) by '$\{\mathrm{I}\}(c)$' is the *individual* JS as in (1a); the character of 'I' is not *itself* a propositional constituent. Hence (1a′) is a bonafide Russellian proposition, indeed the identical Russellian proposition as (1a), although, unlike it, (1a′) *displays* "character-istic information" not preserved in its content. We'll see some examples of the importance of this character-istic information both for demonstratives and metaphors.

Kaplan calls propositions that contain only properties and logical functions but no individuals *general propositions*. This Russellian characterization reflects the fact I mentioned earlier, that discussions of direct reference have concentrated almost exclusively on singular terms. But some New theorists have argued that certain common nouns also *name* natural kinds, substances, and other abstract entities; this suggests that these nouns should also be treated as directly referential terms—but with general rather than individual referents. Closer to home, there are demonstratives that occur in predicative position such as 'is that Φ' (e.g., shape, color, style, speed, etc.) and 'thus' (as in 'the such-and-such Vs (looks, walks, smells, etc.) thus', where the predicate demonstrative is completed by a demonstration of *how* the thing looks, walks, etc.).[15] Should such propositions count as singular or general?

For present purposes, let's restrict our attention to predicate demonstratives. One issue is what to count as their referents. If their referents are their extensions in the usual sense, namely, the sets of things at a circumstance of which the contents of the predicates are true (or to which a predicate, as uttered in a context, applies), then (most) predicate demonstratives are not even rigid, let alone directly referential. Consider the predicate demonstrative 'is that shape' in the sentence 'The coffee table I want to buy is that shape [speaker points at an oval-shaped mirror]'. The predicate demonstrative 'is that shape' has a nonconstant character: depending on the shape demonstrated, it will have different contents in different contexts (being oval, being square, etc.). But unlike the kinds or substances named by natural kind or substance terms that are prima facie essential (or necessary) to any object that falls under them in any one circumstance, the property of having a certain shape is clearly contingent; its extension will vary from circumstance to circumstance. Predicate demonstratives, then, have nonconstant characters but their contents do not determine the same extensions in all circumstances. Hence, if direct reference requires the rigidity of its extension, predicate demonstratives are not even rigid, let alone directly referential.[16]

There is another alternative, however. Instead of taking the referent of a predicate as its extension (at a circumstance), let's think of a predicate (or certain predicates) more like a singular term referring to a property. (We can *also* assign the predicate an extension at each circumstance, namely, the set of individuals at the circumstance who possess the property.) My motivation for this is not metaphysical. I want to articulate the difference between the contents of predicates—the factors they contribute to truth-valuations—that we captured with singular terms by distinguishing direct from indirect reference, that is, by distinguishing between determining the reference by denotation, by satisfaction of a conceptualized representation associated with the expression, and by other ways.[17] Some predicates express (refer to) properties in virtue of there being associated with them a fully conceptualized representation (known by their speaker) that the property satisfies; others express (refer to) their properties in some not fully conceptualized, context-exploiting manner. A predicate demonstrative is directly referential just in case it is *not in*directly referential. The mode of reference- or expression-determination that holds between the predicate demonstrative and its property is not mediated by a purely conceptualized representation.[18]

To return now to the question of whether the proposition expressed by a sentence containing a predicate demonstrative is singular or general: Suppose, following Frege, that all expressions, predicates as well as terms, have referents, and that the referents of predicates are properties. Let's also distinguish, following Russell, between propositions whose constituents include the very individuals, properties, and relations, on the one hand, and those whose constituents are purely conceptualized, qualitative representations whose conditions determine individuals, properties, and relations by denotation (or a suitably generalized relation) at circumstances. Let's call the latter *purely conceptualized propositions*; the former, *referential propositions*. The Old theory holds that all propositions are purely conceptualized; according to the New theory, at least some propositions are referential. The class of referential propositions includes Kaplan's singular propositions, but it also includes propositions whose constituents are properties and relations "themselves" rather than conceptualized representations that denote (or denotationally express) them.

As with the singular direct reference thesis, the distinction between these two kinds of propositions is entirely at the level of content. The "generalized" direct reference thesis holds that, for at least some predicates or common nouns, we should distinguish the property to which it refers from the means by which we conceive of, or express or refer to, that property. In some cases, we want to know whether something falls under a particular property (at a circumstance) regardless of how that property is conceived or expressed; in other cases, our concern is whether something falls under the property expressed or represented by some predicate (or other conceptual representation), whatever particular property that turns out to be. This distinction also reflects our referential skills and capacities. Sometimes we refer to the property by means of a purely qualitative representation we possess in our conceptual repertoire. In other cases, we take advantage of our contextual relations to the property, using a sample we display or demonstrate. And sometimes this is because we do not know, or because there isn't, a label or concept for that property to enable us to refer to or express it in a context-independent mode.

A similar situation, I shall argue in chapter 5, holds for certain metaphors whose context-dependence generates referential propositions. These metaphors, like predicate demonstratives, directly refer or express properties in the absence of, or without employing, fully conceptualized representations of the properties. Through this means, we can explain how metaphors enable us to express novel properties, that is, properties for which we possess no well-integrated conceptualization in our linguistic and cognitive repertoire.

IV   Indexicals and the Parametric Determination of Their Referents

I argued in section III that the direct reference thesis for demonstratives consists in (i) the claim that they rigidly designate their referents or extensions and (ii) the claim that the determination of their referents (at circumstances) is not indirectly referential, that is, by use of a mechanism like denotation. This leaves us with the question: If not by denotation, then by what kind of mechanism do we determine the (direct) referent (which, for Kaplan, simply *is* the content) of a demonstrative? For variables, constants, and proper names, we relegated the assignment of their values, or direct referents, to presemantics. What I'll argue in the remainder of this chapter is that there are significantly different answers to this question for the two kinds of demonstratives that will serve (in ch. 4) as the models for our hybrid analysis of metaphor: the proper indexicals and a new species of demonstrative invented by Kaplan, the dthat-description (or demonstratively interpreted description). (Complete demonstratives are yet another, still more complicated story; for reasons of space I shall discuss them only insofar as it is necessary to present dthat-descriptions.) In this section, I'll begin with the indexicals.

The direct referents of indexicals would seem to be determined (for each context) by their rules of character, such as (I) for 'I'. But exactly how do these rules work? On the face of it, the way that, say, the rule of character (I) for 'I' functions is not very different from the way that the Old theorist's associated representation *C* operates according to its first three roles: It is the linguistic meaning of the word that a speaker understands and it fixes its referent denotationally. In other words, (I) is something any competent speaker of the language is presumed to know as part of knowing the linguistic meaning of 'I', and its rule of character is semantically significant information that the indexical carries beyond its semantically significant direct referent (content). There are at least three reasons for holding this. (1) As I argued in chapter 2, a primary function of linguistic meaning is to *constrain* the intentions we can express with a particular linguistic form on any occasion of use. The character rule (I) spells out exactly what we would expect of the constraints on 'I'. (2) There is a logic specific to the indexicals: There are inferences and sentences (e.g., 'I am here now' and 'I exist') whose "validity" (i.e., truth in every possible context in which they are uttered) depends on their (indexical) characters and not on their contents in any particular context (Kaplan [1989a], 541–553). (3) We know *that* sentences like 'I am here now' are true, or express a truth, in the circumstance of every context in which they are uttered even though we do not always know *what* truth is expressed by each utterance in its context. The explanation for this difference is that we know the former solely in virtue of our understanding of the characters of the indexicals and their formal interrelations; we don't always know the latter because we don't always know the necessary extralinguistic facts, for example, who is speaking, when, and where. The contrast between the two kinds of knowledge lends support to the view that what we know in the former case is linguistic or semantic. Although the linguistic doctrine of a priori knowledge may not be true in general, it tells exactly the right story for these sentences. In sum, the rule of character (I) is, or is a significant part of, the linguistic meaning of the indexical 'I' and what the speaker knows about 'I' as part of his semantic competence.[19]

Like the Old theorist's denotational content C for singular terms that provides conditions that its referent must *satisfy* or *fit*, indexical characters prima facie also seem to specify semantic conditions that their direct referents must satisfy—for example, being the speaker or agent of the context of the utterance of 'I'. The only difference between them appears to be where their respective conditions are laid down: at the level of character or at that of content. So, if satisfaction is the crux of the denotational mechanism of indirect reference determination, an indexical character would seem not to be very different from the content of an eternal denotational term. The mechanism for fixing the indexical referent looks like satisfaction of a descriptive condition (e.g., being the speaker or agent) but (only) in its context of utterance. Put differently, indexicals are directly referential, in that with respect to their evaluation at a circumstance, their content is not indirectly referential. But they are *not* thoroughly nondenotational, in that a mechanism like denotation appears to be operative at the level of their character applied to their context.

Despite this appearance, I want to argue that indexical characters do not determine their direct referents, or contents, through denotation. The reason, in brief, is that the condition explicitly spelled out in the rule of character for an indexical, such as 'the agent (time, location, etc.) of the context', fails to individuate a unique referent in the universe for each utterance of the indexical (e.g., what is *the* context, referred to in the rule?) and no strategy that appeals to the context to pick up the slack succeeds in a way compatible with the requirements of denotation.[20] To avoid a potential misunderstanding, note that this is *not* to say that an indexical determines its referent denotationally only if it determines it fully and exclusively denotationally, in terms of satisfaction of explicitly formulated, purely qualitative individuating conditions. Such a condition would ignore the obvious fact that indexicals are context-dependent; hence, even if indexicals are denotational, context must play some role. The objection instead is that although the rule of character requires contextual supplementation to be denotational, the way in which the context can supplement a rule like (I) is not by furnishing the materials for denotation, that is, satisfaction of linguistic descriptive conditions. Let me explain.

All the plausible strategies to supplement (I) appeal to the extralinguistic context either to "complete" the incomplete description or to supply an appropriate restriction on the universe of quantification. One way the context can do these jobs is by adding more specific descriptive content to the incomplete description or by appending an antecedent condition to the quantifiers. But if there are any descriptively adequate supplementations or restrictions in a given context, there will also be more than one—among which there may be no saying *which* the given speaker had in mind. Potential supplementations and restrictions also presumably vary with the speaker. Both possibilities undermine the status of rules like (I) to be a kind of linguistic meaning.

A second way context can enter is by "supplying" an individual or thing that "anchors" the description, for example, by converting the original to something like 'the agent of the context of utterance of *that token of "I"*' whose content would contain the actual token of 'I', a spatiotemporal sound event. But this alternative runs contrary to the general idea of denotation according to which the condition to be satisfied be conceptualized or qualitative. And even if we overlook that issue, the solution at best substitutes one problem for another. We want to explain how context enables us to determine a referent for the incomplete description 'the agent (time) of the context'. Now we are told that the context "supplies" an anchoring individual for the demonstrative phrase 'that token of "I"'.' But if context can "supply" a referent for this demonstrative phrase, why can't it directly "supply" an individual for the indexical 'I' without invoking a description, period?

Indeed maybe it does. That is, perhaps the context just "supplies" an individual for the indexical without invoking the *satisfaction* of any description. To spell this out, we must say a bit more about the notion of a context or, more accurately, about two conceptions of context current in the literature. These run in parallel with Kaplan's distinction, mentioned in chapter 1, Section II, between *utterances*, or full-bodied speech-acts, and *occurrences* of *sentence(-type)s*-in-contexts.

The first notion of context is the idea of the "total speech situation" that includes "everything" relevant to the "acceptable interpretation" of a particular utterance. Since different utterances call upon different kinds of features for their respective interpretations, we must look first at each utterance to construct its context of this kind. And because we are dealing with actual utterances, real-time speech acts, the context must take into account a wide variety of factors that determine their "success," only some of which are semantic while others are psychological and physical.

The second idea of context, Kaplan's, is an abstraction from this idea of the total speech situation. It accounts only for semantic context-dependence from among the multiple kinds that the more heterogeneous idea of a speech situation aims to explain. On the other hand, this notion of context is concerned not simply with the assignment of truth-conditions to individual sentences, but with forms of inference and with the validity of (sets of) linguistic types.[21] And to account for the simultaneous co-occurrence of multiple propositions in one context, this semantics-oriented notion of context must take liberties that the idea of context appropriate to full-blown utterances does not. What, then, belong to these semantic contexts, and what constraints govern them? To answer this question, we should remind ourselves of why semantics *needs* contexts—contexts in addition to the circumstances necessary for the evaluation of all sentences.

The justification for contexts is that certain sentence-types have se-mantic properties that reflect their specific structure rather than the more general structure of circumstances. For example, each occurrence of 'I am actually here now' expresses a contingent proposition—evaluated at some possible circumstances it is true, at others false—but *each* occurrence of the sentence is true *in* the circumstance of *its* context. Moreover, each occurrence is true in its context in virtue of the fact that, in any context, the individual directly referred to by the indexical 'I' (whoever she may be) is in the position (wherever that may be) directly referred to by the indexical 'here' at the time (whenever that may be) directly referred to by the indexical 'now' in the circumstance (whatever that may be) directly referred to by the indexical 'actually'. So, the semantics singles out contexts as a class of structures because they explain the special semantic properties of certain sentences. But if that is their justification, they should consist of exactly those elements that account for those semantic properties that are not captured by the more general idea of circumstances, relative to which we evaluate the contents of occurrences of sentence(-token)s. These elements are (i) values for parameters corresponding to the indexicals in the language, which (ii) are interrelated according to certain structural constraints. For example, in every context the value of the 'I' parameter must be (located) at the value of the 'Here' parameter at the value of the 'Now' parameter in the value of the 'Actual (circumstance)' parameter.[22] In sum, a (minimal) context is any sequence of four elements, an individual i, a time t, a possible world w, and a position p, such that (a) i is located at p at $\langle w, t \rangle$ and (b) i exists in $\langle w, t \rangle$.[23]

To return now to how the character of an indexical determines its reference: Suppose that a context just *is* (or *supplies*) such a sequence of values for parameters corresponding to the indexicals. When an indexical occurs in a context, the present proposal is that we do *not* survey the context, on the model of denotation, to see which of its elements satisfies the condition stated in its rule of character. Instead, in *situating* the occurrence of the indexical *in* the context—by virtue of the fact that the indexical *occurs* in the context—it is ipso facto assigned the value of its parameter in that context, just as values are assigned to variables. The only difference between indexicals and variables is that the assignment of a value to a variable is entirely unconstrained by the individual's semantic knowledge—hence, it is presemantic—whereas the value-assignment to the indexical in each context is semantically constrained: for 'I' to an agent-value, for 'now' to a time-value, and so on. But denotation, or satisfaction of conditions, plays no part among these constraints. Indexicals, then, are thoroughly nondenotational. However—in contrast to variables, constants, and proper names whose assignments are semantically unconstrained—indexicals are parametric, "filled" by the values of their semantically determined contextual parameters.

To summarize: (1) An indexical is a directly referential term. Each token of an indexical type is a rigid designator of the same referent at all circumstances, and its content *is* that individual referent rather than a representation whose conceptual conditions are evaluated at circumstances to determine that individual as a denotation. (2) Its character is its meaning, an object of the speaker's semantic competence. (3) The character also does not determine the direct referent, or its content (in its context), by way of denotation, via the satisfaction of conditions. Instead (4) the indexical is a parametric expression "filled" by the value of its corresponding contextual parameter. This assignment is semantically constrained, but the indexical, like a variable, is thoroughly nondenotational.

V   Dthat-descriptions and Complete Demonstratives

I now turn to the dthat-description, the second main theme from the theory of demonstratives that shapes my semantic account of metaphor. Dthat-descriptions, like indexicals, are directly referential terms. (1) They are rigid designators and (2) their content is their individual referent; that is, their content is *not* a conceptualized representation that, evaluated at a circumstance, determines the referent by denotation. However, the way in which the character of a dthat-description determines its direct referent—which, as with indexicals, *is* its content—is in sharp contrast to the parametric character of an indexical. As we shall see, denotation does the main work for the character of the dthat-description; therefore, dthat-descriptions are *not* thoroughly nondenotational.

Looking ahead to metaphor, I emphasize this difference because the dthat-description provides us with the model for our treatment of the semantic context-dependency of a metaphor. However, the way the character of a metaphor expresses, or determines, its content, or property, in a context is, unlike dthat-descriptions, not by way of denotation. The characters of metaphors, like those of proper indexicals, are parametric. For this reason, metaphors are a hybrid of the two.

In his first paper on demonstratives, "Dthat," Kaplan was inspired to create the dthat-description through reflection on Donnellan's referential use of the definite description. However, like many other things we humans parent, our creations often take on a life of their own, exceeding our own greatest expectations about their futures. By the time he wrote "Demonstratives" in the '70s, Kaplan writes that he "regards [the] 'dthat' operator as representing the general case of a demonstrative" (Kaplan 1989a, 527), and in the formal "Logic of Demonstratives" the demonstrations that complete pure demonstratives are indeed treated exactly as if they were linguistic singular terms, which, in turn, bears out Kaplan's quoted claim. Nonetheless, despite these considerable parallels, my own view is that there are great *dis*analogies between complete demonstratives (with their extralinguistic demonstrations) and dthat-descriptions, disanalogies that legislate *against* taking the 'dthat' operator as representing the general case of a demonstrative. Here is not the place to pursue that discussion.[24] However, in order to explain Kaplan's insight that motivated the dthat-description, it will be valuable to place it in the context of his analysis of complete demonstratives and, in particular, his Fregean theory of demonstrations. I'll begin, then, with the common ground shared by complete demonstratives and dthat-descriptions, bracketing their many differences and many of the complications that arise in the explanation of complete demonstratives per se.

As I said at the beginning of this chapter, a demonstrative must be completed by a demonstration in order to determine a referent; without the demonstration, the pure demonstrative is incomplete. Let us call the individual demonstrated by the accompanying demonstration its *demonstratum*. The rule of character for a complete demonstrative 'That[Δ]', analogous to (I) for 'I', is, then, a rule like (D):

(D) In any context c, each utterance of 'That[Δ]' directly refers to the *demonstratum* of the completing demonstration Δ in c, and otherwise directly refers to nothing.

(D) raises two main questions. First, what is a demonstration? Second, how should we understand the claim that the demonstration Δ *completes* the pure demonstrative 'That'? What is the syntax and semantics of 'That[Δ]'? Is it syntactically and/or semantically simple or complex? I'll return to this second question at the end of section VIII in connection with dthat-descriptions.[25] The answer to the first question, which is the immediate background to the idea of a dthat-description, is complicated by the fact that two different notions of a demonstration surface in current accounts of demonstratives. Kaplan mentions both notions but unfortunately he equivocates between them.

The first idea of a demonstration is the ordinary idea of a bodily gesture, action, or cue, the paradigm of which is the act of pointing at an object. This is also the popular conception of a demonstration; witness the *Random House Dictionary* entry for 'That': "the person or thing pointed out or mentioned." This act is accompanied by, in Kaplan's words, a "directing intention," and it is a further question whether what really determines the demonstratum is the bodily act itself or the intentional act or state that the bodily act, for communicative purposes, merely externalizes. I also include under this first idea extralinguistic events, happenings, or other contextual occurrences that make something the focus of attention in place of a gesture of pointing, for example, the fact that the thing is in the spotlight or on a podium. The second notion of a demonstration, which may have been first proposed by Husserl, is introduced by Kaplan when he describes a demonstration as "typically, though not invariably, a (visual) presentation of a local object discriminated by a pointing."[26] Here I take the demonstration to be the "presentation"— whatever that is—although the object presented is also "discriminated" by a pointing.

Prima facie these two notions of a demonstration are mutually compatible. Indeed the typical complete perceptual demonstrative involves both: a *gesture* (like pointing) to an object perceptually *presented* in the context in a certain way. However, a number of recent philosophers have tried to pull them apart, seizing on one to the exclusion of the other as the "real" demonstration, depending on the problem the particular author thinks is primary. In general the gesture is given the role to fix the referent, while the presentation accounts for cognitive significance. Of course, if both problems must be solved and each kind of demonstration accounts at most for one, any adequate theory of demonstrations must accommodate both. This is indeed closest to my own view, although I shall not try to defend or elaborate it here. Instead I'll concentrate on demonstrations as presentations, which will lead us to dthat-descriptions.

VI Demonstrations as Presentations

The motivation for the idea of a demonstration as a presentation is the same set of considerations, or data, that prompted the fourth role (and, to some degree, the fifth) that the Old theory assigned to its associated conceptual representations: to explain cognitive phenomena like informativeness (as in Frege's identity puzzle) by positing modes of presentation, or ways of thinking, of their referents. Kaplan, parodying Frege, gives an example of an analogous puzzle for demonstratives. How should we explain the cognitive difference between the informative utterance of

(2) That [the speaker points at Venus in the morning] = That [the speaker points at Venus in the evening],

as opposed to the uninformative utterance of

(3) That [the speaker points at Venus in the morning] = That [the speaker points at Venus in the morning].

Since all the complete demonstratives in both (2) and (3) directly co-refer, they not only have the same referent but also the same content; hence the difference in their information-values must be sought elsewhere.

Back in section I, I said that Kaplan shares the Old theory's perspectivalist epistemology: that we always refer *from* a perspective or think of things *in* a particular way. One way to capture these perspectives or ways of thinking of things is to build them into or encode them in associated representations, be it at the level of content, truth-conditions, sense, or (as we'll see in a moment) character. This strategy I shall call *repre-*

sentationalist. However, a second, and simpler, way to account for certain differences of perspective on a co-referent is by taking the referent to be thought of (or by taking tokens of the co-referring expression to occur) in different extralinguistic contexts. Thus an utterance may be informative because it expresses the discovery that the referent of a term occurring in one context is identical to the referent of the same term (type) occurring in another context. Differences of informativeness would correspond, then, to differences between extralinguistic contexts. I'll call this second strategy of capturing a speaker's cognitive perspective *contextualist*.

The most plausible, and simplest, explanation of the cognitive difference between (2) and (3) is contextualist: In (2) one demonstrative is uttered in the morning in one season, the other in the evening in another season. In (3) they are both uttered at the same place and time. What makes (2) informative is that we thereby learn that the thing referred to at one time and place with a certain appearance is identical to the thing referred to at a different time and place with a different appearance. Likewise, if there were analogous puzzles exclusively involving proper indexicals such as the uninformative

(4) $I = I$

versus the informative

(5) $I = you$

or the uninformative

(6) Tomorrow $=$ tomorrow

versus the informative

(7) Tomorrow $=$ today,

the most plausible explanation for the informative utterances is contextualist. Since it is reasonable to assume that in any one (normal) context, no single thing can fill two parameters, say, simultaneously be agent and addressee or both the day of utterance and the next or previous one, the flanking co-referential indexicals *must* occur in different contexts in order for their utterances ((5) and (7)) to be *true*. To be sure, we generally require a sentence-occurrence to be evaluated in one and only one context, but for these to be *true*, the context must shift mid-sentence. And if their truth requires these sentence-occurrences to split themselves between two contexts, we can also, and most easily, explain their cognitive significance in terms of cross-contextual continuities they track.[27] It would be gratuitous to incorporate different perspectival representations in their structure only in order to account for their informativeness.[28]

However, it is also evident—and this was surely Kaplan's idea—that there *are* informative identities involving complete demonstratives that occur *within* a single context and that cannot be explained cross-contextually. Contrast, for example, the informative identity

(8) He [points to a newspaper photograph of Superman, midair dressed in his blue tights] = he [points to Clark Kent, dressed in mild-mannered suit, standing before us]

with the uninformative

(9) He [points to a newspaper photograph of Superman, midair dressed in his blue tights] = he [points to the same newspaper photograph of Superman, midair dressed in his blue tights].

Here the informativeness of (8), as opposed to (9), that goes beyond their common content must be explained relative to a single context, in which case the natural explanation would be to build representational differences into the complete demonstratives.[29] But how? (8) seems to be informative because of the different visual features, or appearances, "associated with" the co-demonstratum of the two occurrences of 'he'. But what is the nature of this association, and is it a representational, semantically individuated difference between the complete demonstratives? The two occurrences of the pure demonstrative ('he') look like tokens of the same type, with the same character, hence the same linguistically determined mode of presentation. The gesture, the act of pointing at the object, is also the same. All that changes is the visual appearance of the object pointed at. But that is a difference prima facie in what is being represented, not in the representing entity.

Kaplan's proposal is to build these differences in the appearances of the co-demonstratum into the representational structures of the complete demonstratives. The differences in appearance are not just different modes *of* (perceptual) presentation; they constitute different presentations, hence different demonstrations. But what is a presentation? Three basic ideas underlie Kaplan's notion.

1. Let a presentation be enough *like* a linguistic representation (read: re-presentation) to be analyzed with a sense and referent or, in Kaplan's own "corrected" version, with a character, content, and referent. The thing *of* which it is a presentation can be treated as its referent and the mode by which it presents that individual can be treated as its sense, or character/content. (These last two will be distinguished where the presentation "contains" context-sensitive elements like indexicals.) Kaplan calls this the "Fregean Theory of Demonstrations."[30]

2. Presentations, like linguistic expressions, admit a type-token distinction (525). Hence presentations (types) admit replication.[31]

3. Presentations are not rigid designators. A typical presentation is of a particular thing, but it is not necessary that it be of that particular thing (or of anything, to allow for the possibility of vacuous presentations, say, in cases of hallucination). Suppose I am presented with *my* Macintosh (serial) #100C54X129. That machine has a certain appearance, indeed the same appearance as myriads of other Macs. And in some other circumstance another Mac (say, serial #100C54X130) might be the only thing that matches that presentation. In that counterfactual circumstance, the viewer would stand in the very same perceptual relation to #100C54X130 that in fact I stand to #100C54X129. *Which* computer is presented depends, not only on features of the presentation, but also on the contingent circumstances of the presentation. In different circumstances the same presentation might present different, though perceptually indiscriminable, things.

To capture these ideas, Kaplan models presentations after a particular type of linguistic representation, the nonrigid definite description. Thus (9)

(9) He [^{P}the midget with a mustache^P] is a terrorist[32]

contains the pure demonstrative 'he' completed by a presentation in which, say, Y is *presented* with the same qualitative visual properties which he is *described* as possessing in (10)

(10) The midget with a mustache is a terrorist

that is, *as if the presentation were itself a linguistic expression*. The one semantically significant difference between (9) and (10) is that in (10) the nonrigid descriptive condition is part of the content of the utterance; in (9) the content of the complete demonstrative is the individual Y. The qualitative properties of the presentation belong to the character that determines the content without being part of it. So, the proposition expressed by (10) is

(10′) $\langle$ *The M, T* $\rangle$

where the italicized letters M and T stand for the properties of being a mustached midget and being a terrorist, whereas the proposition expressed by (9) is

(9′) $\langle$ Y, T $\rangle$

or

(9″) $\langle \{He[^P\text{The } M^P]\}(c),\ T \rangle$

in which the component corresponding to the complete demonstrative is Y rather than the qualitative conditions that constitute its presentation.

It is the nonrigid content of the definite description that enables the Fregean to account for its cognitive significance and solve his puzzles.[33] By giving presentations the same semantic structure, Kaplan wants to solve the analogous problems for the directly referential terms for which Frege's own solution will not work. Slightly revising Kaplan (see note 31), let's take a presentation to have the following "standard form":

(P) The individual that has appearance A

where an appearance, Kaplan continues, is

something like a picture with a little arrow pointing to the relevant subject. Trying to put it into words, a particular demonstration might come out like: 'The brightest visible heavenly body'. (Kaplan 1989a, 526)

Let's suppose that a linguistic description can serve as a surrogate for the appearance.[34] The character of a complete demonstrative such as (11)

(11) That[^P\text{The brightest visible heavenly body}^P]

is composed from the characters of its parts (or from those of its parts that have their own characters, like the embedded presentation). So, the character of this complete demonstrative (type) is the rule that each of its tokens directly refers to the thing (in its context) that is the brightest visible heavenly body. Presentations with different visual properties substituted for the appearance, A, have different characters and, by composition, so will the complete demonstratives built from them. The only difference between the character of the complete demonstrative and of its constituent presentation is that the former is directly referential and the latter is not even rigid. Therefore, there can be two presentations with different contents in the same context, but, if they are presentations of the same thing, their respective complete demonstratives will have the same content, that is, a co-referent. This excludes an explanation of the difference in the informativeness of the two complete demonstratives at the level of *their* respective contents. Instead, Kaplan argues, we can explain it by their respective characters. For two presentations have different contents *in the same context* iff they also have different characters, and two presentations have different characters iff their two respective complete demonstratives also have different characters. Hence different visual

contents of two presentations will ultimately surface in different characters for their respective complete demonstratives. QED, Frege's puzzle for
demonstratives is solved![35]

VII   Dthat-descriptions

The Fregean Theory of Demonstrations treats the visual presentation Δ
as if it were a definite description, assigning it a character, content, and
referent.[36] Having drawn this parallel, Kaplan next extends it in the
opposite direction. Just as Δ completes the pure demonstrative 'That',
Kaplan introduces a special demonstrative symbol 'Dthat', which is
"completed" by a (nonrigid) definite description Φ.[37] 'Dthat' has two
effects. First, it takes a singular term Φ, whose content is a complex of
descriptive conditions, and yields the directly referential dthat-description
Dthat[Φ] whose content is its individual referent. Second, it takes a singular term Φ whose character (assuming it contains no indexicals) is
constant and yields the dthat-description whose character is nonconstant
determining different contents (= direct referents) in different contexts.
Thus the description 'the midget with a mustache' contributes the same
complex of properties as its content in all contexts, but 'Dthat['The
midget with a mustache']' contributes different contents, that is, direct
referents, in different contexts, depending on who in fact is the midget
with a mustache in the circumstances of its context. The total effect of
'Dthat['The midget with a mustache']' is to make the content of the
embedded description part, not of what is said by its utterances, but of the
character of its utterance, which determines, relative to a context, what it
says. Thus the character rule for dthat-descriptions:

(Dthat)   For every context c and for every definite description Φ, an
occurrence of 'Dthat[Φ]' in c directly refers to the unique individual (if
there is one) denoted by Φ in the circumstance of c, and to no one
otherwise.

Although both effects of 'Dthat' will be important for the application to
metaphor, it is the second—the fact that 'Dthat' generates terms with
nonconstant characters from terms with constant characters—that I shall
work out in greatest detail in chapter 4.

I should emphasize one feature of dthat-descriptions in anticipation of
my account of metaphor. When a speaker learns the rule (Dthat), what he
learns is not the character of a single expression (type) in the language—
as he does when he learns, say, (I) for 'I'. What he learns is a schematic

rule whose instances are the result of substituting particular definite descriptions in the language for the metalinguistic variable Φ. That is, he learns a rule that enables him to interpret any well-formed definite description demonstratively; he acquires a skill of interpretation rather than an individual piece of vocabulary. Although we'll see in a moment some specific difficulties that attend this idea, this aspect of 'Dthat' is also what lies behind the claim that it is an operator on the description rather than a well-formed term in its own right.

The one respect in which dthat-descriptions turn out not to be a model for metaphors, as I mentioned earlier, is that their characters, as the rule (Dthat) shows, employ denotation: At the content generation-stage, it is denotation, satisfaction of the descriptive conditions given in the character of the embedded description Φ, that does the work in fixing the direct referent of 'Dthat[Φ]'. Thus dthat-descriptions, although directly referential, are *not thoroughly nondenotational*. Metaphors, I'll argue in chapter 4, are in this respect like indexicals, which, being parametric, are not only directly referential but also thoroughly nondenotational.

Parallel to the thoroughly–not thoroughly nondenotational distinction, there is a second difference between indexicals and dthat-descriptions that also bears on metaphor—indeed on differences between metaphors. The characters of indexicals are de jure—by their very nature—nonconstant, whereas the characters of dthat-descriptions are only de facto nonconstant. Take indexicals first. The value of an indexical parameter in any one context is entirely independent of its value in any other; for example, the fact that I, JS, am the value of the speaker parameter for 'I' in one context is entirely independent of the fact that DD is the value in another. Of course, the same thing could turn out, as a matter of pure chance, to be the value of the parameter in more than one context, but the characters of the indexicals legislate, as it were, that we look only at the values of the parameter in each context one by one. If a value is preserved across contexts, it is nothing more than accidental homonymy. It follows that, if indexicals are parametric, the character of an indexical *must* be nonconstant, sensitive to each context, one by one. The character of a dthat-description, on the other hand, is (only) de facto nonconstant, because it is only as a matter of fact that its constituent description does not denote the same thing in all circumstances. If the constituent description Φ were such that it turned out (as a matter of fact, physical or metaphysical) to denote the same thing in all *circumstances*, then it would also ipso facto denote the same thing in (the circumstances of) all *contexts*. In which case, the dthat-description 'Dthat[Φ]' would also turn out to have a de facto constant character. Unlike indexicals, there is nothing about the very nature of dthat-descriptions that renders their characters nonconstant.

I emphasize this last point because the de facto context-dependence of a dthat-description is compatible with its being sufficiently rich descriptively or conceptually to uniquely determine its referent at a circumstance—without needing extralinguistic or nonconceptualized contextual aids. Perhaps it would be more accurate to speak of its context-sensitivity rather than context-dependence, but the role of the context in the semantics of the dthat-description is limited to the fact that it is the circumstance of its context, namely, the *actual* circumstance, that is the relevant circumstance for determining (by denotation) its directly referential content.

I'll argue in chapter 8 that the nonconstant character of some metaphors is more like the de jure nonconstant character of indexicals whereas that of other metaphors is more like the de facto nonconstant character of dthat-descriptions. In particular, I'll argue that one kind of dead metaphor is a metaphor whose character is nonconstant and context-dependent but only de facto; the liveliest metaphors are those whose characters are de jure nonconstant.

Finally, I want to return to one issue that arises in part because of the not thoroughly nondenotational character of dthat-descriptions, an issue that, again, marks a difference (as we'll see in ch. 6) between dthat-descriptions and metaphors. This is the question we broached earlier in connection with the character rule (D) for complete demonstratives: If the demonstration Δ "completes" the pure demonstrative 'That,' is the resulting expression 'That[Δ]' syntactically and/or semantically simple or complex? In the case of the dthat-description, where the issues are sharper (since the constituents are all linguistic), we can appreciate the question in all its complexity. There are strong reasons for holding both that it must be syntactically simple or unstructured and that it must be syntactically complex or articulated.[38]

On the one hand, a dthat-description is a directly referential term whose content is simple, namely, its individual referent, as opposed to a merely rigid designator whose content is a complex conceptualized representation that rigidly designates the same individual at all circumstances. Therefore, mirroring its semantic simplicity, its syntax ought to be simple too. For this reason, Kaplan sometimes writes that despite the fact that 'dthat' is provably equivalent in his formalized logic of demonstratives to a rigidifying operator syntactically completed by the description as an operand (1989a, 552, Remark 13), it should be analyzed as a "syntactically complete term that requires no syntactical completion by an operand" (Kaplan 1989b, 581).[39]

On the other hand, there are two good reasons to articulate the character of the constituent description as part of the character of the complete dthat-description. First, as we saw (in section VI), the motivation for positing a constituent presentation in the complete demonstrative was to enable us to account for its cognitive significance, the kind of information that solves puzzles like Frege's. Similarly, the character of the embedded term in the dthat-description carries the mode of presentation that enables us to distinguish informative from uninformative utterances of, say, identity statements flanked by dthat-descriptions, despite the fact that they have the same content. However, to recover this character-istic information carried by dthat-descriptions, they must have constituent syntactic structure. Second, the articulated character of the embedded description determines how the direct referent of the complete dthat-description is fixed, namely, by denotation. But if the description Φ must be discernible as an autonomous denoting unit within 'Dthat[Φ]', there must also be syntactic structure to the whole composite or complex expression.

These two reasons suggest that the characters of dthat-descriptions are articulated and, if their characters are structured, their syntax should be too.[40] Hence the dthat-description is pulled in two directions: Its two motivating ideas lead to the contradictory conclusion that it ought to be both semantically and syntactically simple and complex.[41] One might further conclude that, ingenious as the invention of 'Dthat' is, it is an attempt to do the impossible. Should we therefore abandon it?

The last verdict may be too harsh.[42] There are other constructions in natural language for which philosophers have given competing reasons to hold that they are both syntactically and/or semantically structured and unstructured; examples are quotation, both direct and indirect (that-clauses). In those cases, we certainly wouldn't conclude that we should abandon the constructions. Despite similar theoretical tensions, we wouldn't condemn the natural language constructions as attempts to do the impossible. Rather, the conflicting considerations show that there remain unresolved problems in our understanding, that the fault lies with inadequate theories rather than the phenomena.

Here, too, perhaps we should charitably conclude that 'Dthat' is a successful representation for how we interpret, or use, (nondemonstrative) expressions demonstratively, though we do not yet fully understand how it succeeds at this task. In this spirit we'll also see how 'Dthat' provides us with a technique of great expressive power to import context-sensitivity into interpretation where previously there was none. 'Dthat' gives us a way to understand and explain *demonstrative interpretations* (or *uses*) of arbitrary expressions in addition to the explicit demonstrative and index-ical *expressions.* Demonstrativity is no longer an exceptional, idiosyn-cratic feature of a handful of isolated words, but a general mode of interpretation that can be found—or introduced—throughout all of lan-guage. Nor is it limited to the demonstrative mode of interpretation narrowly character-ized by 'Dthat'. In the next chapter I'll argue that metaphorical interpretation is yet a further mode of the same general type of context-sensitive interpretation of language.

Chapter 4

Knowledge of Metaphor

With Kaplan's semantics for demonstratives in hand, I am now in a position to make good on my promissory notes for metaphor. The "interpretations" of a metaphor (type) are the *contents* its tokens express in their respective contexts. Since there is an unlimited, or not antecedently fixed, number of different possible contexts in which those tokens can occur, there is an unlimited number of different possible contents those tokens can express metaphorically. And because each is a function of its extralinguistic context of utterance, the speaker's knowledge of their contents cannot be a matter simply of her linguistic competence. Yet, as I illustrated in chapter 1, examples (1)–(10), the variations in content seem to follow a pattern of corresponding variations in their respective contexts; and as we saw in chapter 2, there are also constraints on the possible metaphorical interpretations (in different contexts) of one expression (type). Furthermore, those constraints look like those that govern specific kinds of literal interpretations of language. These facts suggest that a speaker has a more abstract kind of knowledge apart from his knowledge of the particular content of each metaphorical token in its respective context. This more abstract piece of knowledge is the *character* of the metaphor.

As with the character of any expression, the character of an expression interpreted metaphorically is a function, or rule, that determines, for each context, its content in that context. Like the nonconstant characters of demonstratives, which determine different contents relative to different contexts, the character of a metaphor is nonconstant. And like the characters of both indexicals and dthat-descriptions, a speaker's knowledge of the metaphorical character of an expression (i.e., the character of the expression interpreted metaphorically), though not of its content, falls within her semantic knowledge; hence it is knowledge of a kind of (linguistic) meaning. Yet, beyond these common themes, the character of a metaphor is a hybrid, in some of its more specific features more indexical-like, in others, more dthat-description-like. I shall mention two of these for now, beginning with a dthat-like characteristic.

First, recall that a speaker's knowledge of the rule of character (Dthat) for the dthat-description is schematic: The rule applies to any description that can be demonstratively interpreted. Hence knowledge of (Dthat) is different from knowledge of the character, or meaning, of a single expression (type) in the language, such as the character of 'I'. Similarly, what the speaker knows when she knows the character of a particular metaphorically interpreted expression is an instance of a character-schematic rule, which applies not only to the particular expression-type interpreted metaphorically on the occasion; what she knows holds for any expression that it is possible to interpret metaphorically. Like her knowledge of dthat-descriptions, what a speaker knows in knowing the *meaning* of a metaphor (*not*: its content in a particular context) is, like a skill of interpretation, a rule that enables her to interpret *any* expression metaphorically, given knowledge of the relevant context.

Let me make this semantic parallel lexically explicit. Just as Kaplan invented 'Dthat [Φ]' to lexically represent the demonstrative interpretation of an arbitrary definite description Φ, I shall now create an analogue 'Mthat[Φ]' to lexically represent the metaphorical interpretation of an arbitrary (literal) expression Φ. Given any (literal) expression Φ, 'Mthat' yields the (to coin a term of art) "metaphorical expression" 'Mthat[Φ]' that has a nonconstant character sensitive to a specific "metaphorically relevant" feature of its context. Thus both 'Dthat' and 'Mthat', completed by their respective expressions, yield lexical representations of specific kinds of context-dependent interpretations of those expressions. Just as the speaker who knows how to generate an interpretation, or content, for a demonstratively interpreted definite description Φ knows the (non-constant) character of the dthat-description 'Dthat[Φ]', so a speaker who knows how to interpret an expression Φ metaphorically—who knows what it is to generate a metaphorical content for Φ in a context—knows the (nonconstant) character of the metaphorical expression 'Mthat[Φ]'.

Second, unlike dthat-descriptions but like indexicals, the metaphorical expression 'Mthat[Φ]' is parametric. Its content in a context is not denoted by Φ, the expression interpreted metaphorically. Instead the content is the value of a parameter in the context to which metaphors are sensitive, just as the content of 'I' in a context is the value of the respective parameter to which that indexical is sensitive. (I shall turn next to the identity of the parameter for metaphor.)

Finally, unlike both singular indexicals and dthat-descriptions whose content (in a context) is an individual, but like the predicate demonstrative 'Thus' or 'is that F', the content of 'Mthat[Φ]', in the basic case where it occurs in predicative position, is a property or set of properties.[1] Therefore, the character of 'Mthat[Φ]' is a function from the set of contexts (or the set of relevant contextual parameters) to a set of (sets of) properties rather than to a set of individuals.

This sketch of the shared and distinct structures of metaphors, dthat-descriptions, and indexicals needs considerable filling in. Two main tasks lie ahead: (i) to describe the contextual parameter on which a metaphorical interpretation depends, and (ii) to spell out the logical structure of metaphorical character, that is, for each expression Φ that is interpreted metaphorically, the character of its corresponding metaphorical expression 'Mthat[Φ]'. In the remainder of this chapter, I shall work out the basic theoretical notions that constitute our knowledge *of* metaphor, the specifically semantic competence that underlies our ability to interpret a metaphor. In chapter 5, I'll illustrate how this theoretical apparatus interacts with, or is applied to, a context to yield a content; this chapter will thereby address one of the two ways by which knowledge is (conveyed) *by* metaphor. Here, I should emphasize, my point is neither to demonstrate nor to test the adequacy of our semantics to produce actual interpretations; it is to show how their semantic structure places constraints on metaphorical interpretations. In chapter 6 I return to apply our account of knowledge *of* metaphor to some outstanding problems that we have already encountered, for example, how an expression interpreted metaphorically nonetheless "has" its literal meaning; how the metaphorical interpretation of an expression "depends" on its literal meaning; why metaphorical character is a type of *meaning*; and the relation of metaphor to other tropes. Finally, in chapter 7, I turn to the second way by which knowledge is (conveyed) *by* metaphor, namely, by way of its character. Here I shall show, as I promised in chapter 1, how a metaphor can convey knowledge by its metaphorical character that is not captured in its (literally paraphraseable) propositional content in a context.

I   The Context of a Metaphor: Presuppositions

Max Black (1962) was the first contemporary author to recognize that what is important for the metaphorical interpretation of an expression Φ is a range of beliefs "associated with" Φ and not, or not only, its "standard dictionary meaning" or "literal sense." After making this observation, Black concentrated his discussion on beliefs he called "the system of associated commonplaces" for Φ. He described these beliefs in a number of ways: as beliefs that would be "readily and freely" evoked by Φ for the ordinary (nonexpert) member of the linguistic community (or, in his terms, "culture"); as "current platitudes" about Φs that are "the common possession of the members of [the] speech community"; and as the kinds of beliefs to which a speaker's literal use of a word "normally commits" him. For example, the system of associated commonplaces for 'is a wolf', in the metaphor 'man is a wolf', is the "system of ideas" of being "fierce, carnivorous, treacherous, and so on." This system, Black observed, is "not sharply delineated" (note the "and so on") though it is "sufficiently definite to admit of detailed enumeration" (ibid., 40–41). None of these properties, he continued, would be properly speaking considered part of the dictionary meaning or definition of 'wolf'. But we would surely expect special pleading by someone who instead interpreted the metaphor to express the proposition that, say, man is a vegetarian. This interpretation would normally be evidence that the speaker is not a member of our speech community or that she falls short of our expectations of common knowledge among competent members of the community.[2]

Much of what Black says is right on mark. His denial that the metaphorically relevant "knowledge" is knowledge of the meaning or definition of Φ highlights the fact that the metaphorically relevant beliefs need not be true (e.g., when the system of commonplaces for 'whale' includes the belief that a whale is a fish), not to say necessary or analytic to Φ. It is much more important that the beliefs be shared and be publicly accessible, although, contrary to his phrase "readily evoked," they need not be effortlessly or instantaneously recoverable. He does not explain why he says it, but Black is also right that the relevant beliefs must be associated with the *word* Φ and not just with its extension or intension. Finally, he emphasizes the systematicity of the metaphorically relevant beliefs, an aspect of metaphorical interpretation that has drawn much recent attention, first through the work of Goodman and lately by Lakoff and his school. We shall return to this last theme in chapters 5 and 7.

Black's emphasis on "associated commonplaces" is, however, unfortunate. Although he acknowledges in the latter part of his (1962) essay that the description "associated commonplaces" only fits the "commonest cases" and that "in a poem, or a piece of sustained prose, the writer can establish a novel pattern of implications for the literal uses of the key expressions, prior to using them as vehicles for his metaphors" (ibid., 43), his emphasis on beliefs linked to membership in the linguistic or speech community tends to blur the distinction he wishes to draw between meaning and belief. It also suggests that, as a rule, there is one kind of pool or system of beliefs—"commonplaces"—for all typical, nonpoetic metaphorical interpretations. This is not true. The range of potentially relevant properties believed to be "associated" with the expression to be interpreted metaphorically is highly variegated. Not all associations are necessarily shared by all members of the community, nor are they always "believed" to be true. Indeed they defy any simple uniform characterization.

Some metaphorically relevant properties do belong to the definition of Φ and are true of Φs, as in:

(1) Shamir was a midget among Israeli leaders

that is, was very small (relative to humans), which is true and even definitional for 'midget'. But other properties may be neither true of nor even believed to be true of Φ's extension; indeed they may be known to be false of Φ's extension. For example,

(2) Kripke is an alchemist of ideas

can be interpreted metaphorically to say that Kripke can produce extremely valuable ideas from the most common, obvious, and prima facie trivial intuitions despite the fact that we know that no alchemist can really produce gold from base metals. In some of these cases that rest on falsehoods, the feature is stereotypical and belongs to a socially shared "meaning" for the term; for example,

(3) Saddam is a gorilla

says that he is fierce and violent, even though we know that in fact gorillas are shy, timid, and sensitive (and violent only when violently provoked).[3] In other cases of socially shared "meaning," the metaphor is based on what we might call, borrowing a term from Marc Crimmins, "normal" as opposed to "idiosyncratic" features.[4] A normal feature of an object referred to by an expression Φ is a feature that belongs to (more or less) community-wide shared knowledge about Φs given a common way of life, for example, a feature associated with Φ that is related to the function of Φ within the general human cognitive system. Thus temperature terms like 'hot' and 'cold' have normal features correlated with our standard sensory modes for identifying temperatures, and these features are routinely exploited when the terms are metaphorically interpreted to apply to, say, emotional states or music. As Crimmins speculates, it is more plausible to expect expressions for properties and relations to have normal features associated with them than names of individuals—although names for "public figures," past or present, universal or local, are also likely to have normal features, for example,

(4) Clinton is a Kennedy.

On the other hand, a feature is idiosyncratic when it is associated with an expression for only an isolated individual, sometimes only through psychological chains of which she may not even be consciously aware. For example, the psychoanalyst Benjamin B. Rubinstein describes the case of a young woman whose father had administered enemas to her until adolescence and, as an adult, could not achieve an orgasm except when masturbating. Her most frequent masturbation fantasy was that she was being given an enema by a young doctor in a hospital. Once, upon being told by her analyst that she apparently preferred an enema to sexual intercourse, "she seemed surprised, as if she had never heard this before" (despite having had the connection pointed out to her on numerous previous occasions), and exclaimed:

(5) Oh, that's awful—I have to wash that out, that desire.

According to Rubinstein, "the remarkable thing is that the patient, who was intelligent and alert, was completely unaware of the metaphorical character of [her] utterance," notwithstanding the fact "that, as a rule, her speech was straight—i.e., nonmetaphorical."[5]

Now, normal (as well as many stereotypical) features are learned, or acquired, by individuals in processes not easily distinguished from those in which they learn the words associated with them. They are shared within a community, and knowledge of certain normal features may even be a qualification to be a competent member of the community. Therefore, one might be tempted to consider a normal feature of its referent as part of the linguistic meaning of a term. On the other hand, features are (normally) normal relative only to a given linguistic community, varying from one to another. Therefore, one ought to resist, I think, the temptation to think of them as truly linguistic—that is, linguistic in the same sense in which knowledge of character proper is linguistic. We should distinguish the kind of knowledge that is the object of a speaker's language faculty—his knowledge of language proper, knowledge of meaning that interacts with the other components of the language faculty, syntax and phonology—from the knowledge he possesses in virtue of belonging to a linguistic community, the knowledge we reasonably expect every speaker in the (linguistic) community to possess on pain of being deemed "incompetent" in a broader sense. Knowledge of normal features associated with expressions (where there are such notions) counts as the latter but not the former. Although we may reasonably expect every speaker of English to know the normal features associated with a term, if he doesn't, he is not necessarily ignorant of something in the syntax, semantics, phonology, or lexical meaning of the word. Consequently I will consider even normal features as extralinguistic knowledge.

The features I have discussed thus far are relatively stable across utterances, given the context of a fixed linguistic community. But many metaphorically relevant properties attach to an expression only in a context, lasting only for the local duration. In the next chapter, I shall discuss at length one class of metaphors I call *exemplification metaphors* that are highly context sensitive in this way. But they are not unique. Poets frequently build up associations around a word in order to exploit them in later metaphorical uses of the same word within the limited scope of one poem.[6] For example, in *Antony and Cleopatra*, Shakespeare first refers to Antony using 'the sun' in order to contrast him with Cleopatra who is described as 'the moon'. Like the sun, Antony has a fixed, predictable, reliable, steady course; Cleopatra, like the moon, is erratic and unreliable. And just as the moon derives its light from the sun, so Cleopatra is subordinate to and dependent on Antony. Later in the play, having already singled out this association of the notion of a regular, reliable, fixed course with 'the sun', Shakespeare then describes the death of Antony in terms of the violent, cosmic catastrophe that would result if the sun were to wander out of its fixed orbit. Thus the two guards:

(6) 2. Guard: The Starre is falne.
    1. Guard: And Time is at his Period. [*Antony and Cleopatra*, IV, xiv, 129f.]

Here the 'falling'—the disappearance or 'falling out of course' of the sun—means the end (or 'period') of Time, the principle of organization governed by the regular motion of the sun.[7] So, having made one, not obvious (and, by our current lights, false) association with 'the sun', Shakespeare turns it around in the later use. The same idea is emphasized by the literary critic, Mario L. D'Avanzo, while commenting on Keats:

Through metaphor words take on a world of possible connotations and, depending upon the precision with which they are ordered in the poem, may precipitate new and surprising networks of reference.[8]

In yet other examples, the history of a metaphor's interpretations may also become one of the properties associated with the expression as it is interpreted metaphorically on a later occasion. The Marxist political philosopher G. A. Cohen reports how another philosopher friend "roused [him] from what had been [his] dogmatic socialist slumber" by "hitting" him with an argument that was to appear in Robert Nozick's *Anarchy, State, and Utopia* (G. A. Cohen 1995, 4). The metaphor 'roused from his dogmatic slumbers' is, of course, borrowed from Kant, who used these words to describe the effect on him of reading Hume's *Treatise*; that is, Hume made him actively rethink and reassess his common, unreflective assumptions. Thus what Cohen wishes to say is, first of all, that Nozick's effect on him was to force him to rethink and reevaluate all his assumptions. But this is not all: He also wishes to convey that Nozick's effect on him was like Hume's effect on Kant. This association with 'roused from his dogmatic slumbers' is not a feature *of* being awakened from one's dogmatic slumbers; rather it is a feature dependent on Kant's use of the (metaphorical) phrase, a historical fact about the metaphorical interpretation of the original token of the phrase, which is now associated with the later metaphorical interpretation of (the later token of) the phrase.

I could go on, but these examples should suffice to convince you that there are any number of relations by which, or sources from which, a property can come to be a candidate for inclusion within a metaphorical interpretation. This will be no surprise to students of metaphor. Glancing through the history of theories of metaphor, one is struck by the variety of principles that have been proposed at one time or another as the so-called grounds of metaphorical interpretation: relations of similarity, analogy, dissimilarity, connotational features, iconic features, semantic fields, features of "interaction," and on and on. In part the explanation for this diversity is that different theorists have focused on different classes of examples, leading them to different grounds to explain their respective data.[9] However, once we see the wide variety of grounds, it should also be clear that if we want to give a *general* characterization of metaphor, it should not be in terms of the specific *content* of any one of its grounds or their genealogy.

Traditional theories of metaphor sought to explain the phenomenon by spelling out a procedure that would yield a literal analysis of each metaphor based on one or another ground, something like an algorithm that would yield, for each metaphor, a synonymous nonmetaphorical expression. Hence, if they took the diversity of grounds to heart, these theories would have had to trim their explanatory sails and confine their analyses to specific classes of metaphors, thus surrendering their generality. And this conclusion would have been fatal for them since it would be tantamount to denying that the many examples of metaphor and their respective grounds constitute a single unified, or cohesive, linguistic phenomenon.

Not so for the present theory, whose aim is not to yield any such procedure or rule but to articulate the semantic structure of a metaphor—the *form* that determines its propositional content (in each context) as a function of certain contextual parameters. From this perspective, the multiplicity of "grounds" poses no theoretical problem. What makes metaphor a single linguistic phenomenon is that one formal semantic relation governs the context-dependence of its interpretation; the multiple grounds that underlie the interpretations of different metaphors simply illustrate the variety of ways in which the relevant contextual parameter can be realized. In what follows, I shall therefore say that a feature related in *any* one of these ways to the expression Φ interpreted metaphorically, the literal vehicle, is *m-associated* with Φ. So, stereotypical, normal, "metaphor-historical," and the exemplified features I shall discuss at length in chapter 5 are *all* m-associated with Φ and are all known (given my earlier comments on normal features) extralinguistically.

Note that there is no circle here: To be m-associated with Φ is to be related to Φ as a stereotypical feature of Φs, or normal feature, or exemplified feature, and so on. None of these relations is itself metaphorical or linguistic; neither are we *analyzing* metaphor in terms of these extralinguistic relations. They simply register the various sources or relations by and from which speakers elicit features that belong to the contextual parameter for metaphor. Although I wish to be conservative in my conception of semantics, I also want to be as liberal, ecumenical, and pluralistic as possible with these extralinguistic pragmatic notions—with the range of features that count as m-associated with the literal vehicle.

How, then, to describe the parameter on which metaphorical interpretations depend? For the indexicals, certain features of the world (the speaker for 'I', the time for 'now', etc.), determine not only the truth-values (or references) of what they (or their utterances) say but also their content. Insofar as they bear on truth-value, those features are functioning as (part of) circumstances of evaluation; insofar as they bear on determination of their content, they function as (part of) their context of utterance (or, if you will, interpretation). An equally important, though not as easily demarcated, fact or feature of the world that plays the same dual set of roles is the existence of certain background beliefs and attitudes against which an utterance takes place. Following Robert Stalnaker, I'll call the shared background necessary for the interpretation of an utterance the set of *presuppositions* of its context (or *context set*).[10] My

proposal is that the contextual parameter on which a metaphorical interpretation depends is a (subset of the) context set of presuppositions.

This general notion of presupposition is based on the intuitive distinction between what is *asserted*, or *said*, by an utterance (roughly, what we
have called its content in a context) and what it *presupposes* (in the context). An utterance of 'the prime minister of Israel is delighted with the
election of Yassar Arafat' presupposes both that there is a prime minister
of Israel and that Arafat has been elected; it asserts, or says, that the
former is delighted with the latter. A standard test to distinguish what is
asserted or said by a sentence from what it presupposes is to negate the
sentence, for example, 'The prime minister of Israel is not delighted with
the election of Yassar Arafat'; what is asserted is obviously different from
its affirmative counterpart, but the presuppositions are the same. Thus the
presuppositions of an utterance are those propositions that can be inferred
from both it and its denial. An analogous test uses a modal variant: 'The
prime minister of Israel might have been delighted with the election of
Yassar Arafat' also preserves presuppositions but alters content. If those
propositions were not presupposed, the affirmative, negative, and modal
utterances would all be inappropriate things to say, either (depending on
one's theory) because they would be false or neither true nor false.

A similar distinction can be drawn between the asserted content of a
metaphor and its "metaphorically relevant" presuppositions—those
properties that must be presupposed to be m-associated with the literal
vehicle because, in their absence, the utterance to be interpreted metaphorically would be metaphorically uninterpretable and therefore inappropriate. Suppose Romeo utters

(7) Juliet is the sun

in a context c (given the identification of 'is the sun' as a metaphor) to
express the proposition that Juliet is, say, the thing around which his life
revolves, that she nourishes him, and that he worships her. This proposition may, of course, be true or false (depending on the facts about Juliet's
and Romeo's relation to each other), but, for it to have one or the other
truth-value, these properties (perhaps among others) must be presupposed
to be m-associated with the word 'is the sun'. These presuppositions are
preserved when we negate (7) (in the same context and where the predicate is still interpreted metaphorically):

(7a) Juliet is not the sun,

meaning that she is not the person around whom Romeo's life revolves,
or that she does not nourish him or that he does not worship her. Like-

wise, the same properties are presupposed when we utter (in the same context, with the same interpretation)

(7b) Juliet might be the sun.

If those properties were not presupposed to be m-associated with the literal vehicle, 'is the sun', none of these three utterances would be successful or appropriate *under this interpretation*. Of course, different properties might be presupposed to be m-associated with 'is the sun', in which case (everything else being equal) the utterance would then have a different metaphorical interpretation whose appropriateness, or interpretability, would also depend on those presuppositions being held. But unless the expression to be interpreted metaphorically is presupposed to be m-associated with *some* such identified set of properties, it won't be knowable at all in the context under what conditions it is true, and hence appropriate.

Now, if the contextual parameter for metaphor is a set of "metaphorically relevant" presuppositions, the character of an expression Φ interpreted metaphorically, or (using the term of art I introduced earlier) the character of the metaphorical expression 'Mthat[Φ]', is a function from the "metaphorically relevant" set(s) of properties presupposed to be m-associated with Φ in its containing sentence S in the context c to a set of properties P.[11] In other words, corresponding to the rule (Dthat) for dthat-descriptions, we can propose an analogous rule of character for metaphorical expressions:

(Mthat) For every context c and for every expression Φ, an occurrence of 'Mthat[Φ]' in a sentence S (= ... Mthat[Φ] ...) in c (directly) expresses a set of properties P presupposed to be m-associated with Φ in c such that the proposition $\langle \dots P \dots \rangle$ is either true or false in the circumstance of c.

(Mthat), like (Dthat) and (I), is a rule of character that a speaker knows simply in virtue of his knowledge of language. As we shall see, in terms of it we can spell out the constraints on metaphorical interpretation described in chapter 2. But because it is a semantic rule, it also doesn't make explicit the pragmatic, extralinguistic notions that describe the context; for example, what it is to be m-associated with Φ, what it is to be presupposed, and exactly what fixes P—what is, as it were, the mechanism encapsulated in the expression-relation. In the coming sections I shall attempt to explain some of these notions in more detail: (i) the attitude of presupposition that is appropriate for metaphor, and how it differs from the simple attitude of belief; (ii) the sense in which metaphorically relevant presuppositions are *pre*suppositions; (iii) the relation between speakers' presuppositions tout cour and the specific presuppositions that are needed for the interpretation of a metaphor; and (iv) the degree to which the mechanism that fixes the content of the metaphor in a context, the set of properties P, is semantic. In chapter 5 I shall discuss at length one particular class of metaphors based on the extralinguistic perception of exemplification-relations. But before continuing, let me add two explanatory glosses.

First, according to (Mthat) the content of a metaphorical expression in a context, the property(ies) P, is determined by two factors: the function that is the character of the metaphor and the context set of presuppositions that is the domain of the function. In setting up the semantics, we therefore have a certain amount of freedom in dividing the labor. At one extreme, we can define the domain of presuppositions as narrowly as we wish, eliminating all but those that actually belong to P, and make the function an identity-mapping. At the other extreme, we can be liberal with regard to membership in the context set of presuppositions, and let the function do all the sorting and selecting of P. In what follows, I tend toward the first strategy. Although it is not yet entirely clear how, and how much, these two ways of cutting up the pie actually make a difference, I have tried to keep the semantics simple and leave messy details to the pragmatics or description of the context. However, one can imagine other ways of yielding the same results.

Second, the content (in a context) of the metaphorical expression is a set of properties such that the proposition expressed by its whole utterance is determinately true or false. But, to anticipate a possible objection, I should emphasize that this content of the metaphor in a context is not, or not always, its full or sole interpretation, or meaning, or significance. As we'll see at length in chapter 7, the characters of many metaphors are equally important for the information or significance they convey; furthermore, not all cognitive significance carried by the character of a metaphor can be expressed propositionally, let alone as part of its propositional content in its context of utterance. As I'll also argue, this character-istic information of the metaphor is generally manifest in a variety of ways other than knowledge of truth-conditions; hence it is best distinguished from the truth-conditions of the metaphor, or its content in a context. At the same time, it is also not always evident precisely where to draw the line between those components of its cognitive significance that are relevant to the truth-evaluation of the metaphor and those that are not. Without trying to draw sharp boundaries around truth-conditions (or content), I'll return to this problem in chapter 5, section III to illustrate how this issue bears on criteria of individuation of metaphors.

II Presupposition, Belief, Pretense, and *Pre*supposition

The pragmatic notion of presupposition I am employing was first proposed as an alternative to the semantic notion that was popular among philosophers and linguists from the 1950s through the 1970s. According to the semantic notion, presupposition is a relation between two propositions P and Q such that P (semantically) presupposes Q iff both P necessitates Q and not-P necessitates Q, where P necessitates Q iff whenever P is true, Q is also true. (Where Q is false, P is claimed to be truth-valueless.)[12] According to the pragmatic notion proffered by Stalnaker and others, we explain the linguistic presuppositions of sentences not in terms of semantic relations between their propositional contents, but by features of their use or properties of their users. The pragmatic notion is guided by two central ideas. The first is that presupposition is a psychological attitude like belief (whose object is, depending on one's theory, either a proposition or sentence). The second is that a central function of presuppositions is to constitute the context on which the appropriateness (including interpretability) of an utterance depends. That is, unlike the semantic notion that takes presuppositions to be required for truth-valuedness, the pragmatic notion requires them for appropriateness. Furthermore, the presuppositions of a sentence that are required for its appropriateness are ultimately to be defined in terms of the presuppositions that a speaker must make for his utterance of the sentence to be appropriate.[13]

Among the attitudes, what distinguishes presupposition is that the subject takes the object of the attitude (be it a proposition or sentence) to be "common knowledge" in the context, part of a doxastic background mutually shared by the other participants. As a first approximation, we might therefore define *presupposition* as follows:

(P1) A proposition p is a presupposition of a speaker S in a context c (or S presupposes p in c) iff (1) S believes that p; (2) S believes that the other members of c believe that p; and (3) S believes that the other members of c recognize that he (S) believes that p.

(P1) captures the relevant kind of agreement for presupposition: agreement among the members of the context about p rather than agreement of p with the world. Thus presuppositions are the "common knowledge" of the participants despite the fact that they need not be true, in which case they cannot, strictly speaking, be knowledge. However, even (P1) is too strong because the presupposition need not even be *believed* by S and by the other conversational participants. Sometimes, of course, it is believed, but, as we saw with the m-associated stereotypical features (e.g., (3)), at times the presuppositions are definitely known to be false. In yet other cases, the participants may *represent* themselves *as* believing propositions they in fact do not believe, adopting the belief only for the sake of the discourse and within its local confines. In some of these cases, Stalnaker suggests that the speaker *pretends* to believe the presupposition; she acts, or makes utterances, in accordance with but without actually believing the presupposition.[14] Without dwelling on all the subtle differences between these cases, I shall suppose that what is necessary for presupposition is neither belief nor even pretending to believe but that the participants *represent themselves as if* they believe that p. So, of the various conditions in (P1), only the third is perhaps necessary: S must believe that the other contextual participants can recognize the presuppositions she represents herself as having, whether or not either she or they actually believe them or she believes that her audience believes them.

It should also be mentioned that even if presupposition were pretending to believe, it would not follow that the contents of metaphorical *assertions* "involve the pretense that something is the case when it is not."[15] The speaker's attitude toward his presuppositions (or the presuppositions of his utterance) should be distinguished from his attitude toward the asserted content of his utterance. Even if we pretend that elephants are delicate, dainty creatures when we know that they are not, I can use the sentence 'The sumo wrestler is an elephant' to assert (under a metaphorical interpretation) with no pretense that the wrestler is delicate and dainty.

Let me turn now to the second clause of (P1), which seems to require that the speaker believe that her fellow contextual participants believe the presuppositions *at the time of utterance*. This is also not in general true and not true in particular for the presuppositions of a metaphor. Let me first discuss a nonmetaphorical case. Often a speaker chooses to convey some piece of information to her audience (*because* she knows they do not share it), not by asserting it, but by asserting something else that presupposes that information. For example, I let you know that Bill in whom you have taken a sudden romantic interest is married by saying: "And let me introduce you to Bill's wife, too." The reason for this indirect form of communication might be either tact or, because it forces the hearer actively to draw out the presupposition, effectiveness. However, from cases like this we should not conclude that presupposition is pretended rather than actual belief. What the example shows is that presuppositions need not be *pre*supposed: they need not be held in common in advance of or initial to the time of the *utterance* that presupposes them. Instead a speaker may come to *make* a presupposition only *after*, or as a consequence of the fact that, she *utters* a sentence expressing a proposition whose appropriateness is contingent on the presupposition. (I'll return in the next section to sentence-presupposition and "making presuppositions.") That is, the only sense in which a presupposition p is pre-, or prior to, its presupposing assertion q is that it is *logically prior* in its respective context; that is, p is a *condition* on the appropriate assertion, or interpretability, of q. We can make this more precise in terms of a model of discourse.

Each contextual participant brings her own *individual context set* of presuppositions to a conversation but, because conversation demands cooperation, individual context sets of different participants typically coincide, at least sufficiently to enable conversation to proceed. Let the intersection of the individual context sets of the participants be the *shared context set* of the conversation. A context is *ideal* just in case the individual context sets of its participants are each identical with the shared context set.[16] Of course, given our different contingent doxastic histories, the ideal is rarely realized, especially if each individual's context set includes all her dispositional beliefs. A context is *close enough to ideal* if and only if the differences that exist do not disrupt the business of the context—do not render utterances inappropriate or uninterpretable and do not block communication or shared understanding. When individual context sets of participants do diverge sufficiently from the shared context set—sufficiently to affect the interpretation or appropriateness of an utterance— there is a breakdown in communication or conversation.

Think of a discourse over time as a series of successive stages, each of which is defined by the shared context set of presuppositions (cs_i) of its participants at that time. At any discourse stage n, the utterance of a sentence s can affect cs_n in two ways. First, if the utterance of s at n asserts a proposition p that does not belong to cs_n, then p is added to cs_n, yielding what is presupposed at the next stage, $cs_{(n+1)}$. But second—and more important for our purposes—the utterance of s will also in general cause its participants to infer various other propositions in addition to p, the proposition it asserts. Among these will be the proposition that the speaker is speaking and any other information that the speaker believes his audience must infer from his utterance in order to interpret and evaluate it as an appropriate assertion in the context set cs_n. These inferred propositions might include ones that are not already occurrently believed in common by all the contextual participants, propositions that belong to the speaker's individual context set but not to the others'. By making a statement that rests on them, the speaker reveals that he believes that the others will add them without challenge to their own individual context sets and that he intends for them to do so.[17] All of this information is presupposed *as part of cs_n*—inasmuch as it is necessary in order for the speaker to express p using s at cs_n—even though it comes to be held only after the speaker opens his mouth and performs the utterance. In these cases, we will say that *by* uttering s the speaker *makes* whatever presuppositions are necessary in order for s to express p. And inasmuch as the presuppositions belong to the context set cs_n relative to which p is asserted, they are prior to the assertion of p for which they are presupposed.[18]

The same story holds for metaphor. The metaphorically relevant presuppositions need not be held temporally before the speaker utters the metaphorical expression or sentence, prior to the speech act. Both the proposition that the speaker is uttering a metaphor at n and all the metaphorically relevant presuppositions that turn out to be grounds for its interpretation are counted as part of the context set cs_n, even if they come to be articulated or held only after the utterance event.

An especially important class of presuppositions of this sort are the properties associated with so-called creative metaphors, those to which Max Black referred when, in the course of criticizing comparison theories of metaphor, he made his now-famous statement that:

It would be more illuminating in some of these cases to say that the metaphor creates the similarity than to say that it formulates some similarity antecedently existing. (1962, 37)

Black has since defended this claim as an ontological thesis,[19] but these creative metaphors may appear to raise a problem for our account even if we understand "creative" in an epistemic sense. On that reading, a metaphor *creates* a similarity or property just in case it makes its speaker-hearer *aware* of a similarity or property he, and possibly everyone else, had not previously perceived. Metaphorical creativity of this sort is closer to the way Hollywood producers create starlets than the way God created the heavens and earth.[20]

Let's grant that some metaphors—especially in scientific and literary contexts—accomplish this intellectual feat. Someone might now object:

"If, as you claim, the interpretation of a metaphor depends on con-textually presupposed properties, any property expressed by a metaphor must occur in some proposition entailed by the speaker's context set of presuppositions; therefore it must be presupposed prior to the metaphor. But then no metaphor can ever be creative or innovative. No metaphor can express a property that its speaker-hearer discovers only by its utter-ance; by hypothesis such a property will not belong to the context set from which the content of the metaphor is drawn. Therefore, your theory only accounts for the least interesting metaphors, those based on what Black called a "system of associated commonplaces." It cannot account for the "vital" interpretations that originate with metaphorical expres-sions themselves."

My response to this objection should be clear by now. The context set relative to which the content of the metaphor is asserted consists of all information inferred from the utterance that is necessary for its inter-pretation; therefore, it will include any proposition or property that is required for its interpretation even if the speaker comes to recognize the property—even if it is "created"—as an outcome of the utterance. These properties may be products of his imaginative efforts as he attempts to construct an interpretation of the metaphorical sentence, or they may be features he notices from the syntax or sounds of the words used. If, as I'll argue in the next section, it is the interpreter of a metaphor who makes the presuppositions necessary for its interpretation, we might also say that the metaphor *makes* the novel properties or similarities—that is, makes us see or notice them.[21] Indeed the speaker himself may not "see" these features until after he has *uttered* the metaphor—or only *by* uttering it—and therefore he will not have presupposed them prior to the *utterance*. Perhaps, then, the speaker, prior to the utterance, also could not have *in-tended* to express the content that depends on these "created" features.[22] None of these properties should therefore count as "antecedently given commonplaces" in Black's sense; yet they count as full-fledged pre-suppositions in our sense inasmuch as they belong to the context set cs_n conditional on which the content of the metaphorical sentence can be asserted at the nth stage—regardless of the real time relation between the utterance and presuppositions or the temporal order in which their actual processing proceeds.

III Utterance-presuppositions and Metaphor

(P1) characterizes presupposition in terms of "common knowledge" or a shared doxastic background. But it should be common knowledge (at least among readers of this book) that not all common knowledge is pre-supposed as part of the context of each particular utterance. There are obviously an innumerably large number of beliefs that are "obviously true, and we each recognize that the other knows that [they are] obviously true";[23] in one sense of the term, these are "presuppositions" we share. But if we want to capture the second idea that underlies the pragmatic notion of presupposition, the idea that a primary function of the presuppositions of an utterance is to demarcate the boundaries within which the utterance is acceptable—which, for a metaphor, would include the presuppositions that enable it to be both interpretable and interpreted with a particular content—then we need some way to limit the context set to the specific body of presuppositions that facilitate and constrain the understanding and appropriateness of the given utterance. For this purpose it is not enough to say that presupposition is an utterer's attitude; we need criteria for what it is for an *utterance to have* (or *make*) *presuppositions*.

Unfortunately, at this point in our story, there is a complication, largely owing to a disanalogy between the general relation of an utterance to its presuppositions and the relation of a metaphor to its presuppositions. Nonetheless I shall argue that there remains enough of a relation to justify thinking of the latter on a model of the former. However, to put the dif-ferences between them in perspective, let me begin with the general rela-tion between an utterance and its presuppositions and then contrast it with the case of metaphor.

To begin with, let's make explicit the relation between a speaker's pre-suppositions (as in (P1)) and her utterance.

(P1*) Speaker S presupposes a proposition p in a context c *by uttering the sentence s* iff (1) S represents herself as believing that p; (2) S represents herself as believing that the other members of c represent themselves as believing that p; and (3) S represents herself as believing that the other members of c recognize that she (S) represents herself as believing that p from her utterance of s.[24]

The last condition of (P1*) requires that the presuppositions of the conversational participants somehow be manifest in the utterance. This condition was the main insight underlying the semantic notion of pre-supposition, although its criterion that the presuppositions be *logically* entailed (by the sentence and its negation) obscured the variety of syn-tactic, semantic, and pragmatic sources of presuppositions. Therefore, instead of saying (pacé the semantic notion) that the asserted sentence is false (or truth-valueless) where the presuppositions fail, we shall say that the utterance is, more broadly, *inappropriate*. Let's also say that we can *reasonably infer* that p from an utterance u of a sentence s by S if and only if it would not be appropriate for S to utter u unless S presupposes p. We can now state what it is for an utterance u of a sentence s to presuppose p or to require p as a presupposition:

(P2) An utterance u of a sentence s presupposes that p (or requires p as a presupposition) iff we can reasonably infer that p from u.

Likewise, we can define sentence presupposition in terms of utterance presupposition:

(P3) A sentence s presupposes that p iff all (or all normal) utterances of s presuppose that p.

Finally, in terms of (P2) we can define a narrower conception of the context set of presuppositions for an utterance:

(P4) The context set of presuppositions for an utterance u are all and only those presuppositions required for (or presupposed by) u.

As I said in section II, all and only those propositions that can be reasonably inferred belong to the context set of an utterance (including those necessary for its interpretation) whether or not they were commonly held by the participants *before* the time of the utterance.

Among the presuppositions required for the appropriateness of utterances, philosophers and linguists have given their greatest attention to those invariantly determined by their respective *sentences*, and, in particular, by conventional features of their form and content. They have concentrated on the presuppositions of, for example, lexical items (e.g., words like 'even', 'only', 'again', the determiner 'the'), syntactic configurations (e.g., cleft and pseudo cleft constructions), and compound sentences as they are computable from those of their sentential components (the so-called projection problem). I shall assume that the best theory that explains and predicts these presupposition phenomena as they arise for the literal use of language carries over to metaphor. However, there is one prima facie difference between the presuppositions of a metaphor and the presuppositions generated by the conventional features of sentences.

Take our earlier example, "And let me also introduce you to Bill's wife," which presupposes that Bill is married. Even if it is not already presupposed by the hearer at the time of utterance, this presupposition will be reasonably inferred by any contextual participant in virtue of the form and meaning of the expression 'Bill's wife'. He'll reason as follows. "Since it *would* be inappropriate (for some reason) for any speaker *nor-*

mally to utter that sentence unless he held that presupposition, the speaker must himself believe it and assume that I (the hearer) either already know it or will accept it without challenge. Therefore, I hereby add the proposition that Bill is married to my presuppositions."[25] The "would" in this piece of reasoning is significant. These presuppositions are *nomically* related to their respective utterances: They *must* be held by *any* (normal) member of the linguistic community if any (normal) utterance of the presupposing sentence is to be appropriate in its context. Given his general intention to belong to the linguistic community and to be speaking English, the speaker *makes presuppositions* simply by uttering sentences that require them. Just as the words 'Bill's wife' *mean* what they do regardless of their speaker's occurrent intentions on a given occasion (but given his general intention to be speaking English, etc.), so the speaker's presuppositions are "read off" his utterance without our examining his own individual occurrent beliefs and intentions—although we assume that, as a competent sincere speaker, he actually holds the presuppositions his utterances require.

Indeed, whether or not a speaker (occurrently) *believes* the presuppositions of his utterances, he is *committed* to them—and can be held responsible for them—just as he is to their meanings. As Stalnaker writes: "[T]he act of *making* a presupposition, like the act of meaning something, is not a mental act which can be separated by an act of will from overt linguistic behavior."[26] The "overt linguistic behavior," the utterance, is not simply *evidence* that the speaker presupposes what the utterance requires to be appropriate; to utter a sentence that requires them *is* to make its presuppositions. Just as meaning (or expressing a proposition) is not an act distinct from uttering a sentence that has that meaning (or expresses that proposition), so presupposing, or making a presupposition, is not an act distinct from using a sentence that requires the presupposition.[27]

The relation between a metaphor and its presuppositions is prima facie disanalogous to this nomic relation that holds for conventionally determined presuppositions. There is no nomic relation between an arbitrary metaphor (individuated by its linguistic form or character) and a particular set of presuppositions. For each metaphorical expression (type) there is no one set of presuppositions that remains invariant across contexts or that must belong to *any* context set in which an occurrence of a token of the metaphor (type) receives an appropriate interpretation. Different sets of presuppositions may each be *sufficient* to determine a (possibly different) interpretation either for different tokens of one metaphorical expression (type) or even for a single token; no single context set is *necessary* for any utterance of the metaphor to have *an* interpretation or an *appropriate* interpretation. There is also no train of reasoning analogous to that rehearsed in the previous paragraph whereby an interpreter who does not already share the speaker's particular set of presuppositions would be drawn to conclude, on grounds of what would *normally* be presupposed by utterances of the metaphor, that he must adopt a particular presupposition set. Therefore, no speaker makes particular metaphorically relevant presuppositions simply in virtue of his utterance of a metaphor, in the way in which he does make their respective presuppositions simply by using sentences with certain conventional forms and meanings.

These prima facie differences are not insignificant. Nonetheless I think we can narrow the gap between the presuppositions of a metaphor and those of general utterances, even if we cannot close it. On the one hand, not all instances of literal language determine particular required presuppositions for their appropriate utterance. On the other hand, and contrary to first appearances, some metaphors do have something like a normal required presupposition, at least as their default interpretation. Finally, the same kinds of rules that govern the appropriateness of utterances in general relative to their presuppositions also govern metaphor. So, although metaphor may be underdetermined relative to its presuppositions (especially compared with the general nonmetaphorical case), these three considerations seem to me sufficient to justify my proposal that the contextual parameter for metaphorical interpretation is a context set of presuppositions. I'll review these considerations in order.

First, metaphorical expressions (types) are not unique in requiring *a* presupposition but no unique or specific one; the same is true of some literal expressions (types). Only after their content on a particular occasion of utterance is determined do they acquire a *specific* presupposition. Not surprisingly, demonstratives are one example. Any utterance of the *sentence* '... He[Δ] ...' requires a presupposition, namely, that there is a unique male demonstratum, without presupposing the existence of a particular thing presented by Δ in its context. Only when we fix the content of the complete demonstrative in its context can we identify its particular presupposition. Likewise, only when we fix a particular content for the metaphor in its context can we identify its particular context set of presuppositions. In this respect, metaphors are no worse off than demonstratives.

Second, contrary to the common impression, some metaphorical expressions do have particular metaphorically relevant presupposition sets they *normally* presuppose across contexts, that is, in all context sets relative to which they are *normally* appropriate. As we'll see in chapter 8, *routinized* (but not yet dead) metaphors are expressions whose interpretations are unquestionably metaphorical (i.e., their content in a context is computed as the value of applying their character to a context set of presuppositions) but they employ, or require, the same presuppositions on all (or on all normal) occasions in which they are used. The same is true of metaphorical expressions whose interpretations rest on m-associated features that are stereotypical (e.g., metaphors whose literal vehicles are natural kind terms, such as 'is a gorilla') or normal (e.g., color terms). Neither of these metaphorical interpretations is context-independent, but they could be called (relatively) context-invariant because they carry their presuppositions with them from context to context. And because they are more easily "accessed" than more context-specific presuppositions (like those involving the exemplified features I'll discuss in ch. 5), these presuppositions may furnish "default" interpretations when others are not, or are not yet, available.

Of course, at this point one might object that these "normal" metaphorical interpretations are, precisely because they are context-invariant, intuitively different from "extranormal" metaphorical interpretations, say, in the way in which poetic metaphors (or poetic metaphorical interpretations) intuitively differ from nonpoetic ones. And, therefore, they are not good examples. Yes and no. Routinized metaphors with their normal interpretations are, I agree, *not* good examples of the relation between poetic, or highly context-specific, metaphors and *their* presuppositions; between the presuppositions of poetic metaphors and the ordinary case of required presuppositions of an utterance there remains a large gap. But insofar as routinized metaphors, which are no less metaphorical for being routinized, may nonetheless serve as examples of how a metaphor can normally require a presupposition, they show that the source of the difference may lie with the specific *kinds* of presuppositions employed in the interpretations of some metaphors, not with the general structure of presupposition that is needed for metaphorical interpretation.

The third consideration that should be taken into account in judging whether the m-associated features of metaphorical interpretations function like the presuppositions required for the general appropriateness of an utterance harks back to Stalnaker's guiding idea, that a primary function of the presupposition set for an utterance is to constrain and enable what the utterance can appropriately assert. Given the structure of a context set of presuppositions, Stalnaker both articulates an abstract conception of communication as a rational activity and, in turn, uses it to justify certain principles or rules of interpretation and communication. The abstract structure has this form: The presuppositions demarcate a range of possibilities (worlds) among which the agent's assertions—his informative utterances—partition those that are actual, those that remain possibilities for the future, and those ruled out as impossible. Assuming that the agent's set of presuppositions is consistent and deductively closed, utterances that express propositions that are either inconsistent with the presuppositions (hence false in all circumstances compatible with the presuppositions) or entailed by them (hence true in all such circumstances) are therefore not informative and hence not assertions: They make no partitions. These statements are inappropriate, at least insofar as they purport to be assertions. But this is not the end of the story. Where an utterance is apparently inappropriate, given this structure, we can draw any of a number of conclusions. Either the presuppositions are not what we have supposed them to be, or the speaker should be interpreted as asserting something else, or indeed there has been a violation that makes the utterance deviant unless we can otherwise explain it, using a Gricean maxim, in terms of some other implicature.

Do the presuppositions of a metaphor have a similar rational structure that constrains its interpretability? To begin with, we should keep in mind that there are two sets of presuppositions at work in the interpretation and evaluation of a metaphor. Or more precisely—although I shall continue to speak of them as if they were two sets—the presuppositions function in two roles. The first set consists in the presuppositions relative to which we evaluate the appropriateness in the context of the proposition that is asserted by the utterance under its metaphorical interpretation. The second set consists in presuppositions relative to which we generate an appropriate metaphorical interpretation for the string. Call the first set the *A(ssertion)-set* of presuppositions; call the second set the *I(nterpretation)-set*. The A- and I-sets can be mutually inconsistent; for example, some m-associated feature presupposed in the second set may be known by the speaker to be false—and therefore not something assertable—relative to the first set of presuppositions. (In other cases, where one presupposition plays two roles, it can belong to both sets.) In general, then, the two sets of presuppositions are insulated from each other. Yet, the A-set can indirectly affect the interpretation of a metaphor and hence the I-set. So, consider two rules of interpretation for metaphor (modeled after Gricean rules of rational cooperative linguistic behavior):

(Inconsistency) Do not interpret someone as to make his sentences express some proposition inconsistent with his presuppositions.

(Redundancy) Do not interpret someone as to make his sentences express some proposition already entailed by his presuppositions.

The relevant presuppositions for both of these rules belong to the speaker's A-set. However, an analogous rule applies to the I-set:

(Presuppositional Inconsistency) Do not interpret someone so that the content of his assertion requires presuppositions that are either inconsistent with his other I-presuppositions at that time or that are internally inconsistent.

Note that all these rules say "do not" rather than "one *cannot*": once we establish rules or maxims of interpretation or appropriateness, speakers tend to exploit those very rules by acting as if what is presupposed is not (representing themselves differently) and thereby overruling them.[28] However, if we listen closely to subtle differences between interpretations, it is possible to become sensitive to nuances whereby we can detect where an interpretation follows a rule governing the context set of presuppositions and where it arises from the violation of a rule by overriding it.

For example, consider the following instance of (one type of) mixed metaphor, composed from two lines, the first by Homer (to express the subject's ability to inspire terror, fear, and the foreboding of the unknown), the second by Byron (to express its subject's gracefulness and elegance):

*(8) Apollo came like night, while Venus walked in beauty, like night.[29]

Or consider the following 'sun' metaphors that we discussed briefly at the end of chapter 2, each of whose (explicit or anaphoric) occurrences of the metaphorical expression makes different, inconsistent presuppositions about the features m-associated with the literal vehicle 'is the sun':

*(9) Juliet is the sun, and Achilles is, too,

(or the even less acceptable)

*(10) Juliet is the sun and Achilles is the sun.

Or imagine the following scenario. A corporate executive impatiently tells his staff:

(11a) Would someone please come up with a green thought.

The staff members scurry to dash out ideas on their notepads but after handing them over, the boss complains:

(11b) You always give me your green thoughts before you have worked out any of the details.

In (11a) 'green' is interpreted relative to a presupposition set in which the predicate is contrasted with the color terms 'yellow' or 'brown' and expresses the properties of being fresh, novel, or original; in (11b) it is interpreted relative to a context set in which 'green' is contrasted with a term for a ripe, mature, or developed (say) fruit, like 'red' or '(bright) yellow'. In the first, the predicate has positive evaluative force, in the second, a distinctly negative one.[30]

Or consider the classic mixed metaphor, supposedly produced by Ronald Reagan:

(12) The ship of state is sailing the wrong way down a one-way street.

There is something unacceptable about (12), but it is not obvious what. Not all mixed metaphors, or sentences containing multiple metaphors, are equally unacceptable; some indeed are not only powerful but appear to be powerful *because* they are mixed: thus

(13) To take arms against a sea of troubles.

What is the difference between (12) and (13)? To begin with, (12) is ambiguous; we can mark the two interpretations in terms of the different scopes of the Mthat-operator (as I shall show further in the next section):

(12a) Mthat['the ship of state is sailing'] Mthat['the wrong way down a one-way street'].

(12b) Mthat['The ship of state is sailing the wrong way'] Mthat['down a one-way street'].

The interpretation of (12a) is that the government is following a path that will inevitably lead to some sort of confrontation or collision; the interpretation of (12b) is that the government is following the wrong policies in an uncorrectable or irreversible manner, in a way that prevents it from changing its direction or turning back. Suppose now that we resolve this ambiguity in context and decide on one or another interpretation. Although there is no difficulty determining its content, (12) sounds decidedly bad—and much worse than (13). Why? One explanation might be along the lines of our present discussion. To interpret the prepositional phrase in (12), 'down a one-way street', we must fill in the context set with the presupposition that the state is an automobile or car. But this presupposition is inconsistent with the presupposition required for the interpretation of the first part of (12), namely, that the state is a ship.[31] Hence the inter-

pretation of the utterance requires that we make inconsistent presuppositions. In (13), on the other hand, although the two metaphors are
different and indeed independent of each other—"independent" in that
the order in which they are respectively interpreted makes no difference—
their presuppositions are not inconsistent. In fact, they oddly complement, and strengthen, each other. Let me briefly explain.

Although it is always possible to ask why an author chooses to use one
particular metaphor rather than another, with mixed metaphors where
she abandons one for another midcourse through the utterance, the
question of choice is inevitable. Moreover, where the different metaphors
could express the same or equivalent contents, an answer must appeal to
their characters and the presuppositions associated with their literal vehicles. If we can show how, by shifting metaphors, and the associated presuppositions, the author was able to communicate further information
she could, or would, not have communicated by sticking with the same
metaphor, the mixing will be justified. In (13) this is indeed the case. Although the content of (13) is ⟨to overcome, or struggle against, vast and
manifold troubles⟩, the character of (13) informs us, in addition, of the
apparent futility of so doing, the prima facie impossibility of taking arms
against seas. This information, communicated precisely by the mixed
metaphor—we might say: category mistake—lends (13) much of its
power as a metaphor. In (12), on the other hand, there is no comparable
redeeming information conveyed by the characters of the multiple metaphors that would justify the change of metaphor midcourse in one context
of utterance. In fact, the inappropriateness or unacceptability of (12) may
also derive in part from the very fact that it raises without answering the
question of why the author chooses to change metaphors in the middle of
his utterance.

To return now to our main line of argument: In all these examples we
interpret the first occurrence of the metaphor relative to one presuppesi-
tion set, and continue, prima facie in the *same* context, to interpret another occurrence of the same metaphor (or a metaphor from the same
family or schema—an idea to which I'll return in ch. 5) relative to presuppositions that are inconsistent with the first set. The result violates the
rule of Presuppositional Inconsistency, thereby generating a mixed metaphor. (To repeat my earlier point, this violation does not render the
metaphor absolutely uninterpretable or incoherent; but we can sense a
difference between the kinds of interpretations that conform to the rules
and those that do not.) Here the rules that govern metaphorical interpretation are the same rules of rational cooperative linguistic behavior that

govern the appropriateness of utterances in general. The one difference is that metaphor does not typically require a unique set of presuppositions like those that may be required by sentences. Unlike speakers' absolute commitments to the presuppositions that depend simply on the conventional form and meaning of sentences, metaphorical interpretation involves conditional commitments given presuppositions set up at one stage that transform the context of interpretation at later stages and thereby constrain the interpretation of subsequent metaphors. In each of (8) and (9), for example, the utterance of the first conjunct P_i under a metaphorical interpretation occurs in a context cs_i that contains all the presuppositions Q_i that are required for the appropriate interpretation of P_i. However, the second conjunct P_j in each of the examples is interpreted relative to cs_j, which results from adding the asserted content P_i to cs_i, and also contains the further presuppositions Q_j required for the interpretation of P_j. If Q_j in turn are inconsistent with Q_i (also in cs_j), either P_j will be inappropriate in cs_j or we must insulate cs_i from cs_j, allowing the speaker to shift between disjoint contexts in the course of a single utterance. Insofar as we seek to avoid either of these consequences, our interpretation of one metaphor relative to a given context *commits* us to certain presupposition requirements for our further interpretation.[32]

To sum up, I have tried to indicate both differences and similarities between the relations of a metaphorically interpreted utterance to its relevant presuppositions and of appropriate utterances to their (conventional) presuppositions. The differences are not mere artifacts of our theoretical apparatus for representing presuppositions; they reflect genuine differences between the role we are asking presuppositions to play in accounting for metaphorical interpretation and the role they play more generally in explaining the appropriateness of utterances. Unlike the presuppositions for the general appropriateness of utterances, which can be identified either by means of logical relations (e.g., entailment) or by means of syntactic or lexical features of the utterance, the metaphorically relevant presuppositions for the interpretation of an utterance cannot be uniquely identified in such a way. Some m-associated features, like stereotypical or normal features, are plausibly known by each competent member of the linguistic community and, if only by default, are there for one to utilize as a metaphorically relevant presupposition. But for metaphors that are more sensitive to their respective actual contexts, and whose interpretations are more specific to their contexts, there are no general rules or recipes to identify their metaphorically relevant presuppositions. For different kinds of metaphors, there are different clues or heuristics we use, the kinds of rules of thumb or start-up techniques that enable us (to the degree to which we are able to) to perceive similarities or, as I'll discuss at length in the next chapter, to perceive what is exemplified or sampled by something. These skills, however, cannot be reduced to rules; on the contrary, they are best put into practice enhanced by a heavy dose of imagination.

Despite these differences, the three considerations I mentioned later in this section give us, I propose, sufficient reason to treat the m-associated features that are employed in metaphorical interpretation as contextual presuppositions, which, in turn, function as the domain on which the character of a metaphor operates, yielding a content in a context. This next part of the story, however, is also more complicated, and controversial, than I have so far let on. In the next section, I shall turn to one question for my claim that the relation between metaphorical character and the context set of presuppositions is a truly *semantic* relation on the model of the relation between an indexical character and its contextual parameter. My answer to this question will, like the conclusion of this section, also be less than conclusive, but I hope the complications and qualifications give the reader a better grip on the issues illustrated in the next chapter.

IV   Is Knowledge of Metaphorical Character Really Semantic?

The character of a metaphor is formally defined as a function from context sets of presuppositions to sets of properties. The value of the function (in a context) must therefore be a determinate truth-conditional or propositional factor, or at least as determinate a factor as those assigned by the characters of the indexicals and demonstratives, a factor that will enable us to evaluate whether utterances are true or false. But (1) is the character of a metaphor sufficiently well constrained to assign it a content that, when evaluated at a circumstance, yields a truth-value? And (2) if it is, is the mechanism that is formally represented by the character function a *semantic* mechanism, again, like the mechanisms for the indexicals, a rule that the speaker knows simply in virtue of his semantic or linguistic knowledge?

The first question is a skeptical challenge to my project tout cour. In chapter 1 I said that the *appearance* is that utterances containing metaphors, no different from exclusively literal utterances, make assertions that are judged true or false. But if they are truth-valued, they must have truth-conditions or content. The burden of argument therefore falls on those who deny that this appearance is reality. Yet there is deep resistance to the appearance. As Davidson puts it: "It should make us suspect the theory that it is so hard to decide, even in the case of the simplest metaphors, exactly what the content is supposed to be" (WMM 262). And now that we have a more precise characterization of the (purported) content or truth-conditions of a metaphor, more precise formulations of the same challenge will hover over us for the remainder of this book. In chapter 7 I shall return to directly address various "transcendental" arguments for this skeptical challenge.[33] In this section, I shall focus on two issues concerning "mechanics": (i) constraints that render it at least plausible that metaphorical character yields determinate contents for at least some metaphors in their respective contexts; and (ii) the further question of whether those constraints are semantic. Let me begin by locating the context-dependence specific to metaphorical character among three (or four) distinct kinds of context-dependence that bear on metaphorical comprehension in general; these correspond to the presemantic, semantic, and postsemantic stages I introduced in chapter 2.

At the *first* stage, we are presented with an event we take to be an instance of a use of a given language; our task is to assign it the linguistic description of an expression type, including a character. Among alternatives, we must determine, or select, whether the utterance is to be interpreted literally or metaphorically and, in the latter case, which constituents of the utterance should be interpreted metaphorically, that is, assigned metaphorical characters—the nonconstant characters of their underlying metaphorical expressions. We can make this picture of selection or determination among alternative expression types more explicit in terms of the structure of a grammar.

Suppose the grammar assigns to every string S under a structural description a character that, in a context (or in conjunction with other "cognitive faculties" or the subject's central belief system), determines the content of S.[34] Suppose also that the lexicon (taken as part of the base of the grammar) contains a metaphorical-expression-generating "operator" (to the status of which we'll return in ch. 6) 'Mthat' such that, for every expression Φ of constant character (at least with respect to the metaphorically relevant contextual parameter), the resulting metaphorical expression 'Mthat[Φ]' has a nonconstant character.

For every string S to which the grammar assigns at least one character that contains no character of a metaphorical expression, let it also generate a set of characters whose members are the characters of all those strings that result from forming all grammatically admissible metaphorical expressions, and combinations of metaphorical expressions, from the expressions in *S*. (For simplicity, I include among these the character of the string containing no metaphorical expressions; we might think of this as the literal character of *S*.) Call this the *metaphor set* of characters for *S*. So, for each metaphorical expression 'Mthat[Φ]' (and combinations of such expressions) corresponding to an expression Φ in *S*, there is a corresponding character in the metaphor set of *S*. (Here I use double angles "$\langle\!\langle\ldots\rangle\!\rangle$" to represent the composite characters of sentences formed from the sequentially ordered characters of their constituents.) For example, corresponding to the string (14) and the character for its "literal" interpretation, represented by (14a), the grammar will also generate a metaphor set of characters for (14b–e):

(14) Juliet is the sun.

(14a) $\langle\!\langle$\{Juliet\}, \{is the sun\}$\rangle\!\rangle$.

(b) $\langle\!\langle$\{Juliet\}, \{Mthat['is the sun']\}$\rangle\!\rangle$.

(c) $\langle\!\langle$\{Mthat['Juliet']\}, \{is the sun\}$\rangle\!\rangle$.

(d) $\langle\!\langle$\{Mthat['Juliet']\},\{Mthat['is the sun']\}$\rangle\!\rangle$.

(e) $\langle\!\langle$\{Mthat['Juliet is the sun']\}$\rangle\!\rangle$.

Most of the characters in its metaphor set will never actually be assigned to any utterance of (14) as its (metaphorical) interpretation. But for every expression (type) in every sentence which it is grammatically *possible* to interpret metaphorically, there will be such an array of characters—its metaphor set—containing the characters of the corresponding metaphorical expression(-type)s generated by the grammar of the language. Each of (14a–e) is, in other words, the character of an alternative type of which an utterance of (14) might be identified as a token. This is the sense in which a metaphorical expression 'Mthat[Φ]' *underlies* an utterance of an expression Φ that can be interpreted metaphorically: To interpret the utterance *u* of Φ metaphorically, one must "recover" or assign *u* the type of the metaphorical expression 'Mthat[Φ]' with its nonconstant character.

Some utterances admit more than one possible structural analysis as a metaphor, ambiguities that are sometimes exploited by authors and poets with great effectiveness. The notational use of 'Mthat' offers a convenient linguistic device to represent these ambiguities. For example, it may be ambiguous whether it is the subject term or predicate in the utterance that is to be interpreted metaphorically. An utterance of

(15) The flowers are smiling in the light

is interpretable either as an utterance about the play of sunlight and shadow on flowers, that is, as

(15a) The flowers Mthat['are smiling'] in the light,

or as a comment, perhaps with sexual innuendo, about some pretty young girls:

(15b) Mthat['The flowers'] are smiling in the light.

Likewise, the scope of the metaphor in an utterance may be (deliberately) ambiguous, another structural feature that we can mark using 'Mthat'. For example, in a famous passage in *Crime and Punishment*, Raskolnikov confesses to Sonia that he has murdered the old money-lender, an act he attempts to justify by depicting his murder victim (perhaps validly) as an utterly worthless human being who merely lived off the suffering and pain of others, a parasite of no value whose elimination will even be a benefit to everyone else.[35] Here is the subsequent dialogue between Raskolnikov and Sonia:

(16) R: I've only killed a louse, Sonia, a useless, loathsome, harmful creature.
S: A human being—a louse!

The exchange plays on an ambiguity in Raskolnikov's utterance to which Sonia strongly reacts. Raskolnikov wishes to justify his action of murder by (metaphorically) calling the money-lender 'a louse'. Yet, even if the money-lender was no better than a louse, Raskolnikov would have only been justified in saying:

(16a) I've only killed Mthat['a louse'],

an act, as Sonia replies, that would still count as *killing* someone, that is, murdering a human being. Raskolnikov, however, seems to believe that his act would be better (structurally) described in different terms, or at least he attempts to depict it as nothing more than a matter of:

(16b) I've only Mthat['killed a louse'],

meaning: I have performed an act that should be judged as no worse than the (minor, justifiable) one of killing a louse, rather than as killing a human being. As Roger White has pointed out, the ambiguity might have been eliminated had Raskolnikov said either

(17a) I only murdered a louse

understood as

(17b) I only murdered Mthat['a louse'],

or

(18a) I only stepped on a louse

understood as

(18b) I only Mthat['stepped on a louse'].

Hence, as White concludes, the ambiguity must have been deliberately intended by Dostoyevsky—precisely to highlight the moral ambiguity of Raskolnikov's action. Be that as it may, for our purposes, the important point is that the structural, linguistic basis for these different interpretations of the utterance is clearly marked by the scope of the Mthat operator. In identifying the utterance as a metaphor, we must assign one or the other character to the utterance as its type—or, as in this example, acknowledge both, leaving open the proper description of the action.

This task—the *identification* of an utterance as a metaphor by *selection* among the alternative characters in its metaphor set, all of which are made simultaneously available to us by the grammar—is what I called our "knowledge *that* metaphor" in chapter 1. To make the identification, we employ all sorts of contextual cues, shared background beliefs, and assumptions about the discourse.[36] Here context plays a definite role but, although it affects what is ultimately expressed, its contribution at this stage is no *part* of what is said. In our earlier terminology, this role of the context is *presemantic*.

Suppose now that we have identified at least one constituent of the utterance as an expression to be interpreted metaphorically; that is, we have assigned the utterance a character from among (14a–e). So, at least one element in the utterance is assigned the linguistic type of a metaphorical expression, that is, the form 'Mthat[Φ]' whose nonconstant character yields different contents given different sets of metaphorically relevant presuppositions. At this *second* stage, the context furnishes the relevant parameter to which the character of the metaphorical expression is sensitive, a context set of presuppositions, the value of which is mapped into the content of the metaphor. If the speaker's knowledge of character is semantic, this role of the context is also semantic. But it is at this stage that the force of the skeptic's question is felt; I'll return to it in a moment.

At a *third* stage, once the content of the metaphor is fixed in a particular context *c,* the context functions again, this time to *evaluate* the metaphor. Here, however, we should distinguish two kinds of evaluation. The first kind of evaluation is whether what is said by the metaphor in the context c is true or false in c. The relevant feature of the context for this task is the *actual* circumstance of the context, not (as it was at the second stage) what is presupposed. But what is "actually the case" is not absolute. The evaluation of an interpretation as true or false itself often depends on context—on the purpose of the utterance and the speaker's intentions, the expectations and knowledge of its audience. However, this kind of context-dependence affects the metaphorical no more and no less than the literal. To use Austin's well-known example, 'France is hexagonal' is true in many contexts and for many purposes—"good enough for a top-ranking general, perhaps"—but false in and for others—"not [good enough] for a geographer."[37] Similarly, 'Juliet is the sun' under its metaphorical interpretation may be true in some situations—say, Romeo's, given his expectations and intentions—but false in other circumstances— say, that for a Shakespearean college admissions officer.[38] This role of the context must also be distinguished from its semantic role at the second stage. The argument for the semantic context-dependence of metaphors turns on their systematic and constrained productivity: the fact that different tokens of one metaphorical expression type, given different context sets of metaphorically relevant presuppositions, express different contents. In contrast, truth-evaluations, as Austin says, are typically "rough." Sometimes we demand strict conformity or correspondence to "the facts," sometimes less stringent standards. But the same context-dependent variation in standards of truth arises equally for evaluations of literal utterances and metaphors. This role of the context is therefore postsemantic insofar as the standards of evaluation (including that of truth) will vary with the further extralinguistic functions of the utterance.[39]

The second kind of evaluation is of the *appropriateness* of the assertion of the metaphor; here too, context plays a central role. This kind of evaluation is broader than the first because the actual truth-value of the utterance in its context—or what the truth-value is believed to be—is only one among a variety of factors that affect judgments of appropriateness. A second set of considerations concerns whether or not the *content* is informative, interesting, redundant, relevant, novel, tired, and so on. A third type of consideration is whether the metaphorical *character* of the utterance, given the presuppositions held in the context, is an appropriate medium for the expression of it content—whether the metaphorical mode of expression in its respective context is effective, too clear or too obscure, accessible or not, witty or trite, and so on. These desiderata will obviously vary with the illucutionary and perlocutionary uses of the utterance and its audience. To give one example, nowadays we tend to rate (at least nonpoetic) metaphors higher if they are relatively accessible and more easily interpretable, but for some ancients and medievals the great virtue of some metaphors was their power to obscure, conceal, or hide metaphysical or theological "secrets."[40] This was also their explanation for certain metaphors and figures found in Scripture and other sacred writings. In these texts, the more transparent and penetrable the metaphor, the worse they judged it to be.

At this third stage, then, the context set of presuppositions bears, not on the determination of what is said—as it did at the second stage—but on its evaluation: whether the content is or isn't *appropriate*. Hence this role of the context is also postsemantic. However, the story is still more complicated. As noted in section III, appropriateness (relative to the I-set of presuppositions) also comes into play, though less directly, already at the second stage: in determination of content. But there is a difference between the two roles of appropriateness. At the third stage we ask whether what is said is an appropriate thing to say in its context; at the second stage we ask whether some content can be appropriately expressed by the metaphorical expression in that context. These latter criteria of appropriateness fill in, I now want to propose, the constraints on the application of metaphorical character: They furnish conditions that restrict the properties generated as the content for the metaphor in a context. However, as I said earlier, if these are indeed the constraints on interpretation, there follows a further question: Are they semantic? To see the problem—whether presuppositional *appropriateness* can *semantically* constrain interpretation—let's look more closely at the "mechanics" of the presuppositions at the second stage.

Back in chapter 1, we observed the divergent interpretations of the members of each of the groups (repeated here) (19–22) and (23–24):

(19) Juliet is the sun.

(20) Achilles is the sun.

(21) Before the sun of Moses had set, the sun of Joshua had risen. (BT *Qedushin* 72b)

(22) The works of great masters are suns which rise and set around us. The time will come for every great work that is now in the descendent to rise again. (Wittgenstein 1980)

(23) Life is a bubble.

(24) The earth is a bubble.

At a first glance, we said, these examples suggest that interpretations of the same metaphorical expression ('is the sun') vary systematically because of their different *linguistic* contexts. But it is easy to see that the relevant context is not (merely) linguistic. Consider Herman Hesse's

(25) He is a shadow over the land,

which, depending on context, might be taken to say either that the subject is a menace and source of gloom or that he is a shade, protection, even relief from a devastating threat or power. Here the linguistic context of (25) remains the same while the interpretation of the metaphor 'is a shadow over the land' varies. So, the metaphorically relevant parameter cannot be its linguistic context per se; it must be the extralinguistic presuppositions associated with the linguistic items. Furthermore, the "metaphorically relevant presuppositions" are not limited to those directly related to, or m-associated with, the literal vehicle of the metaphor (e.g., 'is the sun'); just as important are the presuppositions related to the rest of the linguistic frame of the utterance. In fact, as the variations in the interpretation of (25) suggest, the relevant presuppositions might also embrace presuppositions manifest—even manifest*able*—only nonverbally, hence not directly linked to any verbalized expression in the utterance. These latter presuppositions are also as heterogeneous in content as those associated with the metaphorical expression and, whether they are community-wide (e.g., about stereotypical or normal features) or idiosyncratic, they are not generally part of anyone's linguistic knowledge. Along with those associated with the literal vehicle of the metaphor, I shall therefore also add these to the context set of presuppositions, among the I-presuppositions.

However, there is one significant difference between the roles of the presupposed properties m-associated with the literal vehicle of the metaphorical expression and those associated with its environment. Using the first set of presuppositions, we *generate* the (sets of) properties from among which the interpretation of the metaphor is constituted. But these presuppositions typically overgenerate: Some of the (sets of) properties presupposed to be m-associated with the literal vehicle of the metaphorical expression are inappropriate as the content of the metaphor in its context. Using the second set of presuppositions—associated with the linguistic and nonlinguistic environment of the metaphor—we filter out those unsuitable. I will therefore call the first set, associated with the metaphorical expression itself, the *productive* (p-) presupposition set, and the second set, associated with the environment, the *filter* (f-) set.[41]

The way we use the f-presuppositions to constrain metaphorical interpretations is primarily by application of the same two principles introduced in section III to govern the A-presuppositions: Inconsistency and Redundancy. Suppose (to anticipate an idea I shall discuss at length in the next chapter) that the properties that 'is the sun' in (19) uttered in c metaphorically expresses are those that are presupposed to be *exemplified*— or *sampled*—by the sun in the context c.[42] These properties might include, to begin with, properties such as being the major source of direct, natural light (in contrast to the moon, stars, or a lamp). This property is inconsistent with what we know of human beings and therefore would be inappropriate to assert of Juliet—and, for the same reason, will be excluded from the interpretations of (20) and (21) and, for a similar reason, from (22). But more specific to (19), and possibly as opposed to (20) and (21), among the properties exemplified by the sun in c might be the property of being the one that rises and sets faithfully and regularly, day after day without fail, as well as being the one worthy of worship. Both properties are equally generated p-presuppositions but only the latter, not the former, would be an appropriate property to assert of Juliet in Shakespeare's context. For Romeo's Juliet never declines; she is f-presupposed not to be like other natural, ordinary creatures who rise and wane with time and nature, whose day inevitably ends, like the setting of the sun, after it has run its natural course. (Hence the tragedy of her death, perhaps, and the irony of Romeo's metaphor.) Therefore, to assert *that* p-presupposed property associated with the metaphorical expression would contradict our other f-presuppositions associated with its environment (i.e., associated with 'Juliet'), violating the rule of Inconsistency not to interpret an expression in such a way that what would then be asserted is already presupposed to be false. But the context might have been otherwise. In the Talmudic context of (21), it is presupposed that Moses and Joshua, for all their illustriousness, are equals of a kind; surely that neither ought to be worshipped. Given that presupposition and application of Inconsistency and perhaps Redundancy (which can also function to promote a property otherwise not heavily weighted), the metaphor 'is the sun' in (21) is awarded as its content something like the property of proceeding in uninterrupted succession and continuity—rise, followed by fall, followed by rise.

It should be noted, first, that in all these examples the f-presuppositions interact with the p-presuppositions through the medium of *general* principles of assertion; there is no need to introduce any special techniques of interpretation specific to metaphor.[43] Second, and to avoid a potential misunderstanding, I have described the relation between the p- and f-presuppositions as if the second temporally follows the first, but they need not interact in a fixed order. In impressionistic terms that I'll make more precise in chapter 5, the f-presuppositions not only discourage certain interpretations *already* generated by p-presuppositions; they may block the generation of some and indirectly encourage the generation of others. For example, by limiting the appropriate sets of m-associated features to those attributable to animate and human subjects (presuppositions triggered by our knowledge of the proper names that occupy the subject positions in (19)–(22)), the f-presuppositions already preselect the range of features generated by the corresponding p-presuppositions. As it were, certain features are so far afield that they seem never to arise as potential interpretations; others are eliminated as inappropriate although they are features "in principle" sampled by a scheme. In the former case, we might think of the f-presuppositions as operating *before* the p-presuppositions.

In sum, conditions of appropriateness embodied in rules like Inconsistency and Redundancy constrain applications of the rule of metaphorical character already at the semantic stage. Nonetheless, the skeptic may still not be convinced that these constraints suffice to generate determinate contents for *arbitrary* metaphors. Even where they do, he may also object that Inconsistency and Redundancy are general principles of rational action, not semantics-specific. So, either the speaker's exclusively semantic knowledge of character does not yield knowledge of determinate contents or, to make the contents determinate, we must supplement character by extrasemantic conditions.

Two comments in reply: First, at the third postsemantic stage the potentially pertinent presuppositions can include virtually any presupposition one might introduce, not just the relatively local productive and filter presuppositions of the second stage, presuppositions associated with particular constituents of the utterance in question. Therefore, the presuppositions of the last stage are global and Quinean—no belief can be absolutely ruled out as nongermane—whereas those that are active at the second stage are (relatively) locally partitioned to the task at hand.[44]

Second, rules like Inconsistency and Redundancy do not belong to the constitutive conditions of metaphorical character. They are also not semantics-specific. But they also differ from the various criteria of appropriateness to which we appeal at the third, last stage that depend on the illocutionary and perlocutionary uses of the statement. As general conditions on rational behavior that apply to all applications of the rule of character, Inconsistency and Redundancy are rules that all speakers in all

linguistic or speech communities follow and to which their linguistic behavior should conform. Although they are not rules of language, they are
rules that any speaker of a language must know.

Neither of these comments is a knock-down argument for the thesis
that it is the semantic character of the metaphor—as opposed to or autonomous of all pragmatic considerations—that yields a unique, fixed,
determinate set of properties as its content or (truth-conditional) interpretation. I have also described the different stages as if they were linearly
ordered in real time; in fact, the various kinds of context-dependence
continually interact. Apart from the interaction of the different kinds of
appropriateness at the third stage, considerations of appropriateness of
the last kind—whether a metaphorical character is an appropriate way to
express a given content—also bear on metaphorical identification at the
first stage.

Yet another issue complicates the question whether metaphors have
determinate, semantically fixed contents. The propositional content of a
metaphor—the theoretical explication of *what is said* by the utterance—is
not always distinguished, or distinguishable, from *what is asserted* and
what is intended by the utterance. And in those situations where it makes
a difference whether a metaphor has a determinate content—where we
are called upon to adjudicate disagreements—it is not always clear
whether the disagreement is over what is said, what is asserted, or what is
intended.

The difference between what is said or asserted and what, in addition, is
also intended is clear. Let me illustrate the ambiguity I have in mind between what is said, or content, and what is asserted. What an utterance
asserts is defined for us in contrast to what it presupposes. But depending
on the trade-off between assertion and presupposition, what a given
utterance asserts may or may not turn out to be identical with, or individuated along the same lines as, its propositional content. For example, I
assume that the content, or truth-conditions, of the predicate 'is a bachelor' is the complex property of being an unmarried male.[45] Suppose now
that I ask you whether the man standing to your right is married and you
answer, "No, he is a bachelor." Your utterance presupposes that the
subject of the sentence is a male and it asserts that he is unmarried. In this
case, what is asserted is part of but not identical with what I assume (even
in this case) is the truth-condition, or content, of the predicate.

A similar ambiguity afflicts our talk about what is said/asserted by a
metaphor relative to its context set of presuppositions, especially its f-
presuppositions. What is *asserted* by a metaphor in a context is a function

of the postsemantic considerations of appropriateness (at the third stage) as much as it is of the kinds of appropriateness that bear on determination of semantic content (at the second stage). Depending on how sharply we wish to distinguish what the metaphor asserts from what is presupposed in the context, we can draw the circle more or less tightly around its content. So long as it is ambiguous whether we are concerned with what is asserted or with what is said (i.e., content) by the metaphor, it will be correspondingly unclear whether its "interpretation" is or is not determinate.

I hope I have said enough to allay a skeptic's doubts that the character of a metaphor never yields a determinate content in its context and that, whether we call them semantic in a strict sense or not, the constraints that generate metaphorical contents are sufficiently different from the clearly nonsemantic ones we use to evaluate their postsemantic appropriateness. In the next chapter, I shall turn to more pragmatics to fill out our semantic story and illustrate how the semantics interacts with other aspects of the context in metaphorical interpretation. In chapter 6 I'll return to implications of our semantic knowledge of metaphor, both in order to work out remaining details and to illustrate its explanatory power in articulating various distinctions and notions that run through our pretheoretical concept of a metaphor.

Chapter 5
Knowledge by Metaphorical Content

In chapter 4 I laid out the basic theory of our semantic knowledge of metaphor and the structure of the presuppositions that constitute the context of a metaphor. I located the pertinent notion of presupposition among the attitudes and explained the sense in which presuppositions are *pre*suppositions for an interpretation; the degree to which its presuppositions are *required* for the interpretation of a metaphor; and the various roles of presuppositions in determining an appropriate metaphorical interpretation of an expression. In chapter 6 I'll return to metaphorical character and its status as meaning. In this chapter I'll discuss in greater detail how we apply our semantic knowledge to particular contexts, that is, particular kinds of context sets of presuppositions, to generate content. In the terminology of chapter 1, this content is one type of knowledge (we convey) *by* metaphor. A second type, to which I'll return in chapter 7, is knowledge (conveyed) *by* metaphorical character.

Insofar as these issues are a matter of how speakers apply their semantic knowledge to particular extralinguistic contexts, or use their semantic competence specific to metaphor, they fall in the category of pragmatics of metaphorical interpretation. In more traditional terminology, the issues concern what are called the "grounds" of metaphorical interpretation, for example, the role of similarity judgments. In terms of my theory, these grounds, which are typically not semantics- or language-specific (and introduce additional dimensions of context-dependence), furnish the content of metaphorically relevant contextual presuppositions.

Without this pragmatic story we have no explanation of how an actual utterance of a metaphor has an interpretation—propositional content—in a particular context. Working through these issues will therefore enable us to see how the theory is put into practice. But the point of this chapter is not to test the adequacy of our semantics or to provide recipes to generate interpretations of metaphors. The semantics supplies only the form of, or constraints on, metaphorical interpretations; it does not predict—and therefore does not stand on—the actual interpretation of any metaphor. That will ultimately depend on the ingredients we put into the context set of presuppositions.

My aim in the chapter is, by showing how our semantic competence in metaphor interacts with our extralinguistic contextual presuppositions, to highlight certain differences between our knowledge of character-rules and the kinds of abilities or skills involved in their use or application to contexts. The semantic character-rules apply to all metaphors, while different metaphors rest on different grounds that yield different m-associated features. The diversity of these latter, pragmatic features has persuaded some theorists that there is no general rule-governed explana-tion of metaphor, only case by case stories about individual metaphors. But this is because they focus *only* on the pragmatic aspects of meta-phorical interpretation. This is also not the end of their story. When they next add the assumption that literal meaning, in contrast, *is* a function of linguistic competence, they conclude that there is an untraversable dis-tance between the literal and metaphorical. The moral I want to suggest instead is that the distance is not between the metaphorical and the literal but between the semantic knowledge underlying metaphorical interpreta-tion and the nonsemantic skills that ground their presuppositions.

I have already indicated (ch. 4, sec. I) how wide and varied is the range of m-associated features, corresponding to different grounds, that under-lies the interpretations of different metaphors. I shall not review this here. I shall concentrate on one class of metaphors based on exemplification, a symbolic relation that I'll argue is a source of the (or one class of) simi-larity judgments that are said to ground metaphors. Despite a venerated tradition, similarity has taken a beating during the last thirty years, not only in connection with metaphor but with many topics such as pictorial representation. Yet its critique has significantly improved our under-standing of the relation. I shall briefly trace the history of this discussion, which will lead us to exemplification. My analysis of exemplification, in turn, will introduce the role of networks and systematic family-sized units in metaphorical interpretation, among which I'll distinguish three kinds. This notion of a family of metaphors will, finally, play a crucial role in my explication of knowledge *by* metaphorical character in chapter 7.

I   A History of Similarity in Metaphor

Historically, what I shall call the the *similarity thesis*:

(i) Similarity and comparison judgments play a significant, if not essential, role in metaphorical interpretation has been associated with a second thesis:

(ii) Metaphors are elliptic similes.

I shall return to discuss (ii) in chapter 6 but, in any case, it is important to distinguish (i) from yet a third thesis, also associated with (ii):

(iii) Metaphors (i.e., utterances of declarative sentences containing at least one metaphor) assert similarities.

The similarity thesis (i) contains an important grain of truth even if it is not the whole truth, if only because the m-associated features that enter into metaphorical interpretations include many that do not arise from similarity judgments.[1] But, contra (iii), even those metaphors grounded in similarity judgments need not, and do not, *assert* similarities. The content of the metaphor 'Juliet is the sun' is not that of a relational statement such as 'Juliet is like the sun' or 'Juliet resembles (is similar to) the sun'.[2] If it were, the logical form of the metaphor whose surface grammatical structure is Sj would be that of a two-place relation Rjs. But without compelling evidence to the contrary, there is no reason to abandon the surface grammatical form of the metaphor, which is that of a one-place predication in which we say something about something or attribute the property expressed by the predicate to the subject-referent.

Where, then, is the similarity judgment located? In the *context* of the metaphor rather than as part of its *content*: The similarity judgment generates the presuppositions about the relevant features or properties m-associated with the literal vehicle of the metaphor. The corresponding constituent of the content, on the other hand, is simply the attributed feature or property, not the similarity relation that grounds the context set of presuppositions to which the character of the metaphorical expression 'Mthat[Φ]' is sensitive.[3] Throughout this chapter, I shall therefore continue to assume that "similarity theories" of metaphor are theories about similarity only as a source of contextual presuppositions, setting aside the logical form of the metaphor, which I'll assume is that of a predication rather than a relational statement.[4]

With this role of similarity in mind, any theory of metaphor that employs the notion must address three standard objections.[5]

1. Any two objects share some common property by which they could always be said to resemble each other; therefore, to avoid the charge of vacuity, such theories owe us additional criteria to explain *which* properties count.

2. If a similarity judgment is made by comparing independently known and identifiable features of the objects in question, a similarity theory of

metaphor will be able to take into account only those properties known or identified independently of or prior to the context of the metaphor. It cannot allow for similarities or properties that the utterance of the metaphor, as Black put it (see ch. 4, sec. II), "creates"—even in the epistemic sense of bringing them to our attention or making us notice them—by *likening* the referents of its terms.

3. On the widely shared assumption that similarity is a symmetrical relation, similarity statements should be reversible salva veritate and even salva significatione: *A* is like/similar to *B* if and only if *B* is like/similar to *A*. Metaphors, however, are not reversible. 'This man is a lion' may be true (under its metaphorical interpretation), but it does not follow that 'This lion is a man' is also true (under its metaphorical interpretation).[6] Furthermore, even where the original and its converse both happen to be true, they generally have different meanings: Contrast 'My butcher is a surgeon' with 'My surgeon is a butcher'. Indeed the converse is not always even interpretable metaphorically: Contrast 'John's face is a beet' with 'A beet is John's face'. Therefore, the objection concludes, similarity statements and metaphors must have completely different logical structures, excluding one as grounds for the other.[7]

In reply, let me begin with the third objection, which presupposes a "geometric" model of similarity that represents objects as points in a coordinate space whose (dis-)similarity is a function of their metric distance from each other. (It is arguable that the first objection also assumes such a model.) This is not the only conception of similarity in the literature. In particular, Amos Tversky (1977) proposes a "contrasting feature matching" model, according to which the degree of similarity between two objects is a weighted function of their common and distinct features. An immediate consequence of this model is that, contrary to the metric model, some similarity judgments and statements are asymmetric. Thus Tversky observes that the choice of subject (x) and referent or (as I'll say) predicate (y) in ordinary statements of the form 'x is like y' or 'x resembles y' is not in general arbitrary. We say that the portrait resembles (is/looks like) a person, but not that the person resembles (is/looks like) the portrait; that a son resembles (is/looks like) his father but not that the father resembles (is/looks like) his son; that the ellipse is like a circle but not that the circle is like an ellipse. Likewise, the judged similarity of Bill Clinton to JFK is much greater than the judged similarity of JFK to Bill Clinton. And with similes (or nonliteral similarity statements), the asymmetry or directionality is even more pronounced. Thus, the metaphor 'John's face is (like) a beet' is interpretable, although 'A beet is (like)

John's face' is not; and, even where the two are interpretable, as in 'A man is (like) a tree' (i.e., having roots) and 'A tree is (like) a man' (i.e., having a life history), they have different interpretations. In all these examples, the similarity judgment/statement—literal or not—is directional and asymmetric.[8] Thus the central assumption underlying the third objection fails to hold.

On Tversky's account, a similarity judgment is instead a function of three factors: our "feature representations" of the objects under comparison, the "focus" of the similarity judgment, and the salience of the features. First, we represent each object a and b by a set of features or attributes A and B, respectively. Of course, these sets of features by which we typically represent objects are huge, and only a small number are relevant to a given cognitive task on an occasion. Hence each of the sets of features that enters into a specific similarity judgment must itself be the "product of a prior process of extraction and compilation" (Tversky 1977, 330). Tversky says very little about this process, but I'll return to this part of the story.

Given feature representations for each object, Tversky argues that the perceived similarity of two objects a and b [$s(a, b)$] is a weighted function of their shared *salient* features less the sum of a weighted function of the attributes distinctive only of one and a weighted function of the attributes distinctive only of the other.[9] What determines the salience of a feature? Tversky initially suggests a wide variety of sources—"intensity, frequency, familiarity, good form [for geometric figures], and informational content" (ibid., 332)—implying that there are no general principles that govern such judgments. However, later in the essay Tversky proposes two main determinants of salience; the second of these is context-dependent, the first not:

1. Strength—the intensity of the object or its signal-to-noise ratio (e.g., brightness of a light, loudness of a sound, saturation of a color)—which is relatively stable across contexts and independent of the object of which the feature is an attribute.

2. Diagnostic Value: the classificatory significance or importance of the feature. We sort objects so as to maximize the similarity of those in a class and their dissimilarity from objects outside the class. Features that yield better classifications of this kind have a higher diagnostic value and hence higher salience. But the discriminability of an object by a feature is highly sensitive to context—the function of the classification, the identity of the object, and the realm of objects to be sorted on the occasion. Hence this determinant of salience is context-dependent.

Finally, Tversky argues that we assign different weights to the distinctive and shared features of the things being compared, depending on the "focus" of the similarity judgment. This relative weighting explains why some similarity judgments are symmetric and others not. When the judgment assesses the degree to which a and b are similar to each other, focusing no more on a than on b, the distinctive and shared features of both a and b are equally weighted and the judgment is symmetrical. However, when we judge the degree to which a is similar to b, Tversky hypothesizes that we focus on the subject a, weighting its distinctive features more than those of the predicate b; hence the distinguishing features of the subject reduce the degree of similarity more than those of the predicate. But we also tend to choose as predicate a term whose referent has the more salient features, which thereby increases the degree of similarity, and as subject the term whose referent is the less salient object. For example, the variant in a category is said to be similar to the prototype of the category, but not vice versa. Thus the asymmetry of many similarity judgments is due to the fact that when we judge that a is similar to b, the weighted salient features of b shared by a must be greater than the weighted distinctive features of a and of b. However, when we reverse this order of subject and predicate, and judge whether b is similar to a, we change the focus of the judgment and hence the weighting.

As mentioned earlier, Tversky's observation that many similarity statements are directional and asymmetrical counters the main assumption of the "reversibility objection" to the comparison theory of metaphor.[10] But Tversky also makes an important positive suggestion about the relation of similarity to metaphor. With similarity judgments, he says, we assume a particular feature space and "assess the quality of the match between subject and referent"; with interpretations of metaphors and similes, we assume a resemblance "and search for an interpretation of the space that would maximize the quality of the match" (ibid., 349). This proposal suggests partial replies to the other two objections with which we began. If the quality of a match is a function of the salience of the features—which in turn are a function of their intensity and diagnostic value—we now have criteria to determine which features, relative to the context, count toward determining the relevant similarity. And insofar as the "interpretation of the feature space" is subsequent to the assumption that there is similarity at work, there is the germ of an account for Black's creative metaphors.

This last proposal aside, it should be emphasized that Tversky's primary concern is similarity, not metaphor. For our purposes, his most important contribution is his substantive account of the criteria of salience, the first such account to be proposed. However, other psychologists and cognitive scientists have attempted to modify Tversky's account in order to directly address metaphors and nonliteral similarity statements like similes. To do this job, perhaps the most serious problem facing Tversky's theory is its apparent inability to explain why metaphorical comparisons are not only asymmetric and directional (like all comparison statements) but truly irreversible: Contrast the reversible though directional literal comparison 'Taiwan is like Japan' with the nonliteral 'Israel is like David fighting Goliath' whose reverse is not even interpretable. To account for this difference, Andrew Ortony (1979) next proposed that the salience of a feature is a function not only of its intensity and diagnostic value but also of its "importance," or stereotypical value, for the object of which it is an attribute. For example, redness is a much more "important" or stereotypically characteristic attribute for our notion of firetrucks than for bricks, even though it is frequently true of both and it is necessary for neither. However, this criterion entails that, even apart from diagnostic purposes, the salience of a feature is sensitive to the feature representation of the object of which it is an attribute; hence the salience of one and the same feature may differ in the feature representations of different objects. And this, in turn, raises the question how to compute the salience of a set of shared features in a representation. In particular, where there is significant "salience imbalance" between the feature's salience in A and B, is the salience of the intersection an average of the two or just that of either A or B? Ortony proposes that it is a function of the salience value of the feature in B alone.[11] It follows that if the feature has high salience in B but not in A, the measure of the degree of similarity of A to B will be significantly higher on Ortony's account than on Tversky's.

This fact, Ortony argues, explains why nonliteral similarity statements such as 'billboards are like warts' are not just asymmetric but irreversible. The feature "being ugly" is stereotypically significant for and hence a highly salient feature of warts but not of billboards. Hence there is considerable salience-imbalance—low salience in A, high salience in B. Its high salience in B in turn increases the weighting of the shared properties, including ugliness, of billboards and warts, and thus their degree of similarity. In contrast, in 'warts are like billboards' there are no comparable shared properties with high salience in the representation of 'billboards' and low salience in the representation for 'warts', decreasing the degree of similarity. Therefore, it is impossible to reverse the original nonliteral statement while preserving the same high measure of similarity. On the other hand, with a literal similarity statement like 'billboards are like placards' in which the high-salience features of placards (e.g., being a printed poster, for display in public places) are also high-salience features of billboards, there is relatively little salience imbalance. Hence the statement is reversible despite some difference in degree of salience and perhaps a change of meaning. Generalizing from these cases, Ortony hypothesizes that the greater the "salience imbalance"—that is, the greater the differential in relative increasing salience of a feature from the A to B representations—the more metaphorical, or nonliteral, and the more irreversible we judge the statement.[12]

One moral of this story is that literality and metaphoricity are not discrete values but two poles on a continuum of degrees of salience-imbalance. A second, more important lesson for our purposes is that the key notion in this analysis of metaphoricity is salience (and salience-imbalance), not comparison or similarity. Although Tversky first brought salience onstage to explain certain features of similarity statements and judgments, and Ortony continues to maintain that metaphors should be "analyzed" as "indirect" comparison statements, when we actually turn to their explanations of metaphoricity *all the work is done by the notions of salience and salience imbalance*. The next step in the argument is just to drop the detour through similarity statements and explain metaphors directly in terms of salience or a related notion. This, as I understand their position, is the spirit of a third account recently proposed by Sam Glucksberg and Boaz Keysar (1990) (henceforth G&K).[13]

G&K raise two objections against Tversky and Ortony. First, they point to a disanalogy between literal and metaphorical (e.g., simile) similarity statements. Those who argue that metaphors of the form 'a is an F' are (elliptic) similarity statements frequently point to the possibility of "inserting" 'like' to yield a (literal or metaphorical) similarity statement. G&K point to an important difference in the other direction. In the literal case, we can *never* infer 'A is B' from 'A is *like* B': 'apples are like pears' is true, but 'apples are pears' is false. With metaphorical similarity statements, however, we can *always* infer 'A is B' from 'A is *like* B'; for example, 'Juliet *is* the sun' from 'Juliet is *like* the sun' or 'sermons *are* sleeping pills' from 'sermons are *like* sleeping pills'.[14] This disanalogy suggests, as I'll argue in chapter 6, section VII, that Aristotle's famous statement that "the simile is also a metaphor" should be understood exactly as it is written: Both metaphors and similes are "metaphorical"— unlike literal similarity statements. Furthermore, it follows that what renders similes and metaphors metaphorical must be something that *enters into* a similarity judgment, such as salience, and not something that should be *identified* with similarity.

Second, I mentioned earlier that not all of the innumerable, many of them irrelevant, features of the subject and referent are subject to the matching test in making a similarity judgment. For this reason, you will recall, Tversky posits a prior process to select and extract the relevant features to be put to the matching test. To this G&K object that, if salience plays a role in the matching task, then it—or whatever analogous quality determines which features "come readily to mind" (G&K, 4)— might equally well play a role in the earlier stage of extraction of the relevant features. (To distinguish the weights of the subject and predicate, G&K, like Tversky, also assume a "focusing hypothesis" or similar principle based, say, on the given/new or topic/comment distinction.) Thus we can explain the asymmetry, and even irreversibility, of metaphors and similes in terms of the role of salience in differential feature *selection* rather than feature *matching*, thereby entirely eliminating the extra step through comparison statements. In sum, on all these theories the important lesson is that it is salience rather than similarity that emerges as the key notion for the analysis of metaphor.

II Exemplification

I have now mentioned three determinants of the salience of a feature: (i) its context-independent intensity; (ii) its context-sensitive diagnostic or classificatory value; and (iii) its importance within our stereotypical description or intuitive theory of a thing, its place in our normal notion of the referent, the socially shared way of thinking of the thing that is typically acquired with the linguistic expression for that thing. Of these three sources of salience, the second and third clearly enter into the interpretations of metaphors although there are no hard and fast rules that associate one source of salience with a particular kind of metaphor. There is, however, one difference between the two. Normal notions are typically associated with property and relational terms, natural kind terms, and names of public figures; and within a community, they do not vary significantly from speaker to speaker or utterance to utterance. Where an expression has a normal notion associated with it, its features are therefore available, at least by default, to serve as a metaphorical interpretation for the expression. However, because this source of salience is relatively fixed and contextually stable, it will never be a source of productive, novel metaphorical interpretations that exploit and vary with the resources of their individual contexts of utterance. The other, more context-sensitive source of salience, the classificational or diagnostic value of the feature, is therefore a potentially richer source for metaphorical interpretations. To spell out its contextual parameters, I will now turn to exemplification, a mode of reference to features that is one mechanism by which they are made salient.

The notion of exemplification was first discussed by C. S. Peirce, but in recent years the one who has explored it the most deeply is Nelson Goodman.[15] Allowing ourselves a bit more ontological indulgence than Goodman the nominalist, let's say that an object o exemplifies a property P if and only if (i) o possesses P and (ii) o "symbolizes, stands for, or refers to" P.[16] As Pierce already noted and Goodman makes explicit, the crux of exemplification—and what distinguishes it from mere instantiation—is the second condition. It is a mode of reference rather than mere possession.

Goodman's paradigm of exemplification is the sample, for example, a tailor's booklet of small swatches of cloth. Each swatch in the collection possesses an innumerable number of properties but it is a sample only of some: its color, weave, texture, and pattern, but not its size, shape, absolute value, date of production, or weight. What is necessary for a property to be sampled is not only that the swatch possess it but also that the swatch *refer to* it. I shall not analyze this reference relation. In Goodman's theory of symbols it is a primitive notion, the most general mapping from the items of a symbol system—both linguistic and nonlinguistic, notational and nonnotational—to their correlated field of compliants or referents. There is no one explanation for this reference relation, say, in terms of satisfaction of descriptive conditions or in terms of historical chains. "An element may come to serve as a symbol for an element related to it in almost any way" (Goodman 1976, 65). To the extent to which we can find any account of reference in Goodman's own writings, it is not semantic but psychological, closer to Morris's conception than Frege's: "[E]stablishment of the referential relationship is a matter of singling out certain properties for attention, of selecting associations with certain other objects" (Goodman 1972a, 66). This is, of course, not to say much more than that the sample makes certain properties *salient*. So, by introducing exemplification into the account of salience, my point is not to reduce the latter to something more basic but rather to distinguish one of its brands.[17]

The psychological, or attitudinal, character of this notion of reference—especially as Goodman describes it in the quotation in the previous paragraph—may help explain two curious facts about the relation. First, if exemplification is a matter of bringing agents to selectively attend to something, then, like other objects of the attitudes, what is exemplified must be individuated more finely than (simple) extensions (objects or classes); hence it is properties (or, for Goodman, predicates or labels) that are exemplified. Second, although it is objects that do the exemplifying, how those objects are described or displayed is also not irrelevant to their mode of sampling. For example, a creature with a kidney, but not a creature with a heart, exemplifies the type of living organism that eliminates its own waste despite the fact that anything is a renate if and only if it is a chordate. In this case, however, the description bears not on the individuation of the exemplifying object but identification of the schema to which the exemplifying object belongs on the occasion. To explain this aspect of exemplification, let me turn to its contextual parameters.

Consider again the tailor's booklet of cloth swatches. What determines, of a swatch's innumerable possessed properties P, those that it also refers to and those it does not? Each swatch s_i is a sample not in isolation, but only as part of the whole booklet S. Two relations between the elements of S and the field of properties P prima facie bear on what is sampled by each s_i. First, each s_i in S samples just those features *it* possesses but the other s_j do not, and, second, each s_i in S samples just those properties a *contrary* of which is sampled by some s_j of S. In other words, the features exemplified by any given object o will depend both on the set of things presupposed in the context to be the schema S of referring objects to which o belongs in that context and on the realm of alternative properties P presupposed to be sorted or classified by the schema as a whole. Suppose the schema consists only of a heavy woolen swatch and a light cotton one; relative to the alternative features being-a-summer-dress, being-a-fall-dress, and being-a-winter-dress, the woolen swatch may sample the two latter and the cotton swatch the first. But suppose we add a medium-weight swatch to the schema; the woolen one may now sample only being-a-winter-dress and not being-a-fall-dress. Likewise, a swatch may be a sample of red relative to the alternatives red and purple, but be a sample of pink relative to a feature-space containing red, pink, and purple.

Sampling is a simple case of exemplification, and we cannot generalize its conditions in any precise way. But it indicates the kinds of desiderata that characterize exemplification more generally. The example of sampling may also be misleading insofar as it suggests that what something exemplifies always ought to be immediately evident like the features of the sample that we just "see." This "visual" dimension of exemplification is important: The sample *displays* what it exemplifies.[18] But display does not require instantaneous recognition. For many works of art, it is only after sustained viewing, with the discrimination of the trained eye, that the observer can identify what is exemplified. Likewise, it may only be after considerable analysis and exploration that we can identify what is exemplified in the interpretation of metaphors (especially) in literature or poetry.

Finally, it should be mentioned that one object may simultaneously belong to more than one schema, exemplifying more than one feature relative to the different schemata, all in the same context. The effect can be dynamic, unpredictable, surprising. Wayne Booth describes how he once read the concluding paragraphs of Norman Mailer's *The Armies of the Night*, two paragraphs full of "deliberately scrambled metaphors," to a conference on metaphor, intending to elicit the audience's reaction to the ethical import of the metaphors. To his surprise, the audience instead laughed. The passage was "wrenched out of its context, taken out of its historical moment [the Vietnam war protests] and put into a new context, where attention was focused on deliberately scrambled metaphor as a thing in itself" (Booth 1978, 328). Goodman (1976, 54) gives an example of a tailor's booklet of swatches that, used in the context of a tailors' convention, serves as a sample of being-a-tailor's-booklet. Analogously, Mailer's text is taken here to exemplify the property of being a cluster of "deliberately scrambled metaphors" rather than, or in addition to, a text expressing (among other things) the properties presupposed to be exemplified by its multiple metaphors.

III Metaphors of Exemplification

When Romeo utters

(1) Juliet is the sun

I have argued, first, that its content is *not* that Juliet and the sun resemble each other (in some or another respect) and, second, that it is indeed unnecessary to detour through an underlying judgment of similarity to determine its content. Instead Romeo is saying that Juliet has a certain property—call it P—m-associated with the predicate 'is the sun' and that the crucial explanatory factor that generates P is its salience in the context.[19] I now want to propose that, for at least one class of metaphors (like (1)), the salience of P derives from the fact that it is presupposed to be exemplified by the object(s) that is (are) the extension of the literal vehicle of the metaphor. Here the sense in which the metaphorical depends on the literal is that the content of the metaphorical expression 'Mthat['is the sun']' in a context c is (modulo the filter-presuppositions of the utterance) the set of properties P presupposed to be exemplified by the extension of its literal vehicle.

Which properties are exemplified by the referent of the literal vehicle of the metaphor? What any object exemplifies, we said, is relative to the other elements in the exemplification-schema to which it belongs and to the field of features sorted by the schema as a whole. Metaphors of exemplification are no different; we therefore need to identify the schema and field of features of (1). Let's look again at the context of (1) in Shakespeare's play, Romeo's speech:

But soft, what *light* through yonder window breaks?
It is the *East*, and Juliet Mthat['*is the sun*'].
Mthat['*Arise*'] fair Mthat['*sun*'] and Mthat['*kill*'] the envious Mthat['*moon*'],
Who is already sick and pale with grief,
That thou her maid art far more fair than she.
Be not her maid since she is envious,
Her vestal livery is but sick and green,
And none but fools do wear it; cast it off.
It is my lady, o it is my love,
O that she knew she were.
She speaks, yet she says nothing; what of that?
Her eye Mthat['discourses'], I will not Mthat['answer'] it.
I am too bold, 'tis not to me she speaks.
Two of the fairest stars in all the heaven,
Having some business, do entreat *her eyes*.
To *twinkle* in their *spheres* till they return.
What if her eyes were there, they in her head?
The *brightness* of her cheek would Mthat['shame'] *those stars*,
As *daylight* doth a *lamp*; her *eyes in heaven*
Would through the airy region stream so *bright*,
That birds would sing, and think it were not *night*.
See how she leans her cheek upon her hand.
O that I were a glove upon that hand,
That I might touch that cheek.
(*Romeo and Juliet* II, ii, 2–23; my italics)

In this passage I have substituted metaphorical expressions for some of the expressions interpreted metaphorically; I'll return to these later in this section.[20] I have also italicized the terms for a number of light-related bodies and states that Shakespeare sets up in deliberate contrast with one another: 'the sun', 'moon', 'stars in all the heaven', 'the brightness of a cheek', 'lamp', 'daylight', and the darkness of 'night'. The contrasts among the referents of these latter terms are subtle and intricate; I can touch on only a few of their more obvious connections. The sun and moon are the two referents placed in the sharpest opposition, perhaps because 'the sun' and 'the moon' are the two primary metaphors in the passage, the one referring, of course, to Juliet, the other to Rosaline, Romeo's previous beloved whom he abandons for Juliet. But the opposition between the sun and moon (referred to by the literal vehicles for the two respective metaphors) rests on a variety of literary and mythological as well as natural differences between them. The passage exploits the mythological, symbolic identification of the moon with Diana, the goddess of virginity, who was earlier identified with Rosaline (I, i, 207–209.) and who now is presented as the mistress of Juliet, hence her superior. Romeo's address to Juliet as the sun recalls earlier lines in which the sun is said to be worshipped (I, i, 116f.), and is given quasi-divine features—for example, 'all-seeing' (I, ii, 94), that is, all-knowing. Alternatively, the sun may be all-seeing at this point in that all do see it, it is the center of everyone's attention and field of vision, and it has nothing to hide or of which to be ashamed—in contrast to the end of the play when "The sun for sorrow will not show his head" (V, iii, 305). In this last line indeed even the gender of the sun has changed. The usual relation by which the moon reflects, and is subordinate to, the sun is also reversed in our passage, the sun now being the maid of the moon. But the moon, metaphorically referring to Rosaline, is also described as less "fair than" Juliet, the sun, and envious of her—using the standard of comparison 'fair' which recurs again and again throughout the play (see, e.g., I, i, 204; II, Prol., 3–4)—and earlier was used to describe Rosaline (I, i, 219). Romeo calls upon the sun to "arise" and "kill" the moon, reversing the usual drama in which the moon, or night, kills the sun, or day. There is also a second opposition, in the last eight lines, between Juliet's sun and the stars, heightened by an impossible hyperbole: Romeo imagines that Juliet's two eyes might take the place of two stars and, outshining them, turn night into day. By analogy the difference in their order of brightness is likened to the difference between daylight and artificial light. None of these contrasting descriptions is obviously metaphorical, although, in calling Juliet 'the sun', Romeo is using a metaphor (as well as in his use of 'moon' for Rosaline). The point of the multiple contrasts between the sun, moon, lamp, daylight, and other elements is rather to set up an exemplification-schema composed of the sun and these other objects. What 'the sun' expresses metaphorically depends on what the sun, relative to the schema set up in the passage, exemplifies.

The context of the larger passage, and indeed of Shakespeare's whole play, also circumscribes the range of presupposed features sorted by the schema as a whole, although it does not enumerate or characterize the field explicitly. To begin with, our knowledge that the sun and moon-exemplified features are to be ascribed to human agents (in the latter case signaled by the relative wh-pronoun '*who* is already sick ...') excludes a range of inappropriate features, preselecting one potential space of features. These f-presuppositions function in a way similar to Tversky's process that selects and extracts the relevant features to be put to the matching test for a similarity judgment. However, at a second stage, we again look at the literary context of (1) to identify, from among properties appropriate to humans, those features exemplified by the sun in the schema: We look at the presuppositions of the play about the personality of Juliet, at what makes her Romeo's love and "lady," at the presupposed features that make her "fairer" than all her rivals such as her "vestal" purity and chastity, and, most important perhaps, at all the features that seem to draw the envy of the moon, Rosaline, and of Juliet's other peers.

So, to interpret the metaphor 'is the sun' in (1), its metaphorical character (or the character of the underlying metaphorical expression) directs us to the actual p- and f-presuppositions that constitute its context of interpretation. These are p-presuppositions about the other elements in the schema relative to which the referent of its literal vehicle exemplifies what it does and about the range of features sorted by the schema, and f-presuppositions about Juliet and possibly other elements in the schema that rule out inappropriate features, both for generic and specific reasons. Notice that these presuppositions need not (although they might) include any that specifically, explicitly state the feature presupposed to be exemplified by the sun in the context. Rather the only way to identify the complex of properties exemplified by the sun in the context may be by way of the description 'the complex of properties exemplified by the sun relative to the schema $\langle x, y, z, \ldots \rangle$'. And indeed the complex of properties may be one that has no simple adequate linguistic expression. As I'll argue in section VI, the property might be expressible by us only by relation to the sample, relative to the specific schema that obtains in the context; we describe the schema which, in turn, shows us what it samples. Our grasp of the property itself may lack the abstractness that is a precondition for a fully conceptualized linguistic expression to express it, an expression that would mark the fact that we can determine whether the property is possessed across contexts by arbitrary objects. But these strictures on our verbal, linguistic, or conceptual ability to express the property need not imply that the property itself, or the content of the metaphor in that context, is necessarily indeterminate or vague.

As I noted in our discussion of sampling, we cannot generalize from its necessary and/or sufficient conditions to exemplification in general. If that is true even of relatively uncomplicated exemplification systems, how more so of the subtle, complex exemplification involved in literary texts of the kind we have been examining. There are no general instructions how to determine what is exemplified, and discovery of what something exemplifies may take "time, training, and even talent,"[21] but especially imagination. As our discussion in the previous paragraphs hopefully illustrates, discovering what is exemplified is often the result of balancing out our various p- and f-presuppositions, adding, subtracting, and canceling presuppositions, often without arriving at one round figure as the result. Yet, the lack of rules or instructions and the trouble and effort necessary to state definitively what is exemplified on an occasion should not lead us to conclude that nothing is exemplified (and hence that nothing is metaphorically expressed). As all of us know from our experiences in interpreting original, challenging metaphors, especially in literary texts, these sorts of difficulties and complications are endemic to the enterprise. The point of a theory of metaphor (or at least ours) is not to furnish rules that eliminate this hard work, or even make it easier, or that make it possible to grind out interpretations; rather the theory aims to specify the parameters and factors knowledge of which will enable us to *understand why* the practice and process of interpretation *is* (and ought to be) difficult. Two of these parameters are the schema and field of features with which exemplification varies.

To illustrate the context-specificity of these parameters, contrast the above passage from *Romeo and Juliet* with another set of 'sun' metaphors based on a different exemplification-schema sorting a different field of features. Shakespeare frequently uses 'sun' metaphors in his historical plays; in the following passage, the Welsh Captain and Salisbury describe the end of Richard II's reign:

Cap. 'Tis thought the king is dead; we will not stay.
The bay-trees in our country are all wither'd,
And *meteors* Mthat['fright'] *the fixed stars of heaven*;
The pale-faced *moon* Mthat['looks'] bloody on the *earth*,
And lean-look'd prophets whisper fearful change;
Rich men look sad and ruffians dance and leap,
The one in fear to lose what they enjoy,
The other to enjoy by rage and war:
These signs forerun the death or fall of kings.

Farewell: our country men are gone and fled,
As well assured Richard their king is dead.
Sal. Ah, Richard, with the eyes of heavy mind
I see thy glory Mthat['like *a shooting star*']
Mthat['Fall to the base *earth* from the firmament'].
Mthat['*Thy sun*'] Mthat['*sets*'] *weeping* Mthat['*in the lowly west*'],
Witness Mthat['*storms*'] to come, woe and unrest;
Thy friends are fled to wait upon thy foes,
And crossly to thy good all fortune goes.

(*Richard II*, II, iv; my italics)

The exemplification-schema to which the sun belongs in this passage is markedly different from that of *Romeo and Juliet.* Here the sun is not one among a set of sources of light—"fairness"—but one among a class of celestial "signs" that prefigure crisis and tragedy, the "death or fall of kings": "meteors," "wither'd bay-trees," the "fixed stars of heaven," "moon," "earth," "storms to come," and "a shooting star." Whereas Romeo's sun is rising in the East, the sun of this passage is setting in the West. The range of features sorted by the schema are predominantly negative: fear, sadness, the anxiety and insecurity of lawlessness; states of ephemeral greatness, aging glory, slow, inevitable decline, imminent disaster and crisis. Relative to this schema, the (setting) sun exemplifies (and thus the metaphor "thy sun" expresses) (declining) glory, (lost) authority, and insecurity. Again, the passage does not explicitly enumerate these presupposed features. Instead it *depicts* a scene, or scenario, in which the exemplifying elements in the schema *display* for us the properties they exemplify.[22]

The properties (presupposed to be) exemplified by the sun (and then metaphorically expressed by 'the sun') in these two passages are highly specific to their respective schemata. The author deliberately designs and sets up the schemata, which, for all we know, hold only within these passages. In contrast, normal and stereotypical features, as we said in chapter 4, are associated with expressions (hence with literal vehicles of metaphors) invariantly across contexts, hence regardless of schemata to which their referents belong. Although there are no strict criteria to distinguish exemplification-metaphors from, say, metaphors based on normal notions or stereotypes, where the schema is more or less explicit as in these examples, we might also use its degree of schema-relativity as one way of diagnosing its metaphorical kind. Where the schema is not explicit, there may also be default features that a given object exemplifies. Out of context, 'the roses of her cheeks' may sample fragrance, pinkness, and softness, not thorniness or deep red.[23] Similarly, animal metaphors for character-traits (e.g., 'fox' for sly, 'gorilla' for violent and dangerous, etc.) or occupational or craft metaphors for manners ('butcher' for messy and destructive, 'surgeon' for careful and precise) exemplify relative to more or less contextually fixed schemata that sort contextually fixed ranges of features. But the less context-specific and more widely shared the schema of exemplification, or where the metaphor has default interpretations, the more difficult it is to distinguish a metaphor of exemplification from one that draws on presuppositions concerning normal or stereotypical notions. Who is to say, when Wittgenstein remarks

(2) The works of the great masters are suns which rise and set around us. The time will come for every great work that is now in the descendent to rise again[24]

whether 'suns' is a metaphor that *exemplifies* cyclical rise and decline, or whether it simply builds on presuppositions that belong to our *normal* notion of the sun?[25]

The larger issue raised by this question concerns the degree to which the metaphorical interpretation of any single expression is necessarily relative to a schema, network, system, or family of expressions to which it belongs. In recent years this issue—the systematicity of metaphor—has become a leitmotif among philosophers, linguists, and psychologists. Nelson Goodman, perhaps the first to press the point, argues that in metaphorical transfer, "a label functions not in isolation but as belonging to a family"; that it is always "a label along with others constituting a schema [that] is in effect detached from the home realm of that schema and applied for the sorting and organizing of an alien realm."[26] Goodman's own argument for the family-relativity of metaphor is rooted in his general theory of predication, which he treats as a form of categorization or classification, the basic cognitive activity in his lights. Since all classification is relative to a set of either implicit or explicit alternatives, the predication 'a is an F' is also a matter of classifying a as an F rather than as a G, H, etc. The metaphorical application of a predicate is, in turn, no different from other types of predication; hence it too is relative to an assumed schema of alternatives, hence relative to a family. We need not saddle ourselves with Goodman's theory of predication and, to be sure, most contexts are not as explicit as our Shakespearean speeches in enumerating the members of the schema and the field of features relative to which a given metaphor should be interpreted. However, if exemplification is an underlying mechanism by which a significant class of metaphors is interpreted, the fact that all exemplification is relative to a schema would offer independent support for Goodman's insight.

There is also indirect evidence for Goodman's insight from the practices we employ in interpreting metaphors whose exemplification schemata are not explicit. The first step we typically take is to recover such a schema, guided by the principle that what is metaphorically expressed is a feature that some referent in the context, relative to a schema, exemplifies. To interpret the metaphor, we therefore enrich the context by adding such a referent with its schema to our presuppositions. Consider, for example, Hamlet's statement, "What should such fellows as I do crawling between heaven and earth?" (*Hamlet* II, 2, 129). The statement could, to begin with, be interpreted literally in its context. Yet, as I. A. Richards remarks, it also has a definite metaphorical interpretation: "[T]here is an unmistakable reference to other things that crawl, to the motions of foul insects, to vermin, and this reference is the vehicle as Hamlet, or man and his ways, are the tenor" (Richards 1936, 119–120). The force of the metaphor 'crawling', Richards continues, "comes not only from whatever resemblances to vermin it brings in but at least equally from the differences that resist and control the influence of their resemblances. The implication there is that man should not so crawl" (ibid., 127). That is, other metaphors personify their inanimate or non-human agents; this metaphor dehumanizes or depersonifies its agent by attributing features of insects or vermin and, with them, a negative evaluation.

Suppose Richards is right: Suppose the kind of agent whose crawling Hamlet attributes to himself here is that of an insect or vermin. The question we still need to answer is: why that subject rather than something else that crawls—babies, soldiers under siege, snakes, other animals? How do we, as interpreters, know that this is the relevant agent of crawling? In our choice, we can see the influence of exemplification as a mechanism of generating interpretations. In interpreting the metaphor, we try to identify a referent, or extension, for the expression (e.g., 'crawl') that exemplifies a property or kind of property we think appropriate for the subject of the metaphorical statement. Our schema of alternatives might consist, then, of the various things that crawl and a correlated set of features those different kinds of crawling things sort. Thus the crawling of snakes exemplifies deceit; the crawling of babies—immaturity, innocence, clumsiness, perhaps lack of control; of soldiers—stealth and surprise in attack. None of these features would be appropriate to express of Hamlet (the referent of 'I') in this context; for it is f-presupposed in the context that Hamlet loathes himself and mankind in a fit of misanthropy. So, what is (appropriately) expressed is a kind of repulsive degradation that only the crawling of insects *exemplifies*. Hence we fill in the context to make the crawling of the agent insect- or vermin-like, and the "insectification" of the subject in turn brings in its train the other associations Richards notes. Here exemplification guides the way we fill in, or transform, the context in order to yield a metaphorical interpretation.[27]

If we think of Goodman's thesis of the family-relativity of metaphorical interpretation in terms of exemplification-schemata, we can also clarify an obscure point in his conception of metaphor as transfer. According to Goodman, when we use, or apply, any one expression metaphorically, what is transferred is "a whole set of alternative labels, a whole apparatus of organization [that] takes over new territory" (Goodman 1976, 73). That is, the whole schema in which the given expression functions is metaphorically "transferred" to the alien realm. But does that mean that each member of the schema is "transferred" in exactly the same sense as the individual metaphor used on the occasion—that each element in the schema is itself interpreted metaphorically on the occasion? In our example from *Romeo and Juliet*, 'moon' as well as 'sun' is interpreted metaphorically. But do *all* the terms for the other elements in the exemplification schema, for example, 'the brightness of a cheek', 'lamp', 'daylight', and 'night' have metaphorical interpretations? (What would they be?) In my own quotation of Shakespeare's passage, I identified only 'sun' and 'moon' (and their governing verbs 'arise' and 'kill') as metaphorical expressions, because only those expressions obviously undergo a change of content, a change in their respective contributions to the truth-conditions of their utterance. On the other hand, if not all elements in the schema are in fact metaphorically interpreted, how should we understand Goodman's idea that every time we use a single metaphor, its whole family or schema is *transferred*?

I want to suggest that, in putting forth his thesis, Goodman's real concern is with the individuation of a metaphor. What counts as one metaphor and what counts as two, and by what criteria? When do we have the same and when different metaphors? I have touched on this question earlier.[28] We obviously cannot individuate metaphors by the number of words used (one word, one metaphor); in this sentence from a *Time Magazine* film review, all the words in the italicized phrase (which is not an idiom) constitute one metaphor:

(3) [The movie *That's Dancing!*] is filmed dance *with one leg tied behind its back*. (*Time*, Jan. 28, 1985)

Likewise, it is arguable that in Conrad's statement

(4) Into that narrowed circle furious seas *leaped in, struck,* and *leaped out*

it is all three italicized verbs that together constitute one metaphor. (In (4), 'furious' is, of course, also metaphorical, and metaphorically related to the italicized verbs, but it is a distinct metaphor.) We also cannot individuate a metaphor by surface phrasal constituency; on one reading of Davidson's example (discussed earlier in ch. 4, fn. 35):

(5) Tolstoy was a great moralizing infant,

the metaphor is discontinuous—only 'a great infant' is metaphorical— violating the phrasal structure.[29] Similarly, it is arguable that Luke's proverb

(6) Physician, heal thyself (*Luke*, iv, 23)

is one metaphor, despite the fact that 'physician' and 'heal' belong to syntactically distinct surface phrases.[30] In short, we cannot individuate metaphors either simply by word units or by surface phrasal units.

In terms of my theory, we can distinguish at least three different criteria for the individuation of a metaphor; Goodman's intended criterion is the third of these. I would also argue that, depending on our other interests and purposes, we employ each of these criteria at one or another time. The first criterion is sameness of character; thus the three 'sun' metaphors in *Romeo and Juliet, Richard II,* and the Wittgenstein passage, or any of the other pairs of metaphors cited in chapter 1, examples (2)–(10), such as (repeated here)

(7) Life is a bubble

(8) The earth is a bubble

count as one metaphor since each expression interpreted metaphorically is a token of one metaphorical expression type, for example, 'Mthat['is a bubble']'. It is in this sense that we say that a (i.e., one and the same) metaphor can have different interpretations (contents) in different contexts. Formally:

(i) Two occurrences of Φ and ψ are the same metaphor iff $\{Mthat[\Phi]\} = \{Mthat[\psi]\}$.

The second criterion requires sameness *both* of character *and* of content in their respective contexts, that is, relative to their respective context sets of presuppositions. By this standard, (7) and (8), as well as each of our 'sun' metaphors, each count as a different metaphor, since their respective contents in their respective contexts are different. Here we individuate the metaphor by *what* is metaphorically expressed (in the context) as well as its metaphorical form of expression. Formally:

(ii) Two occurrences of Φ and ψ are the same metaphor iff
(a) $\{\text{Mthat}[\Phi]\} = \{\text{Mthat}[\psi]\}$ and
(b) in their respective contexts c and c', $\{\text{Mthat}[\Phi]\}(c) = \{\text{Mthat}[\psi]\}(c')$.

The third criterion for individuation of a metaphor takes into account not only the character and content of the individual expression interpreted metaphorically (or its corresponding metaphorical expression) but also (where there is one) the family (say, exemplification-schema) of the literal vehicle of the metaphor. This criterion is also, I propose, what Goodman is trying to capture with his thesis about family transfer. To appreciate the force of the intuition that drives it, let's look again at the quotation from *Romeo and Juliet*. I have identified only a few words ('sun', 'moon', 'arise', 'kill') as metaphors, as I said, based on their content, that is, truth-conditions, in the context. But is it really clear that the metaphors begin and end with these individual expressions? Suppose we fix the content of the metaphor 'is the sun' in its context. 'Juliet is the sun', interpreted metaphorically, says that she is far 'fairer' than any rival, so far fairer that her competitors are virtually eliminated from the competition. She 'kills' and 'shames' them in competition. (Again, this is not meant to be any-thing like a definitive interpretation, merely exemplary of what a fixed content could be.) Yet, however we fix it, this content of the metaphor does not exhaust—far from it—all the information or cognitive signifi-cance it conveys. In chapter 7, I'll return to the theoretical nature of this additional information or cognitive value of a metaphor and its differen-tiation from its content in a context. For now it is sufficient to observe that there is clearly much more metaphorically conveyed by the various ways in which the sun is said to be related to the other elements in its ex-emplification schema, for example, the way in which the sun's bright-ness—violently?—'shames' the stars and 'kills' her rivals, especially the envious moon. Or the contrast between her natural 'daylight' and the artificial, indirect light of a 'lamp'. Or between her sustained brightness and the twinkling of the stars. This third criterion tries to incorporate all these added dimensions of significance, shown or displayed by the exemplification-schema, into its conditions of individuation.

The other terms in the exemplification-schema may be used (only) lit-erally, but passages like this challenge a neat line of separation between the metaphorical and the literal (which is not to deny the distinction), that is, a simple division between expressions used on an occasion that are to be identified as metaphors and those to be typed as literal. Furthermore, although 'is the sun' is interpreted metaphorically, it must also have, in some sense, its literal meaning. For the literal vehicle of the metaphor, together with its schema, is what generates the m-associated presuppositions (about what is exemplified by the sun) out of which we produce the metaphorical interpretation. (Recall our discussion in ch. 2 of the difficulties in demarcating this sense of "have"; I shall return to the appropriate sense in ch. 6.) We could then include all other members of the schema (under their literal characters) in our criteria of individuation for the metaphor. For the character, and resulting interpretation, of the metaphorical expression depends on its literal vehicle, and its literal vehicle contributes to the metaphorical interpretation by way of its contrasting relations to the other members of the exemplification-schema.

Another way to focus on this third criterion would be to contrast the 'sun'-metaphor (in this extended sense) determined by its whole exemplification-schema with a second metaphor (in the same extended sense) in the same passage. In lines 12–14 Romeo appeals to a second metaphor based on the widely used Elizabethan metaphor that people (or human faces) are books (or, in this case, oral speech):

She ?Mthat['speaks'], yet she ?Mthat['says'] nothing; what of that?
Her eye Mthat['discourses'], I will not Mthat['answer'] it.
I am too bold, 'tis not to me she Mthat ['speaks'].[31]

I count these, the extended 'sun'-metaphor and the 'face'/'speech' metaphor, as two different metaphors: Each set of expressions constitutes one, internally coherent schema of metaphorical interpretation, and they are different metaphors because, as schemata, they are independent of each other.[32] Again, it is not entirely clear where to draw the line between the metaphorical and the literal. We can fix the content of the individual metaphor, but when we try to spell out its undeniable additional cognitive significance, it is impossible not to appeal to what is conveyed by its whole schema of interpretation, including its literal elements.

Yet another aspect of the schematic nature of a metaphor suggests that it be individuated by a larger, more systemic unit. Consider the following passage from *Time Magazine* (cited earlier in ch. 1):

Propelled by the engine of the postwar Wirtschaftswunder, the capitalist Federal Republic of Germany is a sporty blond racing along the autobahns in a glittering Mercedes-Benz. The Communist German Democratic Republic, bumping down potholed roads in proletarian Wartburgs and Russian-built Ladas, is her homely sister, a war bride locked in a loveless marriage with a former neighbor. (*Time*, March 25, 1985)

This passage contains at least two exemplification schemata (each with two explicit elements): 'a sporty blond' vs. 'her homely sister, a war bride locked in a loveless marriage with a former neighbor' and a sequence of cars—Mercedes-Benz, Wartburgs, and Ladas. Numerous expressions are individually interpreted metaphorically. Yet if one (somehow) failed to see that this whole passage, with all its rich parts and complex inter-relations, constitutes *one* metaphor, some kind of unity as a metaphor, she would miss a crucial part of its interpretation and power.

On my theory, the schema is not itself strictly speaking part of the metaphor; it is part of the context necessary to generate the m-associated presuppositions about what the referent of the literal vehicle for the metaphor exemplifies. So, according to this third criterion, we might say that we individuate the metaphor by its *character* and *content-in-its-context*—which collapses onto the second criterion. Formally, however, we might distinguish this third criterion from the second by building its mode of generation (including its contextual schema of exemplification) into our representation of the content. Recall that back in chapter 3, section III, I suggested a way of representing logical but nonpropositional structure in Russellian (or referential) propositions. Although the propositional constituent for a metaphorical expression Mthat[Φ] is, say, a property P, we can *display* the character-istic information that yields P as its value in its context c (or, more specifically, context set) by representing P as the value of the character of the metaphorical expression in its context: that is, as {Mthat[Φ]}(c). By the same token, we can make explicit in our representation all the contextual parameters that yield P, given the character of the metaphorical expression. Let the context set cs_i for the metaphorical expression Mthat[Φ] contain, among other presuppositions, the presupposition that Φ (or Φs) belong to an exemplification-schema E. We can represent that presupposition as $\langle \Phi, E \rangle$. So $cs_i = \langle \ldots, \langle \Phi, E \rangle, \ldots \rangle$. Thus

(iii) Two occurrences of Φ and ψ are the same metaphor iff
(a) {Mthat[Φ]} = {Mthat[ψ]} and,
(b) in their respective contexts c and c',
    where $c = \langle \ldots, \langle \Phi, E \rangle, \ldots \rangle$ and
    $c' = \langle \ldots, \langle \psi, E^* \rangle, \ldots \rangle$, {Mthat[$\Phi$]}($c$) = {Mthat[$\psi$]} ($c'$), &
(c) $c = c'$, i.e., $\langle \ldots, \langle \Phi, E \rangle, \ldots \rangle = \langle \ldots, \langle \psi, E^* \rangle, \ldots \rangle$.

In other words, not only must the same metaphors have the same characters and contents; their contexts, in particular where they involve verbally explicit schemata of interpretation, must also be the same.

Goodman's family or network that is transferred in metaphor is specifically the set of alternative predicates by which a realm of objects is sorted into categories. Structural linguists sometimes call such networks *contrast sets*.[33] Another example of a contrast set is my notion of an exemplification schema. But this is not the only kind of network or set of systematically related expressions that enters into metaphorical interpretation. In the next sections, I shall turn to two others. These networks supplement rather than compete with the exemplification schema for metaphors of that kind.

IV Thematic and Inductive Networks

To borrow a metaphor from Quine, metaphors do not face the tribunal of interpretation one by one but as a corporate body. Indeed there are different kinds of corporate bodies into which metaphors organize themselves. Some of these other systems or networks have been discussed by recent authors—including George Lakoff, Mark Johnson, Eve Sweetser, Mark Turner, Eva Kittay, Adrienne Lehrer, Lynne Tirrell, and Roger White.[34] The details of their respective accounts vary widely, and they draw on different kinds of metaphors to support their respective theories. I shall not review them in detail, nor shall I argue for one to the exclusion of others. As I have said, there does not seem to be a single network or one set of systematic relations that explains, once and for all, how metaphors work. Under the rubric of a single semantics, there can be different kinds of networks subsumed as different aspects of context. Semantic orthodoxy is compatible with broad, variegated pragmatic heterodoxy. However, the more different kinds of networks we can identify, the better feel we shall have for the multiple forces acting from different directions that shape metaphorical interpretations.

Two additional networks or metaphor-systems, which I shall now discuss, interact in various ways, but they differ in one important respect. The first network, the *thematic* scheme of a metaphor, supports predictions as do the semantic constraints of character; our knowledge of this network is also linguistic: semantic or lexical. The second kind of network is built on associations of different degrees of inductive strength. This network of inductive associations (for short, inductive network) does not furnish us with the means to lay down law-like claims about

metaphorical interpretations, but the fact that it does not support predictions makes it no less important. If we fail to see that a number of
metaphors belong to one inductive network, we will still have missed a
significant generalization.

The idea of a thematic metaphor scheme, or a system of thematically
related metaphors, is not new. In Eva Kittay's (1987) version of semantic
field theory, the notion corresponds roughly to the set of syntagmatic
relations of a word, its relations to the words that constitute its linguistic
context, with which it either obligatorily or optionally collocates.[35] For
example, the syntagmatic field related to the verb 'to fish' (in Kittay's
terminology: the conceptual domain of fishing) contains phrases for an
agent ('fisherman'), patient ('fish'), instrument ('with rod/line/bait', 'line
and hook', 'net', 'angling reed'), goal ('catching a fish'), and location ('in
the water', 'in the crystal brooke', 'river'). In metaphor, this field of words
structured according to these grammatical relations is transferred as a
whole to another conceptual domain, for example, courtship, as Kittay
([1987], 263–275) illustrates with Donne's "The Bait."

In current theoretical linguistics, the notion of a thematic relation or
role corresponds roughly to the role identified by a syntagmatic relation.[36] Thematic relations concern the number and grammatical type of
(phrasal) arguments required by the verb of a sentence (where the verb
refers to an action, process, or state) and the semantic and syntactic relations the arguments bear to the verb. Thematic roles typically include
Agent (the initiator or doer of an action), Goal (that *toward* which some
concrete or abstract event moves or changes), Source (that *from* which
some concrete or abstract event moves or changes), Location (the place
where something is), Experiencer (the individual who feels or experiences
the event), Recipient (that which receives, where there is change of possession), Instrument (the means with which an action is performed),
Benefactive (the one for whose benefit an event or action takes place),
Percept (what is experienced or perceived), Patient (what undergoes an
action), and Theme (what moves or changes in any abstract or concrete
motion or change). On at least some theories a single phrase can also bear
more than one thematic role. These relations and roles are not determined
by the structural position of a phrase in a string; rather they are determined by the meaning of the verb. That is, we know the thematic roles to
be assigned in a given sentence and the role to be borne by each phrase
(only) by knowing the meaning of the dominating verb. However, this
knowledge is not necessarily of each verb one by one. Verbs also organize
into classes, each of which has its respective lexical and syntactic proper-

ties according to which its members interact with the syntax in predictable ways. So, in addition to knowledge of the idiosyncratic meanings of individual verbs, a speaker also knows the properties of these verb classes and the membership of each class. All this knowledge of verb-assigned thematic roles is linguistic, hence in contrast to our extralinguistic knowledge of exemplification-schemata. In other words, the significant point for us is not (as it is for Kittay) that the thematically or syntagmatically related noun phrases, given their standardized names (e.g., 'fish', 'fisherman'), belong to one semantic field corresponding to a unified *conceptual* domain, but rather that the noun phrases are linguistically determined arguments for verbs with certain general properties of meaning.

To see how the thematic network of a metaphor affects its interpretation, let's focus on verbs.[37] When one uses a verb metaphorically, as in (9):

(9) Sleep ... knits up the raveled sleeve of care (*Macbeth* II, ii)

the idea is that not only the verb ('knits up') is "involved" in the metaphorical interpretation, but also the noun phrases in the sentence that play the thematic roles it assigns. First, 'knits up', whether interpreted metaphorically or literally, requires an Agent (in the subject position) and a Patient or Theme in object position. Hence the unacceptability of, for example,

*(9a) Sleep knits up;

*(9b) Knits up the raveled sleeve of care.

Thus the metaphorical interpretation of the verb preserves its thematic structure. Second, while 'sleep' still (literally) refers to sleep, its Agent thematic role personifies or 'agent-izes' it; by virtue of its thematic role of Agent, 'sleep' acquires whatever features are necessary to be an agent. Likewise, the patient or theme of the verb 'knits up' (metaphorically as much as literally) must be an appropriate kind of object. 'Knits up' (literally) means 'to compose or repair by knitting, that is, by tying by fastening with a knot (as in weaving)'. Therefore, its patient must be the sort of thing that has disconnected or thread-like parts that are composed or repaired by knotting, interlacing, or intertwining them. This, in turn, excludes as patient or theme any noun phrase referring to partless kinds of things, such as 'care'; hence the unacceptability of

*(9c) Sleep knits up care.

In this respect, contrast (9) with (10):

(10) He bathes in gladness.

The verb 'bathe' requires an agent (if 'bathes' is an action) or experiencer (if 'bathes' is a state) and (optionally) a location (here the prepositional phrase 'in X').[38] However, the location (or instrument) argument for 'bathe' can either have as its "head" a mass noun ('water', 'oil', 'mud') as in (10) or a count noun '('a bathtub', 'a pool of water', 'a puddle') as in (10a):

(10a) He bathes in a tub/pool/sea of gladness.

Either (10) or (10a) is acceptable. In contrast, (9) does not admit these options. 'Care' *must* be incorporated into a complex noun phrase whose referent is of a kind that has parts that can be tied or fastened together, for example, 'the raveled sleeve of care'.

   To be sure, the requirements of the thematic roles necessary for a verb, together with these additional semantic features, do not uniquely determine a single noun phrase. Any candidate that satisfies the relevant conditions would be equally acceptable. Shakespeare might have written 'the raveled sweater of care' or 'the tangled loose threads of care', for example. It is in choosing or discriminating among these alternative possibilities that the true master of metaphor demonstrates his skill. However, what is not up to the metaphor-maker is that there must be some noun phrase with these semantic properties to fill that thematic role.[39] The thematic network of a (verb) metaphor thereby both implicates other expressions in its interpretation and constrains their involvement.

   It should be emphasized that these network relations can be captured only in terms of the character of the metaphor, not in terms of its content. Thus the content of (9) is roughly:

(9d) Sleep restores (repairs, composes) the calm and composure of confused, exhausted, weary people.

Since 'restores', 'composes', and 'repairs' do not require a theme or patient with parts,

(9e) Sleep restores (repairs, composes) calm (to the weary and confused)

is also acceptable. It is only at the level of the character of (9), that is, the character of

(9f) Sleep Mthat['knits up'] Mthat['the raveled sleeve of'] care,

that we can represent the kind of semantic structure relevant to these thematic roles that explains why the metaphor takes the form it has.

Attending to the thematic argument structure of a metaphor can also influence the interpretation we give it. Consider Aristotle's chestnut:

(11) The ship ploughs the waves.

On the face of it, the subject ('the ship') is agent and the direct object ('the waves') is patient, analogous to the literal

(12) The oxen plough the field.

This is also how the literary scholar Hugh Kenner reads the metaphor whose content, he says, has to do with the "similarity in two dissimilar actions: the ship does to the waves what a plough does to the ground."[40] But it is not at all clear what it is that a ship *does* to waves that resembles what oxen do to a field when they plough. Instead I would suggest a different metaphorical interpretation of (11) based on a different thematic structure: The motion of the ship through the waves is in the manner of a plow, rising and descending with the waves as a plow rises and descends with the furrows in the ground. That is, the metaphor expresses the effect of the waves on the motion of the ship, rather than, like (12), the effect of the ship on the waves. On this reading, the subject is not the Agent but the Theme, while the object noun phrase is the Source and/or Location of the action. 'Ploughs', in turn, is a verb of a manner of motion.

The moral to be drawn from this example is, again, that it is not always enough to interpret a single expression metaphorically; we must also take into account the other expressions that discharge its thematic roles, the whole system of relations between the words used in the context. Only when we interpret, in this example, the main verb as part of its whole network of thematically related words can we arrive at its correct metaphorical interpretation.

Thus far we have discussed only verbs in connection with thematic networks because only verbs directly assign arguments with thematic roles. One might try to extend this story to nominals derived from verbs, for example, to 'fisherman' which is derived from (verb) 'fish', such that the thematic roles assigned by the verb are inherited by the noun. Where, for example, there is an agent signified by 'fisherman', it would be implied (even if it is not verbalized) that there is a patient (signified by 'fish' or some subordinate class, e.g., 'trout' or 'salmon'), location ('water', 'lake', etc.), and instrument ('hook', 'bait', 'line', 'net', etc.). And to extend the idea even to underived nominal phrases, one might argue that many common nouns or noun phrases have characteristic or "normal" actions associated with them; for example, 'the sun shines/warms/blazes'. Given these associated verbs, the thematic roles they assign might, in turn, be inherited by the respective noun, yielding a network of associated roles that can be assigned to still more nouns or noun phrases. To spell this out, I now turn to the second kind of network based on inductive associations.

As several writers on metaphor have noted, all the metaphors in the following lines in T. S. Eliot's "The Love Song of J. Alfred Prufrock" presuppose an enthymematic metaphor: 'fog is a cat'.

The *yellow* fog that *rubs its back* upon the window panes,
The *yellow* smoke that *rubs its muzzle* on the window panes,
Licked its tongue into the corners of the evening,
Lingered upon the pools that stand in drains,
Let fall upon *its back* the soot that falls from chimneys,
Slipped by the terrace, *made a sudden leap,*
And *seeing* that it was a soft October night,
Curled once about the house and fell asleep.

(my italics)

Tanya Reinhart (1970, 391) makes this point, using I. A. Richard's terminology, by calling a cat (or another animal with similar behavior) the metaphorical vehicle. Lynne Tirrell (1989, 26–28) proposes that the implied 'fog is a cat' metaphor functions as an "antecedent," or governing, metaphor (the "metaphor-proper," in her words) for the extended set of (italicized) metaphorical expressions, roughly in the way that a noun phrase serves as antecedent for co-referential pronouns in anaphoric chains. What both authors have in common is the idea that the constituent metaphors in the passage belong to one interrelated complex, one system or network. Someone who interprets each expression metaphorically but fails to recognize that they are part of one network misses an important fact about them as metaphors—even if he assigns the same interpretation to each individual metaphorical expression as the one who recognizes their network-structure. In chapter 7 I'll return to the cognitive significance of the network-structure carried by the characters of its members. Here I want to look at the status of the connections between the predicates in these networks or, more precisely, the relations between the properties they express.

One way to explain the connections between the italicized phrases in the above "Prufrock" passage would be to take them to be deductively related. Each of the phrases belongs to one 'fog is a cat' metaphor because our concept of a cat can be explicated or analyzed by or decomposed (exhaustively or not) into the following set of meaning postulates:

(i) (x) $(x$ is a cat $\rightarrow$ x is yellow)

(ii) (x) $(x$ is a cat $\rightarrow$ x rubs its back)

(iii) (x) $(x$ is a cat $\rightarrow$ x makes sudden leaps)

(iv) (x) $(x$ is a cat $\rightarrow$ x licks its tongue)

(v) (x) $(x$ is a cat $\rightarrow$ x curls up to sleep), etc.

But the obvious problem with this approach is that it is not at all clear which properties to include in our concepts. To make the approach descriptively adequate to capture all the kinds of cat-scheme predicates that can be used in one such extended metaphor, it would be necessary to include *every* property that is empirically true of a cat in its concept (and perhaps even more, such as false stereotypical properties). But once we include all such properties, every change in our (empirical) knowledge about cats would constitute a change in our concept of a cat. On the other hand, if we restrict the properties we take to be constitutive of the concept to some privileged subset, we need some criterion to distinguish those constitutive properties from all others. For lack of a good criterion, a sharp division runs the dangers of an unprincipled analytic-synthetic distinction.[41]

A more plausible explanation of the fog-is-a-cat network is that it is inductive in character. That is, all the properties are inductively related to our experiences of cats, but to different degrees of confirmation or probability. So, 'x is licking its tongue' and 'x is curling up' can be more strongly inductively inferred from 'x is a cat' than 'x is rubbing its back' or 'x is lingering', and all of these more than 'x chases dogs'. Inversely, from 'x is yellow', 'x licks its tongue', and 'x is curled up to fall asleep' we can infer, though again with different degrees of likelihood, 'x is a cat'. Here the nature of the inference from each of the italicized phrases, and from all of them as a group, to 'x is a cat'—as the "governing" or "controlling" metaphor—would not be deductive but that of an inference to the best explanation.

All the cat-associations mentioned above are more or less community-wide and socially shared, rather than personal and idiosyncratic. Indeed they are not just relative to one—that is, our—community but are more or less constant across communities. And they are established rather than novel associations. Other inductively based extensions might be established only relative to a given community, and yet others may be novel rather than established. Had Eliot metaphorically described a fog as a cat because—like a cat for a community in which it is a sacred, awesome animal—it is off-limits, feared, and terror-inspiring, the metaphor would be foreign to our community. Had he described it as a sometime black cat because it is an omen of bad luck—when it crosses or blocks our paths— it would be more of a novel than extended interpretation of the metaphor, yet native to our community rather than foreign. In any case, unlike the linguistic connections established by thematic relations, all of these links are based on inductive, empirical grounds.

In sum, all three of the kinds of networks or schemes we have discussed—exemplification, thematic, and inductive—belong to the context that generates the presuppositions from which metaphorical interpretations are drawn. This is not to suggest that these three should exclusively and exhaustively be taken to be *the* sources of metaphorical presuppositions. On the contrary, given the ways they differ among themselves, there is good reason to expect that there are more sources, a variety of different contextual factors that generate metaphorically relevant presuppositions, factors that cannot be systematically reduced or even unified into one overarching system. This state of pragmatic affairs, as I said earlier, stands in contrast to the genuine semantic constraints that belong to our semantic competence in metaphorical character.

Before leaving the pragmatics of metaphorical interpretation, it would be helpful to contrast our networks with those in the best-known account that analyzes metaphors in terms of large-scale, systematic networks: the theory of "conventional" or "conceptual" metaphor developed by George Lakoff and his co-authors Mark Johnson and Mark Turner.[42] In what follows I shall refer to the theory of this school simply as "Lakoff et al." or as "Lakoff" (with no slight intended to the others).

V   Lakoff et al. on Metaphor

Lakoff et al. have collected to date the largest corpus of data in the literature on metaphorical networks with which they have constructed a valuable taxonomy of metaphor systems. Although the idea that metaphors work in networks (or families) is not original with Lakoff et al., until their research no one, I think, had a full appreciation of the ubiquity and variety of these families. Lakoff et al. have also drawn some very strong conclusions about the philosophical significance of their descriptive material—about the bankruptedness of "objective truth," classical "Western" philosophy of language, epistemology, and metaphysics, and much contemporary theoretical linguistics, as well as a slew of other theoretical claims. These polemically charged claims have not only failed to convince philosophers; they have also had the unfortunate effect of discrediting the authors' empirical theory in the eyes of many beholders. For reasons of space, I shall not discuss their philosophical claims.[43] But it would be helpful to examine Lakoff's metaphor networks to see whether they constitute a genuine alternative to those we have discussed.

According to Lakoff et al., there are three fundamental ways in which their "contemporary" theory of metaphor differs from "classical theories" for whom "metaphor was seen as a matter of language, not thought" (Lakoff 1993, 202):

1. On Lakoff's view, metaphors are not linguistic expressions (or interpretations) but cross-domain mappings in the conceptual system. One domain, the source, is used to "conceptualize" a second, the target, (i) by individuating the entities of the latter in terms of its own (source) entities (sometimes indeed "making," or constituting, entities in the target domain), and (ii) by "sanction[ing] the use of source domain language and inference patterns for target domain concepts" (ibid., 207). A "metaphorical expression" is simply "a linguistic expression (word, phrase, sentence) that is a surface realization of such a cross-domain mapping" (ibid., 203). To designate the mappings, Lakoff et al. use capitalized slogans, for example, ARGUMENT IS WAR or LOVE IS A JOURNEY or TIME IS A MOVING THING. However, the verbalized slogans should not be mistaken for the true metaphors, that is, the conceptual mappings and restructurings of the target domains. I'll refer to the capitalized clauses as *metaphorical slogans.*

2. On Lakoff's view, metaphor is not restricted to "novel or poetic linguistic expression." Instead "everyday abstract concepts like time, states, change, causation, and purpose also turn out to be metaphorical" (ibid.). Because these metaphors are ubiquitous, automatic, and often communally shared in ordinary language, Lakoff et al. call them *conventional* metaphors. *Poetic* metaphors are typically "based" on the same mappings as the conventional metaphors but they are not automatic; instead they are often original or novel, requiring effort to be understood. These differences should not, however, obscure the basic fact that both conventional and poetic metaphors are realizations of the same mappings.

3. The primary evidence for Lakoff that metaphor is "conceptual" rather than "linguistic" are the many complex and systematically organized networks of metaphorical expressions with which we talk about domains or topics. For example, aspects of love relationships are expressed using metaphors from the domain of journeys:

Our relationship has hit a dead-end street. Look how far we've come. We're at a crossroads. We'll just have to go our separate ways. We can't turn back now. I don't think this relationship is going anywhere. We've gotten off the track. We are spinning our wheels.

These are not unrelated, independent individual metaphors. Rather "we have one metaphor, in which love is conceptualized as a journey. The mapping tells us precisely how love is being conceptualized as a journey. And this unified way of *conceptualizing* love metaphorically is realized in many different *linguistic* expressions" (ibid., 209). Thus lovers correspond to travelers, their relationship to the vehicle, their shared goals to their common destination, and difficulties in the relationship to impediments in their way. Given these correspondences, "inference patterns used to reason about travel are also used to reason about love relations" (ibid.). And similarly for other topics like argument, which is conceptualized as war, or time, conceptualized as money, and so on.

I (and most philosophers, I think) would agree with most of these claims. Metaphors are not restricted to poetry; they run through all uses of language. Metaphor is also not linguistic *as opposed to* conceptual if that means that language is merely decorative or that it does not express cognitive content. Metaphorical interpretations can not only express cognitive content, including novel properties, that would not be expressed literally; they also bear cognitive significance—that bears on action as well as knowledge—by way of their (metaphorical) character, as I'll argue in chapter 7. Finally, I share Lakoff et al.'s conviction in the existence and importance of large-scale systematic networks to which metaphors typically belong that bear on their interpretation. Much of the work done by my thematic schemes and inductive networks is done by Lakoff's "experiential gestalts," constrained by his Invariance Principle that ensures that structural (many of them thematic) relations among the expressions taken from the source domain continue to hold in their metaphorical application to the target domain. For example, in the LIFE IS A JOURNEY mapping, the source domain (JOURNEY) includes an argument place for paths, sources/places of origin, and goals/destinations, none of which is clearly found in the target domain (LIFE). A primary effect of the mapping is to "create" and structure argument-places for those thematic roles in our (metaphorical) language for the target domain.

Despite its descriptive riches, Lakoff et al.'s explanation still has serious gaps. They do not explain why a particular metaphorical expression ought to be subsumed under one rather than another mapping or how the proper level of mapping is decided.[44] Even in the LOVE IS A JOURNEY example, it is not clear why it is specifically love rather than any relationship or indeed any goal-directed activity (of which love might then simply be an instance) that is conceptualized as a journey. They also fail to explain why, given a conceptual metaphor, only some but not other "parts" of the metaphor are mapped or, when interpreted, appropriate. Indeed, despite their sometimes inflated rhetoric, in their more sober moments, Lakoff et al. acknowledge that their schemes and their structural relations are not predictive and that they only provide constraints on the class of possible metaphors (ibid., 215).

The main difference between Lakoff et al.'s account and mine concerns the relation between context and the metaphorical networks.[45] One small expression of this difference is that even though the cross-domain mappings are the real metaphors for Lakoff et al., the realizations of those conceptual metaphors in language are always in linguistic *expressions*, that is, linguistic *types*. On my account, metaphors are never expression types per se but interpretations (or uses) of expression *tokens in contexts*, although those interpretations may depend on the networks, or mappings, to which the token belongs. Consider Lakoff et al.'s examples of the *non*-metaphorical: *sentences* (i.e., types) such as 'the balloon went up' or 'the cat is on the mat'. Yet, it is obvious that even these "literal" sentences or expressions can, in some context with a little imagination, be used metaphorically. T. S. Eliot might have continued his famous depiction of fog as a cat with 'the cat is on the mat' or we might summarize the impact of a stock market run on a vulnerable economy with 'the balloon went up'. Contra Lakoff et al., there are no *expressions* (types) per se that are either metaphorical or nonmetaphorical.[46]

Lakoff et al.'s conception of metaphor as *any* cross-(conceptual) domain mapping is also both too broad and too general. It is too broad because there are too many different kinds of context-independent mappings, not all of which plausibly underlie metaphor specifically. And it is too general because even multiple mappings are inadequate to account for certain differences of metaphorical interpretation for which it is necessary to appeal to the role of context. Let me illustrate both shortcomings.

Among Lakoff et al.'s conceptual metaphors, or cross-domain mappings, is a large number in which various domains (birth, states and changes of state, death, life, form, progress, and time) are conceptualized as, or structured, using (thematic) relations and concepts drawn from the domain of space and motion in space. Lakoff et al.'s primary evidence for the existence of these metaphor systems, or cross-domain mappings, is the variety of linguistic expressions in context-invariant conventional language that realize them. Thus people come into the world when they are born and leave it or depart when they die, we go in and out of states, progress is moving forward, covering ground, and so on. These expressions, they claim, are all metaphorical and they are metaphorical *because* they realize an underlying cross-domain mapping. This, however, is not the only possible explanation. Ray Jackendoff (1983) and Jeffrey Gruber (1965/1976) have, as an alternative, argued for what they call the *Thematic Relations Hypothesis*: that there is one neutral, primitive structure that is used both for the analysis of spatial location and motion and for a large number of event and state semantic fields (including temporal, possessive, identificational, circumstantial, and existential fields). The only differences that exist among the semantic fields that possess this one structure consist in (i) the things assigned to the roles of theme and location and (ii) the semantic values of the referential expressions. All other predicates in the different fields can be analyzed or decomposed (though not always exhaustively, allowing for idiosyncratic differences) into the same spatial primitives for motion (e.g., GO, REMAIN/STAY, FROM, TO, TOWARD) and a small number of general primitives (e.g., CAUSE, BE, LET). Their evidence for this hypothesis is lexical, as well as the many syntactic regularities that recur across these fields.

In large measure, Jackendoff-Gruber and Lakoff et al. are in agreement. Spatial notions and their thematic relations, both of which constitute systematically organized linguistic or conceptual networks, structure our thought and talk in many other domains. Their disagreement is whether the evidence warrants calling all this talk and thought *metaphorical*. For Lakoff et al., the large number of expressions that linguistically realize the cross-domain mapping is primary evidence for the ubiquity of metaphor. Jackendoff denies this for four reasons. I am sympathetic to his conclusion, but his arguments do not, I think, make the case. The first two reasons can be dealt with quickly. The third and fourth are illuminating for where they go wrong.

Jackendoff's first objection is that, "unlike metaphor, thematic parallels [i.e., the spatial thematic relations paralleled in the event and state fields] are not used for artistic or picturesque effect" (1983, 209). True; but Lakoff et al. (and we) would, of course, deny that metaphor need be used only for artistic or picturesque effect.

Second, "thematic structure is the only means available to organize a semantic field of events and states coherently—it is an indispensable element of everyday thought" (ibid.). True again (or at least, let's grant the point). However, the apparent assumption that metaphor *is* dispensable is false. As I'll argue in the next section, a classic motivation for the use of metaphor is catachresis: to fill gaps in the vocabulary of the language for which there are (at a given time) no (literal) expressions. This may also be true of whole systems or networks of metaphors that serve to structure domains that (at the time) possess no structure "of their own." Metaphors of this kind would be ineliminable and indispensable.

Third, and more interesting, Jackendoff argues that Lakoff et al. "stretch" the term "metaphor" when it should be limited to expressions that manifest "some overt" or "literal incongruity," be it semantic anomaly or a pragmatic incongruity (Jackendoff and Aaron 1991, 325). As a test, he proposes that we construct "diagnostic" sentences whose first clause "acknowledges the incongruity of the mapping" and whose second clause "constructs a hypothetical invocation of the mapping that motivates the metaphorical reading." For example, to capture the metaphoricity of

(13) Our relationship is at a dead end,

which would be an instance of the mapping A RELATIONSHIP IS A JOURNEY, Jackendoff proposes the diagnostic sentence:

(14) Of course, relationships are not journeys—but if they were, you might say ours is at a dead end.

A number of Lakoff et al.'s "metaphors," he argues, fail this test. The purported temporal metaphor

?*(15) Christmas is approaching,

based on the mapping TIME IS A MOVING OBJECT, only questionably passes the diagnostic test:

(16) Of course, times are not a medium in motion—but if they were, you might say Christmas is approaching.

The difficulty with this argument and diagnostic, as I noted back in chapter 1, is its presupposition that all metaphors are literally or overtly incongruous, either pragmatically or semantically. This assumption has been roundly criticized for the last twenty years, and it is not at all clear how the diagnostic would apply to sentences that can be both literally and figuratively true (even in the same context), such as (17) and (19). Neither (18) nor (20) does the job.

(17) The painting is blue.

*(18) Of course, paintings don't have colors—but if they did, you might say that the painting is blue.

(19) Jesus is a carpenter.

*(20) Of course, people aren't craftsmen—but if they were, you might say that Jesus is a carpenter

Finally, Jackendoff's fourth argument is based on the observation that

the most remarkable aspect of metaphor is its variety, the possibility of using practically any semantic field as a metaphor for any other. By contrast, thematic relations disclose the same analogy over and over again.... That is, the theory of thematic relations claims not just that some fields are structured in terms of other fields, but that all fields have essentially the same structure. (1983, 209)

It is not entirely clear how we should understand this last passage. On one reading, the claim is that there is one semantic field (source), the spatial, in terms of which all, or many, other semantic fields (targets) are structured. But this fact (if it is one) does not count against that single source-field applying metaphorically to all the others; on the contrary, such a fact would simply testify to its power as a metaphor. Nor would it exclude the possibility that there are additional mappings (sources) that might structure those targets, compatible with what Jackendoff calls the "variety" of metaphor. Nor does the Thematic Relations Hypothesis deny the possibility of another field (metaphorically) structuring the spatial. On this reading, the argument is moot against Lakoff et al.

On a second reading of Jackendoff's objection, the Thematic Relations Hypothesis is not a claim to the effect that one field, the spatial, is used to conceptually structure other fields. Rather it is the claim that there are a set of "abstract parameters" that structure all (or many) semantic fields, among them (and perhaps more clearly than elsewhere but, in no interesting sense, primarily) language about space. There is, then, no *mapping* at work, just one structure realized in different fields. Contra Lakoff et al., the existence of *parallel* thematic relations is no evidence specifically for metaphor.

One problem with this reading is that it leaves unexplained why nonetheless there surfaces so much explicit spatial language in the other domains, but no or little, say, temporal or possessive language in the spatial domain. If there were simply one common abstract structure underlying all these different fields, no one of which is privileged over the others, we would expect much more reciprocal language than we find:

existence or temporal language for the spatial field, circumstantial talk for the temporal, or temporal for the circumstantial. The omnipresence of specifically spatial language is significant.

Despite these difficulties, I agree with Jackendoff's conclusion: Lakoff et al.'s spatial "metaphors" for time, states, and events are not metaphorical. But the reason is not that Lakoff et al.'s mappings do not exhibit the "variety" of metaphor, where that is understood as "the possibility of using practically any semantic field as a metaphor for any other" (Jackendoff 1983, 203). The real "variety" of metaphor rather consists in its context-dependence: the fact that any semantic field—that is, any expression from one semantic field—can, in different contexts, metaphorically express different contents; or that given (almost) any two semantic fields, with appropriate context sets of presuppositions, expressions in one can metaphorically co-occur with the other. What makes it questionable whether Lakoff et al.'s spatial mappings are metaphors *at present* is that there is no evidence that context plays a role in their present interpretation. Hence there is no reason to think—as there ought to be if they were metaphors (i.e., if they had context-sensitive metaphorical characters)— that if there were different presuppositions in their contexts, they would have different interpretations. I emphasize "at present" because I do not wish to make any claim about their history; the claim that they are not metaphors at present is compatible with the fact that they originally entered the language as metaphors. On the other hand, I am also not objecting (as many others have objected in reaction to Lakoff et al.) that Lakoff et al.'s conventional metaphors are at present nothing more than dead metaphors. By denying that they are metaphors, I do not wish to imply that as a system they are in any way "dead." The mappings are very much alive in that, as both Jackendoff and Lakoff et al. demonstrate, they actively interact with syntax, and hence with the language faculty, as well with our other belief systems and action. Yet, although the mappings are alive, they are not metaphorical—because they exhibit no (propensity to) context-dependence. For this reason, Lakoff et al.'s mappings are too broad to capture the specifically metaphorical.

Lakoff et al.'s mappings are also too general. They fail to account for the specificity of different metaphorical interpretations—and, again, precisely because they fail to take into account the role of the context. To illustrate the problem, let's take a closer look at Lakoff et al.'s analysis of a metaphor discussed at length by Glucksberg and Keysar (1990):

(21) My job is a jail.

G&K analyze this metaphor as a "class-inclusion" statement, or predication, in which the subject referred to by 'my job' is assigned to a category referred to by 'a jail'. Now, psychologists like G&K speak of categories where we speak of properties or concepts—largely as a function of our different theoretical interests: theirs with the processes governing categorization, ours with the content of utterances. But the idea is the same: The phrase 'a jail' is used here to refer, not to its ordinary extension (jails) but to a superordinate category (or property) of which that extension is an exemplary member—in our terminology, the predicate expresses a property (presupposed to be) exemplified by its (literal) extension.[47]

But how do we know which superordinate category or property is referred to by 'a jail'? Although G&K do not mention exemplification or sampling, they note correctly that the category referred to depends on the other objects with which the (literal) object is classified and on the other categories, or alternatives, with which the given category-expression is grouped. For example, (1) a jail can be (more or less literally) a spartan, unluxurious dwelling, in contrast to palaces, hospitals, resorts, dormitories, and hotels. Or (2) a jail can be a kind of punishment, classed along with scoldings, spankings, traffic tickets, and capital executions. This is what 'jail' means when my five-year-old son, who has hit his brother, angrily blurts out when I tell him to go to his room:

(22) OK, send me to jail!

Or (3) a jail (or prison) can contrast with open roads, a life in which people can freely come and go as they choose. Thus a Palestinian official once described his town of Bethlehem as a prison, because he could not come and go without rarely approved Israeli permits. Or, finally, (4) a jail can be classified among psychologically pleasant, neutral, and unpleasant situations. For lack of a better name, 'a jail' in this last scheme of classification would refer to situations that hold individuals against their will, that offer no satisfaction, that the individual would leave if he only could (but can't), that are psychologically confining. The contrasting elements in this schema include, perhaps, honeymoons, holidays, and vacations. This also may be the sense of 'prison' when Hamlet announces

(23) Denmark's a prison. (*Hamlet* II, ii, 260)

As these examples illustrate, the specific superordinate category to which a given expression refers depends on the schema of alternatives with which it alternates. If we think of the exemplification-schema for an object (or for its term) as its context, this is one way in which this kind of reference is context-dependent. But, in a broader sense, the classification of 'a jail' with one or the other of these exemplification-schemas also depends on context—on other features of the discourse, identities of the participants, etc.

Thus in different contexts, depending on what we presuppose about the job, speaker, and discourse, we will assign 'a jail' in (21) to different schemas relative to which it exemplifies different properties and meta-phorically expresses one or the other of the following contents: Either that my job is a punishment with a term (say, for having committed a crime-like act like dropping out of school as a youth, thereby committing me to the consequences of my error); or that my job involves a spartan exis-tence, with few amenities, low pay, no frills or perks; or that the job is claustrophobic, heavily constrained, with little opportunity for spontane-ity; or, last of all, that it is simply an unpleasant situation in which I am trapped. In short, exemplification metaphors like (21) are highly context sensitive, expressing different contents given different presuppositions concerning the exemplification-schema involved.

Now, Lakoff (1993, 236) claims that he can neatly explain the same metaphor 'my job is a jail' in terms of the interaction of three conceptual metaphors: ACTIONS ARE SELF-PROPELLED MOVEMENTS (an instance of the event-structure metaphor), PSYCHOLOGICAL FORCE IS PHYSICAL FORCE, and GENERIC IS SPECIFIC. His reconstruc-tion of the interpretation falls into five steps:

1. We begin with our "knowledge schema," that is, our community-wide presuppositions about jails that includes "knowledge that a jail imposes extreme physical constraints on a prisoner's movements" (ibid.).
2. The GENERIC IS SPECIFIC metaphor next applies, "factoring out" what is specific to prisoners and jails, thereby yielding: X imposes extreme physical constraints on Y's movements.
3. The ACTIONS ARE SELF-PROPELLED MOVEMENTS metaphor next applies to the result of 2 to yield: X imposes extreme physical con-straints on Y's actions.
4. The PSYCHOLOGICAL FORCE IS PHYSICAL FORCE metaphor next applies to the result of 3 to yield: X imposes extreme psychological constraints on Y's actions.
5. Substituting 'my job' for X and me for Y yields as an interpretation for 'my job is a jail': "my job imposes extreme psychological constraints on my actions."

This analysis raises a number of questions, beginning with the first and second stages. First, GENERIC IS SPECIFIC may be a "mapping," and even a mapping involved in the interpretation of some metaphors, but it is not itself a metaphor. If the mapping were a metaphor, it ought to be realized or realizable linguistically in a metaphorical expression. What would it be? Lakoff's own example of a generic metaphor is, say, 'death is destruction'. Analogously, we might propose: 'A situation that imposes extreme physical constraints on someone's movements is a jail'. A bit odd, yes; but a metaphor? Hardly. The problem lies in the origins of Lakoff's idea of generic structure, which he first introduces as a *constraint* on mappings: as a set of generic-level conditions (overall event shape or causal and aspectual structure) roughly like thematic relations.[48] Only later, when he proposes a "mechanism" corresponding to "our ability to extract generic-level structure," and attempts to assimilate all such mechanisms to his rubric of mappings, does he invent the GENERIC IS SPECIFIC "metaphor." This is unnecessary. We already have the needed "mechanism" in the (not-language-specific) relation of exemplification, which in the case of events is, as we all agree, constrained by thematic or generic-level structure.[49] Hence there is no evidence that the GENERIC IS SPECIFIC mapping is itself a metaphor.[50] And insofar as Lakoff's own account that rests on mappings like GENERIC IS SPECIFIC also relies, as we just said, on a reference-relation like exemplification (whether or not he calls it by that name), it is no genuine alternative to G&K.[51]

The main and least controversially metaphorical mapping in Lakoff's analysis is PSYCHOLOGICAL FORCE IS PHYSICAL FORCE. But this metaphor enters into the story only because Lakoff *begins* by assuming that our "knowledge schema" about jails specifically includes *only* the "knowledge that a jail imposes extreme *physical* constraints on a prisoner's movements" (ibid., my italics). Why couldn't the ur-schema equally well include the knowledge that a jail imposes extreme *psychological* constraints (social isolation, limited access to family and outsiders) on a prisoner? Once we include that information in our initial knowledge-schema there is no work left to be done by the PSYCHOLOGICAL FORCE IS PHYSICAL FORCE metaphor.[52]

Finally, let's assume that Lakoff et al.'s interpretation for 'my job is a jail'—namely, "my job imposes extreme psychological constraints on my actions"—is in fact one of its metaphorical interpretations. Still it is only one among a number—depending on the exemplification schema in which jails are taken to function in the context of utterance. As we have just seen, different schemata yield rather different metaphorical interpretations for the one sentence. Compared to these riches of alternative interpretations, Lakoff et al.'s interpretation is much too thin, monolithic, and one-dimensional.[53] The reason, as I hinted earlier when I said that their linguistic metaphors are expression types rather than interpretations of tokens, is precisely that their theory of conventional, conceptual metaphor fails to do justice to the role of the context in metaphorical interpretation.

In conclusion, Lakoff et al.'s theory of conceptual metaphors draws from a rich body of evidence about metaphorical networks. But it is far from evident that the "mappings" to which the theory appeals are specifically metaphorical, that the principles that govern its mappings are really different from those of opposing accounts like G&K's, and that it does justice to the role of context, which is necessary to account for the full variegated range of metaphorical interpretations. On the other hand, those who characterize the difference between Lakoff et al.'s theory and G&K's (or mine) as a dispute over whether metaphor "involves the construction of novel categories" or whether it "always relies on preexisting conceptual mappings" are, I think, also off the mark.[54] Just as Lakoff et al.'s theory must be supplemented by (or already involves) context-sensitive factors like exemplification, so the notion of exemplification itself relies on and interacts with networks like Lakoff et al.'s. Some of these networks, such as exemplification-schemas, may be specific and novel to the context of the metaphorical utterance. Others, like the thematic relations of the metaphor and its inductive network, may preexist the particular context, either because they are built into our language faculty or because they are based on established communally shared associations. In either case, the different networks, and different accounts that focus on different networks, complement rather than compete with each other.

VI Exemplification, Catachresis, and *De Re* Knowledge *by* Metaphor

With the analysis of exemplification in hand, I can now draw out an analogy between metaphors and predicate demonstratives to which I alluded in chapter 3. In the course of our discussion of the direct reference thesis for demonstratives, I pointed out that Kaplan's characterization of a singular proposition, as a proposition that contains at least one individual in contrast to a general proposition that contains only properties (or universals) and logical functions, fails to do justice to sentences containing natural kind or substance terms or predicate demonstratives like 'is that Φ' (e.g., 'the table in Classics 12 *is that shape*[points at a long rectangular board]' or 'thus' (e.g., 'he broke the board *thus*[snaps a thin twig between his two fingers]'). On the one hand, the contents of these expressions are properties (kinds, substances, other abstract entities)—the stuff of general propositions. On the other, these expressions appear to express (or refer to) their respective properties just as directly referential terms refer to their individual contents: without the mediation of a purely conceptualized representation whose conditions are *satisfied*, the kind of relation that characterizes *in*direct reference. In this respect, the contents of predicate demonstratives are more like the constituents of singular propositions.

To address this problem, I proposed a broader distinction between *referential* and *purely conceptualized* propositions (under which we would subsume the singular/general distinction). Following Frege, we assign all expressions referents, the referents of *n*-ary predicates being *n*-ary properties. The class of referential propositions now includes all singular propositions, but it also includes all propositions at least one of whose constituents is a property and relation "in itself"—a bare property or relation—rather than a conceptualized representation whose qualitative individuating conditions in turn determine the property or relation via satisfaction at a circumstance. This distinction is more epistemological than Russell's, which distinguishes the two classes of propositions solely by the identities of their constituents. Ours also takes the different classes of propositions to mark differences between the means by which we conceive of their constituents. As I said in chapter 3, the distinction might reflect a number of different epistemic situations. Sometimes we possess a purely qualitative conceptualization of the property that enables us to denote it. At other times, as with many directly referential (singular) terms, it is only by employing our contextual relations to the property that we are able to express a proposition containing it. We may be able to express the property only by way of a sample that we demonstrate in context or by way of applying the property to a particular object in a context, without knowing, and perhaps even without there being in the language, a label or concept for that property. In these cases, to borrow a usage of Tyler Burge (1977), we refer *de re* to the property. On the other hand, we refer to the property *de dicto* where we express or refer to it by using a purely conceptualized individuating representation, where we express it by using vocabulary in our linguistic, or conceptual, repertoire that is determinately true or false of arbitrary things without depending on features of its context of application. This difference between *de re* and *de dicto* expression of or reference to properties is a matter of how they are expressed or referred to in the utterance and by its agent. The same property expressed *de dicto* by one sentence on one occasion may be expressed *de re* by another. *De re* expression via the context may also have other virtues not due (simply) to the lack of *de dicto* conceptual or linguistic resources. Context-sensitive character, as I'll show in chapter 7, may also carry its own cognitive significance in addition to its propositional, truth-conditional content (in a context). A speaker may therefore choose to express a given property *de re*, using a context-sensitive expression, in order to communicate this additional character-istic information.

Some utterances containing metaphors also express referential propositions. Like predicate demonstratives, they express or refer to their contents by exploiting (via their nonconstant characters) features of their nonlinguistic contexts, without the mediation of purely conceptualized representations denoting their respective contents (in extension) at each circumstance of evaluation. As linguists have often observed, one important function of metaphor is *catachresis*:[55] to fill in lexical gaps or to compensate for the lack of vocabulary in a language for a concept or property. The deficiency is not simply a shortage of words. Rather it signals the lack of representations in our conceptual or linguistic repertoire whose characters are characters *of* those properties, characters that would determinately express (or refer to) those properties in all contexts, independently of their application to a particular thing in a particular context. Instead the metaphorical expression expresses the property by exploiting features specific (and sometimes unique) to its context. In particular, the metaphor may employ contextual presuppositions about what property (whether or not we know a name for it) is sampled or exemplified by things in the context. Given my account of exemplification, we can fill in the details of this picture more fully.

Let me begin with a superficially similar example of nonmetaphor, which Glucksberg and Keysar (1990, 1993) compare to the mechanism by which metaphor enables us to express, or refer to, novel superordinate categories (or properties). The difference between the two cases is instructive.

G&K (1990, 1993), following Rosch (1973), point out that all languages have simple names for basic level objects (such as 'table', 'chair', 'bed') although some languages such as American Sign Language lack (or did, until recently) names for superordinate categories (such as 'furniture'). To refer to the superordinate category of furniture, ASL signers use compounds or concatenations of the "basic objects signs that are prototypical of that category" (1993, 409) such as 'table-chair-bed'. So, to say 'I lost all my furniture in the house fire but one thing was left: the bed', ASL signers produce the string:

House fire [+] lose all chair-table-bed etc., but one left, bed. (Newport and Bellugi 1978, 62)

ASL, then, contains a mechanism to compensate for its gaps in lexical vocabulary, by using concatenations of names of prototypical or exemplary basic level objects of a category as a name for the category itself. Similarly, G&K claim, metaphor serves as a compensating mechanism in natural language. Lacking a name in English for a novel superordinate category, we use the name of a prototypical or exemplary member of the category (e.g., 'is a Kennedy' or 'is a walking time bomb') to (metaphorically) name the category itself.

There is a difference, however, between the two cases. In ASL the lack of simple superordinate category names is purely lexical. This lexical deficiency is not because users of ASL do not *understand* the concept of furniture, not because they lack knowledge of the conditions under which something belongs to the superordinate category. It may be vague whether something borderline is furniture because it is vague whether it is a bed or vague whether it is a chair or vague whether it is a table, etc. But the vagueness of the superordinate category of furniture is neither more nor less than the vagueness of the basic level object categories—bed, chair, table. There is no more deficiency in the ASL user's understanding of the superordinate category 'furniture' than there is in his understanding of the basic level categories. It is, to be sure, striking in the ASL case that the lexical deficiency is not simply of one particular piece of vocabulary but of names of categories of a whole type or level, namely, the superordinate. Nonetheless the catachresis is simply lexical.

Metaphor is a different story. With metaphors of exemplification, we also use an expression that (literally) refers to one thing to express or refer to a property that (it is contextually presupposed) the referent exemplifies in the absence of a (simple) predicate that (literally) expresses the property. But in at least a central set of cases of this sort, the property has no linguistic expression to call its own, not simply for lack of a word but for lack of adequate *understanding*. This is especially true when the metaphor is used to express or refer to a "novel" property. What makes the property novel is not that it is being applied for the first time to a particular object but that we can apply it only in relation to the particular object that samples, exemplifies, or displays it in context. Such a property is not yet fully conceptualized. We lack at the time of utterance a concept, or representation, of the property that would enable us to determine what possesses it in a context-invariant or transcendent manner. We lack knowledge of the conditions that would enable us to determine whether an arbitrary object possesses the property regardless of the extralinguistic context in which we make the determination. We can only express or refer to, say, a color *as* the color of an object to which we demonstratively refer or gesture. Like a complete demonstrative that enables us to refer to an individual by employing nonconceptual nonlinguistic features, the character of the metaphor, given a complementary set of presuppositions, enables us to "point" to the property even when we don't possess the fully conceptualized linguistic means to express it independent of context.

What would it be to have such a fully conceptualized—in one sense of the word: literal (as I'll argue in ch. 8)—means to express a property? I don't have a good answer to this question. But to return to our point of contrast with ASL, it is not *merely* a matter of having a (literally interpreted) *word* for the property, although the availability of and ability to apply such a context-independent word is frequently evidence of having such an epistemic capacity. It is therefore misleading to think of the *de re* use of metaphors of exemplification as nothing more than *verbal* catachresis, a matter of plugging a hole in the literal vocabulary. Instead the capacity is a function of the extent to which our knowledge of the concept, or conception, of the property transcends any particular application of the predicate that expresses it. Among other things, this capacity is related to the degree to which the concept of the property is integrated within our conceptual repertoire, roughly, the degree to which we know what the concept entails and what entails it among a relatively rich number of logical relations to other concepts and beliefs. This is, to be sure, a very rough statement of the idea of fully conceptualized understanding, but where metaphors serve to introduce properties to which we are related only *de re*—not fully conceptualized properties—it is important that we have some sense of what would be required to transform the metaphorically expressed property into one that is (more) fully conceptualized.[56]

Let me illustrate the epistemic difference between the *de re* and the *de dicto* with another example. Typical novel metaphors express not just one property but, as G&K (ibid., 421) note, "a patterned complex of properties in one chunk," all those the literal referent of the metaphor exemplifies. The, or a frequent, way the metaphor expresses that complex property, or complex of properties, is not by expressing the totality of constituents as one conjunction or articulated compound but simply as the undifferentiated chunk of properties exemplified by Φs. The distinction between these two modes of expression parallels Gareth Evans's (1982, 284–289) distinction between two types of memory, recall and recognition. In some tasks, when asked to remember or identify Φs, sub-

jects have the capacity to recall—and list serially—descriptive features of
Φs individually and without prompting, features the satisfaction of which
would make something a Φ. In other tasks, however, subjects cannot recall the individual features, but they can recognize Φs on presentation.
Evans argues that memory and identification need not require recall, that
recognition is frequently sufficient, and, furthermore, that even where
subjects *can* recall the features of something, they often identify it by
simply recognizing *it* without employing knowledge of the features they
can recall.

Similarly with metaphors of exemplification: Speakers and interpreters
can often *recognize* the property-complex metaphorically expressed by
'Mthat[Φ]' in a context c—the property exemplified by Φs in c—without
being able to recall, or articulate, the constituents of the property-complex. Ted Cohen (1990) describes how his father could immediately and
repeatedly recognize whether a beer was green. But he could never tell you
why, or state in other terms what that metaphorically expressed property
was. This was not because he was just guessing, nor a matter of a single
occurrence of the metaphorical predication, nor something idiosyncratic
or necessarily subjective about the metaphor. There was a common taste
or feel to the beer, a taste or feel he could recognize on different occasions
and that he could even induce others to recognize. But he (and others)
didn't have any way to articulate that metaphor—explicate the features
that make a beer green—except by applying it to particular beers in context. One function of metaphors is just this: to refer to categories (or
properties) for which we do not *at the time* have the capacity to articulate
explicitly the conditions in virtue of which things belong to (or have) it.[57]
The interpretation of such metaphors involves a kind of *de re* grasp of
their contents, recognition that relies on and is sensitive to the cues
afforded in the context, the "lighting" and "angle" in and from which the
property is presented.

With this idea of *de re* knowledge by metaphor, we can also understand
better one well-known applied problem of metaphor: "irreducible" metaphors in theological discourse.[58]

The problem of irreducible metaphors in theological language arises
from a combination of assumptions. First, there is the assumption that "it
is possible to make true statements about God, ... to convey in words
some apprehension, however inadequate, of what God is like."[59] Second,
it is assumed that it is impossible to say anything true about God
expressed by language used literally, that is, language whose conceptual
content is fully determined by the linguistic meanings of the words used.

Given these two premises, it is next proposed that one—perhaps the only—way to make true statements about God is by metaphor. But given the second assumption, it is further inferred that "what is said in the metaphorical utterance cannot be said, *even in part*, in literal terms" (ibid.). Hence, if there are true metaphorical statements about God, they must be irreducible. Their content cannot be said, even in part, in literal language.

The "problem" of irreducible theological metaphors is that this conclusion, it is next argued, is indefensible. "What is said" by the metaphor that is claimed to be irreducible is also claimed to be its propositional content, its truth-valued content. (Recall that, according to the first assumption, the metaphorical statement is indeed true.) But if the theological statement, say, 'God is a rock', has propositional content, then corresponding to the (metaphorically used) predicate, there must be a property P that is attributed to God. But if there is such a property P, there should also be, at least in principle, a predicate that can be *literally* used to attribute P. That is, there may or may not always be available to the speaker such a predicate expressing P (depending on a variety of linguistic and extralinguistic factors), but a speaker who attributes P to God must at least have a concept, or conceptual representation, of P—and once she has such a concept, it always ought to be possible at least in principle to associate it with a predicate as its meaning, that is, with a literally used predicate. Therefore, there *could not be* a property expressed by a metaphor that cannot be expressed *at all*, even in principle, by a literally used expression. Hence there are no irreducible metaphors.

Another way of putting the argument would be this: Either the metaphor expresses a truth-valued proposition or it doesn't. If it doesn't, it is irreducible only in the trivial sense that it has no content to express literally. If it does, then it must be possible to state that content, like that of any proposition, in literal language—for that is the very nature of propositional content. Either way there can be no irreducible metaphors about God. The theologian cannot have his metaphorical cake and eat it, too.[60]

The fallacy in the argument is, of course, its assumption that all propositional content must be *fully* conceptualized, if it is conceptual at all. In referential propositions, the constituent corresponding to a metaphor may be a bare property for which the speaker possesses no fully conceptualized representation. Nonetheless there is definite reference to, or expression of, the property, and there should be a fact of the matter whether *that* property is true of God, even though we may not *know* whether it is. Indeed, in light of our epistemic gloss on *de re* attitudes, divine properties would be exactly the sorts of things we ought to expect to be expressible (only) *de re*. Theologians (or other believers) who want to attribute properties to God do so on the basis of various kinds of arguments. But given the transcendence of the deity, they must also acknowledge that, despite their arguments, we can't really fully understand the nature of those divine properties. Propositions about divine properties are, then, paradigms of beliefs or thoughts that we incompletely understand (or even completely fail to understand), that is, of not fully conceptualized beliefs or thoughts. Nonetheless, through the context-sensitive mechanisms of metaphor, we can "point" to those properties despite our conceptual deficiencies.[61]

Let me add one more loop to this story to drive home the point that it is identifiable properties that are the constituents of these metaphorically expressed *de re* propositions, that is, properties that, despite our lack of concepts, theologians appear to believe we can identify or reidentify (if only in context) on different occasions.[62] Although divine properties are properties true of God, not all metaphorically expressed propositions containing divine properties need be propositions *about* God. Consider the biblical verse, "There will you worship gods made by human hands out of wood and stone, gods that neither see nor hear, neither eat nor smell" (Deut. 4, 29). Although this verse is true under its literal interpretation, the great medieval Jewish Talmudist, mystic, and biblical commentator R. Moses Nahmanides argued that what are denied of the false gods in this verse—that is, the properties expressed by 'seeing', 'hearing', and 'eating'—are the properties expressed by these predicates when they are interpreted metaphorically as applied to God, say, in a sentence like 'God sees' or 'God eats [your sacrificial offerings]'. For Nahmanides, then, we can meaningfully speak of the *same* property truly attributed to God and denied of false gods. But such a divine property is not purely conceptualized, not fully understood, and it is assumed that there is no literal expression for it. To generate the proposition, we need, then, a context of interpretation in which we hold certain presuppositions about God, even though the (negated atomic) proposition itself predicates the divine property of something other than God.

In concluding this chapter, let me add two final comments: First, the not fully conceptualized properties that a speaker can express or refer to *de re* using metaphors of exemplification constitute only one kind of knowledge—propositional content—expressed by metaphor. Not all metaphors are of this *de re* type, and this is also not the only kind of knowledge conveyed *by* metaphor. Many metaphors express properties for which we do have fully conceptualized representations. And even some metaphors of exemplification express or refer to contents we could express *de dicto*, using a fully conceptualized representation. In some of these cases, as well as with *de re* metaphors of exemplification, the character of the metaphor carries a second kind of knowledge *by* metaphor. This kind of cognitive significance is additional to its propositional content in a context—or so I'll argue in chapter 7.

Second, I have emphasized how exemplification can reveal, or render cognitively accessible, bare properties that we have no fully conceptualized means to express. But exemplification (and metaphor) can also serve to *conceal* a fully conceptualized and independently understood property. This second function of metaphor, concealment, is hardly mentioned nowadays, but it was a classical and widely cited explanation for the use of metaphor in Scripture and other sacred writings by medieval philosophers, especially those in the Islamic and Jewish Aristotelian traditions. Moses Maimonides, for example, explains that "Plato and his predecessors . . . concealed what they said [from the multitude] about the first principles and presented it in riddles. . . . [E]ven those upon whom the charge of corruption would not be laid in the event of clear exposition used terms figuratively and resorted to teaching in similes" (1963, 42–43). In these traditions, then, metaphors and other figures are primarily used—and note, by no less than philosophers—in order to conceal philosophical truths from the community at large, both to protect the uneducated from knowledge for which they are unprepared (on the assumption that a little knowledge can harm) and to protect themselves from charges of corruption leveled by the uneducated. In a slightly different vein, Pascal also writes that

God being unwilling to reveal these things to these people who were unworthy of them, and yet wishing to effect them so that they should be believed, foretold the time clearly and at times expressed them clearly, but very often in a figurative way, so that those who loved the symbols should go no further and those who loved what was symbolized should see it.[63]

For Pascal also, metaphors simultaneously conceal from some, the unworthy, and reveal to others, believers. The latter, who know and seek the content of the metaphor, "see" it in the figure. Knowing the intended content and that the expression is a figure, they recover the context that must obtain in order to interpret the figure that expresses the content. The unworthy, however, simply love the symbol itself, perhaps without even recognizing that it is a metaphor. Being unworthy, they cannot grasp its content.

Here, again, a comparison with demonstratives is helpful. Suppose I have a delicious piece of gossip about Phil to tell a colleague at a crowded party but I am afraid that the wrong ears may pick it up. Instead of using Phil's proper name, I use the complex demonstrative 'that abusive liar'. The demonstrative both enables me to communicate the identity of my intended referent to any listener who shares my context (i.e., pre-suppositions) and conceals that identity from everyone else outside that context. Likewise metaphors of exemplification. Knowing the property exemplified on an occasion depends on knowing its context: the relevant sample schema and the range of features the schema sorts. A speaker may therefore choose to use a metaphor of exemplification in order to restrict the audience to those who can identify its context. Were she to express that property with a literal expression, she would not be able to exercise the same control over its dissemination. In sum: The specifically contextual orientation of a metaphor enables it both to extend our powers of expression and to restrict the reception of their contents. That these two complement each other may be no accident.

Chapter 6

Metaphorical Character and Metaphorical Meaning

In the course of my critique in chapter 2 of Donald Davidson's use theory of meaning, I formulated a number of semantic problems involving metaphors in order to motivate the turn to metaphorical meaning. If, as I argued, one task of meaning is to (semantically) constrain the contents of possible interpretations, and we can demonstrate the need for semantic constraints on possible metaphorical interpretations, that would be an argument for the existence of metaphorical meaning. With our semantic theory in hand, we are now in a position to say more precisely how these constraints work and, thus, what we know when we know the meaning of a metaphor. We know the metaphorical character of the expression, that is, the character of the expression used, or interpreted, metaphorically (or, equivalently, the character of its underlying metaphorical expression). Like the character of an indexical, the character of the metaphor constrains its content by limiting its contextual source to actual presuppositions—even when we evaluate its truth in nonactual circumstances. As with the character of an indexical, there is also knowledge conveyed specifically at the level of metaphorical character, information or significance in addition to that conveyed by the (propositional) content of the metaphor in a context. In this chapter, I'll discuss the first of these roles of character *qua* meaning, its role in our knowledge *of* metaphor. In chapter 7, I'll address the second role, its part in our knowledge *by* metaphor.

I begin by explaining the kind of meaning with which the 'Mthat' operator equips us, by analogy to Kaplan's 'Dthat'. I next turn to the different ways we can fail to "get" a metaphor in order to sharpen our focus on what we know when we know the character of a metaphor. Of these various kinds of metaphorical *in*competence, lack of knowledge of character turns out to be a failure of understanding best described as not knowing the meaning, or semantic incompetence. Using the metaphorical character-content distinction, I then show how we can explain the data and solve the problems introduced in chapter 2. In contrast to those who take metaphor itself to be a kind of speech act, I also argue that an independent notion of metaphorical meaning is necessary precisely to account for (indirect) speech acts performed with metaphors. Finally, I'll turn to metaphors whose character does not seem to fit our model (e.g., nominative metaphors like 'the sun', referring to Juliet, in 'the sun is ascending') and to tropes other than metaphor (such as simile and irony) to raise the question of whether our semantics ought to be extended to them. Put differently, this is the question of whether there is one natural kind that subsumes all tropes and whether all figurative interpretations should be explained in one way.

I   Knowledge of 'Mthat'

Suppose a speaker S knows the metaphorical interpretation of one expression Φ but no others—and suppose that the reason is *not* that S doesn't know the relevant m-associated presuppositions for the others. Even if S's interpretation of Φ is an interpretation that would unquestionably count as metaphorical were it produced by a speaker with metaphorical competence (e.g., someone who can freely interpret expressions metaphorically), S's own interpretation of Φ is not metaphorical. Metaphorical competence involves mastery of a general skill that one can apply to arbitrary expressions across the language. More theoretically, metaphorical competence consists in knowledge of a schematic rule that applies to all expressions that admit a metaphorical interpretation.[1] This schematic rule governs the characters of all metaphorical expressions of the type 'Mthat[Φ]', for each substitution-instance of Φ. The metaphorically competent speaker knows how to generate metaphorical expressions given her knowledge of the expressions Φ to be interpreted metaphorically. So, if Φ is an expression of a syntactic category C (e.g., a one-place predicate) with an interpretation of type T (e.g., a property), she knows that 'Mthat[Φ]' will belong to the same syntactic category and have an interpretation of the same type.[2] Either one knows this schematic rule and has the general skill or one doesn't. It makes no sense to say that one could know this rule, or have this skill, for some expressions but not for others. Thus part of what the speaker knows when she knows how to interpret a metaphor Φ is not simply something about the single expression Φ. Her knowledge of metaphor is closer to knowledge of an operator, of an interpretive operation she can perform on any (literally interpreted) expression. And in this respect the character of a metaphor is more like that of the demonstrative interpretation operator 'Dthat' than of that of any individual indexical (type) such as 'I' or 'here'.

If we recall our earlier discussion of 'Dthat', however, other issues may prima facie appear to complicate the question whether 'Mthat' is an operator. Both dthat-descriptions and metaphorical expressions, we said, are attempts to construct *lexical* representations corresponding to, or encoding, *uses* (or interpretations) of language. In chapter 3, I mentioned various difficulties that arise with dthat-descriptions stemming from this shift from use or interpretation to lexical representation. On the one hand, dthat-descriptions are meant to capture directly referential interpretations of the descriptions, on the formal model of directly referential complete demonstratives (i.e., pure demonstratives like 'that' completed by extralinguistic demonstrations). That, in turn, would suggest that dthat-descriptions are syntactically and semantically simple expressions—like the individuals who are their simple propositional contents—and I mentioned two ways to cash out this suggestion. Either treat the complete dthat-description as syntactically and semantically (though perhaps not lexically) unstructured, or let 'Dthat', like 'That', be the only syntactic and semantic unit and the embedded description, simply a pragmatic "aside," in Kaplan's words, a parenthetic stage direction.

On the other hand (as I argued in ch. 3), there are various reasons to structure the character of a dthat-description as a complex built up from the character of the constituent description. First, the dthat-description is formally constructed (in Kaplan's "Logic of Demonstratives") as an operator taking the definite description as operand. Second, only if we can recover the character of the embedded description as a separable semantic entity can we account for the cognitive value of the dthat-description (and thereby solve Frege's puzzle). Third, because dthat-descriptions are directly referential but not thoroughly nondenotational, we need to acknowledge the description as a significant constituent in order to explain how the direct referent of the dthat-description is fixed in (the circumstance of) its context as a function of the denotation of the description. All these reasons argue that dthat-descriptions ought to be articulated as syntactically and semantically complex expressions.

There are, then, conflicting properties of and motivations for the dthat-description that pull us in opposite directions. However, rather than condemn the dthat-description itself as an incoherent attempt to represent lexically how we use, or interpret, nondemonstrative expressions demonstratively, we concluded in chapter 3 that (like the notion of quotation

that is beset with similar tensions) the fault more likely lies in our understanding, and theory, than in the construction itself.

Some of these difficulties plaguing dthat-descriptions do not carry over
to metaphorical expressions. Unlike dthat-descriptions, metaphorical
expressions are thoroughly nondenotational; like indexicals, they are
parametric. The contextual feature that the character of the metaphorical expression 'Mthat[Φ]' maps into its content—the context set of
m-associated presupposed properties—is not something its constituent Φ
denotes; neither are the presuppositions directly related to the *object(s)*
denoted by the expression Φ in c, or its extension. If they were, we ought
to be able to substitute a co-denoting or co-extensive expression for Φ
without affecting the truth-value of the metaphorical interpretation; but
as we saw from the failure of substitutivity arguments back in chapter 2,
that is not the case. Instead, like the parametric values of the indexicals,
the content of a metaphor is assigned or mapped from a given kind of
contextual parameter, namely, the presuppositions m-associated with the
word Φ (in c) or, more precisely, the presuppositions associated with the
character of Φ (in c). This assignment, like that of its value to a variable,
involves no *satisfaction* or *fitting* of conditions spelled out in the character
or content of the metaphor. But, unlike variables, it involves semantic
knowledge. As with the indexicals (e.g., 'now', whose relevant parameter,
the time of the context, is known by the speaker as part of his semantic
knowledge), the relevant parameter (namely, a context set of presuppositions) is semantically specified, known by the interpreter as part of his
knowledge of language. Nonetheless, because metaphorical expressions
are parametric and thoroughly nondenotational, we don't have the same
compositional motivation to acknowledge an autonomous semantic contribution by the embedded expression (via denotation) to the semantic
value of the metaphorical expression. In this respect, there isn't the
same motivation to separate off 'Mthat' as an operator from the embedded expression as operand. Although 'Mthat' lexically generates
Mthat-expressions, we can treat them as syntactically simple.

On the other hand, it should be kept in mind that the character of each
metaphorical expression of the form 'Mthat[Φ]' that results from substituting an actual expression for Φ is individuated by the character of
that constituent expression; hence each distinct expression (type) interpreted metaphorically will yield a metaphorical expression with a distinct
character. For example, the character of 'Mthat['is the sun']' is different
from that of 'Mthat['is the moon']'. Therefore, our semantic knowledge
of metaphor—the semantic knowledge represented by the schematic rule

for 'Mthat[Φ]' that underlies our ability to interpret *all* expressions metaphorically—is the same for *all* expressions we interpret metaphorically.
But because each particular metaphorical expression that is a substitution-instance of 'Mthat[Φ]' has its own respective character, the knowledge *by* metaphor that is conveyed, and individuated, by the character of
each such metaphorical expression will be distinct to it.

Despite its differences from 'Mthat', 'Dthat' furnishes us with a valuable model of how we can represent context-dependent interpretations (or
uses) of classes of expressions that are not otherwise indexical or demonstrative. This is the primary point of the parallel with 'Mthat'. So long as
we keep in mind that the content of the metaphorical expression is not
determined compositionally from the contents of its constituents, there
is no reason not to think of a metaphorical expression, like a dthat-
description, as a complex expression formed by an operation on the
constituent expression, that is, as an expression whose character is individuated by the character of its embedded expression.

II Metaphorical Incompetence[3]

One way to articulate the kind of meaning an interpreter grasps when he
knows the character of a metaphor is to identify what he *fails* to understand when he *lacks* competence in metaphorical character. We can locate
that kind of incompetence among four basic ways in which a speaker/
interpreter can fail to "get" a metaphor, four species of metaphorical *incompetence* and four correlative sources of possible disagreement among
interpreters over claims expressed metaphorically. The fourth of these is
best described as a failure to know the meaning of the metaphor.

1. Cases where we fail to recognize or identify an utterance *u* of a sentence *s* as containing an expression Φ that is to be interpreted metaphorically. This is a general failure to know-*that*-metaphor (ch. 1, sec. I), but
we might distinguish three special subcases:
A. I hear *u* but fail to recognize that it can be interpreted metaphorically,
that it has a (grammatically) possible interpretation that contains at least
one metaphorical interpretation of a constituent. Such a failure to assign *u*
any of the grammatically possible metaphorical characters in its metaphor
set borders on linguistic incompetence.
B. I hear *u*, recognize that it has a possible metaphorical interpretation
but, given what else I know about the speaker (e.g., that he is hopelessly
literal minded and never uses metaphors), I fail to recognize that this is
how *he* intended it. Therefore, I fail to interpret *u* metaphorically. Here I

rule out the possibility that u is to be, or might be, interpreted metaphorically because of my other presuppositions. This failure is not linguistic, but empirical.

C. I recognize that at least one expression in u is to be interpreted metaphorically but I do not know which one. Or perhaps I identify the wrong constituent. For example, I fail to get your metaphor because, while we both know that 'S is P' (e.g., 'the sun is smiling') is to be interpreted as a metaphor, you interpret S literally and P metaphorically while I interpret S metaphorically and P literally. This failure falls between the linguistic and extralinguistic, depending on the reason that the correct constituent is not identified.

2. Cases where we fail to know the context-set of presuppositions, and hence the content of the metaphor in its context. This is failure to grasp one kind of knowledge *by* metaphor.

Here we know *that* u is to be interpreted metaphorically. We know that it is to be assigned a metaphorical character and we know how metaphorical character works. Hence there is no linguistic incompetence. But, for whatever reason, we fail to learn the relevant presuppositions about its m-associated features that determine the content of u in that context. This failure is of extralinguistic knowledge, but we can differentiate further between cases.

Sometimes the interpreter is at a total loss to know the relevant presuppositions. Ted Cohen's late father says 'That beer is green' and I don't have the foggiest idea of what associations with 'green' and/or 'beer' are appropriate or relevant to interpreting his utterance. I can't identify the presuppositions his father is making, and I can't come up with any of my own. This is an extreme case of failure to know the context set of the metaphor, and thus failure to understand its content—though I know *that* the utterance is a metaphor.

In a second set of cases, I identify a context set of presuppositions and thereby assign u an interpretation. However, the interpretation differs from the speaker's; hence I fail to understand how *he* intends u to be understood. And where I fail to realize that our context sets differ, I fail even to realize that our interpretations differ.

This case is a frequent source of failure to get literary metaphors, where the main interpretive task is recovering the relevant presuppositions. (I won't take a position on what counts as legitimate evidence for a literary interpretation; for our purposes both extratextual beliefs and intratextual information can count as contextual information for the interpretation of a given metaphor.) But it may not always be necessary for a correct interpretation of a metaphor that I know or give the author's intended interpretation (as some schools of literary criticism tell us). It may be more important to give the most informative, interesting, illuminating interpretation possible in the context, regardless of what the author intended. To obviously different degrees, failure to do so may be counted by some as a type of failure to "get" the metaphor.

3. Cases of failure to know the truth-value of the metaphorical utterance. Here I correctly identify u as a metaphor, identify a context set of presuppositions, know a content of the metaphor in the context, but then either fail to know its truth-value (on the metaphorical interpretation) or mistake the truth-value. Many philosophers would not count this failure as a failure of understanding, but I think a case can be made that it is, especially for those metaphors whose process of interpretation has a strong constructive element. Suppose I interpret u with presuppositions that yield a metaphorical interpretation that is obviously false or absurd. Suppose the propositional interpretation is so obviously false or absurd that if it were the literal meaning of an utterance, it would be possible grounds to identify it as a metaphor. If I give the metaphor this absurd interpretation—without a collateral reason to so interpret it (because, say, of some additional information communicated by its metaphorical mode of expression)—then one might argue that I have also failed to "get" the metaphor. If I can't believe the irrational or absurd, I also can't interpret someone as expressing the irrational or absurd—or, if I so interpret someone, at least the burden of responsibility falls on me to show that I have not misinterpreted her.

4. Cases where we fail to know what metaphorical character is. In this last class of cases, we may know that some utterance is *not* to be interpreted literally but not yet know *what it is to interpret it metaphorically*; say, we do not know that a metaphor depends for its interpretation on a contextual parameter (as opposed, say, to its literal meaning), or on a particular contextual parameter (i.e., presuppositions) different from that which determines whether its content is true (i.e., the actual circumstances), or only on its actual context set of presuppositions (and not the features m-associated with the expression in a counterfactual context in whose circumstances we also want to know whether *what* the metaphor *actually* expresses is true). In these last sets of cases, we have not yet mastered the function of metaphorical character. A speaker in this position might be said to lack an "entry" for 'Mthat' in his mental lexicon. Although he knows that the utterance is not to be interpreted literally, he is in no better position to interpret it metaphorically than he would be

with respect to a string that he knows to be in a foreign language but of which he does not know a single word.

Of these cases, the incompetence exemplified by the fourth is solely due to *linguistic* incompetence; the lack of a kind of knowledge of language proper, similar to the linguistic incompetence of one who does not know that the content of (a token of) the indexical 'now' depends on its time of utterance—and on the actual time rather than, say, the time the speaker believes it to be. This fourth kind of incompetence is also best described as lack of knowledge of *meaning*, not of content or truth-conditions and not of the context, but of how one goes about interpreting a metaphor. This case of linguistic incompetence in metaphor is also especially interesting precisely because it is so hard to imagine. It asks us to conceive of a speaker who is fully competent "speaking literally," a full member of our linguistic community, but incompetent "speaking metaphorically," a radical foreigner. From the point of view of our theory that draws such a tight connection between metaphorical interpretation and other types of context-dependent interpretation (e.g., of demonstratives), it also asks us to think of a speaker who has the general repertoire for contextual interpretation (assuming that is also part of his semantic competence in the literal interpretation of his language) but who has somehow failed to realize that metaphorical interpretation is of the same ilk. Without special pleading, it is difficult to see how such a speaker could evolve.

Of the four cases, the source of most inter-interpreter disagreements—the kinds of hard-to-resolve disputes that make many philosophers skeptical about there being determinate metaphorical content—is the second, although it may often appear that the disagreement is instead over truth-value. Suppose, for example, that 'Juliet is the sun' is asserted by Romeo and denied by Paris. How can they settle their disagreement? Or, better yet, what is the *source* of their disagreement? Romeo points out Juliet's unparalleled qualities and her presence that inspires hope. Paris denies neither that these properties are true of Juliet nor that they are true of the sun. But Paris points out other properties of the sun: its remoteness or the monotonous regularity and mathematical predictability of its motion. That *those* properties are true of the sun and false of Juliet is, in turn, admitted by Romeo. There is no disagreement between them, then, over what is *true* either of the sun or of Juliet. Where they disagree is over the question: Which of these individual context sets of presupposed m-associated features ought to be adopted as the shared context set for the metaphorical interpretation of 'is the sun' on the occasion? Although they appear to disagree over the *truth-value* of the utterance, in reality their disagreement is over the *proposition* expressed. Insofar as they each hold different interpretations of the metaphor in their respective individual context sets, they are talking past one another, inhabiting different contexts, not disputing the truth-value of a single proposition expressed in a shared context. To resolve their disagreement, Romeo and Paris must first agree on a shared context set of presuppositions. Only then can they agree on the propositional content of the metaphor, and only having fixed on a common proposition can they raise the question of whether the facts make *it* true.

A good, or even just adequate, theory of metaphor should have the conceptual resources to articulate and explain the differences between these cases. But to do this, it is necessary to invoke the character-content distinction, which presupposes *a* distinction between linguistic knowledge and extralinguistic information, between meaning and the presuppositions that (jointly with the meaning) determine the content of the metaphor in its context.

III   The Interpretation vs. Evaluation of a Metaphor

The crux of our semantic theory lies in the distinction between the character and content of a metaphor or, equivalently, between the second and third of the three (or, if you wish, four) stages of metaphorical comprehension and roles of the context distinguished in chapter 2: between the interpretive role of the context, given the character of the metaphor, in generating what is said, and its evaluative role, given a content generated in a context, in determining the actual truth-value of the utterance. (For this last role of evaluation, it is the circumstances of the context that do the work, for the former role, the context set of presuppositions.) Without this distinction, there would remain no part of the speaker's knowledge of metaphorical interpretation that could count as part of his semantic competence proper, or as knowledge of metaphorical meaning.

One strategy for arguing that we should draw this distinction for metaphor is by way of the same kind of argument that requires that we distinguish character from content (and the corresponding roles of the context) for demonstratives. In their case, you'll recall, Kaplan argues for the distinction from the difficulties that result either when we simply combine contexts and circumstances in complex indices or when the rule describing the character of a demonstrative is taken as its propositional content.[4] If pointing to Romeo, I say

(1) That man might not have loved Juliet,

(1) will be true if and only if there is some counterfactual circumstance in which *Romeo*, the *actual* referent of the demonstrative in its context of utterance, does not love Juliet, not if there is some counterfactual circumstance in which whoever would be demonstrated *there* doesn't love Juliet. Likewise, if I say

(2) I might not be speaking

my utterance is true if and only if there is some counterfactual circumstance in which I, JS, am not speaking, regardless of the fact that in that circumstance I could (and would) not be fixed there as the direct referent of the indexical given its character. The character of the indexical functions only to generate its content in a context; it plays no part in the evaluation whether that content is true at any circumstance. Now, this argument is especially forceful applied to singular demonstratives and indexicals, for their context-dependent contents are the very individuals who are their direct referents. But an analogous claim holds for the properties that constitute the propositional contents of predicate demonstratives and of metaphors. The content of the predicate demonstrative and of the metaphor is always the property fixed in its context of utterance. Suppose Paris disagrees with Romeo's utterance of (3)

(3) Juliet is the sun

in *c* but concedes that

(4) Juliet might have been the sun.

(4) is true just in case there is some counterfactual circumstance w' in which Juliet has the particular set of properties P, which is the content of 'is the sun' interpreted metaphorically in its *actual* context of utterance c. Juliet must fall in the extension at w' of the relevant property P, but the relevant property P is fixed relative to c, not w'. It is not sufficient if there is some counterfactual circumstance in which Juliet possesses whatever property happens in *that* circumstance to be the content of 'is the sun' *had it been* interpreted metaphorically *there*. All that is relevant to determining whether (4) is true in its *actual* circumstance, $w(c)$, is whether Juliet has P at w', regardless of the truth-value in w' of the proposition, if any, that *would have been expressed* had the sentence been interpreted there at w'. Likewise, it matters not at all whether the denizens of w' are able to express the property using their linguistic resources—whether the prop-

erty P, fixed in c, is metaphorically expressed (or expressible) at w' by 'is the sun'.

If your intuitions agree with mine about this example, you should also agree with the following claims. Since sentences that contain metaphors, like demonstratives, express different propositional contents in different contexts, we must distinguish between the content *actually* expressed by such a sentence in its context of utterance and the content that it *would* have expressed in some other context. We must also distinguish between the truth-value of the proposition *actually* metaphorically expressed *were* it evaluated at a counterfactual circumstance and the truth-value of the proposition that *would have been* metaphorically expressed at that counterfactual circumstance. And for both metaphors and demonstratives, the *relevant* or *appropriate* propositional content—that is, the proposition asserted, to which the speaker's utterance commits him—is always that content expressed in its context of utterance, regardless of the circumstance at which we evaluate its truth.

One prima facie counterexample to these theses—and, in particular, to the thesis that a metaphor is always interpreted relative to its actual context—is the occurrence of a metaphor in counterfactual statements. The context relative to which we interpret the metaphorical expression 'Mthat['the Rolls-Royce of']' in the consequent of the subjunctive conditional, (5):

(5) If Rolls-Royce starting building really rotten cars, SONY would be the Rolls-Royce of television

cannot be its actual context of utterance, since we actually presuppose—hence the counterfactual—that a Rolls-Royce is the best car now made.[5] But, in fact, these cases can be handled nicely by our account if we make two additional (relatively innocuous) assumptions about the pragmatic analysis of conditional statements.[6]

First, assume that the antecedent of a conditional is an explicit supposition that is added (at least for the duration necessary to evaluate the consequent) to the initial context set of presuppositions. Second, assume that the subjunctive mood in English is a conventional device for indicating that prior presuppositions to the contrary are being (temporarily) suspended. Here, then, we add the presupposition that Rolls-Royce has started building rotten cars to our initial context (set) c and simultaneously "contract" c by dropping the initial presuppositions that associate features of excellence with the name 'Rolls-Royce'. Call the resulting context (set) c^*. This context, c^*, not the original (actual) context c, is now the *actual* context—the context in which the consequent of (5) occurs and is interpreted—just as our theory predicts. As we said in chapter 4, section II, the members of the context set are *pre*suppositions, not because they are presupposed *prior* to the time of the utterance, but because they are conditions required for the interpretation of the utterance.

A potentially more problematic philosophical assumption is implicit in our claim that *the* property relevant to evaluating the truth of a metaphorical sentence at an arbitrary circumstance is always *that* property actually expressed by the metaphor in its context of utterance. This claim assumes that it is possible to identify the property at counterfactual circumstances other than the actual circumstance in which it is generated. Here we might distinguish two cases. Where the property is *rigid*, always yielding the same extension at all possible circumstances, this problem reduces to that of cross-world identification of individuals (or sets of individuals). But, in the second case, where the property is not rigid and its extension itself changes over circumstances, how do we determine *the* property that is reidentified? How are such properties individuated?

It is important to distinguish semantic from metaphysical issues raised by this question. The property P that is actually expressed by one expression interpreted metaphorically may not be expressed by that very same expression interpreted metaphorically in a counterfactual circumstance w'. We might also lack a context-*in*dependent (or nonmetaphorical) expression for P that would enable *us* to express that property were we in w'. Nonetheless, even if we cannot actually *express* P except by using a predicate sensitive to its context, the semantic question of whether we can express the property at w' is independent of the metaphysical question of whether the property P exists in w'. The latter is the question whether P can be evaluated at w'. Evaluation is independent of expression.

Evaluation of a property, in turn, raises its own set of questions. Is it *meaningful* to talk of evaluating a property, or of the property "existing," at a counterfactual circumstance even if the property applies to no individual at that circumstance? Does the property itself, then, not apply (refer, denote)—hence "exist"—at that circumstance? Or is it simply the case that the thing that it purportedly applies to does not exist in that circumstance? (In the latter case, choose your favorite theory of nonreferring terms.) This issue is not specific to metaphor. Indeed it is the same problem that arises for nondenoting singular terms and, among them, nondenoting directly referential terms. So, choose your own favorite theory to handle the whole set of cases but, whatever your line on this question, keep the semantic and metaphysical issues separate. The former is our exclusive concern here.

A last set of cases that illustrates the importance of the distinction between interpretation and evaluation are metaphors that occur in the propositional attitudes, for example, belief reports and indirect discourse.[7] Because I do not have a theory of belief to propose, a full account of these cases is out of the question here. However, I would like to point out certain parallels between the behaviors of metaphors and demonstratives in these contexts; whatever ultimate account works for the latter should also work (unless proven otherwise) for the former. It would also be helpful, for a start, to distinguish two sets of questions raised by metaphors in these linguistic constructions. The first concerns the individuation of their truth-conditions; the second concerns whether their truth-conditions exhaust the information they convey: their knowledge *by* metaphor. I shall return to the second of these in chapter 7; here I'll address their truth-conditions.

Under what conditions can I truly state (6)?

(6) Romeo asserted (believes) that Juliet is the sun.

There are at least four different interpretations or readings of this sentence. On the first and perhaps least problematic reading, the metaphor in (6) is only the speaker's; the metaphor is simply his way of expressing a property in his own context (i.e., relative to his own presupposition set).[8] The speaker intends to attribute this property (as a constituent of a believed or asserted proposition) to the subject (Romeo) but without imputing that the subject would himself have expressed that property in those metaphorical terms. According to that reading:

(6a) $(\exists P) (P = \{Mthat['is the sun']\} (c_s) \& R$ asserted (believes) the proposition $\langle j, P \rangle)$

where c_s is the speaker's context (set of presuppositions), the context of utterance of (6). Apart from the fact that this involves quantification in (of the second-order quantifier), there is nothing problematic about this reading.

On the next three readings, the metaphor used is ascribed to the subject. That is, what is ascribed to Romeo is not only *what* he believes or asserted—the (propositional) content of his belief—but also *how* he believes or asserted that content, its metaphorical character.[9] Each of these three readings must also solve one problem. Because metaphorical character is nonconstant, its content will vary across context sets of presuppositions. *Whose* context is, then, the relevant context for the interpretation of metaphors in indirect discourse and the attitudes?

Two different assumptions prima facie come into tension here. On the one hand, we presume that the content expressed both in indirect discourse and in belief reports is the same as that of the subject's (reportee's, e.g., Romeo's) original utterance and belief in their respective contexts. But because that content is expressed by a (indeed the same) context-sensitive expression (such as a metaphor) with one character, the context of utterance of (6) must be that of the original utterance. On the other hand, there is also the general constraint on the interpretation of indexicals and demonstratives according to which their relevant context of interpretation—the context to which their characters apply—is *always* their context of utterance, the context of the speaker of the indirect-discourse sentence or belief report, no matter how deeply embedded the indexical or demonstrative may be.[10] The problem is to resolve, or accommodate, these prima facie incompatible desiderata.

To give an example, suppose Romeo asserts (repeated here)

(3) Juliet is the sun

whose logical form is

(3a) Juliet Mthat['is the sun'].

By disquotation and standard principles of indirect discourse and belief-reporting, I say (6), whose logical form therefore is

(6b) Romeo asserted (believes) that Juliet Mthat['is the sun'].

Both (3a) and (6b) contain a metaphorical expression with a nonconstant character. Under what conditions is (6b) true?

There is one sense of 'said' (and perhaps 'believe') according to which what is said is (only) the sentence (under an assignment of a character)—even where the sentence contains an indexical—rather than its content (in a context). So, if two politicians say 'I am the best presidential candidate', in this sense of 'say' they said the same thing. Similarly, both Romeo and Paris might be said to say the same thing when they each utter 'Juliet is the sun' despite the fact that the presuppositions they respectively associate with 'the sun' are different, even incompatible, yielding different, even incompatible, contents in their respective contexts. In general, however, this is not the relevant sense of 'said' (or 'believe') in indirect discourse or belief reports. If Russell tells Frege

(7) You are wrong

and Frege reports this fact, he cannot say

(8) Russell said (that) you are wrong.

He must say:

(9) Russell said (that) I am wrong.

Here the reporting sentence—to be a *report*—must preserve the content of the original utterance in its context. And because the content (or direct referent) of the indexical is always determined relative to its actual context of utterance, the shift in contexts, or contextual parameters for 'you' and 'I', forces a corresponding shift in the expressions used with their respective characters.

In the case of indexicals this is especially clear, for, as Frege (1984) originally noted, there are systematic rules according to which we convert and replace one indexical by another in order to preserve the content of one utterance in a different context. In the case of metaphors—despite their parametricity—there are no analogous rules that enable us mechanically to replace a metaphor with one character by another in order to preserve the content of the original across variations in the relevant contextual parameter. But, again, metaphors are not unique among context-dependent expressions in this respect. There are no fixed, mechanical rules for complete demonstratives, complex demonstratives, and dthat-descriptions that legislate how one of these should be replaced by another to preserve the original content in a different context. Yet, the same constraint applies: Their contents (e.g., direct referents) are always determined relative to their contexts of utterance, no matter how deeply embedded they are in indirect discourse or attitudinal operators. The speaker's context, not that of the subject of report, is what matters.

The only way to explicitly and unequivocally ensure that the reported utterance, preserving the original sentence uttered, is interpreted relative to the subject's or reportee's original context of utterance, is to quote it directly:

(6c) Romeo asserted (believes) (that): 'Juliet is the sun',

where what is quoted is not just an uninterpreted expression but the expression with its original interpretation. And perhaps some uses of indirect discourse border on direct discourse uses, thereby shifting the relevant context of interpretation from the context of actual utterance to the original context of the reported utterance. Bracketing these cases, however, let's return to our original question: Under what conditions will (6) be true?

The problem, as we said earlier, is that if we try to preserve both the character and content of the original reported utterance, we violate the constraint that the interpretation of the metaphorical expression, like that of indexicals and demonstratives, always cleaves to its context of utterance, the context of the speaker, not of the subject of the report. (I'll call that condition the *actual context constraint*.) So, if we analyze (6) as expressing what it presumably does, namely,

(6d) R asserted (believed) the proposition $\langle j, \{Mthat['is\ the\ sun']\}(c_r)\rangle$

where c_r is Romeo's context (set of presuppositions), not the speaker's, we violate the actual context constraint. On the other hand, if we interpret (6) as (6e)

(6e) R asserted (believed) the proposition $\langle j, \{Mthat['is\ the\ sun']\}(c_{js})\rangle$

attributing to Romeo the proposition generated by my (JS), the speaker's, presuppositions c_{js}, we respect the constraint but attribute to Romeo a proposition he may never have held, given his different presuppositions associated with the expression interpreted metaphorically.

One option lies between merely (directly) quoting the original utterance's character and generating a full-blown content that would require shifting to a context other than the actual one. I may truly report Romeo's original utterance if I merely claim that he said something, relative to his presuppositions, using the same words (with the same character). Thus (6f):

(6f) $(\exists\ P)\ (\exists\ c)\ (c = $ Romeo's context set of presuppositions and $P = \{Mthat['is\ the\ sun']\}(c)$ and R asserted (believed) the proposition $\langle j, P\rangle)$

If we want to do more, to ascribe a specific, fully determined content to Romeo, either we can preserve the original content at the expense of the character, or we can try to replicate the context c^* of the original utterance by making our (the speaker's) context of utterance c sufficiently similar to c^* in all respects relevant to determination of the content of the original utterance given its original character. On the first alternative, we abstract the content away from the context; on the second, we put ourselves in, or take the point of view of, the original context, yielding the same value for the same character.[11] Let me say a bit more about what "putting ourselves in" or "taking the point of view of" the original context might involve.

Suppose I report

(10) Shakespeare said that the world is a stage

which, in its original context of utterance (reconstructed from *As You Like It*) expressed, say, that the men and women of this world seem to follow rehearsed patterns of action throughout the course of their lives, patterns that divide into distinct parts, with beginnings and ends like the acts of a play. And suppose that I have rather different presuppositions, according to which the interpretation of the metaphor is that life and action in this world is all pretense and illusion, that humans are all vain creatures and their actions mere spectacle.

Not only do I intend to report Shakespeare's utterance, and not only do I use *his* metaphor to express its content; my use of the linguistic construction for reporting thereby commits me to using the metaphor with his intentions and presuppositions—even where that commitment requires that I suspend the presuppositions I myself would associate with that metaphor. After all, to disregard the subject's presuppositions for my own, the reporter's, would defeat the objective of giving a report. Therefore, on pain of either acting irrationally (contrary to my own desire to *report* his belief) or exposing a kind of linguistic incompetence on my part (with respect to either or both metaphor and belief reports) I must adopt the reportee's point of view. There may be an appearance that the content of the metaphor is determined relative to the context of the *subject* of the report *rather than* relative to that of the speaker, the actual context of utterance. But because the speaker must suspend the presuppositions he otherwise, by default, would hold in order to adopt the local presuppositions of his subject, in fact the metaphor is interpreted relative to its speaker's presuppositions, albeit his adopted rather than native ones; nonetheless relative to what is for the utterance its actual context. The actual context constraint is upheld.

At the same time, for a speaker to enlist presuppositions by "taking the subject's point of view" is evidently not the same as making those presuppositions himself. Taking the subject's point of view is not simply a matter of adding presuppositions to my own context set, even temporarily. Adopted presuppositions are insulated from the speaker's general context set of presuppositions. What holds according to the adopted presuppositions (say, in the circumstances that would obtain were the presuppositions true) cannot be assumed to hold according to the speaker's native presuppositions.[12] Hence, although in general we do not assert anything that contradicts the presuppositions of our prior assertions, there is nothing to prevent us from explicitly denying the adopted pre-suppositions of a belief report or indirect discourse, for example,

(11) Shakespeare said that the world is a stage, but our lives are nothing but sheer chaos.

Perhaps with metaphors in belief reports, we could also say, then, that pretense or pretending is at work in the relevant attitude of presupposition—despite our general reservations expressed in chapter 4. But note that this is not specific to metaphors in belief reports; it is true of all belief reports. We can also cancel nonmetaphorical presuppositions adopted to take the subject's point of view:

(12) Bill said that Mary's husband stopped beating her, but Mary is not married and she is a well-known masochist.

This brief discussion suggests that although adopted presuppositions are not native, they are no less actual, that is, held (if only in a slightly broader sense) in the speaker's context of utterance. Where the speaker enlists such presuppositions, it is not necessary to hold that the interpretation of the utterance shifts to a counterfactual context, a different context than that of the speaker. Therefore we can still maintain that the general features that characterize demonstratives and indexicals apply also to the interpretation and evaluation of a metaphor. Indeed the simplest explanation why metaphors cleave so closely to their contexts is that, just like demonstratives and indexicals, they are distinguished by their nonconstant character.

IV Metaphorical Meaning

The various arguments for the character-content, or interpretation-evaluation, distinction reviewed in section III constitute one way to argue for the claim that there is metaphorical meaning, that there is knowledge of meaning specific to metaphors, apart from their contents (or truth-conditions) in particular contexts. But there is also a second way to argue for metaphorical meaning. Harking back to our discussion of Davidson, one might argue that precisely because metaphors are highly context-sensitive and context-variable, they *need* meanings to constrain their possible interpretations. That is, meanings are constraints on possible contents that display their structure. The actual contents (truth-conditions) of a metaphor are never part of its meaning, and the conditions that constitute the meaning of the metaphor are never *part* of its content (truth-conditions) in any context. But the two—meaning and content—are intimately related. The task of the metaphorical meaning of (a token of) an expression is rather to constrain the possible content the expression expresses qua metaphor in a context.

For example, I argued in chapter 2 that there are constraints on the possible metaphorical interpretations that can be assigned to verb phrase anaphors jointly with their antecedents. These constraints also seem to be identical to those that apply to nonmetaphorical verb phrase anaphora, where the antecedent allows multiple interpretations but only the interpretation it is actually given can serve as the interpretation of the anaphor. Thus, recall that 'may' can be interpreted with the sense of either permission or possibility in

(13) John *may* leave tomorrow

but in

(14) John *may* leave tomorrow, and Harry, *too*

the antecedent and anaphor must both be interpreted with the same content: Either both must mean permission or both possibility. The explanation for that constraint is that in cases of anaphora the interpretation of the antecedent is copied onto the anaphor; hence, although the interpretation of the antecedent may be free, once interpreted, its anaphor will be obligatorily assigned the same interpretation.

Similarly with metaphorical antecedents and anaphors. Consider, first, the literal statement

(15) The largest blob of gases in the solar system is the sun

and the two (I shall assume) different metaphorical interpretations of 'is the sun' in (repeated)

(16) Juliet is the sun

and

(17) Achilles is the sun.

(The substantive differences between the two interpretations need not concern us, so long as there is *a* difference.) Now, consider these (unacceptable) examples of verb phrase anaphora:

(18) *The largest blob of gases in the solar system *is the sun*, and Juliet *is, too*

(19) */?Juliet *is the sun*, and Achilles *is, too*.

On our account, the explicit representations underlying (16) and (17) and their respective propositions (in their contexts) are

(16*) Juliet Mthat ['is the sun'].
          $\langle j, \{Mthat \text{ ['is the sun']}\}(c_1)\rangle$

and

(17*) Achilles Mthat ['is the sun'].
          $\langle a, \{Mthat \text{ ['is the sun']}\}(c_2)\rangle$

Although the two occurrences of 'is the sun' have the same character, they have different contents in their respective contexts. Hence the propositions expressed by the antecedents and anaphors of (18) and (19) are

(18*) 《The definite description operator$\langle$Being-a-blob-larger-than-any-other ...$\rangle$》, Being-the-sun$\rangle$&$\langle j, \{Mthat \text{ ['is the sun']}\}(c_1)\rangle$》

(19*) 《$j, \{Mthat \text{ ['is the sun']}\}(c_1)\rangle$&$\langle a, \{Mthat \text{ ['is the sun']}\}(c_2)\rangle$》

We can now explain why (18) and (19) are unacceptable, although (18) is still worse than (19). In (18) the purported antecedent and anaphor are expressions with different characters; failing to stand in an anaphoric relation, the "meaning," or character, of the first cannot be copied onto the second. In (19) the antecedent and anaphor do have the same character but have different contents; hence, as marked, they must occur in different contexts. This raises two problems. First, in utterances like (19), the statement must "shift" contexts in the course of its interpretation, splitting itself between two contexts. This is at odds with a general assumption that complete sentences are always interpreted relative to a single context. For the same reason, (20) will be unacceptable where each conjunct has the same interpretation it would have in isolation.

(20) *Juliet is the sun and Achilles is the sun.

Here too we must assume that the interpretation of the string as a whole requires context-shifting midway. Second, the character of the antecedent, but not its content, can be copied onto the anaphor, suggesting that only where there is full identity of character *and* content can the copying that underlies anaphora completely work. Where there is less than complete identity between character and content, the interpretation of the anaphor is blocked, rendering the result unacceptable (at least to a degree).

To explain these constraints on interpretation, it is necessary, then, to appeal to the notions of character and content. Since the differences in interpretation clearly make a difference to the truth-values of the sentences, the constraints are semantic. And if meaning is what captures semantic constraints, this is to say that there is meaning specific to the metaphorical interpretations of metaphors.

A similar explanation applies to the failure of substitutivity discussed in chapter 2. Suppose that Romeo utters (to repeat)

(21) Juliet is the sun

in a context c in which 'is the sun' is interpreted metaphorically to express the property P of being unequaled by one's peers. Suppose also that (21), so interpreted, is true in the circumstance of its context, namely, the actual world, $w(c)$. But

(22) The largest gaseous blob in the solar system is identical with the sun

interpreted literally, is also true in $w(c)$. Yet, from (21) and (22) it does not follow that

(23) Juliet is the largest gaseous blob in the solar system

will be true in $w(c)$ even if 'is the largest gaseous blob in the solar system' is interpreted metaphorically (to say, e.g., that she is liable to explode at any moment).

Here the explicit representation underlying (21) is more precisely

(21*) Juliet Mthat ['is the sun'].

The representation underlying (22) is the same as its surface form, but (23), like (21), ought to be represented as

(23*) Juliet Mthat['is the largest gaseous blob in the solar system'].

Thus (21*) and (23*) involve different (though homonymous) expressions than (22)—that is, expressions with different characters, and what is necessary for substitutivity is that the substituted and substituting expressions be *both* character- and content-equivalent. It should also now be clear why, as I first conjectured in chapter 2, one might be tempted to propose that the explanation for the failure of substitutivity is something like a fallacy of equivocation. However, as I also argued in chapter 2, the metaphorical interpretation of an expression is not just an additional sense of a polysemous expression. Nor does metaphor fit neatly into the received typologies of ambiguity. The proposed analysis of metaphorical interpretation in terms of character, or meaning, and content explains why.

Finally, the character-content distinction provides an elegant solution to a classical problem about metaphorical meaning. Most of us (unless we are philosophers with jaded conceptions of truth) share the intuition (or act as if it is the case) that utterances of declarative sentences containing metaphors are truth-valued. When two people argue over a claim expressed by a sentence containing a metaphor, one of them is correct, the other incorrect; there is a "fact of the matter" (at least as much as with literally interpreted sentences) to which metaphorical statements are accountable. So, for example, when Paris disagrees with Romeo's utterance 'Juliet is the sun', they are disputing the *truth* of Romeo's statement. (Which is not to say that they could not *also* be disputing the value of expressing that claim by way of that metaphor, as I'll argue in ch. 7. However, that dispute is *additional* to their disagreement over the truth of the claim.) The classical problem this intuition raises is this: *What* is it in these utterances of metaphor that is true or false? If metaphors are truth-valued, what is the vehicle that bears their truth-value?

The most obvious candidate is the sentence. But if we individuate a sentence by its "meaning" (i.e., those aspects of its interpretation that are a function of its linguistic form), the relevant truth-bearer cannot be the sentence unless we also specify its meaning or, more precisely, *which* meaning it has on that occasion. It clearly cannot be the sentence with its literal meaning because many metaphors are, as a matter of fact, literally false but metaphorically true. Hence taking the literal sentence as vehicle yields the wrong truth-value.

The truth-vehicle also cannot be the sentence with its metaphorical meaning. First, as in the literal case, the same sentence with one metaphorical meaning can express different contents with different truth-values in different contexts. Hence it would be necessary first to specify the relevant context. Second, this candidate raises a slew of difficulties having to do with shift and change of meaning. If the claim assumes that the metaphorical interpretation (or use) of the sentence is *the* meaning of the sentence, that its metaphorical meaning is the only meaning of the sentence—hence, that it "loses" its literal meaning as it "gains" the metaphorical one—then the claim is at best highly implausible. If that is the case, every time a speaker uses a word metaphorically to express something other than its literal meaning, the word would change its *meaning*. (Deconstructionists may indeed hold a view like this, but such a vacuous notion of meaning has no explanatory power.) Furthermore, if the metaphor loses its literal meaning, we have lost the means to explain—except historically or diachronically—how the metaphorical interpretation *depends* on the literal meaning of the word, a relation central to our idea of metaphorical meaning/interpretation. If the metaphorical interpretation of an expression Φ depends (synchronically) on its literal meaning, Φ must "have" (in some sense) that literal meaning even while it is interpreted metaphorically. But if the sentence "has" its literal meaning, we are back at our original problem of identifying the relevant truth-vehicle.

We need something, then, to serve as the truth-vehicle for metaphors, and none of the usual candidates will do. One philosopher who appreciates the difficulty is Robert Fogelin, who wonders "how it could be possible for an utterance to be false when taken literally, but true when taken metaphorically without there being any shift of meaning from the one reading to the other" (1988, 91). In reply, he

first note[s] that parallel situations arise with non-figurative language. If I say "I am James Jones," and James Jones says "I am James Jones," then, unless I happen to be named James Jones, what I say is false and what he says is true, even though there is no shift in the meanings of the words used. Less controversially, and closer to the present case, if 'x is good' means something like 'x satisfies relevant standards of evaluation,' then saying that x is good could be true in some contexts, but not in others, without there being any shift in the meaning of what is said. This, it seems to me, is how likeness claims—both literal and figurative—function: what they say is that one thing is like another, and whether that's true or not will depend upon canons of similarity determined by the context.[13]

There is much in this passage on the mark: the analogy with indexicals, the implicit relativization of the attributive adjective 'good' to a reference class, the context-dependence of similarity judgments. But it is difficult to see how Fogelin puts these ingredients together to solve the problem with which he started: the problem of identifying the truth-bearer—sentence, meaning, or whatever—of sentences containing metaphors. Fogelin's claim is that "a metaphorical utterance of the form 'A is a Φ' just means, and literally means, that A is like a Φ"; yet both the metaphor and its corresponding elliptical simile can be true in one context and not another, not because their meaning changes, but because the "modes of relevance and evaluation governing the likeness claim" (ibid., 75–76) shift.

Now, as I argued in chapter 5, similarity judgments (that depend on criteria like salience) are context-dependent. But it does not solve the original problem of the identity of the truth-bearer to say that the "canons of similarity" shift from context to context. The truth-bearers are obviously not the canons themselves. Nor is the problem solved by the suggested parallel to sentences of the form 'x is good'. Even if the semantics of the latter were analogous to that of metaphor, there would remain the same question about the identity of the truth-vehicle for utterances of sentences of that form.[14] Finally, because the modes of evaluation of the *truth* of likeness claims shift across circumstances (including the circumstances of contexts of utterance), it also cannot be the corresponding likeness sentence '*A* is like a Φ' with its invariant meaning but shifting "modes of relevance and evaluation" that is the truth-bearer for the metaphorical statement '*A* is a Φ'. Such an explanation, once again, runs afoul of the distinction between contexts of interpretation and circumstances of evaluation. Contrast the following modal metaphorical and likeness sentences whose respective evaluations make reference to alternative circumstances, circumstances distinct from those of the contexts in which their respective interpretations are generated. If (as Fogelin claims) '*A* is a Φ' (where Φ is interpreted metaphorically) means that A is like a Φ, it follows that '*A* might be a Φ' (where Φ is interpreted metaphorically) should just mean that *A* might be like a Φ. But '*A* might be a Φ' uttered in *c* is true in *c* just in case there is some alternative world or context *c'* in which *A* has whatever property is expressed by Φ *in c* (say, the way in which *A* is like Φ *in c*). In contrast, the sentence '*A* might be like a Φ' is true uttered *in c* just in case there is some world or context *c'* in which *A* has whatever property in virtue of which it is like Φ *in c'*. Here the metaphor and its respective likeness-statement clearly have different truth-conditions, a difference that emerges only when we separate (as in these modal linguistic contexts) the tasks of interpretation and evaluation.

Fogelin's own conclusion notwithstanding, it is in fact his first parallel, to indexical sentences, that is "less controversial ... and much closer" to metaphor. Furthermore, I would conjecture that Fogelin correctly sees what needs to be argued in order to solve the dilemma he raises, but lacking adequate semantic distinctions—in particular, something like the character-content distinction—he cannot articulate the solution.[15] Just as the *meaning* of the indexical sentence 'I am James Jones' does not change when it is spoken truly by Jones and spoken falsely by me, so with metaphors. But what that shows is that there must be a distinct truth-bearer, "what is said," that is neither a meaning nor a sentence. In other words, we must distinguish the propositional content of the indexical or metaphor—which is the truth-bearer—from its character; we must distinguish what is evaluated from what determines the interpretation.

Only if we distinguish the different elements—context (or contextual parameter, e.g., similarity- or salience-presuppositions), character, and content—can we adequately solve the problem of the identity of the truth-bearer for metaphors. The explanation on my account of how it is possible for an utterance to be false when taken literally and true when taken metaphorically *without a shift of meaning* is straightforward: The different truth-values are a function of the different contents of the utterances (in their respective contexts), and contents are not meanings. Characters are meanings. As with indexicals, one meaning/character of a context-sensitive expression can determine different contents in different contexts, and the same content can be determined even in the same context by different meanings/characters. Hence a difference in content does not entail a difference in the meanings/characters of the utterances.[16] On the other hand, on my account Romeo's utterance of 'Juliet is the sun' does have a *different* meaning on its metaphorical interpretation (under which it is true) than it has on its literal interpretation (under which it is false). But it would be misleading to describe this difference as a *shift* in the meaning of a single expression (type). The type 'is the sun' (the type the utterance would be assigned were it interpreted literally) itself undergoes no *change* of meaning; it retains the (literal) meaning/character it always had. What is different is that, when the utterance is interpreted metaphorically, it, the utterance, is *assigned to a different type*, namely, the type of the metaphorical expression 'Mthat['is the sun']' whose character/meaning is different from that of 'is the sun'. What changes is not the character of the expression 'is the sun' but the expression to be identified with the words 'is the sun'—although, with difference in expression (type), there is also a corresponding difference in character.

I can also now explain how, according to my account, the metaphorical *depends* on the literal. I have already argued that neither the content nor extension (in its context) of the metaphorical expression 'Mthat[Φ]' is determined compositionally from the content or extension (in its context), respectively, of its constituent Φ. Metaphorical expressions, like indexicals, are parametric. Yet, notwithstanding the fact that they are semantically simple, they may be lexically complex. The characters of 'Mthat['is the sun']' and 'is the sun' are different, but the former is "built up" from the latter. Metaphorical expressions are individuated by the characters of their constituent expressions, and the relevant presuppositions are those m-associated with their literal vehicles, the component expressions under their literal characters/meanings. Therefore, there is a *change* of character when a word is interpreted metaphorically rather than literally, but the vehicle interpreted metaphorically synchronically *retains* the literal meaning on which its metaphorical meaning, or interpretation, *depends*. This way in which the metaphor still *has* its literal meaning should not be taken to mean (contra Davidson, as I argued in ch. 2) that the vehicle is *used* literally, that is, interpreted and understood with that literal meaning. Although the literal meaning of the vehicle plays a role in *determining*, and individuating, the character of the expression under its metaphorical interpretation, the vehicle is not itself understood, or interpreted, literally on the occasion of its metaphorical interpretation or use. If it were, then we should also say that the literal *sentence*, say, 'Juliet is the sun' is understood, or interpreted, literally on the occasion. But, as I argued (in ch. 2, sec. III) following Margalit-Goldlum and White, it is far from clear that we have an *understanding* of this literally interpreted *sentence*, that we know under what conditions it would be true. The difference in question—between the vehicle having its literal meaning and being understood, or interpreted, literally—is marked in my formal construction of metaphorical expressions in which, it should be noted, the vehicle, or word interpreted literally (the operand), occurs in single quotes, metalinguistically. This is not Tarski/Quine-quotation (in which there is no internal structure to the complete quotation and what is mentioned is an uninterpreted word); think of this kind of quotation as *displaying* its value, which is identical to the word-token (with its literal meaning) occurring in the metaphorical expression.[17] Even while it is not being *used* literally, that value *has* its literal meaning, which is necessary to determine, or individuate, the character of the complete metaphorical expression. It is this special intermediate standing of the literal—according to which the metaphorical depends on the literal—that we sought to capture in chapter 2. The same standing is, I believe, what some authors are attempting to pin down when they describe a "metalinguistic" aspect of metaphor in which we attend to the literal meaning of the word.[18] But it is only with the character-content distinction that we can clearly articulate the idea.

V Metaphor and Indirect Speech Acts

Yet another way to argue for the character-content distinction and the claim that a metaphor's meaning is its character is through an analysis of indirect speech acts performed by utterances containing metaphors. Suppose, for example, that one Trojan warns another to flee the battlefield by saying 'the sun is blazing today', with the content that Achilles is furiously angry. Or suppose I say: 'this room is an icebox' on a wintry morning in order to ask you to close an open window. How should we account for the *meaning(s)* of these utterances?

On the standard explanation, the meaning of an utterance as an indirect speech act is a kind of speaker's meaning—what the speaker means by uttering the words or sentence—which is communicated in *addition* to (although clearly related to) its sentence meaning—what the words or sentence means. Furthermore, in most cases the sentence meaning is its literal meaning. For example, when I say 'can you please pass the salt', I am not asking a question about your ability but making a request; nonetheless the sentence uttered retains its literal meaning, which is supplemented by the meaning of the request. In John Searle's (1993) words: in indirect speech acts, "the speaker means what he says but he means something more as well. Thus an utterance meaning includes sentence meaning, but extends beyond it" (110). With metaphors, however, the story is more complicated. According to most use or speech act theorists like Searle (as we saw in ch. 2, sec. I), metaphorical meaning is also a variety of speaker's meaning.[19] The speaker says S is P (whose sentence meaning is that S is P), but he metaphorically means (as its utterance meaning) that S is R, where R is related to P by one of the variety of "principles" we reviewed back in chapter 2. What is the relation between these two kinds of utterance or speaker's meaning when a metaphor is used to perform an indirect speech act?

Commenting on Searle's analysis, Robert Fogelin notes that it is one question whether an utterance is to be interpreted literally or not; it is another question whether the speaker's utterance meaning (or the "point of the utterance") is "exhausted" by the sentence meaning or whether the utterance meaning contains more. Fogelin calls any speech act performed with a sentence whose meaning is only, or exclusively, (determined by) the sentence meaning *direct*. A speech act whose (utterance) meaning is not exclusively determined by its sentence meaning is *indirect*. Since the literal/nonliteral and direct/indirect distinctions cross-classify, we can now distinguish four possible types of speech acts. Fogelin (1988, 39) suggests the following examples:

i. Literal direct: "Saying 'the cat is on the mat' just [i.e., exclusively] meaning that the cat is on the mat."
ii. Nonliteral direct: "Reciting nonsense poetry."
iii. Literal indirect act: "Saying 'this hike is longer than I remember" meaning (primarily but not exclusively) that I need a rest."
iv. Nonliteral indirect: "Saying 'You're a real friend,' meaning you're a louse."

Examples (i) and (iii) are unproblematic. However, (ii) and (iv), the two cases of nonliteral interpretation, bring our difficulty to the fore. Fogelin (ibid.) argues that irony falls in (iv) because "the speaker expects the respondent to reject the actual utterance and replace it with another that corrects it or modifies it in certain ways." He claims that Searle would also locate metaphor in this category. Metaphorical meaning is utterance rather than sentence meaning and "we typically mean more than what we actually say and it is this 'more' that really matters." Fogelin himself, however, claims that metaphor falls under (iii) because, on his comparativist theory of metaphor, the sentence is "intended literally" but "the point is largely indirect."

Suppose that I utter the sentence 'this hike is longer than I remember' to a colleague after making my way, for the nth time in as many years of job searches, through a tall pile of job applications. Here 'hike' is interpreted metaphorically, but the primary (if not exclusive) "point" of the utterance, as with its literal interpretation in (iii), is that I need a rest. It is difficult to know how Fogelin would (or could) classify this utterance. If he takes it to be literal—as a comparison between hikes and the process of reading job applications—he has lost the means to capture a significant difference between the cited example in (iii) and our example, namely, the difference between the metaphorical and the literal. Likewise, although Searle would place our example in (iv), his reason would be that *all* utterances of metaphors fall in that category. He cannot account for the difference between this use of the metaphor to perform a genuine indirect speech act and uses of metaphors that are direct—that exclusively assert their metaphorical content.

An analogous problem arises, on Searle's and Fogelin's accounts, for the treatment of nonsense poetry. Searle does not explicitly comment on this case, and it is not clear what he would say. However, Fogelin explains that he classifies it under (ii), the nonliteral direct, despite the fact that his

first (wrong) instinct was that nothing could fall in this category, for if someone intentionally utters something without meaning it literally, then it would seem that there must be something *else* he is literally trying to get across, else why produce an utterance at all? Nonsense poetry is a counterexample to this claim. (1988, 40)

Notice, to begin with, that Fogelin shifts from talking of "meaning [an utterance] literally" to "literally trying to get [something else] across." It is not clear what he means by the latter phrase, but I assume that the sorts of things we "try to get across" with utterances, apart from expressing (asserting?) their meanings or contents (their locutions), are their illocutionary and perlocutionary effects. Those are neither literal nor nonliteral.

What is more significant is Fogelin's "first (wrong) instinct" to which he refers in the above passage. Presumably the explanation for his instinct is that he (and, for that matter, Searle) assumes that all sentence meaning is literal meaning and that the literal meaning of a sentence is its truth-condition (relativized to a context). Therefore, where a sentence is transparently false (e.g., a category mistake), it is difficult to imagine that a rational competent speaker could intentionally utter it directly, that is, exclusively and exhaustively, to mean by the words used what, and only what, the words themselves mean. But this is difficult to imagine only because he assumes that the only sentence meaning is literal meaning. Once we acknowledge the character-content distinction, and allow for metaphorical character as the meaning of a metaphorical expression, there is no difficulty finding nonliteral (e.g., metaphorical) direct utterances. Romeo's utterance of 'Juliet is the sun' is one of them. Its sentence meaning is the character, or (metaphorical) meaning, of 'Juliet Mthat['is the sun']'. And Romeo wants simply to assert that meaning or, more precisely, its content in its context without *doing* anything further with his utterance. Similarly, to return to the fourth class of cases, with the character-content distinction we can give, and explain, genuine cases of indirect nonliteral acts. Leaving aside irony, our earlier examples 'the sun is blazing today' and 'this room is an icebox' are nonliterally interpreted utterances whose point is not to assert their content or truth-conditions (as determined by their metaphorical character/meaning) but to "get across something else," a warning and a request, respectively.

In sum, with a richer semantics for metaphors—one that captures the character-content distinction and identifies their characters with their meaning—we can not only represent their proper truth-vehicle but also account for the speech acts we perform with them.[20]

VI Nominative Metaphors

Metaphors like

(24) The sun is furious

whose subject term 'the sun', in nominative position, metaphorically refers to Achilles prima facie pose an additional problem for my notion of metaphorical character. In the case of a predicative metaphor Φ, its content (in a context) is the value of the character of its underlying metaphorical expression 'Mthat[Φ]' in the context, namely, a set of properties. But if *all* metaphorical characters are functions from context sets of presuppositions to sets of properties, the character of the nominative metaphor 'the sun' in (24)—whose value in its context is the *individual* Achilles, not a set of properties, indeed not even a set of properties uniquely satisfied by Achilles—will not be metaphorical. On the other hand, if the character of 'the sun' in (24) is a function from the context to an individual, it is not clear how to represent the fact that it is also a mode of metaphorical reference—rather than, say, simply a Donnellan-like referential definite description in which the speaker succeeds in referring to someone even though the referent does not satisfy its denoting conditions.[21] Somehow we need to capture both facts: that the nominative term is metaphorical and that its content is an individual. How can we accomplish this?

To sketch a solution to this problem, let me first review some basics about nominative terms. When I utter

(25) The prime minister of Israel in 1998 was a former furniture salesman

I presuppose that Israel had a unique prime minister in 1998, and I assert that he was a former furniture salesman. But (25) is ambiguous or, more precisely, can be used in either of two ways, and the same ambiguity carries over to the presupposition. The subject term 'the prime minister of Israel in 1998' can contribute as its content to both the presupposition and assertion *either* a denotational conceptual complex, namely, the complex consisting of the one and only one individual with the unique property of being prime minister of Israel in 1998, *or* the actual individual who in its context was the prime minister of Israel in 1998, call him, Bibi (b). Thus the content of (25) (ignoring tense) can be either the general (or purely conceptualized) proposition

(25a) $\langle$The $P, F\rangle$

(where P and F are properties) or the singular proposition

(25b) $\langle b, F\rangle$.

Likewise, an utterance of (25) will *either*

(i) presuppose that there exists a unique P and assert that he is F

or

(ii) presuppose that b exists and assert that b is F.

If we use 'Dthat' to generate directly referential terms from otherwise general definite descriptions, we might also represent the ambiguity in terms of the different surface subject terms 'The prime minister of Israel' and 'Dthat['The prime minister of Israel']'.

Apart from this semantic distinction, there is a second pragmatic distinction with which it intersects (and with which it is sometimes confused):

the distinction between terms (either denotational or directly referential) used teleologically (or *referentially*, in Donnellan's sense), with a particular individual in mind to whom we use the term to refer, and those used nonteleologically (or *attributively*), to refer to whoever fits the descriptive conditions of the term or whoever turns out to be referred to (e.g., whoever is the historical or causal source of the term). It is worth emphasizing that the denotational–directly referential distinction cross-classifies with the teleological-nonteleological one: Both general descriptions and directly referential terms like dthat-descriptions can be used teleologically, with someone in mind, or nonteleologically, to refer to whoever it is to whom the term refers.[22]

With this background, let's return to nominative metaphors. To begin with, if we distinguish between teleological and nonteleological metaphors, then (contrary to what I said in setting up the problem) perhaps we should allow for propositions like those generated by (24), which contain as their constituent for the nominative metaphor a conceptual complex whose properties, or descriptive conditions, are those expressed metaphorically. For example, one might use 'the sun' to refer to *whoever* turns out to have (uniquely) those properties it metaphorically expresses. On this use, (24) would mean something like

(24a) The sun, whoever it/he/she may be, is furious.

We might represent the proposition it expresses as:

(24b) $\langle$ The S^*, $F \rangle$,

whose constituents are all properties and logical expressions, and S^* stands for the properties metaphorically expressed by 'the sun' (*not* including the literally expressed property of being the sun). That use of (24) can, in turn, be contrasted with its metaphorical but teleological use

(24c) $\langle a, F \rangle$,

where a is the individual Achilles (even if Achilles is the individual who uniquely satisfies S^* in the context). (24b) raises no problems beyond those raised by predicative metaphors. Our problem cases are exemplified by (24c). It is not clear how we can semantically represent the metaphorical character of 'the sun' while also allowing Achilles to be its propositional content.

Here are two possible solutions. The first rests on the assertion-presupposition distinction. When I utter (24), I presuppose that there exists a unique sun and that he is furious. Or, more accurately, I presuppose that there exists a unique thing that has the properties that are the content of 'Mthat['is the sun']' in c, and I assert that it/he/she is furious. Here the content of my *assertion* is the singular proposition (24c), which does not reflect its metaphorical mode of expression. However, the assertion *presupposes* a proposition whose representation does convey its metaphorical mode of expression:

(24d) ⟨There is exactly one thing that possesses {Mthat['is the sun']}(c)⟩

A second solution employs a dthat-description. On this proposal, the logical form of the sentence that generates (24c) is

(24e) Dthat['The x: x Mthat['is the sun']'] is furious.

Here we first determine the content (and, assuming the sentence contains no other indexical elements, thereby recover the metaphorical character) of the constituent-denoting description whose uniquely denoting descriptive conditions are the properties metaphorically expressed by 'is the sun'. We then let the individual uniquely denoted by those conditions in the context of utterance be the propositional constituent for the containing dthat-description.

Both of these proposals apply not only to definite descriptions but also to proper names interpreted metaphorically in nominative position. We can represent the metaphorical character of

(26) Khomeini is coming

where we refer with the proper name to the Dean, either as a predicative metaphor in the sentence expressing its presupposition

(26a) There exists an x such that x {Mthat['is a Khomeini']}(c)

or as part of a dthat-description

(26b) Dthat['The x: x Mthat['is a Khomeini']'].

Finally, on both proposals, the metaphorical content (a set of properties) of the nominative metaphor 'the sun' is not itself an immediate constituent of the content asserted by (24). But it has a place in the full explanation of its semantics. On the first alternative, we *make* the presupposition that contains the metaphorical content as an immediate constituent in the course of our assertion. And in making the presupposition, we *communicate* the specifically metaphorical character-istic information. On the second alternative, the character of the assertion is built up from the metaphorical character, again giving it a place in the communication. On both proposals, it might be added, predicative metaphors play a role explanatorily prior to that of nominative metaphors. We explain the semantics of metaphors in nominative position in terms of the "same metaphors" in predicative positions. If either of the two proposed solutions is on the right track, predicative metaphors are, then, the more basic construction in terms of which the other is to be explained.[23]

VII Metaphor and Simile

Given the proposed semantic theory of metaphor, the next question is whether the same account applies to all kinds of nonliteral interpretation, including simile, irony, metonymy, synecdoche, meiosis, and understatement. *Can* and *should* we treat all these varieties of figuration as instances of one kind of context-dependent semantic interpretation, which depends on sets of presuppositions that differ from each other only in their respective contents? Should we invent cousins of 'Mthat' for each of these tropes?

I will divide this question into two. In this section I'll address the special relation between metaphor and simile; in the next section, I'll turn to the more general question of whether metaphor is representative of a single natural kind of figures.

The history of the relationship between metaphor and simile goes back at least as far as Aristotle: "The simile also is a metaphor; the difference is but slight" (*Rhetoric* 1406[b]20). Note that Aristotle does not say that metaphors are similes, or statements of comparison, but that similes are metaphors.[24] As I said in chapter 5, this way of putting their relation is just right—and I shall return to it. But most recent authors who have appealed to the authority of Aristotle (or criticized him) have taken him to hold the inverted thesis, that metaphors are (elliptic) similes or comparison statements. In turn, they interpret Aristotle's claim to mean either that the *metaphorical* meaning of statements of the form '*a* is (an) *F*' is the *literal* meaning of corresponding statements of the form '*a* is like (an) *F*', or (on a more sophisticated reading) that the literal meaning of the metaphor is the literal meaning of the simile or comparison statement *and* the figurative meaning of the metaphor is the same as the figurative meaning of the corresponding simile or comparison statement.[25]

In evaluating the claim that metaphors are (elliptic) similes, let's remind ourselves of the three theses distinguished in chapter 5, section I:

(i) Similarity- and comparison-judgments play a significant, if not essential, role in metaphorical interpretation.

(ii) Metaphors and similes differ only by the occurrence in the latter of the (superficial) 'like'.[26]

(iii) Metaphors (i.e., utterances of declarative sentences containing at least one metaphor) "assert" similarities.

As I argued in chapter 5, thesis (i) contains an important grain of truth even if it is not the whole truth, but, in any case, it does not follow, contra (iii), that metaphors *assert* similarities. The similarity judgments are part of the *context* of the metaphor—the subject matter of the relevant presuppositions about the relevant properties related to the word used metaphorically—rather than its *content*. The corresponding constituent of the *content* is simply a set of properties, not the similarity relation in virtue of which those properties were singled out or identified.[27]

What of thesis (ii)? The surface grammatical form of a metaphor '*a* is (an) *F*' is that of a one-place predication in which we say something (expressed by the predicate) about something (the referent of the subject term). It is not a two-place relation as the comparativist holds, and, without compelling evidence, there is no reason to say that the underlying logical form of the metaphor is different from its surface structure. Nonetheless we can endorse (ii), so long as we understand it as saying not that metaphors are (elliptic) similes, but that similes are metaphorical predications and that they should be explained on the model of metaphorical predications. If the 'like' of the simile is grammatically superficial, similes, like metaphors, have (one-place) predicative structures in which the predicate is interpreted metaphorically. As Goodman (1976) puts it: "Instead of metaphor reducing to simile, simile reduces to metaphor; or rather, the difference between simile and metaphor is negligible" (77–78).

This also enables us to explain the observation (noted in ch. 5) made by the psychologists Glucksberg and Keysar (1990) that it is always possible to "transform" a nonliteral comparison or simile (e.g., 'my kid's bedroom is like a war zone') into a metaphor ('my kid's bedroom is a war zone'), unlike literal comparisons (e.g., 'my kid's bedroom is like the kitchen'), which cannot be so transformed (*'my kid's bedroom is the kitchen'). The reason is that the literal comparison statement really is a two-place relational statement; but the logical form of the simile is that of a one-place predication. The 'like' may be rhetorically or even grammatically effective, but it is not semantically significant.

Why might one think that semantically metaphors are similes or comparison statements? Sophisticated comparativists like Fogelin begin with the correct assumption that similarity plays a central role in working out (some) metaphorical interpretations, from which they then infer (a) that metaphors *assert* similarities as their propositional content, and (b) that beneath the surface structure of the one-place metaphorical predication there lies a relational statement that would be explicitly expressed by a simile. Hence metaphors are "elliptic similes." But this story fails for at least two reasons. First, as Fogelin himself notes, it is not the literal meaning of, or literal similarity expressed by, the simile that expresses the figurative meaning, or figurative similarity, expressed by the metaphor; rather it is the figurative meaning of the simile. Furthermore, the figurative meanings of the metaphor and simile are also assumed (e.g., by Fogelin) to be of one kind. But if so, the claim that metaphors are elliptic similes does not *explain* the figurative meaning of the metaphor, say, in terms of something nonmetaphorical or even in terms of something of a different semantic kind. The analysis merely pushes the problem of explanation one step back. Second, if the simile is the logically prior of the two, and if the metaphor really expresses a (figurative) similarity relation, some explanation must be given for the fact that the relational 'like' is *not* realized in the surface structure of the metaphor. Fogelin argues that the metaphor is "elliptic" for the simile containing the overt 'like', "elliptic" in the same sense in which (28) in reply to (27) in the following exchange is elliptic:

(27) Are you coming?

(28) In a little while.

Here (28) is "understood" as and thus elliptical for

(29) I shall come in a little while.

However, this parallel is not sufficient to make the metaphor/simile case. For examples like (28), there is syntactic evidence for the presence of the phrase 'I shall come' in its underlying structure and evidence that it is deleted in the surface structure. There is no analogous evidence that 'like' is really present in the underlying structure of a metaphor. Contrast

(30) Mary is coming now, and Jane in a little while

in which the deleted or copied verb 'is coming' is understood, with

?(31) Mary is like the moon, Jane (is) like the stars, and Juliet is the sun.

Here there is no evidence that the last clause is "understood"—cannot be interpreted except—as containing an unrealized 'like' and therefore contains an elliptic 'like', as does

(32) Mary is like the moon, Jane like the stars, and Juliet the sun.

Likewise, there is nothing incoherent about saying

(33) Juliet is not like the sun, she is the sun

in which the predicate is interpreted metaphorically in both clauses. However, on the elliptic simile view, this statement is elliptic for

(34) Juliet is not like the sun, she is like the sun

which is self-contradictory. On my view, that similes are metaphors, (33) is not incoherent. Semantically, 'is the sun' and 'is like the sun' express the same content (in the same contexts) but they differ rhetorically or pragmatically. As many authors suggest, a simile is less direct and forceful than its corresponding metaphor. The reason is not that the one is "shorter" or more concise than the other, but that 'like' functions as a hedge, or qualifier, on the content. What is denied in the first clause is the qualification, not the content simpliciter, which in turn is affirmed with emphasis in the second clause. Both clauses, however, are interpreted metaphorically.[28]

VIII   Is There One Natural Kind of Trope?

Let me now return to our opening question in the previous section. Are metaphor, irony, simile, metonymy, and the rest of the tropes all members of one natural kind of nonliteral interpretation or figuration?[29] If they are, then if a given analysis works for one member of the kind, it ought to work for all—and failure to do so would ipso facto count as evidence against the analysis, even for the case where it does prima facie apply.

The issue whether there is one natural class of figures is also important for another reason. It motivates a further argument in the literature for the view that metaphor is an illocutionary act or force, a kind of use that falls under pragmatics rather than semantics. For if metaphor and, say, irony are figures of one stripe, they both ought to be explained by one kind of account. Now, whatever controversy surrounds the status of metaphorical meaning, the ironic "meaning" of an utterance is surely not a semantic meaning. If my wife comes home on the day on which I was supposed to cook dinner, finds me working at the computer, the raw chicken still in the freezer, and says, "I could smell the aroma of roast chicken blocks away," its semantic meaning is what the sentence carries on its literal sleeve. It is not (solely) in virtue of our semantic knowledge that we understand her utterance to mean that raw chicken does not make a meal or that I have been utterly derelict in my duties. Nor are we even tempted to posit an ironic meaning in the utterance in addition to the ordinary literal meanings of the words used. However the ironic interpretation is explained, it is a function not of the speaker's semantic knowledge but of his use of his words to say more than they mean in virtue of their force or illocutionary capacity. Assuming it is one of a kind with irony, a similar story is then taken to apply to metaphor. Had my wife said instead: "You run on an Italian train schedule," it would be no part of our semantic knowledge but a matter of the force or illocutionary capacity of the utterance that would tell us that what she said is that I am unreliable and always late. Thus, given this natural classification of the figures, it is widely believed that their common account would be a theory of use or pragmatics.

Whatever turns out to be the correct explanation of irony—whose full account lies beyond the scope of this book—what primarily concerns us is the step from irony to metaphor. Let's grant for the sake of argument that irony is a kind of force (whether or not force is itself a kind of [speaker's] meaning) or an illocution. It still does not follow that the same is true of metaphor. In other words—to put the claim back in the terms in which I first framed the question—the account we have proposed for metaphor does not generalize to all the other tropes because, I shall now argue, they do not constitute a single natural kind. Instead I propose to divide the received class of tropes into two main groups. The paradigm of the first is metaphor, of the second irony. The account I have proposed for metaphor is generalizable to the other tropes in its class, but it will not apply to irony and its family.

Before turning to differences between the two subclasses of tropes—which, for simplicity, I shall treat as the difference between metaphor and irony—let me mention two respects in which they are similar. It is also, perhaps, because of these common features that others have tended to lump them together. First, both are context-dependent. I have already argued that this characterizes metaphor, but it may not be evident for irony. Indeed several authors have claimed that irony, in *contrast* to metaphor, is context-independent. Thus Ted Cohen writes that irony "typically incorporates a function that leads from a given meaning to its *reverse* or *opposite*" (my italics).[30] H. P. Grice proposes that, although contextual inappropriateness (in light of the conversational maxims) may indicate *that* an utterance is ironic, to determine the ironic interpretation all we need to know is that the speaker must be trying to get across some proposition other than the one he purports to be putting forward. This must be some obviously related proposition; the most obviously related proposition is the *contradictory* of the one he purports to be putting forward.[31]

And John Searle says:

Stated very crudely, the mechanism by which irony works is that the utterance, if taken literally, is obviously inappropriate to the situation. Since it is grossly inappropriate, the hearer is compelled to reinterpret it in such a way as to render it appropriate, and the most natural way to interpret it is as meaning the *opposite* of its literal form.[32]

Neither Cohen, Grice, nor Searle acknowledges the role of context in determination of the ironic interpretation (as opposed to its role in *recognition that* the utterance should be interpreted ironically). But as the differences between their accounts show, context must be brought in. In particular, for Grice the ironic interpretation is the *contradictory*—that is, the negation—of the interpretation purported to be put forward; for Searle and Cohen, it is the *opposite or reverse*—that is, an interpretation at the other end of the scale. Which of these is correct? Both, but each only some of the time—*depending on the context*. Irony is a context-sensitive function that yields a *contrary* from among a set of alternatives themselves determined in the context. Very frequently, the relevant contrary is the opposite. For example, after having been beaten 80–0 in a football game, one fan of the defeated team bitterly tells another, "Well, *we* really beat *them*, didn't we?" However, in other cases, the ironic interpretation may be closer to the contradictory, as Fogelin points out in an example like the following. Suppose my son brings home an exam with a grade of 80, for which he studied a bit, but not enough, because he believed (and assured me) that he already knew the material cold. I comment: "Well, you really aced that one." The ironic meaning of my utterance is neither its opposite, that he failed the exam—for he did know some of the material; nor is it simply the bare contradictory that he did not *completely* master the material. For, as Fogelin indicates, the irony would be inappropriate if the individual had missed just a single question (e.g., received an A–). Rather, it means something like: You have a long way to go if you think you know that material and could do well on the exam without studying. Yet, in another context, where my son did not even *try* to learn any of the material, we can imagine the same utterance meaning its opposite. Thus, as Fogelin also argues, irony, no less than metaphor, seems to be a context-dependent figure.[33]

The second feature common to irony and metaphor, as Fogelin has also argued, is that both involve mutually recognized intentions and beliefs—that is, what I have been calling presuppositions. These presuppositions enter into both recognition and interpretation of the two figures. For both figures, the speaker intends his utterance to evoke, or stimulate, in the respondent (who, in the case of irony, may or may not be the target) a response, or adjustment to its literal meaning, which the respondent, in turn, believes was intended by the speaker. Likewise, the interpretation of the metaphor or irony must draw on beliefs, or intentions, that the speaker believes his audience shares (or could share) and that he believes his audience will believe he intends them to recognize.

Yet, despite these two features common to metaphor and irony, I now want to turn to a difference between them that points to their having distinct semantic statuses.

Consider the following *complex figurative statement*, that is, a statement interpreted by more than one trope.[34] Trying to decipher my clumsy, awkward, sloppy, thick, and messy handwriting on a public document, you say: "What delicate lace work." In this context, the utterance is interpreted both metaphorically and ironically. The same sentence might, of course, be uttered on another occasion simply to say that someone's handwriting shows care and carefulness, craft and training, a wonderful attention to subtle calligraphic flourishes. In that context the utterance would be a simple, hence nonironic, metaphor. And in yet a third context, the same sentence might be uttered only ironically, say, as a comment on some expensive curtains that your dog has just ripped to shreds. However, let's imagine a context in which the speaker utters the sentence both ironically and metaphorically. How should we describe the utterance? Is it an ironic metaphor, or a metaphorical irony? The issue concerns the logical order of interpretation. Do we first interpret the utterance metaphorically and only then determine its ironic interpretation? Or do we first determine the ironic interpretation of the literal vehicle used in the utterance—say, find the contextually appropriate contrary (i.e., a predicate) to 'lace work'—and then determine the metaphorical interpretation of the contrary expression? The question is not one of temporal order or of actual psychological processing (although it may have implications for these); the issue is rather whether one interpretation is conditioned on the other.

Speakers I have polled unanimously seem to think that the ironic interpretation is conditioned on the metaphorical interpretation of the utterance: First we determine the metaphor and only afterward the irony. The reason for this ordering seems to be that the other "irony first" order is not only more difficult to compute; there is a conceptual difficulty in selecting the relevant ironic *contrary* to the literally interpreted term. Would the contrary to "delicate lace work" in our earlier example (according to the complex interpretation) be "course rags" or "rough sheepskin" or "a heavy shawl" or "stiff polyester"? The difficulty is that we have no context-independent formula for deciding in a given case whether the contrary is the contradictory or a polar opposite or some contrary midway on the continuum from the mere contradictory to the polar opposite. The element of the context that is most relevant to determine the appropriate contrary at this first stage is information related to the feature in terms of which the expression will then be interpreted metaphorically at the second stage. So, to select an ironic contrary, it is necessary to have some knowledge already of the metaphorical interpretation of the expression.

This example is a relatively "live" metaphorical interpretation (in the sense of "live" of chs. 1 and [as we'll see] 8, namely, an interpretation that involves applying the character of the underlying metaphorical expression to the presuppositions of its context to determine its metaphorical content). With dead, or dying, metaphors, the same problem does not arise. If I say "Shamir is a towering figure," intending the utterance to be interpreted both ironically and metaphorically, we might be able to interpret it in either order. Either first metaphorically—a man of impressive ability and accomplishments, that is, of great stature, who commands great respect—and then ironically—an unimpressive man of little ability and accomplishments who commands little respect. Or first ironically—a diminutive figure—and then metaphorically. Even here, however, there may be subtle differences in interpretation. And there is no guarantee that there will—always or ever—be a literal (ironic) contrary of the original expression, which, under its subsequent metaphoric interpretation, will express a feature contrary to the feature metaphorically expressed by the original expression. However, the degree to which it is possible to reverse the order of interpretation appears to vary with the degree to which the metaphorical interpretation of the expression is dead, suggesting that there may be no (or less) actual metaphorical interpretation taking place, or that the interpretation may already be "lexicalized."

There is much here that is still not theoretically well understood. However, we might draw a few tentative morals. First, and most important, if irony and metaphor were straightforwardly two figures of one natural kind, it is difficult to explain why there should be a prima facie fixed order of interpretation. One would expect, at the very least, much more free ordering or more inversion of the order. That the order of interpretation should *always* be metaphor first and irony second suggests that there is a difference in kind between metaphor and irony as kinds of interpretations. Furthermore, metaphor and irony do not appear to be isolated figures in this respect. Similar results obtain with other figures, suggesting that the received class of figures of speech can be divided into the following two subclasses:

(M)	Metaphor	(I)	Irony
	Simile		Meiosis
	Synechdoche		Hyperbole
	Metonymy		Understatement
			Overstatement

I cannot conclusively demonstrate the hypothesis, but I shall tentatively propose that whenever we have complex figurative interpretations, all M-figures are interpreted prior to I-figures, that the latter are conditioned on the former. There are ironic/hyperbolic, etc., interpretations or uses of metaphors/similes, synechdoches, etc., but no metaphorical/similaic, synechdochic interpretations or uses of ironies/hyperboles, etc.

The existence of a fixed order of interpretation at most implies that there is *some* difference between the two classes of figures. It does not explain the difference or even determine what the difference is. As a second conjecture, I want to propose that the (M)-figures are all character-istic operations of interpretation, that is, operations on sentences (or their tokens) that assign them nonconstant characters that, in turn, yield propositional contents in their contexts. The (I)-figures are operations on propositional contents to yield (different) propositional contents. So, for the other (M)-type figures, we might also posit operators like 'Mthat' that take arbitrary context-independent expressions and yield metaphorical-like expressions whose nonconstant characters are sensitive to a corresponding contextual parameter—a context set of relevant presuppositions. (Where there is no (M)-type interpretation, the literal meaning of the sentence directly generates the content of the sentence.) The contents generated by the characters of the various M-type expressions, in turn, can be interpreted by an (I)-figure, say, ironically. Hence (M)-type figures are semantic interpretations, interpretations determined by the semantic structure of the language; whereas (I)-type figures are postsemantic, that is, *uses* of the semantic interpretations of sentences, namely, propositions, to yield further propositions.[35] This difference between the two classes of tropes also explains our intuition that sentences meant ironically nonetheless are understood literally, whereas metaphors are not understood literally even if, in some sense, they still "have" their literal meaning. In any case, even apart from this final conjecture, it should be clear there is good reason not to draw an inference from the pragmatic status of irony to a similar conclusion for metaphor—which answers the objection with which we began. Despite received opinion, there may be no single natural kind of figures of speech.

IX Three Semantic Theories of Metaphor: A Comparison

In recent years, semantic theories of metaphor have not been nearly as fashionable as pragmatic theories—and (as I argued in ch. 1) they are also not the natural first candidates to which we would turn for an explanation of metaphor. But mine is also not the first or the only semantic theory in the field.[36] To emphasize its distinctive features, I'll conclude this chapter by contrasting it with three other semantic theories in the literature and, in the next section, by replying to several potential objections.

The first kind of semantic theory of metaphor, or class of theories, had its greatest appeal and strongest influence in the early 1970s. To explain both metaphorical recognition and interpretation in one fell semantic swoop, theories in this vein diagnosed the "tension" frequently identified with metaphor in terms of the then almost universally accepted claim that a metaphor is, taken literally, semantically anomalous or grammatically deviant.[37] That is, its constituent expressions violate various semantic (or perhaps syntactic) co-occurrence conditions if the utterance is taken literally. This fault of the sentence uttered, it was argued, excludes its literal interpretation, from which these authors also concluded that the utterance is ipso facto identified as a metaphor; and through the same violation of co-occurrence conditions the metaphorical interpretation is generated. According to some authors, a new metaphorical sense emerges from secondary connotations to which the interpreter shifts when the literal meanings fail; according to others, it is the result of cancellation-, weighting-, and transference-operations performed on component features of the lexical entries of the words. On all these accounts, however, metaphorical meaning is a reinterpretation of language that cannot be understood in its primary, privileged literal sense. The metaphorical interpretation is nevertheless semantic, for it is a function of violations of *semantic* conditions, conditions the speaker knows as part of his linguistic competence. Metaphorical interpretation falls within the grammar, or semantics, of a language because all we need to know in order to explain how it works are the linguistic or semantic rules that it violates.

As I noted back in chapter 1, the fatal weakness of all these theories is their ruling assumption that all, or most, or at least typical metaphors are grammatically deviant, semantically anomalous, or just plain false under their literal interpretation. In the mid-1970s this dogma was decisively challenged. In Ted Cohen's apt phrase, there are many "twice-true" metaphors, utterances that are perfectly fine and equally true in the very same context whether they are interpreted literally or metaphorically. More generally, the import of the critique is that there need be absolutely *nothing*—syntactically, semantically, or even pragmatically—deviant or irregular about the literal meaning of a sentence used or interpreted metaphorically. (Of course, it would not help a *semantic* account of metaphor even if metaphors were *pragmatically* odd.) Hence neither the recognition nor interpretation of a metaphor can be explained by way of its literal impossibility, let alone its literal *semantic* impossibility.

Unlike these accounts, mine does not assume that metaphors are semantically or grammatically (or, for that matter, pragmatically) deviant or anomalous under their literal interpretations, or that they should be interpreted in terms of violations of semantic (or indeed any) rules. Furthermore, my theory is diametrically opposed to the view that metaphors are *re*interpretations of strings that cannot be taken according to another prior, privileged sense. On the contrary, the metaphorical expressions of the form 'Mthat[Φ]' that underlie metaphorically interpreted utterances are *fully* grammatical; they are generated by the grammar as a subset of the set of expressions of nonconstant character, indeed in parallel and simultaneous with the nonmetaphorical characters in the metaphor character set under which the utterance can be typed (ch. 4, sec. IV). Knowledge of the characters of metaphorical expressions falls squarely within the domain of a grammar, or our linguistic competence, like that of the characters of context-dependent but literally interpreted indexical expressions. To be sure, the propositional content of the utterance of a metaphor requires appeal to an extralinguistic parameter (i.e., its presupposition set), but so does the content of 'I' (its agent) or 'here' (its time) in its context. Thus knowledge of these contents, determined by their respective extralinguistic parameters given their nonconstant characters, is also extralinguistic or not purely semantic. But to be *extra*grammatical in this way is not to be *un*grammatical.

In claiming that metaphorical expressions are grammatical, I do not merely mean to say that it is possible to accommodate metaphor within a grammar by making revisions or additions compatible with standing syntactic or semantic rules. On my account, metaphors require an absolute minimum of semantic apparatus beyond what is *already* in the grammar, in addition to what is *independently* necessary for the semantic interpretation of nonmetaphorical language. Because 'Mthat' is simply a variant of 'Dthat,' the main apparatus is already available for the semantics of demonstratives. All that needs to be altered in the grammar is the addition of the one operator 'Mthat' to the lexicon, together with a rule that (optionally) spells it out either as the word 'metaphorically' or with appropriate stress. On this count, my theory differs from previous approaches that attempted to incorporate metaphor within grammar by rewriting or adding substantively new grammatical rules. Unfortunately, in making the grammar descriptively adequate for metaphor, these theories in turn weakened its explanatory power.[38] A distinct virtue of my account is that it leaves the grammar and semantics in place; because it adds no significantly new rules, there is no cost to the explanatory power of the grammar.

The second kind of semantic theory of metaphor begins from the assumptions that the literal is semantic and that the metaphorical depends on the literal. It assigns each expression in the language a set of component features ("selectional features" or "semantical hypotheses") that constitute its lexical description or entry, which it in turn identifies *in toto* with the literal meaning of the word. The various metaphorical interpretations of the word are then derived by dropping or deleting one or another feature, thereby highlighting or weighting the remaining ones. Thus "the metaphorical meanings of a word or phrase ... are all contained, as it were, within its literal meaning or meanings. They are reached by removing any restrictions in relation to certain variables from the appropriate section or sections of its semantical hypothesis."[39] That is, a metaphorical interpretation is the result of *cancellation* of features given in the literal, or lexical, meaning of the expression.[40] And because a speaker presumably knows the literal, or lexical, meaning of a word as part of his linguistic and semantic competence, it follows ipso facto that he knows its metaphorical meaning as part of his semantic competence as well.

One attraction of this approach is its straightforward explication of the way in which the metaphorical "depends" on the literal, in terms of its idea that the one is *contained* in the other. But this claim is also the major shortcoming of this account. The difficulty is that we must *both* specify the literal or lexical entry of a word broadly enough to include the wide, variegated range of properties that it can express metaphorically *and* yet remain faithful to the idea that these properties are known by a speaker as part of her semantic competence. It is impossible to satisfy both of these descriptive and explanatory desiderata simultaneously. One need not assume a sharp analytic-synthetic distinction to make this point. Even if one takes common knowledge to be part of the "dictionary meaning" of a word—including false but stereotypical features (such as Searle's example of the stereotypical features of being mean and prone to violence associated with the name 'gorilla')—what many metaphors express in context are not antecedently accepted beliefs but properties noticed on and restricted to that occasion.[41] Indeed the problem is exacerbated insofar as we make cancellation of features depend on relations between the features of the metaphorical vehicle and features of other expressions in the string. Consider the different metaphorical interpretations of 'is a fish' in

(35) Grace Kelly was a fish

(36) Richard Nixon was a fish

—say, 'is at home in water' in (35) and 'is slippery and hard to catch' in (36). These two strings raise two problems. First, the two different metaphorical interpretations of 'is a fish', as I have stated them, are themselves expressed (at least arguably so) by metaphors.[42] Suppose, moreover, that it is only possible to express the metaphorical interpretations using metaphors. I'll argue in chapter 7, section VI, that this is not problematic for my account but, rather, typical and indeed necessary in order to capture the cognitively significant "perspective" on its content contributed by the character of the metaphor. However, for a lexicalist semantic theory like the one under consideration, it poses a serious problem if the content of a given metaphor can only be adequately expressed by employing other metaphors. If the lexical entries must themselves consist in features that can only be expressed by metaphors, then the theory must surrender its stated motivation to explicate how the metaphorical "depends" on the *literal* in terms of (feature) "containment" in a lexical entry.

The second problem raised by (35)–(36), to return to my main line of argument, is that the difference between their interpretations is in part prima facie dependent on presuppositions associated with the proper names for the respective individual subjects of the sentences. But proper names cannot be lexically represented by the necessary features to mark these differences without making every presupposed property of an individual a lexical feature of her name. Indeed, if we try to build all these features into lexical entries, it soon becomes clear that the notion of lexical feature is simply doing the work of encoding what presuppositions are made in a given context, including many that are extralinguistic. The theory that results is hardly semantic.

The third semantic theory I will discuss is Eva F. Kittay's "perspectival theory," which, using the lexical semantics of semantic field theory, takes the meaning of a term to be a function of its relations of affinity and contrast to other terms in its field.[43] According to Kittay, the interpretation of a metaphor (like 'Juliet is the sun') involves the transference, or mapping, of the semantic field associated with the vehicle of the metaphor (e.g., the field of terms for celestial bodies such as 'the sun') onto the domain of the semantic field associated with the topic of the metaphor (e.g., the domain of women or humans associated with 'Juliet'). In mapping the former onto the latter, the speaker reconceives, or restructures, the latter in terms of the intralinguistic relations that hold within the system of expressions in the former. With this restructuring of the topic domain, there emerges what Kittay calls the *second-order interpretation* that constitutes the meaning of a metaphor.

There are several similarities between Kittay's theory and mine. Both of us emphasize the motif that metaphorical interpretation involves systematic families or sets of expressions. The central role I assign to networks in the interpretation of a metaphor parallels the role Kittay assigns to semantic fields, although she is more inspired by Black, I by Goodman. As I also mentioned in chapter 5, section III, the semantic field theoretic notion of paradigmatic relations that hold among members of a contrast set corresponds to that of the exemplification relations that hold for members of the sample scheme to which the referent of the literal vehicle of the metaphor belongs. The syntagmatic relations of semantic field theory can also be analyzed more generally as the network of expressions that are candidates to fill the argument places marked by the thematic relations that underlie the expression interpreted metaphorically. Kittay's detailed analyses of a number of complex metaphors offer good illustrations of the rich interpretations that can be captured when, and only when, we pay attention to the systems of expressions, and their relations, in which individual metaphors function.

Yet there are also several deeper differences between Kittay's theory and mine that reflect our different conceptions of semantics and context, two notions that are intimately related in both of our accounts. On the one hand, I have argued that metaphorical interpretation is highly sensitive to contextual presuppositions, some of which may be known by the participants as part of their lexical knowledge but most of which are extralinguistic. To avoid drawing a sharp analytic-synthetic-like distinction, I have treated all of these together under the rubric of presuppositions, hence (for all theoretical purposes) as a nonlinguistic parameter of semantic interpretation. On the other hand, I have also argued that speakers possess semantic competence specific to their ability to interpret metaphors that is central to their knowledge of language (as opposed to empirical beliefs). This is their knowledge of metaphorical character, which constrains their interpretations. Insofar as metaphorical character is an instance of character in general, which is central to speakers' knowledge of language, I have argued that this account has genuine explanatory force. It subsumes metaphorical interpretations under the interpretation of context-dependent expressions (demonstratives and indexicals) tout cour. The main difference between Kittay's theory and mine is that she (apparently by design) does not draw any sharp distinction between speakers' knowledge of language or semantic competence, on the one hand, and their empirical, extralinguistic beliefs and the kinds of skills that enter into their use of language, on the other—what I call "context."[44] Hence her explanatory aim must be rather different than mine. In giving what she calls a "semantic theory of metaphor" her point does *not* seem to be to give a theory that attempts to isolate what speakers know specifically as part of their knowledge of language or semantics. Therefore, despite the descriptive riches of her analyses, there is no specific *explanatory* force to her claim to have given a semantic theory of metaphor. Let me illustrate this difference between our theories by reference to two of Kittay's explanations and certain problems they raise.

Like the first kind of semantic theory we discussed, Kittay claims that a metaphor "breaks certain rules of language, rules governing the literal and conventional senses of terms" (ibid., 24). She employs this assumption of literal incongruity first to explain how we identify a metaphor, but it is also deeply entrenched in her conception of metaphorical interpretation insofar as the literal incongruity reflects the conceptual differences that demarcate the semantic fields of the vehicle and topic, the differences in terms of which she characterizes the tension distinctive of metaphor. This assumption of literal incongruity is already one issue that sharply distinguishes Kittay's theory and mine, but let me grant it for the moment in order to focus on a deeper difference between us that emerges from her replies to the various counterexamples that have been raised against the assumption.[45]

To defend her claim about literal incongruity, Kittay argues that the purported counterexamples mistake the proper unit that is literally incongruous. Sometimes it is an immediate constituent phrase (e.g., Eliot's 'a slum of bloom'), at other times the sentence uttered, but, where neither of these is prima facie incongruous, the relevant unit is the utterance in its situational context. In these cases, however, Kittay is not satisfied simply to uncover *some* kind of incongruity, such as pragmatic or conversational oddity. She tries to demonstrate further that the presence of one of these latter kinds of oddity is simply symptomatic of the presence of genuine semantic incongruity. To construct her case, she proposes the *Expressibility Principle*: All salient elements of a situational context can be expressed in linguistic terms. So, if the context of a metaphor does not consist in a linguistic text (e.g., an explicit verbal discourse) containing a semantic incongruity, Kittay claims that the salient features of the non-linguistic context can always "be rendered linguistically as an utterance of a level of complexity higher than that of the given expression" (62). This linguistic context, she then conjectures, will contain a violation of the *semantic* combination rules that govern first-order literal language, hence a semantic incongruity. As a consequence, she concludes, this "places the identification of metaphors squarely within the province of semantics" (75).

This conclusion is symptomatic of the problems with Kittay's conception of semantics and context. Consider the example:

(37) The rock is becoming brittle with age

where the subject description is used metaphorically in a context to refer to an aging professor, "accompanied perhaps by a gesture, for example, a nod in the direction of the professor" (71).[46] The *sentence* (37) violates no semantic or linguistic rules and contains no incongruity but, Kittay claims, the *utterance* in its situational context does. Therefore, she proposes that we "render" the gesture, as part of the situational context, "linguistically," and thereby provide an incongruous frame for the sentence (37) as metaphorical focus. For example, she imagines (37) in the "context" of (38):

(38) He responds to his students' questions with none of his former subtlety.

Here Kittay reasons that the pronoun in (38) must be anaphorically coreferential with 'the rock' if the two utterances are to cohere conversationally. Therefore, we ought to be able to substitute the antecedent for

the pronoun in (38). However, this immediately creates a semantic violation since 'the rock' is [-animate] and the verb 'responds' requires a subject that is [+animate]. To make the incongruity explicit, she suggests that
we construct a "conversion sentence" that states the identities and equiv-
alencies of terms:

(39) The rock is the professor.

This is a possible description of an interpreter's reasoning. But as an
explanation of how we identify an utterance of (37) as a metaphor, the
utterance in a situation (37)–(38) and the conversion sentence (39) fail to
show that it is by means of exclusively semantic knowledge. First,
although it is *possible* for the pronoun in (38) to corefer to the referent of
'the rock' in the previous sentence, it is not linguistically, or semantically,
obligatory that it do so.[47] The pronoun might equally well be functioning
as a demonstrative, demonstrating the individual rendered salient in the
context (e.g., by the independent metaphorical reference to the person in
the previous utterance). Hence to link the two we already need to know
that 'the rock' refers to the professor in its context, that is, we need to
know the very information that is expressed by the conversion sentence
(39). However, knowing (39) or the fact that in the context 'the rock'
refers to the professor requires nonsemantic empirical knowledge. Hence
there is no conceptual or linguistic connection between (39) and (37), only
an empirical one, and the fact that (39) involves an incongruity does
nothing to explain away (37) as a congruous counterexample to the incongruity thesis. Second, Kittay argues that when we sense an oddity
we construct a linguistic context like (37)–(38) that violates a semantic
rule. But it is clearly only because we *already* believe that (37) is metaphorical that we recover the context (38). Therefore, we cannot appeal to
the violation involved in (37)–(38) to explain why we take (37) to be
metaphorical.

In short, the problem with this explanation is that even granting Kittay
the assumption of literal incongruity, one cannot assimilate the role of the
extralinguistic context of an utterance into semantics as she does without
robbing the attribution of semantic knowledge of its explanatory
power.[48] On my view, recognition of a metaphor—the knowledge *that* an
utterance is to be interpreted metaphorically—is a matter of recognizing
that an utterance is a token of one rather than another type, where the
types are individuated (in part) by their respective meanings (or characters). Our semantic knowledge is knowledge exclusively of the types with
their characters; what enables us to subsume utterances as tokens under

types introduces nonsemantic knowledge, for example, about the purpose of the utterance and other features of the extralinguistic use of the sentence. This task falls to a theory of speech or pragmatics.

There is a similar problem for Kittay's use of semantic fields to explain metaphorical interpretation. Although there is considerable controversy over the exact definition of a semantic field in all its complexity, the basic idea is that it is a set of contrast sets and possibly a permutation relation defined over the members of the sets.[49] A (basic) contrast set $\langle L: E_1 \ldots E_n \rangle$ is a sequence containing a linguistic expression L that serves as a covering term for the set and a set of expressions $E_1 \ldots E_n$ such that the extension of each E_i is a subset of the extension of L and the extensions of each E_i are disjoint. Examples of (basic) contrast sets are: $\langle$colors: red, green, blue, yellow, orange, brown, purple, black, white$\rangle$ and $\langle$days: Sunday, Monday, Tuesday, ..., Saturday$\rangle$.

As long as we limit ourselves to (basic) contrast sets like the two examples just mentioned, it is plausible to hold that knowledge of the semantic field to which a given expression belongs is part of a speaker's lexical and, therefore, linguistic knowledge. However, as we already saw in connection with the second kind of semantic theory, as soon as one tries to extend the idea even to relatively simple metaphors, it becomes less and less plausible that the networks in which the terms are functioning could possibly be known by speakers in virtue of their linguistic or semantic competence. Again, consider one of Kittay's own examples.

(40) The seal dragged himself out of the office.

Let's grant Kittay the assumption that in its (verbally explicitated) context an utterance of (40) contains a semantic incongruity, say, between the vehicle 'seal' and topic 'human beings'. However, as Kittay herself shows, it is possible for utterances of (40) to be interpreted metaphorically with two distinct contents. On the first interpretation, let 'seal' express the property of being a performing creature who knows all the tricks and is constantly put on display, subject to its captor's purposes. On the second interpretation, 'seal' metaphorically expresses a number of features concerning physical appearance and manner: wearing a black shiny suit, having dark slicked-down hair, a waddling walk. Further, let's grant that utterances of (40) in their respective contexts could have either of these two metaphorical interpretations. In virtue of what kind(s) of knowledge will the speaker know the content of either of these distinct metaphorical interpretations of (40)? Kittay proposes that the contexts in which the two interpretations result would include the different networks of expressions to which 'seal' respectively belongs. On the first interpretation, the network might include seals as captive, performing animals exploited by their owners for the latters' amusement and benefit, as opposed to free, noncaptive, unexploited animals who are masters of themselves. On the second interpretation, the network includes the features of seals' physical appearances, both in contrast to each other and to those of other creatures, features like a lion's mane or an elephant's wrinkled, saggy skin.

As a description of how the interpretations are determined, this story is entirely plausible. The question for our purposes is whether knowledge of these networks or sets of expressions that determine these interpretations is *semantic*. If the semantic field of an expression is determined by its lexical/linguistic/conventional meaning, 'seal' in (40), even as it is used to yield these divergent interpretations, ought to belong on both occasions to one semantic field. But relative to one constant semantic field, we cannot explain the different metaphorical interpretations of (40). In reply to this issue, Kittay writes that, as these examples illustrate, "most terms belong to a large number of semantic fields. Which semantic fields come into play in the interpretation of the metaphor depends on what [literal/conventional] interpretation we have chosen for the term" (165), and this, in turn, depends on the literal/conventional senses of the other terms in the discourse. Yet, for an example of this process of selection, all she says is that in the case of 'seal' "we tend to eliminate the sense of 'seal' which is an 'inanimate stamp'" (165–166). Yes; but that sense of 'seal' differs in its syntactic and semantic feature components from the sense of 'seal' in (40). An explanation of different interpretations of (homonymous) tokens that in fact belong to different types with different syntactic and semantic features hardly explains our two metaphorical interpretations, whose literal vehicles have *identical* syntactic and semantic features. Perhaps to fill in this lacuna, Kittay next argues that the semantic field of an occurrence of the term is only "fully specified when we obtain the most complete [literal/conventional] interpretation of the utterance in which the term's [literal/conventional] sense is a constituent" (166). By a "full specification" she seems to mean: making verbally explicit the context of the utterance according to her Expressibility Principle, an explicitation that will make explicit the term's contrast set. How interpreters accomplish this, she concludes, is the "difficult question of how a context selects out relevant semantic fields" (ibid.). About this, unfortunately, she has nothing more to say other than that "work has yet to be done in this area" (ibid.), although she herself concedes that the relevant considerations will be in large measure pragmatic. In short, if we want to appeal to different contrast sets or fields to explain the different metaphorical interpretations of tokens of one expression type, we must introduce nonsemantic, extra-linguistic information—such as the different exemplification relations of seals relative to different sample/exemplification schemata to which they belong. Again, the moral is that there is no explanatory force to Kittay's notion of a *semantic* field.[50] Of course, a speaker may know as part of his semantic lexical competence that a term like 'seal' belongs to *a* contrast set with other captive and noncaptive animals. But knowledge of the content of the contrast, the particular features in virtue of which the expressions stand in contrast, goes far beyond what speakers know in virtue of their semantic or lexical competence.

If we want to capture a body of semantic knowledge that underlies metaphorical interpretation, we cannot look, then, only to the networks in which the metaphorical vehicle and topic function (even if knowledge of some of the relevant networks may be part of our linguistic compe-tence). Making the contrast sets verbally explicit and then arguing that it is our knowledge of the intralinguistic relations between the explicitated terms that determines the interpretation simply disguises the fact that we know *what* to make explicit in virtue of extralinguistic knowledge and beliefs—that is, contextual presuppositions.[51] On my theory, on the other hand, what is known by the speaker in virtue of his semantic competence is not the schemata or networks but the character of the metaphor, the appropriate function, with its constraints, from contextual presupposi-tions to contents. Finally, note that Kittay also employs a function that maps the first-order literal/conventional interpretation onto the second-order metaphorical interpretation. However, she also emphasizes that this function is just one member of a whole set of functions that yield second-order interpretations, including indirect speech acts, irony, and non-figurative utterances with two illocutionary forces. The latter are, quite clearly even on Kittay's account, nonsemantic, pragmatic interpretations. She gives us no reason to believe that the function specific to metaphorical interpretation is any more semantic.[52]

X Objections and Replies

Objection: Our ultimate goal is to account for the acceptability or success of metaphorical utterances. Semantic theories like yours promise to do this by tying acceptability or success to truth (and unacceptability or failure to falsity). But this move presupposes that we have at least as good a grasp, if not a better grasp, of the truth and falsity of metaphors—

hence of their truth-conditions or content—as we have of their success and failure. Yet, we all know how difficult it is to know with certainty that a metaphor means one thing rather than another. Metaphors can often be interpreted in multiple, sometimes incompatible, ways ("depending on context"), and metaphorical interpretation seems endless at least in the sense that we often don't know when to stop. As Donald Davidson puts it, it is an error to think that metaphors have fixed, determinate truth-conditional contents, for if they did, why is it "often so hard to decide ... exactly what the content [of a metaphor] is supposed to be" (WMM, 262)? On the other hand, if metaphors do not have determinate contents or truth-conditions, we cannot condition their success (or failure) on well-defined criteria of satisfaction of those conditions. Invariably we must have recourse to pragmatic, nonsemantic desiderata to explain their success and failure. But in that case truth-conditional semantics does no *explanatory* work. Hence there is no need to advert to semantics or truth-values for metaphors, indeed good reason (viz., Ockham's razor) not to.[53]

Reply: The objection charges that without a firm knowledge of metaphorical contents or their truth-values, we cannot hope to explain why metaphors succeed by attributing semantic knowledge to their speakers. To begin with, it is important to keep in mind that it was never claimed that a speaker's *semantic* knowledge of metaphor is sufficient for him to interpret a given utterance of a metaphor, hence, to account for its content and its actual truth-value. For that purpose, knowledge of the context, or presupposition set, is also necessary. So, if we don't know, or "it's hard to decide," the truth-value or truth-conditions of the metaphor, the difficulty may be due to at least two possible reasons. One possibility is that metaphors do not have "determinate" interpretations and therefore really do lie beyond the scope of semantics. Or it might be that we simply do not know the relevant aspects of the context that must be known to interpret the metaphor, that is, we lack extralinguistic knowledge. Before rejecting the semantics, we need to discount the latter possibility.

Of course, even if we shouldn't conclude from the fact that we don't know the content or truth-value of a metaphor that it has none, one may still object that it is not obvious what advantages accrue from the assumption. My proposal is twofold. First, by assuming that metaphors are truth-valued and have contents, we can articulate more clearly what we don't know when we don't know how to judge at least one kind of *success* of a metaphor, the kind of success that turns on the metaphor having a determinate metaphorical interpretation. One such factor that might enable us to explain what makes it so "hard to decide" on the content of a metaphor is its context set of presuppositions, the extralinguistic parameter of its interpretation that we can separate out *only* by distinguishing it from the speaker's semantic knowledge (of character). For example, where the metaphor originated in a historically remote or culturally foreign context, what can make it so hard to decide on its content is that we often do not know the author's presuppositions unless a good literary historian tells us or an anthropologist discovers them. Another reason it can be difficult is that there is more than one possible set of presuppositions among which we have no good reason to choose one rather than another as *the* context for the metaphor. Furthermore, even when we can begin to spell out presuppositions, we often don't know when to stop: how to delimit the presuppositions and thereby delimit the content. Because of the interpretive power of metaphorical character, the longer we dwell on many metaphors, the more, and the more novel, presuppositions we frequently make.[54] (Again, for rich, vital metaphors, there may be not just one but alternative, even mutually incompatible, kinds of potential presuppositions.)

How, then, do we know when to stop to settle on a fixed metaphorical content? What determines what does or does not belong to the context of a given metaphor so we can be confident, at least as an idealized standard, that there are some metaphors with determinate truth-value-bearing content, relative to which we can then explain why the ideal is not realized in other cases?

In a word, *we* do: We fix the contexts of our metaphors. 'Juliet is the sun' out of context *could* mean that she is to be worshipped *or* that she can burn up her admirers *or* that she follows regular predictable motions *or*.... But fix the *context* of the utterance—that is, the specific context set of presuppositions—and ipso facto we fix its *content* in that context.[55] The fact that the metaphor *could* mean this in one context and mean that in another does not show that *within* a given context it has more than one of these interpretations. And to the further charge that metaphorical interpretation even within a context is endless and indeterminate, my reply is: only if we let it be so. It is up to us to impose a closure. To be sure, given a fixed context set of presuppositions, it is always possible for us to add new ones. But from the point of view of the semantics, each such addition constitutes a different context relative to which the metaphor has a distinct interpretation.

The second half of my proposal centers on what we should and what we should not expect of a semantics of metaphor. The semantics, on our account, does not furnish a unique method or procedure to generate the presuppositions, an algorithm—something like the traditional grounds of metaphor—that would enable us to produce a (literal) explication or explicit statement of the content of a metaphor in terms of the presuppositions. For that we need a pragmatics or theory of context. But this should not count against a semantic theory of metaphor any more than the fact that we cannot individuate the contents of 'here' and 'now' without theories of locations and times should count against a semantic theory of the indexicals. The point of the semantics is not to generate actual interpretations, let alone give rules or recipes that will make it easier for us to interpret metaphors. The semantics only explains *constraints* on possible metaphorical interpretations by spelling out their *form* or *structure* relative to certain parameters. This structure of metaphorical interpretation—metaphorical character—is just as rich (and as impoverished) as the structure of interpretation of indexicals; so I argued earlier in this chapter (secs. I, III, and IV). By the same token, if the semantic structure of a metaphor underdetermines its interpretation—and allows for an interval of alternative interpretations rather than a unique content (for some metaphors)—this kind of vagueness or indeterminateness should not count against the truth-valuedness of metaphors any more than it should count against the truth-valuedness of literal utterances containing indexicals or demonstratives that their "neighborhoods" are also sometimes vague or indeterminate. The constraints for the two classes of expressions stand (or fall) together.

Objection: If the reason we sometimes do not know a determinate content for a metaphor is that we do not know its contextual presuppositions, it is no surprise that once we know the presuppositions, we know the content—they are one and the same. Hence your *semantics* tells us nothing more about the interpretation of a metaphor than we already know when we know the context set of presuppositions. Furthermore, isn't the reason we don't know the context set of presuppositions *because* we do not know, independently of knowing the content, which presuppositions we must hold? Without an independent account of how to identify the extralinguistic presuppositions, the semantics is trivial.

Reply: You are right insofar as a theory of our *semantic* competence in metaphor does not *itself* generate the interpretation of a particular metaphor in a context. For that we need extralinguistic knowledge. But if the semantics tells us that the (content of an) interpretation of a metaphor depends on its actual context set of presuppositions, *and on nothing but that*, it is hardly fair to charge that now that we know the context set of presuppositions, and thereby the content of the metaphor, what *more* does the semantics tell us.

There is also a second point to the objection. I have emphasized that the semantics must be complemented by a pragmatics—by a theory of how we apply our semantic competence to particular contexts, that is, sets of presuppositions—and I have rehearsed various stories (in ch. 5) about the kinds of desiderata (e.g., the various networks to which the vehicle belongs) that ground the presuppositions for some kinds of metaphors. So, to the extent to which we can describe these factors that yield the presuppositions, we *can* give an independent characterization of the metaphorically relevant or m-associated presuppositions, as the objection demands. However, as I have also said, there is no sure-fire criterion to pick out a unique set of relevant presuppositions for a given metaphor. Indeed this is one way I suggested that our semantic competence that consists in knowledge of the constraints that govern character differs from the kind of extralinguistic knowledge of the context that constitutes our pragmatic skills.

It is also true, as the objection says, that we generally don't know which presuppositions we must hold independently of knowing the content of the metaphor. In some contexts we do have independent means of knowing the m-associated features presupposed to be associated with the literal vehicle. But the presuppositions that *must* be held are those that are "required" (or at least are sufficient, even if not uniquely so [see ch. 4, sec. III]) for the interpretation of the metaphor, just as the pragmatic presuppositions of utterances generally are those *required* for their appropriateness. Indeed, as I suggested in chapter 4, we accommodate our contexts to the interpretation of our metaphorical utterances. This, however, is not an objectionable way in which metaphors are exceptional, but a general characteristic of the interaction between contextual presuppositions and utterances.

Objection: According to your theory, the interpreter of a metaphorically used expression Φ is said to *know*, as part of his semantic competence, the character of the metaphorical expression 'Mthat[Φ]', that is, a rule from the context set of presuppositions to the content of the expression in that context. But other than readers of this monograph, surely no speaker of English or of any other natural language has ever heard of 'Mthat'. Therefore, no such speaker has knowledge of 'Mthat' or of metaphorical character.

Reply: It is helpful to distinguish two issues here. The first issue is whether it is theoretically fruitful to attribute cognitive states to speakers in order to explain their ability to interpret metaphors. I have tried to argue that it is both productive and necessary to posit such cognitive states, insofar as accounts that purport to account directly for our use of metaphors in terms of speech act, conversational, or verbal abilities are inadequate; see chapter 2 and earlier in this chapter. But whether or not you agree with those arguments, it should be understood that being in such a cognitive state or having such knowledge does not require that speakers or interpreters also be able to verbally articulate or explicitly state the content of those states, such as the rule of character for 'Mthat' or indeed any semantic principle that is the content of the state they are in when they are semantically competent in a language. Nobody but readers of this book, admittedly, are likely to be able to do the latter. That, however, hardly counts against my theory as the best explanation of the cognitive state of interpreters inferable from the data at hand. Furthermore, on this score, knowledge of the rule of character for metaphorical expressions is no different from knowledge of any rule or principle of grammar (e.g., of the sort spelled out in generative grammar), none of which can be assumed to be explicitly known or statable by those bearing the cognitive states of which they are the content.

The second issue is whether the cognitive state that consists in grasping the character of Mthat-expressions, or any principle of grammar or semantic competence, should be described as *knowledge*, that is, whether it is appropriate to say that interpreters *know* the characters of metaphors. If you do think that "knowledge" is an appropriate term for this state, the knowledge—which, again, is of the same kind as linguists attribute to speakers when they say that they know a language or its grammar—must be allowed to be tacit, implicit, or unconscious. If you don't think it is appropriate, the moral to be drawn is not necessarily one about the state in question; it may equally well reflect the poverty of our ordinary notion of knowledge, insofar as it cannot subsume prima facie cognitive states of this type, attitudes toward propositions or concepts.[56]

Objection: Is it your claim that metaphors *are* demonstratives or indexicals, or that they are simply *like* them in some general respects? The latter might be true, but it is uninteresting. The former obviously does not fit ordinary usage (unless 'metaphors are demonstratives/indexicals' is a metaphor!), and, despite the parallels you have pointed out, there are great differences between metaphors and demonstratives. It is simply implausible to consider them one class of expressions (or interpretations) falling under one theory.

On the one hand, demonstratives and indexicals have explicitly statable rules that determine definite direct referents relative to their contexts of utterance. Each utterance of 'I' directly refers to its speaker or the agent of the context, an individual. Similarly, 'now' and 'here' each has a definite value in each context. These rules are what we take to be the meanings of indexicals and demonstratives. Hence *anyone* who masters the language acquires knowledge of these rules, enabling her to assign the expression a referent/content in each context without any additional special skill or knowledge. Therefore, there is good reason to take such knowledge of demonstratives and indexicals to fall under a semantic theory.

On the other hand, is there anything analogous for metaphor? Even your own candidate rule (Mthat) (see ch. 4, sec. I) is much less definite and determinate than the rules for the indexicals. The rule that each token of the metaphorical expression 'Mthat[Φ]' expresses as its content properties P presupposed to be m-associated with Φ leaves unexplained what it is to be m-associated with each Φ. It is also not straightforward to apply the rule, even given an account of what it is to be m-associated. As you indicated back in chapter 4, we must still select from among the m-associated properties those that are appropriate in the context. There are no rule-governed procedures to instruct us how to make this selection or how to compute the final value of the metaphorical character. Indeed, selection for appropriate properties, and more generally the kind of complex interpretation that metaphor demands, requires insight, guesswork, intuition, fitting or accommodating features to one another, skills of detection and discovery not captured by rules and certainly not by rules of language. Does anyone who masters a language plausibly acquire *as part of her semantic knowledge* rules that *suffice* to interpret a novel, context-sensitive metaphor (even in its context)?

Reply: First of all, my claim is that metaphors and demonstratives (including the full range of proper demonstratives and indexicals) fall under one natural *semantic* kind; I am not sure whether that means that metaphors *are* demonstratives or just *like* them. In either case, to say that is not to deny that there are also significant differences, and especially pragmatic differences, between them.

But before I turn to those differences, and their significance, I want to clarify (at the risk of repeating myself) two potential confusions. The objection claims that *anyone* who masters a language acquires knowledge of the character-rules of indexicals and demonstratives that *enable* her to *assign* them referents or contents in each context. In contrast, the skills of interpretation (including intuition, insight, guesswork) involved in metaphor cannot be expressed by rules that could both assign metaphorical interpretations and count as semantic, part of what every speaker of a

language knows. First, the characters *both* of demonstratives and indexicals and of metaphors, like meanings generally, express linguistic *constraints* on possible contents of interpretation. Because they must be
completed by their respective contextual parameters, their (nonconstant)
characters or meanings do not themselves self-sufficiently generate any
contents or referents for their expressions; they merely exclude impossible
candidates, things that *cannot* be expressed by the words whose character
they are. Even someone who masters indexical language is not, then,
thereby enabled to *assign* referents or contents to the expressions apart
from context. The same is true of metaphors, but, by the same token, they
are no worse off with respect to their constraints. (To be sure, their
respective constraints differ substantively; the demonstratives and indexicals refer to *actual* speakers, times, locations, and demonstrata, whereas
metaphors express properties *presupposed* to be associated with the literal
vehicle.)

Second, when a speaker knows the character of an indexical, she knows
a rule that constrains the referent/content of the indexical in a context;
but *knowledge* of that character-rule still does not furnish her with
knowledge of its referent/content unless she *also* knows who is speaking,
the time and location, and so on, knowledge of the context that is extralinguistic. Don't think that just because the content of a fully determined
indexical is determined by its character that the semantic *knowledge* of the
latter is also sufficient for *knowledge* of the former. By the same token, it
cannot count *against* the determinate status of the character rule (Mthat)
for a metaphor that *knowledge* of it is not sufficient to *know* its content,
for which we must also know its extralinguistic context, that is, context set
of presuppositions. Hence neither for demonstratives and indexicals nor
for metaphors is semantic knowledge of their respective characters sufficient for speakers to have knowledge of their assigned contents.[57]

Turning back now to the differences between the demonstratives and
metaphors, I want to argue (i) that the differences between them are of
degree rather than of kind, and (ii) that there are also significant differences within the class of proper demonstratives and indexicals. The differences between demonstratives/indexicals and metaphors are easy to
overstate because we tend to focus on the most determinate indexicals at
one pole and the most indeterminate metaphors at the other. But when we
compare the full range of metaphors and demonstratives, we find a continuum of context-sensitive interpretations. Pure demonstratives may be
no less indeterminate than some metaphors and the metaphorical interpretations of many expressions are far more determinate than it first

appears. I'll argue for this by pushing from both directions: from below—
from the alleged determinacy of demonstratives—and from above—from
the alleged indeterminacy of metaphors.

In discussing these examples, it is important to distinguish between how
determinate (as opposed to vague) is the content of the interpretation and
(keeping in mind that characters do not assign but constrain possible
interpretations) how the content is *determined* by the rule of character,
even though these often hang together.[58] 'I', for example, has a determinate content (an individual, possibly at a time), and typically its content is
also fully determined by its character—although even for 'I', there are
problematic applications, for example, its answering-machine uses in 'I
am not here now'. When we move on to 'here' and 'now', as well as 'you'
and 'we', the relevant "unit" of content suffers from vagueness or indeterminateness about the interval of its "neighborhood" (Is 'now' the second, minute, hour, day, or an even longer interval?), although the rule of
character is still fully determining. And when we move from the indexicals
to the complete (singular) demonstratives, not only may the indeterminateness of the content grow (depending on what is demonstrated); the rule
of character, which requires a completing demonstration (either or both
presentation and ostensive gesture), is significantly less determining. For
example, we inevitably point at an indefinite number of things when we
point at any one thing. Hence it is arguable that all complete demonstratives require a sortal modifier, one that is often not verbalized, leaving
open a range of alternatives among which it may not be clear which (or
whether any) was specifically intended by the agent. Add to that the natural imprecision of many ostensive gestures and the topiclessness of presentations. With dthat-descriptions, there can be a further indeterminacy
of character if the description is incomplete, failing to fix a unique referent
in the actual context. Moreover, identification of the referent depends on
who/what is known (or believed) to satisfy the description, knowledge
that may be as allusive as knowledge of shared presuppositions. Finally, if
we turn from the singular to predicate demonstratives (e.g., 'thus', where
it is a property that is ostended) there are all the old theoretical worries
associated with the individuation of properties in addition to the many
practical difficulties in applying the rule of character. Here matters are not
much better off than with metaphor.

In short, there is a continuum of demonstrative and indexical expressions, or interpretations of expressions, of more or less indeterminacy. At
one extreme there are the singular indexicals, at the other the predicate
demonstratives. Despite the fact that we clearly do have semantic knowl-

edge of their characters, in all these cases this knowledge needs to be supplemented by, and to some degree cannot always be distinguished from, the same kinds of insight, guesswork, and skill in rules of thumb that we tend to associate with metaphor.

At the same time, we should not deny or even understate the fact that metaphorical interpretation involves, as I tried to show in chapters 4 and 5, many non-rule-governed skills and abilities—the skills and abilities that come into play, for example, in identifying and working out the networks to which the vehicle of the metaphor belongs. This is precisely what a pragmatics of metaphor must capture, although it is unlikely for the very reasons cited by the objection that these skills and abilities can be put into the form of rules or a theory (see ch. 5, sec. I). My aim is not to ignore these non-rule-governed aspects of metaphorical interpretation but to argue that, because of them, we also should not lose sight of the semantic constraints that are equally important. These constraints, captured by characters that we know as part of our semantic competence, are what become evident when, as with indexicals, we focus not on the interpretation of one token in a context but on the systematically related interpretations of different tokens of one type in different contexts (see chs. 1, 4, and earlier in 6). When we ascend to this semantic vantage point, we observe regularities and systematic constraints relating contents to their respective contexts no different from those of indexicals. And as with indexicals, the most plausible explanation is that our knowledge of these constraints and rules constitutes our semantic competence in metaphor. In these (and only these) respects I claim that metaphors and indexicals form one natural semantic kind.

Objection: On your view that metaphors express propositional contents, given that propositional contents are the very sort of things that admit literal articulation (at least in principle), shouldn't it then be possible to express literally *everything* a metaphor conveys—in your terminology, all knowledge *by* metaphor? And isn't this at best true of trite, common, or dead metaphors, not novel, live ones?

Reply: No, it does not follow on my account that all knowledge *by* metaphor is expressed in its propositional content, let alone that it can all be stated literally. To explain why not, I now turn to chapter 7 and to our knowledge *by* metaphorical character.

Chapter 7

Knowledge by Metaphorical Character

I Marie's Problem—and Ours

Marie, a young woman in her teens, suffered from the eating disorder *anorexia nervosa*. In treatment, she explained to her therapist that her mother had forbade her to continue seeing her boyfriend. Angrily, she reported, she had said to herself:

(1) I won't swallow that [referring to her mother's interdiction].

Let's assume that in the context in which she uttered (1) it was clear that Marie's use of the word 'swallow' was metaphorical.[1] Let's also suppose that *what* Marie *said*, the content of (1) interpreted metaphorically, is expressed by

(2) Marie won't obey her mother's interdiction.

Does (2) adequately express everything said by Marie's utterance of (1)? Does it exhaust the information conveyed by her utterance? Yes and no. Yes, insofar as (1) is true, spoken by Marie referring to her mother's interdiction, if and only if Marie does not obey her mother's interdiction. No, insofar as her utterance of (1) is meant to contribute to an *explanation* of her anorexic behavior, albeit as an irrational way of resisting her mother's command. For to explain why Marie stopped *eating* in terms of a belief we would ascribe to her on the evidence of her utterance of (1), we must somehow include as part of the representation of her belief the fact that what she said, namely, that she would not obey her mother, was expressed metaphorically using the verb 'swallow'. Only under that metaphorical mode of expression of what she said—only if we include *how* she metaphorically believed, or expressed, *what* she believed—can we see any connection, conscious or unconscious, between her belief and her subsequent anorexic behavior. To be sure, Marie's behavior and the connection she made are not rational, and no explanation should make it so. But only by acknowledging the cognitive and explanatory significance of the metaphorical way in which she expressed her belief can we explain her behavior at all.

This example may not be as innocent as we might like, but it gives us a glimpse of how a metaphorical use or interpretation of language can convey a kind of information, or bear cognitive significance, above and beyond what we might all agree is *what it says*, its propositional content (in a context).[2] The metaphorical mode in which Marie expressed her belief is essential, not to determine whether what she said is true or false, but for our folk-psychological purposes of explaining her behavior. Information of this kind, conveyed specifically by the metaphorical mode of expression of a word interpreted metaphorically, is an example of what I called, back in chapter 1, "knowledge *by* metaphor."

Here is a second, more innocent example of knowledge *by* metaphor, taken from the *Book of Samuel* II, 12.[3] After David has Uriah killed in battle in order to cover up his indiscretion with Bathsheba whom he then took as his wife, God sends Nathan the Prophet to reprimand him. David, as far as we can tell from the text, feels little regret, shame, or guilt for the act he committed. He is now married to Bathsheba, and he seems to dismiss and forget the gravity of his offense. Nathan tells him the story of a rich man and a poor man. The rich man has countless flocks of sheep and herds of cattle, the poor man only one little lamb whom he loves as dearly as his own child. When a traveler comes to town, the rich man takes the poor man's one little lamb to feed the guest rather than use one of his own large flock. Hearing this, David explodes with anger. He tells Nathan that the rich man should be killed as punishment and that he should compensate the poor man fourfold. At this point, Nathan points his finger at David and tells him (here I translate with a little liberty): "You are the rich man." David then confesses his sin and repents.

Now, what has David learned when Nathan tells him, using what I take to be a metaphor, "You are the rich man"? Surely Nathan has not told David anything he did not know already (in at least one familiar sense of "know")—that he has all the wives and women that any man could wish for, in contrast to Uriah who had only Bathsheba whom he dearly loved; that it is wrong to take another's property, let alone his beloved wife; that it is surely wrong to have someone else killed to save one's own honor and satisfy one's own desires. What, then, is it about this metaphor—or the knowledge somehow carried *by* the metaphor in that context—that brings about this radical change of feeling and action in

David?[4] Whatever the specific information consists in, I want to argue that it is knowledge *by* metaphor.

In chapter 1, I pointed out that most contemporary theories hold that our knowledge *of* metaphor and knowledge *by* metaphor go hand in hand. Those who hold that a speaker's knowledge *of* metaphorical interpretation is part of his linguistic competence also hold that any meaning or concept he is able to express *by* a metaphor should belong "in principle" to the stock of linguistic, or literal, meanings or concepts he knows in virtue of his knowledge of language (and specifically lexical knowledge). Therefore, whatever can be expressed metaphorically ought to be equally well expressible literally; no additional knowledge ought to be communicated specifically by the metaphorical mode of the metaphor that could not be communicated by some literal utterance. On the other hand, those who hold that someone's knowledge *of* metaphor is something other than, or in addition to, his general linguistic competence at least allow for the possibility that some kinds of information or knowledge conveyed *by* some metaphors might not be expressible by a literal expression. And indeed those who hold that our knowledge of metaphor violates rules that constitute our linguistic competence may even be committed to a stronger position, according to which it is impossible to express literally any knowledge *by* metaphor. Both of these last two positions acknowledge a kind of knowledge conveyed specifically and essentially by the metaphorical mode of expression of a metaphor.

My own view, which I promised back in chapter 1 to argue for later in this book, is that the component of a speaker's ability to interpret a metaphor that falls within his semantic competence proper is precisely what enables him to express knowledge *by* the metaphor that is *not* equivalently expressible except through its metaphorical mode of expression. The time has now come to pay off my promissory note. I shall argue in this chapter that it is our semantic knowledge of the character of a metaphor that enables us to express knowledge and information by the metaphor in addition to that expressed in its (propositional) content (in a context). The propositional content of a metaphor, like any propositional content, can always be expressed literally "in principle," that is, given the availability of a sufficiently rich literal vocabulary. But the "character-istic" knowledge or information carried by the metaphor—the knowledge or information that depends on and should be individuated by the character of the metaphor—is additional to the propositional content of the metaphor (in a context) and is not always equivalently conveyed through other linguistic means. Even if *what* the metaphorical character conveys can be put differently, *how* it conveys that information is also significant—and not literally duplicable.

Indeed, as we'll see toward the end of the chapter, even our formal semantic notion of character is not always fine enough to capture all the philosophically intuitive differences of significance we wish to register between modes by which metaphors present their contents. To that extent the "character-istic" information we wish to express outruns the expressive power of our formal notion of character. But, as we saw earlier at the end of chapter 3, section VII, similar shortcomings of the formal apparatus emerge in the theory of demonstratives. These reflect as much the limits of formalization as our theory in particular.

I'll begin by clarifying the problem posed for our knowledge *by* metaphor by a semantic theory of our knowledge *of* metaphor. In the past this problem has usually been presented in terms of literal paraphrasability. But this way of framing the issue has tended to obscure rather than clarify. In the remaining sections of this chapter, I'll try to recast the problem in a different mold.

II   The Rise and Fall of Literal Paraphrasability

The theme of knowledge *by* metaphor is not new to the literature. It has been taken up by way of a number of subjects: the cognitive significance (or insignificance) of a metaphor; the surprise occasioned by a metaphor; and its figurative, or pictorial, versus its descriptive aspects. However, by far the most attention has focused on whether metaphors are literally paraphrasable: whether the meaning of a metaphor can be equivalently stated in literal words. This emphasis is not surprising in light of the history of theories of metaphor, but it has not been helpful in furthering our understanding of the nature and scope of the problem.

Historically, it appears to have been the rhetorical origins of the investigation of metaphor that gave rise to the idea that metaphors are paraphrasable. Beginning with Aristotle (though this was hardly his full view) through the rhetorical tradition in antiquity and the middle ages, a metaphor was mainly viewed as a decoration or ornament—a matter solely or primarily of form—superadded to the content of language, which, it was thought, could always be extracted from the metaphor and then expressed literally. Thus the Andalusian Hebrew poet and literary theorist Moses ibn Ezra (c. 1055 to after 1135) wrote in praise of biblical metaphors:

Know that ... metaphor is the most beautiful [of the literary figures] for both [poetry and prose]. And although that which is stated explicitly is fundamentally more accurate whereas metaphor is an irregularity, [the latter] is nevertheless possessed of elegance. When discourse is covered with the garments of metaphor and embellished with figure, its silken embroidery is made comely and its enameling, beautiful. The difference between ornamented and naked discourse is like the difference between eloquence and stammer.... Whoever among the contemporary men of understanding rejects this [use of] metaphor, denigrates the certain and the obvious and departs from the straight path.... For metaphor is used frequently in our [sacred] texts.... There is no harm in this; indeed it is inescapable.[5]

Here a metaphor is said to provide beautiful clothing for the naked body of discourse, its "unembellished" content, which we can identify from its expression in "naked discourse" or plain speech, bare of all ornaments and decorations. As the modern critic A. E. Housman says, metaphor and simile "are inessential [even] to poetry"; they are "accessories," employed by the poet "for ornament" only because the image contained possesses an "independent power to please."[6] If we strip off the metaphorical surface of an utterance or inscription, there exists beneath it a statement that would express its content explicitly. It is this possibility of an explicit literal paraphrase that underwrites the distinction between form and content presupposed by the rhetorical conception of metaphor as a purely stylistic device.

In Renaissance rhetoric, the ornamental conception of metaphor seems to have meant something different. Brian Vickers explains that while figures were described as "ornaments of rhetoric," an ornament was not, as we mean nowadays, "a decoration not functional to the overall aim," but rather a piece of equipment or accoutrement, an instrument to make discourse more intense and effective, even if primarily emotionally. Thus figures were "functional, persuasive, not decorative."[7] It is, perhaps, against this background that we should also understand the famous negative comments of Hobbes and Locke, who charge that the essentially rhetorical function of metaphor makes it dangerous, deceptive, and undesirable, something to be eliminated wherever and whenever possible.[8]

The rhetorical conception of metaphor as ornament, in any of these versions, is rarely held today. However, its noncognitivist motivations survive in the guise of two contemporary cognitivist arguments for literal paraphrasability. The first of these is semantic eliminativism. If we can state everything the metaphor says in a literal paraphrase—say, by substituting literal for metaphorical terms or by expanding the metaphor into a literal comparison statement—we can eliminate the need to posit a special kind of metaphorical meaning. Instead we can explain how metaphor works either as a species of our knowledge of the literal or as one kind of speaker's meaning. The second argument originated as a reaction to the view that metaphors are merely expressions of feeling or emotion that lack all cognitive content, a view that was held by movements as disparate as the Romantics and logical positivists. In response to these positions, in order to legitimate metaphor as the expression of "serious thought" (Black 1962, 25), it was argued that they make truth-claims no different than literal language. But where there is truth and falsity, there must be truth-conditions or propositional content. Assuming that the language contains a sufficiently rich literal vocabulary, any such metaphorically expressed propositional content should therefore be "in principle" literally expressible. For, despite its metaphorical *means* of expression, *what* the metaphor expresses should be the same kind of language-independent or language-neutral propositional content that can be expressed literally. After all, the very nature of propositional content is to be an abstracted object of understanding that admits, and can be equally well expressed by, different inter- and intralinguistic expressions.[9] All metaphors should therefore be literally paraphrasable.

The intentions of these proponents of metaphorical cognitivism were honorable, but the net effect of their arguments was to reaffirm the old view that there is no increment of information added to the literally expressible propositional content of a metaphor by its metaphorical means of expression. The metaphorical mode of expression turned out, once again, to be of no cognitive value, even if the function of metaphor was no longer thought to be essentially rhetorical, ornamental, or decorative. It was in reaction to such "decoration" theories of metaphor that figures like I. A. Richards, Cleanth Brooks, and Max Black, in the 1950s, insisted on the *cognitive autonomy* of at least some metaphors.[10] As Black put it:

Suppose we try to state [their] cognitive content in "plain language." Up to a point we may succeed.... But the set of literal statements so obtained will not have the same power to inform and enlighten as the original.... One of the points I most wish to stress is that the loss in such cases is a loss in cognitive content.... [The literal paraphrase] fails to be a translation because it fails to give the insight that the metaphor did. (1962, 46)

Black defended his view by proposing on the same page his own "interaction" theory of metaphor. However, even if we reject his defense, there is no denying that he identified a compelling intuition that (at least some) metaphors are, for some reason, unparaphrasable. No matter how complete, how detailed, how subtle a literal paraphrase one provides for a particular metaphor—indeed the more detailed and fuller, the longer, the more prolix the paraphrase—*something* seems to be invariably lost, at least a significant difference in structure and effect, however hard it is to spell out the relevant idea of structure and in what this effect consists. Hence no literal expression can serve as a "full" paraphrase of the cognitive content of a metaphor and thereby substitute for it.

I share Black's forceful intuition, but it remains for us to make sense of this differential information. The cognitive autonomy theorist lumps all differences between the metaphorical and literal into one category he labels *cognitive content*. But when asked to be more precise and explicit about the difference in cognitive content between the metaphorical and the literal, he is pushed to more and more obscure defenses. Black, for example, says that the "insight" fostered by the metaphor that is not expressed by its literal paraphrase results from "a distinctive intellectual operation" (ibid.). However he immediately—and paradoxically—adds parenthetically that this operation is "familiar enough through our experiences of learning *anything whatever*" (ibid.)! One quickly begins to suspect that the autonomy theorist's view of the distinctive insight of a metaphor is less and less distinguishable from the view that what metaphors distinctively express is really *non*propositional—feeling, emotion, or (in Frege's terminology) coloring. In sum: Neither of the two traditional camps—the decoration theory or the cognitive autonomy theory— do justice to both intuitions and theory. We end up with either descriptively inadequate paraphrases of metaphors or hopelessly obscure explanations of their unparaphrasability.

Consequently, the general dilemma for accounts of knowledge *by* metaphor is to show how the following two theses jointly hold.

(A) Metaphors (i.e., utterances in which at least one constituent is interpreted metaphorically) are truth-valued utterances; hence metaphors have truth-conditions or propositional content no different from that of literally interpreted utterances.

(B) The information or knowledge or cognitive content (i.e., content that is either true or false, or true or false *of* things) communicated by a metaphor is at least in part a function of the specifically metaphorical mode by which the utterance is interpreted.

Contemporary theorists have reacted to this dilemma in different ways. Davidson's reply, for example, is to defend (A) by denying (B). As we have seen, he argues that a metaphorical utterance expresses nothing other than what the utterance expresses with its literal meaning (according to which it is typically false). The purported information cited in (B) is really an *effect* of the utterance rather than content "contained" in it, and typically it is not even propositional. A second extreme, taken (in different ways) by Lakoff and Johnson (1980) and by Ricoeur (1962, 1978), appears at first to defend both (A) *and* (B). However, they also claim that the received notions of truth and propositional content assumed by (A) are based on an illegitimate paradigm of literal meaning and objective truth and must, therefore, be rejected. In effect they defend (B) by denying (A).

My own position assumes (A), the thesis that (assertions of declarative sentences containing) metaphors are true—in the same sense of 'true' in which 'snow is white' is true. And some of the arguments in this chapter will lend this assumption additional indirect support. But my main aim is to show how my semantic conception of our knowledge *of* metaphor—a conception built on (A)—supports (B): how the very same semantic competence in metaphor underlies the speaker's ability to express knowledge, or information, *by* the metaphor that is not expressed as part of a literal statement of its propositional content in its context of utterance.

Before turning to this positive project, one last preliminary comment: I alluded several paragraphs back to reservations about the usefulness of literal paraphrasability as a device to explain our knowledge *by* metaphor. Let me say a word about my doubts. To begin with, the very idea that literal paraphrasability should be a necessary condition for a metaphor to have cognitive content or to convey information undercuts the function of specific metaphors. As daily experience demonstrates and as historians of language remind us, metaphors are frequently used to express contents for which no literal expression is available at the time of utterance. So why *require* that all metaphors always be literally paraphrasable?[11] Furthermore, it is never made clear what constitutes an adequate literal paraphrase of a metaphor. Must the paraphrase be a single simple expression or can it be a complex string or phrase? Apart from the fact that which concepts are lexically represented by simple expressions and which by complex phrases is itself an idiosyncratic fact that varies from language to language, the first alternative would seem too strong, the second too weak.[12] Finally, there is a deeper problem with literal paraphrasability as a litmus test for the cognitive status of a metaphor. The condition achieved its prominence against the background of a set of assumptions about meaning and linguistic competence that prevailed earlier in the century among Anglo-American philosophers of language. It was assumed that each competent speaker has complete, context-invariant, and determinate understanding of all the meanings of all the expressions in his language; that this knowledge of meaning consists in knowledge of truth- (or satisfaction-) conditions; and that a competent speaker should be able either to articulate the cognitive meaning of any expression in an explicit definition or synonymous paraphrase or, where that is not feasible, to manifest his knowledge of meaning by demonstrating that he recognizes when sentences (containing the expression) are established on particular occasions to be true or false.

Few philosophers of language nowadays would accept all of these assumptions, and many would accept none of them. The requirement that the cognitive meanings of expressions should be generally definable and paraphrasable is subject to many of the same kinds of criticisms leveled by Kripke and others against description theories of proper and general names. Quine's critique of synonymy and analyticity back in the 1950s undid the explanatory usefulness of talk of paraphrase as part of accounts of knowledge of meaning. The identification of meaning with truth-conditions does not hold in general, as we have seen with demonstratives. And, last of all, the assumption that a speaker's linguistic competence consists in complete and determinate knowledge of meanings rests on an unacceptably strong individualistic conception of mind and knowledge. I shall not review objections to this view, but my account gives more central place to the extralinguistic context in individuating the contents of one's knowledge *by* metaphor.[13] In short, the ability to articulate explicitly in a (literal) paraphrase what one knows when one understands a use of language is not to be expected *even for literal language*. On pain of enforcing a double standard, we should not demand more of metaphor.

These reservations do not show, of course, that literal paraphrasability has no value in understanding knowledge *by* metaphor. Rather my point is to displace it from center stage, to situate it within a broader arena of discussion that includes other ways in which knowledge *by* metaphor is manifest. The first claim I shall discuss, the "endlessness" of metaphorical interpretation, was traditionally offered in support of the unparaphrasability thesis; in recent years philosophers have employed it to draw a diametrically opposed conclusion about the nature of metaphorical meaning. However, neither side of the dispute has paid sufficient attention to the nature of the purported endlessness. To get a better look at this feature, we must also look at other ways in which knowledge *by* metaphor is displayed. In the next section I'll take the first step toward these other approaches to the topic.

III   The Endlessness of Metaphorical Interpretation

According to a widely shared intuition, metaphors admit endless or at least open-ended interpretations; what they mean or communicate is never antecedently fixed. William Empson describes metaphors as "pregnant" with meaning. Stanley Cavell calls a metaphor "burgeoning" with meaning; he insists that paraphrases of metaphors significantly end with 'and so on'.[14] Davidson writes that what a metaphor conveys is not

finite in scope.... [T]here is no limit to what a metaphor calls to our attention.... When we try to say what a metaphor 'means', we soon realize there is no end to what we want to mention. If someone draws his finger along a coastline on a map, how many things are drawn to your attention? You might list a great many, but you could not finish since the idea of finishing would have no clear application. (WMM, 263)

However, despite their common premise, these authors draw opposing conclusions. Empson and Cavell conclude that metaphors must have a special kind of cognitive content or meaning. If metaphors are true, they must be "wildly true—mythically or magically or primitively true" (Cavell 1967, 81). Davidson, on the other hand, infers from the fact that they lack a finitely specifiable set of truth-conditions that metaphors cannot be used to make true or false assertions in the received senses of "true" and "false"; hence they have no cognitive or propositional content (other than their literal one).

Nonetheless all these authors seem to agree that in fact there *is* no end to the number of properties, features, or things a metaphor expresses. But what is the nature of this purported "infinitude," "endlessness," or "inexhaustibility" of whatever it is that a metaphor conveys? Before we draw conclusions from a phenomenon, we must secure its existence.[15]

One relatively noncontroversial way in which a metaphor (type) Φ admits limitless interpretation is that there is no fixed upper limit on the number of different *contents* (tokens of) Φ expresses in different *contexts*—relative to different context sets of presuppositions—because there is no upper bound on the number of different contexts in which Φ can be used. Recall, again, our examples (1)–(10) in chapter 1, section II. In each example, one character for a single metaphorical expression (type), say, 'Mthat['is the sun']', determines different contents in the different contexts—given different sets of presuppositions—in which it is uttered. Thus a single metaphor (type) is capable of apparently endless or at least an indefinitely large, unbounded number of interpretations, contents, in its respective contexts. However, apart from knotty questions about how to individuate contexts, note that *in* each respective context, the interpretation, or content, of the metaphor is finite and fixed. The conditions under which the utterance is true or false in that context are determinate and finite. If we know the context set and our literal vocabulary is rich enough, it even ought to be possible for us to state the content finitistically. Hence this kind of limitlessness of metaphorical interpretation neither conflicts with the finitistic requirements of a semantics (as Davidson seems to argue) nor requires a different kind of truth or content sui generis to metaphor (as Cavell suggests).[16]

This explanation also suggests an additional way in which the knowledge conveyed by a metaphor is not exhausted by its fixed, finite content in a single context. Besides knowing the specific content each utterance of the metaphor generates in each context, the speaker also knows (in each context) that its context-sensitive character *would* determine a different content given a *different* context. And he knows that if he knew what the alternative presuppositions were, he could also figure out, or calculate, what its content would be. This knowledge, corresponding to the character of the metaphorical expression, resembles the "directions" contained in the characters of indexicals like 'I'.[17] Both instances of character-istic information endow their respective types with a *power* or *potential* for further, future interpretation lacked by the characters of expressions (types) that are context-*in*dependent. But for both types of expressions, indexicals and metaphors, the "directions"—how to interpret them in arbitrary contexts—that we know in knowing their characters are never themselves part of their contents in any particular contexts; therefore they will not be expressed by any (literal) statement of the content of an utterance, be it a metaphor or indexical, in a particular context. This, I propose, is Cavell's insight when he insists on the significance of the "and so on" that comes at the end of any example of a literal paraphrase of a metaphor. Obviously this "and so on" cannot be eliminated by a specific supplementation of content, no matter how much content we add. What the "and so on" signals is a *potential* for a different or additional interpretation that, by hypothesis, no *actual* interpretation can capture or exhaust.

This potential for further interpretation is essential in order to understand properly how metaphors function in science. One scientist proposes a metaphor based on a content it expresses in an initial context, a context in which, say, he notices, and so (in our sense) presupposes, that the literal referent of the vehicle exemplifies some feature to be attributed. What he says, relative to that presupposition set, is taken to be true or false in that context. But in proposing the metaphor, he may *also* intend for others to adopt it as their own: to accept the truth expressed by the metaphor (in that context) as a hypothesis in order to explore it, both by extending the metaphor in subsequent contexts relative to expanding presupposition sets built on his own and by following out the associations made by the various networks to which the literal vehicle belongs.[18] However, notice that the content of the metaphor in future contexts is neither determined nor constrained by the original author's *intention* in choosing the metaphor with its respective character, or meaning. In the course of exploring the metaphor in subsequent contexts, later interpreters are not revealing, or recovering, content originally intended by the one who introduced the metaphor. Once proposed, the metaphor possesses a life of its own, its life span limited only by the degree of potential carried by its character and by the presuppositions that depend on the creativity, imagination, and powers of discovery of its users in their respective contexts. Metaphors may be pregnant with meaning, but that need not mean that all potential interpretations are "embryonically" contained in the initial content or in the original *Sinn* in the mind of the one who first conceived the metaphor.

Yet these explanations for the endlessness of metaphorical interpretation are not the end of the story. What many writers, Davidson and Cavell included, have in mind is not only the countless number of different interpretations that a single metaphor (type) might have in different contexts. Nor is it the potentiality for further interpretation carried by the character of the metaphor. They also want to claim that what a metaphor expresses *within* one context has no end. This fact, if it is a fact, does conflict with the requirements of a finitistic semantic theory, thereby constituting a major difference between metaphorical and other kinds of semantic interpretation. And, as we saw earlier, different authors draw different morals from this alleged intracontextual interpretive endlessness. For some, so much the worse for finitistic semantics. For others, so much the worse for metaphor, or for metaphorical meaning, or for the possibility of a semantics of metaphor.

But what could this kind of intracontextual interpretive endlessness consist in? Are these authors claiming that if we actually try to state the content of a particular metaphor, we in fact find ourselves going on and on, mentioning feature after feature, proposition after proposition, literally never coming to an end? As a matter of practice, I know of no evidence (fortunately) that this is ever true.[19] To borrow the metaphor of a few paragraphs back: metaphors may indeed be pregnant with meaning, but it would also be a strange pregnancy if it had no term and if it issued forth in endless streams of progeny.

Although we have not yet found evidence that metaphorical interpretation is endless in an objectionable way, there is nonetheless a widespread sense that metaphor is semantically anomalous because (as

Davidson put it) it is so hard so much of the time to say "exactly"—determinately—what the content of a live, vital metaphor is supposed to be, especially in poetry and literature. Can we explain (away) this *apparent* endlessness or indeterminacy in some other way?

One account would begin with the explanation of how context or, more precisely, the force of the utterance fixes determinate content for other uses of metaphor. An utterance that purports to make an assertion, or to communicate information (or to perform another speech act that presupposes assertion), purports to have a determinate content or truth-conditions. So, when a metaphor occurs in a prima facie assertion (or utterance presupposing assertion), that use typically exerts pressure on the participants to fix their presuppositions in order to generate a determinate content for the metaphor that must be satisfied for the utterance to be true, to be assertible.[20] But by the same token, if the utterance does not itself have the force of or presuppose assertion, indeterminacy can be the result. Metaphors in poetry or literature whose point is *not* assertion may, on the contrary, aim at a multiplicity of alternative contents (and thereby ostensible truth-values).[21] Rather than pressure us to fix and delimit the presuppositions, these contexts may nurture the very plurality of possible contents that results when we leave a unique selection of the presuppositions unresolved, a range of alternative sets of presuppositions left open. For these metaphors, there may indeed be no one unique proposition asserted. But the *coherence* of such indeterminacy presumes that in some context and used in another way, the content of a metaphor *is* fixed and determinate: that the content of the metaphor in some context does uniquely determine one or another truth-value. The most plausible way, in other words, to account for *in*determinacy of metaphorical content—the difficulty we sometimes have (and some critics and readers welcome) in deciding on the content of some metaphors—is by assuming, at least under a reasonable idealization, that there are metaphors with determinate contents.

In any case, we have not yet discovered a sense in which our knowledge *by* metaphor *within a single context* is "endless" in a way that would conflict with the requirements of semantic knowledge *of* metaphor. But this is not the end of our story. In the following sections I shall turn to other ways in which our knowledge *by* metaphor is manifest, including other ways in which a literal statement may not capture "everything" conveyed by a metaphor. This will eventually lead us back to a different dimension of the character of a metaphor in terms of which we will be able to explain its "endlessness."

IV   Metaphorical Mode of Presentation

Throughout this book (e.g., in ch. 1, examples (1)–(10)) we have seen how one metaphorical character can determine different contents in different contexts, that is, relative to different sets of presuppositions. Inversely, one content (say, one property) can be determined by different metaphorical characters relative to different sets of contextual presuppositions. For example, in Nigeria people use the metaphor "She is my bedbug" as a term of affection for their lover (or beloved)—ostensibly because bedbugs are cute there.[22] Of course, given *our* presuppositions about bedbugs, if we Americans were to "translate" the same metaphor, we would be saying that she is a nuisance. To express the same content as the Nigerians with a metaphor, we (or at least W. C. Fields) might say: "She is my little chickadee."[23] In short: different contexts, same content, different metaphorical characters.

This relation between metaphorical character and content is reminiscent of the relation between Frege's notions of sense and reference (see ch. 3, secs. I, VI). Frege, you'll recall, posits the notion of sense in order to solve his puzzle of identity (among other reasons): to explain how true identity statements like

(3) The Morning Star = The Morning Star

(4) The Morning Star = The Evening Star

might differ in their cognitive significance or informational value. (3) is known a priori to be true; learning (4) might be and, for some ancient Babylonian, presumably was a genuine empirical discovery. Frege's explanation of this cognitive difference is to distinguish between the referents of the terms and the different modes under which they present their referents. The *mode of presentation* of the referent, which Frege locates in the *sense*, or *Sinn*, of the expression, constitutes the qualitative perspective from which the speaker is epistemically related to the thing. This epistemic difference between the senses of the terms flanking the identity sign in (4) accounts for its informativeness, unlike the uninformative (3) whose flanking terms have the same sense as well as referent.

Frege's own examples involve proper names and definite descriptions, that is, eternal singular terms. However, as we also saw in chapter 3, section VI, Kaplan shows that the same puzzle arises with demonstratives:

(5) That [the speaker points at Venus in the morning sky] = That [the speaker points at Venus in the morning sky]

(6) That [the speaker points at Venus in the morning sky] = That [the speaker points at Venus in the evening sky]

(where (6) is uttered *very* slowly). Because Frege's solution in terms of sense won't work for these directly referential terms, Kaplan proposes that we look to the different *characters* of the respective complete demonstratives, where those characters are individuated by their different demonstrations or presentations. One presents Venus as seen in the morning sky, the other as seen in the evening. Just as Frege views sense as the mode of presentation of its referent, so Kaplan proposes that we view the character of a complete demonstrative as a mode of presentation of its content.

To pursue our explanation of metaphor on the model of demonstratives, I want to propose that metaphorical character also provides a mode of presentation of its content (in a context). That is, there is information or cognitive significance carried and individuated by the character of the expression interpreted metaphorically, or its corresponding metaphorical expression, above and beyond its propositional, truth-conditional content in a context, "character-istic" information that is never captured in a statement of the content alone. But from that it does not follow, let me immediately add, that the character-istic information is different in cognitive kind from the information contained in propositional content. Everything else being equal (which, we shall see in a minute, is also *not* entirely the case), there is no reason that information or cognitive value should not be expressible by some (other) proposition; it is just not part of the content generated by that utterance in its context.

If we turn back for a moment to the old problem of literal paraphrasability, it is now tempting to try to recast it in the mold of Frege's puzzle. Recall that the problem of paraphrasability was that, on the one hand, if metaphors have propositional content, it ought ("in principle," given a rich enough literal vocabulary, etc.) to be possible to state that content without change (loss *or*, for that matter, gain) in informativeness in literal language. On the other hand, the information or knowledge expressed by a metaphor also appears to be a function of its metaphorical mode of expression, which is *not* preserved in literal paraphrases (as the many descriptively inadequate literal paraphrases attest). Now, in light of our parallel with demonstratives, why not treat that difference in informativeness between a metaphor and its literal propositional paraphrase on the model of our account of the difference in informativeness between the identity statements in the demonstrative version of Frege's puzzle? Why not treat the difference in information or cognitive significance between a statement containing an expression interpreted metaphorically such as

(7) Phil is an eel

or, equivalently,

(7*) Phil Mthat['is an eel']

uttered in a context c and a literal statement with (let's suppose by hypothesis) the same content in c, for example,

(8) Phil is stealthy,

just as we would treat the difference between the two identities

(9) The proposition that Phil is an eel = The proposition that Phil is stealthy

or, equivalently,

(9*) The proposition that Phil Mthat['is an eel'] = The proposition that Phil is stealthy

and

(10) The proposition that Phil is stealthy = The proposition that Phil is stealthy.

(where the context c in which (7)–(10) are all uttered is a context in which 'is an eel' is interpreted metaphorically to express the same content expressed by 'is stealthy' interpreted literally)? The same solution proposed to account for the difference in informativeness between the two demonstrative identity statements (5)–(6) with the same content should carry over to the difference in informativeness, or cognitive significance, between the statement containing a metaphor and the literal statement with, by hypothesis, the same content. In both cases, the difference in informativeness is a function of their different characters, which present their common content under different modes. It is precisely this characteristic difference that is felt to be lost in paraphrase.

V Surprise

Surprise is another feature associated with metaphor on which we might also be able to throw some light using the Fregean account of informativeness in terms of differences in mode of presentation. According to Frege (1966), the relevant notion of informativeness that distinguishes (6) from (5) is manifest in the fact that it is a *discovery* for someone to learn that identities like (6) are true, that such statements "contain very valuable extensions of our knowledge and cannot always be established a priori" (56). Something similar happens when we hear or learn a metaphor (or a metaphor/literal identity like (9)). As philosophers since Aristotle have observed, some metaphors have a particular power to occasion surprise.

> Liveliness is specially conveyed by metaphor, and by the further power of surprising the hearer; because the hearer expected something different, his acquisition of the new idea impresses him all the more. His mind seems to say, 'Yes, to be sure, I never thought of that.' (*Rhetoric* 1412a 18–21)

But not all notions of surprise are relevant for metaphor. One idea makes it a function of the probability of the sentence (type) being tokened; the lower the probability, the greater the surprise. This notion won't work for us since there is no plausible way to assign probabilities to the tokening of sentences on occasions.[24] A second notion makes surprise a matter of unpredictability. But we have argued that, constrained as they are, metaphors are not absolutely unpredictable. A more promising idea for our purposes takes surprise to be a "cognitive emotion": an emotion that presupposes that its subject has certain accompanying beliefs and expectations that purport to justify it and that would be unjustified if the beliefs and expectations turn out to be false.[25] In the passage quoted, Aristotle proposes two cognitive conditions for the surprise occasioned by a metaphor: (1) the subject must believe that he has acquired a "new idea" through the metaphor; and (2) his acquisition of the new idea must somehow differ from his prior expectations. But what is the new "idea" he must believe he has acquired with the metaphor, and how must it differ from his prior expectations? When the hearer expresses his surprise by saying "I never thought of *that*," what does the demonstrative refer to? Is it the content (in that context) of the metaphor: that Juliet has some property P—that she is worthy of worship and of Romeo's undivided attention? No, what is new cannot simply be the unprecedented attribution of the property in question to the subject; it cannot be a function simply of the content of the utterance. If it were, the surprise occasioned by the metaphor would be no different from what follows any novel application of a literal predicate—that is, any literal attribution of a previously unattributed property. This kind of surprise or novelty is not insignificant but it is hardly specific to metaphor. Instead, the surprise must be a function, at least in part, of its metaphorical mode of expression or attribution, that is, the character of the metaphor. What the hearer never thought of is that *Juliet is the sun*—not literally, of course, for that is not surprising. We all know that the (literally expressed) proposition is false. But what may be surprising—both new and different from a prior expectation—is that Juliet Mthat['is the sun'], that she can be truly ascribed a certain property under the mode of presentation conveyed by 'Mthat['is the sun']' given the contextual presuppositions associated with the metaphorical expression. The property itself may be one we could express literally or it may be expressible only metaphorically. But even if we could express the same content some other way, it would still be a substantial cognitive accomplishment to see that we can express or refer to it by employing that metaphor in that context. In either case, the new idea is a function in part of the contribution of the character of the metaphor, the context-specific perspective from which it enables us to grasp and express the feature ascribed.

It is more difficult to say exactly what the hearer must have expected differently that contributes to its surprise when he hears the metaphor. Once again, if the surprise in question is occasioned by the utterance *because* it contains a metaphor, it cannot be a difference only between its content (in the context) and prior beliefs. But the divergence from prior expectations might also not be of one kind for all metaphors. One kind of divergence would presumably be where the utterance expresses a "semantically anomalous" proposition, or category mistake, under what would have been its literal interpretation. In that case, the surprise or novelty would be, as Goodman (1976) puts it, "a matter of teaching an old word new tricks" (69). In previous accounts, the point in appealing to such literal anomalousness was to explain why the utterance is *identified* as a metaphor; here I am suggesting that the anomalousness registers the "distance" (however that is measured) between the characters of the expressions employed in the utterance, not to show how literally *unlike* they are from each other, but to signal how *unlikely* it is that we would antecedently think that we could say something true about the content of the one using the other. As Aristotle says (ibid., 10–12), a resemblance perceived between "things far apart" is more striking, and hence surprising, than one between things closely related. On this view, the expectations need not contradict or conflict with the metaphor; it is sufficient if the resemblance is simply unanticipated given prior expectations.[26] In either case, the departure from prior expectations is not what makes the utterance a metaphor, but what makes the metaphorical interpretation surprising.[27]

VI Metaphorical Perspective

Can we now say more specifically what the cognitively significant difference between the characters of metaphorical and literal expressions consists in? And how the metaphorical mode of presentation of a content (in
a context) is different from the content itself? Let's begin with another
example from *Romeo and Juliet*. When Lady Capulet entreats Juliet to
take a greater interest in Paris, she tells her:

Read o'er the *volume* of young Paris' face
And find delight *writ* there with beauty's *pen*.
Examine every married lineament
And see how one another *lends content*;
And what *obscur'd* in this fair *volume* lies,
Find *written* in the *margent* of his eyes.
This precious *book* of love, this *unbound* lover,
To beautify him only lacks a *cover*.
The fish lives in the sea; and 'tis much pride
For fair without the fair within to hide
That *book* in many's eyes doth share the glory
That in *gold clasps locks* in the golden *story*.
(I,iii, 81–92; my italics)

Here Lady Capulet presents Paris to Juliet as if he were a book, drawing
on the metaphor network that people are books, a metaphor scheme that
was especially popular among the Elizabethans (and is still used today).[28]
People can be 'read' like books, hence truly known by those and only
those who have 'literate' skills. Their facial features are 'signs' that 'communicate' 'content'. Eyes are 'margins' in which 'commentary' and 'emphasis' are 'written', clues how to interpret what is 'hidden' in the 'pages'
of the person's life. Its 'covers' complete the book here; hence Paris without a lover is 'unbound', incomplete—and, with some implied sexual
connotation, naked.[29] Furthermore, as important as these many book-
like properties ascribed to Paris is the opening directive of the passage to
Juliet to 'read' Paris. Not only are (some) people books; others are (related to them as) readers and authors. (It is not obvious what the sortal
alternatives to the 'people are books [to be read]' metaphor would have
been for Shakespeare ['people are pictures to be viewed'?] but clearly the
scheme would be different, as it might be nowadays, if the alternatives to
'books' were 'software' or 'a computer program/file' or 'a video'.)

These are the terms in which Lady Capulet metaphorically describes
Paris to Juliet. Were we to try to state the *content* of her speech (as literally as we can), it would be something like: 'Study Paris closely, both his

natural features and his behavior, and you'll discover his many natural virtues, attractive qualities, his capacity to love. To learn his inner virtues and character traits, pay close attention to his outward acts and features—and, realizing all this, you'll realize that all this wonderful man lacks is a wife. Indeed the woman who marries him will share in his universal admiration and glory. Therefore . . .'.

Shakespeare does not express this content literally. Nor does he use a set of independent individual metaphors. Instead he uses a single systematically intraconnected metaphor network. In chapter 5, I argued at length that metaphor networks are essential to determining the *contents* of the individual metaphorical expressions that belong to them. Here I want to focus on a second role of metaphor networks that turns on the information carried by the sums of their constituent characters. By employing this network that determines the contents of its member expressions, Shakespeare also adds a cognitive significance to Lady Capulet's speech in its entirety. But this additional significance is not more *content*; rather it is a *perspective* on, or a *way of seeing*, that content. Let me try to explain what I mean by (the metaphors) a "perspective on" or a "way of seeing or presenting" content, beginning with one class of nonmetaphorical expressions: not surprisingly, indexicals.

Consider the context-oriented perspective that is a feature of indexical language. A crucial part of what a speaker knows when she knows the meaning, or character, of one indexical is knowledge of its *inter*indexical relations and the mandatory conditions under which one indexical must replace another. For example, a speaker knows that when she utters a sentence S of the form '. . . today . . .' on day d to express one propositional content, then in order to express that same content on day $(d + 1)$, she cannot use S but must shift (assuming she wants to use an indexical) to S', which contains 'yesterday' in place of 'today'. If she does not know that required transformation, she fails to know something essential to the meaning of 'today'. Thus one knows the meaning of any one indexical only if one knows the meaning of the indexical system to which it belongs. To borrow an image from James Higginbotham (forthcoming), the set of indexicals constitutes a set of coordinate points marking their respective parametric positions as they are interrelated in a context. When we change perspective by referring to the same individual from a different position—calling today 'yesterday' tomorrow—to preserve the reference we must shift, not just the one indexical, but its whole coordinate system. Here, then, we individuate the perspective offered by each individual indexical by the unit of its containing system, not by the unit of the individual term.

For indexicals, this systematic feature of their perspectives is, of course, especially striking because, as Frege (1984) first observed, there are *oblig-atory* rules that direct the replacement of one indexical by another to preserve referent, or content, under change of context. "If someone wants to say today what he expressed yesterday using the word 'today', he will replace this word with 'yesterday'.... It is the same with words like 'here' and 'there' " (40). And, I would add, 'I' and 'you', and 'today' and 'to-morrow'. These content-preserving substitutions are mandatory in all linguistic contexts, including embedded that-clauses, under the relevant change of extralinguistic context. So, if Jack says on Monday morning:

Jill is going up the hill

I can report later that day:

Jack said that Jill is going up the hill today

but on Tuesday I *must* say:

Jack said that Jill was going up the hill yesterday.

These transformations are routine. Indeed the routine, mandatory shifting of indexicals might also be taken to show that the perspective preserved across these substitutions, whatever it is, is also *all* there is to the charac-ter-istic cognitive significance of indexicals. For if there were additional cognitive differences semantically individuated at the level of the charac-ters of the individual indexicals, we would expect them to make a differ-ence in the substitution-behavior of the indexicals in attitudinal contexts. The fact that they do not, that the referent/content-preserving replace-ments are *mandatory,* suggests that there is no additional cognitive per-spectival or character-istic information semantically associated with the indexicals at the level of their characters. But, in any case, in adopting the use of an indexical, the speaker *commits* himself to its entire coordinate system, which must be systematically changed with shifts in context.

Something similar is at work with metaphor, although there is nothing nearly as perspicuous as the perspective determined by the indexical sys-tem. Metaphor networks—whether they are the schemes of exemplifica-tion or inductive networks or even thematic relations—are not governed by *routine*, let alone *mandatory*, transformations of terms to accommo-date changes of context. (Note, on the one hand, that in this respect metaphors are more like complete demonstratives, for which there are also no obligatory, routine rules. On the other hand, for the thematic networks, we can predict required thematic arguments for verbs but not unique candidates to discharge those roles.) Yet the perspective furnished by a metaphor network shows itself in the many ways that it guides, directs, even *commits* us to go on metaphorically, to extend and elaborate a given metaphor. When we adopt a metaphor, we adopt—or inherit—its respective scheme(s) and network(s). If we change the relevant feature of context for a metaphor—the context set of presuppositions we associate with the vehicle of the metaphorical expression—we must change not only that individual expression but its whole family to preserve the content. Although you could obviously read each of the (italicized) expressions in Lady Capulet's speech independently of one another *and* each metaphorically, to do so would leave out something significant about them *as metaphors*: that they are all members of a single interrelated scheme organized and weighted relative to each other. To borrow again from Quine, the cognitive significance specific to the metaphorical mode of expression of a metaphor is awarded to it not as an individual term but as a member of a corporate body (or bodies)—its network or scheme.

The set of schematic, network-oriented commitments of a metaphor is a central element in the idea of a perspective (on its content) that is contributed by the metaphorical character of the metaphorical expression 'Mthat[Φ]'. It is no accident that, when asked what Romeo meant by 'Juliet is the sun', we reply with something like: "Romeo means that Juliet is the warmth of his world; that his day begins with her rising; that he can flourish only when she shines her light on him." Simply to give the content of the metaphor (which we might do "in principle" in a literal paraphrase) would not capture the additional perspective in which Romeo stands toward what he says. And the only way to give that perspectival information is by spelling out its metaphorical consequences and commitments: by elaborating the place of Φ in its various schematic inferences and networks, drawing out its metaphorical extensions and the other members of its family. So, the fact that we frequently explain a metaphor with more metaphors—not breaking out of the metaphorical circle—should not be taken to be objectionable. Nor should the fact that we sense the inadequacy of literal paraphrases or explications of metaphors be seen as a problem (as many seem to have thought in the past) for the cognitive status of metaphor. On the contrary, these facts are characteristic of the very way in which a metaphor furnishes its cognitive perspective on, or mode of presentation of, its content. Indeed we have now come full circle. Not only is it not necessary (as philosophers used to think) that we be able to literally paraphrase a metaphor in order to manifest our knowledge of its "meaning"; the—perhaps only—way we can manifest our understanding of the mode of presentation provided by a metaphor is by elaborating the other metaphors in its scheme or family.

As with indexicals, a metaphor's perspective on its content is context-oriented. Therefore, it is a function of the character of the metaphorical expression rather than of its content (in that context). But it should be noted that context interacts with the mode of presentation carried by the character of the metaphor at two points. First, the scheme to which the utterance of a given metaphor belongs, and as a member of which it comes to have its particular mode of presentation, depends on and may vary with the context. Second, like the character of a demonstrative, the character of the metaphor, which carries its perspective on its content, is nonconstant and context sensitive. Only someone occupying Romeo's context, someone who makes (even if he does not himself believe) his presuppositions about the sun—say, that it is the center of the universe and that everything else revolves around it—can express what he does with his metaphor: that Juliet is the one on whom all his actions are focused. The mode by which the metaphor presents its content requires the figures in Shakespeare's play, and us as interpreters, to adopt a common contextual perspective by making particular shared presuppositions. But, to use our earlier terminology, some of these contextual presuppositions are presemantic, involved in assigning its character to the metaphor, and others are semantic: given the character, they function as its contextual argument to yield content. And not unlike the problem we faced in chapter 4, section IV in apportioning presuppositions among the semantic and pragmatic determinants of appropriateness, here, too, it may not always be absolutely clear how to distinguish the role of a particular presupposition. This difficulty will recur in the coming sections.

VII Metaphor and Seeing-as

In chapter 3, we saw how Frege's notion of sense reflects his perspectivalism. In the same vein, the (additional) cognitive significance individuated by the character of a metaphor should be conceived as an epistemic "perspective" on its content. Although Frege only hints at the systematic character of his perspectivalism in his brief remarks about indexicals, metaphorical perspective, I argued in the previous section, is deeply rooted in the networks and schemes to which the interpreter (speaker, user) of the metaphor commits himself in his interpretation of a metaphor. In this and the next two sections I want to discuss three ways in which this network-individuated perspective corresponding to the character of a metaphor provides both different information and information of a different kind than its propositional content (in a context). The first two of these are, I want to suggest, ways to work out the often-repeated (but rarely explicated) claim that metaphor is connected to the phenomenon of seeing-as: that when Romeo utters 'Juliet is the sun' he *sees* (and invites his interpreters to *see*) Juliet *as* the sun. The third way will return us to our opening example of Marie and the semantic status of metaphor in belief.

What is meant when we say that Romeo's utterance of the metaphor 'Juliet is the sun' makes us *see* Juliet *as* the sun? One thing is that Romeo is not simply asserting the single belief that is its content in its context. By seeing Juliet *as* the sun, Romeo commits himself, and asks his interpreters to commit themselves, to a *way of thinking of* Juliet and her properties that is broader than the content of a single belief. To think of Juliet *as* the sun, as opposed to merely thinking that she *is* the sun, is to direct oneself to think of her in terms of the scheme(s) to which the metaphor 'Juliet is the sun' (in its context) belongs.[30] This commitment—to think of Juliet and her properties in terms of a complete, complex metaphor scheme—cannot be adequately cashed out simply by *enumerating* each of the contents of the individual beliefs that would be expressed by utterances of the metaphors that belong to the scheme in question (even on the supposition that we could exhaustively list all the members of the scheme). For what that enumeration of contents would leave out is the structure of and relations between the metaphors in the scheme, the way in which the scheme packages those metaphorically expressed properties, including the weighting, ordering, and organizing that expresses the speaker's and interpreters' comparative evaluations of the properties. It is this kind of structure that Black may have had in mind when he wrote that to use chess vocabulary (which itself is vocabulary transferred from talk about medieval knightly battle, a fact that curiously enough Black does not mention) to describe a battle

will lead some aspects of the battle to be emphasized, others to be neglected, and all to be organized in a way that would cause much more strain in other modes of description. The chess vocabulary filters and transforms.... The metaphor selects emphasizes, suppresses, and organizes features of the principal subject....

Suppose we try to state the cognitive content ... in "plain language".... The set of literal statements so obtained will not have the same power to inform and enlighten as the original.... [T]he implications, previously left for a suitable reader to adduce for himself, with a nice feeling for their relative priorities and degrees of importance, are now presented explicitly as though having equal weight. (Black 1962, 42–46)

Black goes on to say that this kind of information conveyed by a metaphor is sui generis. However, as Martin Davies (1982a) has persuasively argued, the kind of structuring or restructuring of properties achieved by a metaphor can be equally well achieved with literal language. Suppose I have a quiet, polite neighbor—call him Philby—always responsible in paying his bills and doing his duties, who prizes his privacy and, though not unfriendly, keeps to himself and does not make it easy for his neighbors to get to know him well; a fairly innocuous neighbor who does not bother or disturb anyone else and who does little to attract attention. Then one day we learn that he has been arrested as a spy for The Enemy. Now *seeing* Philby *as* a spy, that is, *thinking* of him *as* a spy, puts all his familiar properties in a new light. We see his dutiful, responsible, polite behavior in light of an ulterior motive—designed to give us a certain impression. We understand differently than we did before why he was so guarded about his privacy and why it was so difficult to get to know him well. We reinterpret all his efforts at anonymity and innocuousness in terms of his newly discovered occupation. The novel piece of news that Philby is a spy is not just a single new belief we acquire (although it is also that); for it restructures and reorganizes all of our other (prior) beliefs about him—and will also lead us to discover, or uncover, other beliefs we might not have noticed otherwise (say, about his passion for electronic gimmicks and high-frequency radios).

Similarly, Davies argues, with metaphors: Seeing Juliet *as* the sun restructures our complex of beliefs and attitudes about Juliet. It puts her and her properties in a completely new light, a light that both displays her familiar properties in ways we did not see before and reveals new properties. What is this new light? It is thinking of Juliet in the terms of the metaphor schema to which one's utterance of 'Juliet is the sun' (in that context) commits one. As we have seen, this way of thinking of the subject and its properties may entail revisions in our conception of the relations between the properties expressed by the members of the schema, sometimes large-scale changes that involve redescriptions of the properties, sometimes more subtle ones about their relative weights. Davies is certainly right that metaphor is not unique among devices that can achieve such global, complex reorganizations and restructuring of beliefs. But a metaphor, via its character, is especially well suited to this task because of its place, essential to its identity as a metaphor, within a larger governing schema: because its use carries along with it the macroscopic way of thinking of contents that is spelled out by its network(s). As Davies also notes (though not in these terms), this way of thinking of Juliet and her properties is not itself the *content* of any single metaphor in its context; yet it is cognitive significance nonetheless—cognitive significance that can be identified only when we attend to the level of the character of the metaphor.

Insofar as the structured schema to which a metaphor belongs creates an organized, and thus unified, way of thinking about the properties that are the contents of its individual members, we might say that it subsumes them under a new complex category or concept. However, this kind of novel categorization or "conceptualization" achieved by a metaphor should be distinguished from the other way (discussed in ch. 5, sec. VI) in which a metaphor can "introduce" novel properties: through the *de re* (in Burge's sense) expression of properties for which we possess at the time of utterance no context-independent, conceptualized (if you will, "literal") means of expression, properties to which we can be epistemically related only by exploiting the extralinguistic context, like the properties expressed by predicate demonstratives. Where the knowledge by metaphor is *de re* in this sense, the further cognitive significance, or perspective, contributed by the schema of its character, may complement it—and help define the "bare" property (in terms of its schematic role). But even where the individual properties expressed by the metaphors that belong to a schema are such that we *could* express them by fully conceptualized means, the effect of the metaphor-schematic perspective will be to *present* them in a different, unanticipated form (as in the Philby example) that furnishes knowledge *by* the metaphor we did not otherwise have.

A good example of this information conveyed by the structure of a schema beyond that of its constituent metaphors can be seen in the metaphorical language at work in discussions of a recent U.S. Divorce Court case over the value of a corporate wife's work, her contribution to her husband's career. According to Judith Dobrzynski, writing in the *International Herald Tribune* (January 25–26, 1997; all italics mine), the issue is "how much is [the corporate wife's] *contribution* [to her husband's career] *worth?*" And "its resolution will be a verdict on the institution of marriage itself and on the value of the supportive duties traditionally known as 'women's *work*'"; "Invoking economic theory, [the plaintiff, a wife who turned down a $10 million settlement] is arguing that her performance as a corporate wife was an *investment, entitling* her to half the family fortune.... 'Gary wanted to *buy out my partnership, and I didn't want to be bought out,*' [she said, using language she learned in her role]; 'It's *like a hostile takeover—he offered me a very small percentage, I said that's not the price of the buyout.*' According to Prof. Martha Fineman, "the important public policy issue here is: What is the nature of the marital *partnership?... Is it an equal partnership* or is a housewife *a junior partner?*" In each of these statements, there would be no difficulty interpreting (and literally explicating) the contents of the individual (italicized) metaphors. But the cognitive effect of the metaphor schema as a totality is powerful in its own right. Playing on the traditional *literal* description of marriage as a partnership, the metaphorical application of the contemporary legal/economic schema—none of whose constituents is inductively related to the nonlegal/noneconomic term—furnishes a novel way of thinking of the marriage institution. It selects and reorganizes the not unfamiliar properties expressed by each of the constituent predicates to fit the legal/economic partnership model. And, to anticipate section IX, the metaphorical schema also explains the *behavior* of the parties to the divorce in ways that the received notion of marriage as (literally) a partnership, of course, never would.

This is also, perhaps, the cognitive significance of Lady Capulet's use of the 'people are books' metaphor schema. It is difficult to think that the contents of any of the individual metaphors in that passage were not known by Juliet independently. But by reorienting her relation to Paris to that of a reader to a book, Lady Capulet makes Juliet see her relation to Paris as something different than what the contents of those metaphors singly would have meant to her. And, again, this differential information can be captured only by looking at the character of the metaphor beyond its content (in the context).

VIII Metaphor and Pictures I

There is a second significance that Donald Davidson, among others, has attached to the claim that a metaphor makes us see one thing as another: the idea that metaphors are pictorial or picture-like.[31] The metaphor/ picture analogy is an old and rich one—metaphors are, after all, *figures* of speech—and, I shall argue, it is crucial to understanding how the character-istic perspective furnished by a metaphor is distinctive. However, it is also primarily from this analogy that Davidson draws his well-known denial that metaphors have propositional content. Apart from his objection that what a metaphor conveys should not be given the status of *meaning* (the objection we addressed back in ch. 2), Davidson argues that the so-called content of a metaphor is just what it makes us "notice" or "see"; that what the metaphor makes us notice or see, in turn, is no different in kind from what a picture makes us notice or see; and that what a picture makes us notice or see is not content. In particular, he singles out two features common to metaphors and pictures that legislate against their expressing content. First, like a picture, "there is no limit to what a metaphor calls to our attention."[32] Second, as with a picture, when we hear a metaphor "what we notice or see is not, in general, propositional in character." As with Wittgenstein's duck-rabbit, when I get you to *see* one thing *as* something else, "no proposition expresses what I have led you to see.... Seeing as is not seeing that." Analogously, "metaphor makes us see one thing as another" but this is not "recognition of some truth or fact" (ibid., 263), that is, something contentful of the kind addressed by a semantic theory.

Although I shall argue against Davidson's conclusion that metaphors do not express metaphorically specific propositional contents, I do think that he puts his finger on a pictorial dimension that distinguishes the *character* of a metaphor from that of nonmetaphorical expressions. And despite the fact that we have rejected (in section III) a number of arguments for the endlessness of metaphorical interpretation, there is also a kind of endlessness we have not yet examined that falls out of Davidson's analogy between metaphors and pictures. But before turning to that argument, I shall briefly discuss another argument—best formulated by Richard Moran, although it expresses a widely felt intuition (which Davidson also hints at)—that metaphors do not have "definite" propositional content because the "irresistible" force of their picture-like seeing-as violates a condition on the assertion and communication of content.[33] In section IX, I'll return to Davidson's main argument.

According to Moran (1989), an assertion is characterized by the fact that, having understood it, one is always in a position to accept or reject it. "There is no category of utterances that necessarily produce, when understood, agreement or belief in what they assert" (92). In the same vein, "communication involves a relation between assertion and belief, and is always resistible. And part of what this means is that the notions of communication and of saying require that a distinction can always be drawn between understanding and belief" (99). On the other hand, metaphors—and here Moran has in mind live, successful metaphors that make us see (or "frame") one thing as (or in terms of) another—have a "compelling power" or force that makes them "irresistible" (ibid.). Once understood, they compel acceptance (as true) or rejection (as false). This "compelling" force or power of a metaphor, Moran further argues, is best explained by its pictorial dimension. To understand or interpret a metaphor is, like viewing a picture, to *see* things a certain way, to *see* one thing *as* another, and, where that seeing-as is successful, thus to *believe* them to be that way. Both successfully seeing what a picture depicts and understanding what a metaphor expresses have factive implications. So, when a speaker interprets the metaphor '*a* is *F*', if he succeeds, he sees *a* as an *F*. But then he must also believe *a* to be *F*, not literally of course, but metaphorically. He must believe *a* to have a particular feature metaphorically related to *F*. Therefore, there remains no space between understanding, or interpreting, the metaphorical utterance and believing it; if we "get" the metaphor, or understand its interpretation, we cannot but believe what it says. But if all assertions are, by hypothesis, "resistible"—if all assertions leave open the possibility of belief or acceptance—*and* what the metaphor makes us see is not resistible, it follows that no metaphorical utterance can express the content of an assertion.[34]

In reply, we can agree, to begin with, that there is a close connection between the interpretation of a metaphor and belief. To "get" a metaphor, to understand it, is to *give* it an interpretation, and gifts of metaphorical interpretation, like other gifts of interpretation, are governed by charity. We take speakers to mean what, in light of our beliefs, is (or is compatible with what is) true—as well as informative, interesting, and appropriate. Unless we have a story to explain why it was nonetheless reasonable for the speaker to say something false by our lights, falsity counts against a purported interpretation. As a rule, then, our interpretations of metaphors express what (for all we know) is true. (Of course, what we, or the whole community, *believe* to be true may turn out to *be* false.) So, what a metaphor is interpreted to assert will, by and large, be something we *ought* to believe.

Moran, however, seems to have something yet stronger in mind. If it is necessary to successfully see *a* as an *F* in order to interpret the metaphor '*a* is *F*', we must already *believe* that *a* has some particular feature—the feature that in turn is the content of the metaphorical assertion—in virtue of which it can be seen as an *F*. Thus the very *interpreting* of the metaphor puts us in its doxastic grip; having generated the interpretation by way of seeing one thing as another, there is no further (open) question whether or not it is true, to be accepted or rejected, whether, say, *a* has the feature in virtue of which it can be *seen as* an *F*.

But does this show that metaphors cannot be used to make assertions? I would still resist this conclusion. Suppose the understanding of a metaphor already presupposes belief in its interpretation. Contrary to Moran's blanket claim that *no* class of utterances "necessarily produce, when understood, agreement or belief in what they assert," there is a venerable (even if criticized) tradition that there is a significant class of utterances with this very property: the so-called analytic (and, depending on one's philosophical position, a priori) truths. When one grasps their meaning, or what they assert, she already knows (hence believes) that they are (and must be) true. It is for this reason that if someone sincerely and knowingly denies (and, perhaps, even doubts) one of these to be true, there is often sufficient reason to doubt either her rationality or her linguistic competence—whether she truly understands the utterance.

Metaphors are not analytic truths, but the case suggests that there is some normative relation for at least some propositions between understanding and belief. A second class of utterances, whose status is still closer to that of metaphors, is that of the "pragmatically necessary" truths, such as 'I am here now', which are true on every occasion on which they are uttered, and which speakers are assumed to believe in virtue of their knowledge of language, for example, their understanding of the meanings of the words 'I', 'here', and 'now' and their structural relations to each other. Whenever I utter this sentence, I know that it expresses a truth, something that I cannot but believe—even if (for lack of empirical knowledge of where or who I am) I do not know *what* proposition I am asserting. With these utterances as well, there is no gap between understanding them—at least understanding what they mean, if not their truth-conditional content, or what they say—and believing them to be true. One can resist assent on understanding them only at the cost of casting doubt on one's rationality or linguistic competence. Here, too, there is no further question whether the utterance is true or false, should be believed or not, once we understand its linguistic meaning.

There remain, to be sure, differences between metaphors and pragmatically necessary truths. However, the two examples of analytic and pragmatically necessary truths suffice to show that we need not worry that we are violating a *general* condition on assertion if it should turn out that, given our practices of (charitable) interpretation, our understanding of a metaphor, or even our knowledge that the metaphor has an interpretation (even if we do not know precisely what it is), is accompanied by belief in or assent to its truth. Metaphors do not "create" facts (or similarities), but their interpretation may be self-verifying or self-fulfilling. What a metaphor makes us see does not make what we see, but what is there to be seen may explain why the metaphor makes us see it. Therefore, the fact that the seeing-as involved in generating the content of the metaphor may presuppose belief need not impugn its assertability, nor should it be taken to show that the content of a metaphor is nonpropositional.

IX   Metaphor and Pictures II

I now turn to Davidson's argument against the propositional status of metaphors on the grounds that they make us see aspects or features by way of picture-like seeing-as that is not propositional seeing-that.[35] As I said in section VIII, Davidson has drawn our attention to a feature that distinguishes the network-oriented cognitive perspective carried by metaphorical character—which in turn enables us to make sense of the endlessness of metaphor—although his argument does not show (I'll argue, contra Davidson) that metaphors do not have propositional content. Let's begin by putting aside two ways in which seeing-as *cannot* make the difference Davidson wants it to make.

First, there is an uncontroversial sense in which seeing-as is not seeing-that. The object of seeing-that is a sentential clause, whereas the object of seeing-as is a predicative clause (or an open sentence)—the subject is seen as having some property. This difference, however, cannot support Davidson's conclusion that what the metaphor (or picture) makes us notice is not propositional if what we mean by "propositional" is not only (in the narrow sense) a complete proposition (or closed sentence), one that is either true or false, but also a propositional constituent like a property that is true or false *of* things and that can figure in singular (or our referential) propositions.

Second, although we do say that Romeo's metaphor makes us "see" Juliet as the sun, this obviously cannot be taken to mean that we (literally) see her as the sun in the same way that we do (literally) see the physical medium of a picture as what it is a picture of. There is no evidence that metaphors are visual in their functioning, that they make us visualize their content, that they evoke mental images, or that they visually depict what they say.[36] Neither this nor the previous consideration, then, supports Davidson's claim that metaphors are pictorial in a way that would render them nonpropositional.

Nonetheless, I agree that there *is* a pictorial dimension to metaphor and that the perspective it generates cannot be expressed propositionally. We can begin to see what this perspective might be from Davidson's comment that when the metaphor 'he was burned up' was "active, we would have *pictured* fire in the eyes or smoke coming out of the ears."[37] Would we have? Well, yes and no, depending on what we mean by "pictured." If we mean 'formed a mental image or picture', then perhaps some of us but not others would have (if only because of the well-known variation among individuals' capacities to construct mental images). This reading of the claim is at best inconclusive. On the other hand, what almost certainly is the case is that when the metaphor 'he was burned up' was active, or alive, we would have also *said* that the subject had fire in the eyes or smoke coming out of the ears. That is, when the metaphor was alive, it would have functioned as part of a productive network in which we would have drawn extensions like these from the antecedent metaphor. This relation between a metaphor and its schema, I want to argue, is the key to its pictorial dimension and its distinctive character-istic cognitive significance. Let me explain.

What makes a symbol pictorial is neither that it is perceived in a visual medium or modality, nor that it visually depicts its subject matter.[38] Instead it is a matter of its mode of expression. Like a picture, a metaphor *displays* rather than *describes* its content. There are a number of proposals in the literature that attempt to articulate this distinction between pictures and descriptions; the most common technical formulation is that pictures or the contents of the visual experiences they depict are analog, while discursive symbols and linguistic descriptions are digital. Unfortunately, there is also little agreement over the theoretical explication of the analog-digital distinction. For the sake of exposition, I'll follow Nelson Goodman's version of the distinction—with a little help from John Haugeland.[39]

Goodman defines the distinction in terms of the finite differentiability of symbol schemata (sets of basic characters and rules of composition) and symbol systems (schemata correlated with fields of reference); Haugeland formulates it in terms of write-read computer procedures, that is, the procedures for replicating or repeating tokens of a type. For our purposes, the crucial issue is syntactic, but to fill out the picture I will also lay out some of the parallel semantic notions. Three notions are basic for us. (1) A system exhibits syntactic finite differentiation if it is the case that whenever a mark doesn't in fact belong to both of two characters, one can always determine at least in principle that it doesn't belong to one or the other. It exhibits semantic finite differentiation if it is the case that whenever an object doesn't in fact comply with both of two characters, one can always determine at least in principle that it doesn't comply with one or the other. (2) A system exhibits syntactic density if between every two characters a third always exists, thereby assuring that the system isn't syntactically differentiated. It exhibits semantic density if between every two compliance classes a third always exists, thereby assuring that it isn't semantically differentiated. (3) A system is replete (as opposed to attenuated) to the extent that the features of a mark pertinent to determining the character or characters it instantiates (if any) are many and varied. The first two characteristics of symbol systems are in principle all or nothing; repleteness and attenuation are matters of degree.

With these distinctions in place we can begin to capture various antecedently familiar and functionally important distinctions between symbol systems. In particular, analog systems are syntactically and semantically dense, since they are set up so as to denote arbitrarily small continuous changes in one quantity by means of sufficiently small continuous changes in another. Digital systems, by contrast, exhibit syntactic and semantic finite differentiation. Linguistic systems, once they have been suitably disambiguated, exhibit syntactic disjointness and syntactic finite differentiation, but they lack semantic disjointness and semantic finite differentiation: arbitrarily small changes in an object can require large changes in its accurate description, for example. Pictorial systems are highly replete analog systems, since arbitrary and arbitrarily small changes in almost any of a picture's pictorial properties correlate with real (typically small) changes in what an object needs to be like for the picture in question to depict it. (Less replete analog systems are at work in maps, diagrams, and the like.) In general, then, except by explicit fiat, no feature can be ruled out ahead of time as irrelevant to the individuation of a picture; every difference can potentially make a difference.

For our purposes, the main consequence of these conditions is that the tokens of characters in analog schemata like pictures cannot be *replicated* and that tokens of digital characters can be. In the pictorial case, it is impossible to determine to which type a given token-picture uniquely belongs; hence it is impossible to determine unequivocally that another token-picture is of the same type. Here, it should be emphasized, "determine" means *know*. Even if by chance we did produce a replica of a pictorial inscription, we would lack a theoretically possible test to ascertain that we did. Furthermore, as Haugeland emphasizes in his formulation, even if we *might* on an occasion somehow succeed in producing such a replica, for analog schemata like pictures we lack the requisite *procedures* to do so, procedures that produce absolutely perfect replicas ("positive procedures," in Haugeland's terms) that can be relied on to succeed every time.

What we need for a positive procedure is a notion of type defined for a particular criterion or along a particular dimension (such as spelling) that lets us disregard all other differences along other dimensions. (If we always had to take into account *all* differences along *all* dimensions, no two things could ever be "perfect copies" of each other.) Replicas, then, are anything but perfect copies of each other. Just the opposite: It is because replicas of a type are individuated by a specific criterion, such as spelling, that it is unnecessary for two tokens to be copies to pass as replicas. With pictures, on the other hand, no feature (unless ruled out by explicit fiat) can be ignored or abstracted away and, because variations are continuous or smooth, the least difference will matter. Hence the best available procedures produce approximations to the original, not perfect copies. On the other hand, for lack of a single or restricted set of parameters or dimensions (e.g., spelling) to define pictorial types, no two tokens can unequivocally be said to belong to one type. Hence there are no procedures to produce either pictorial replicas or perfect copies of other pictures.[40]

It follows that no description can state exactly what a picture displays, not simply because their respective individual characters (types) are different but because the one is digital, the other analog, that is, because the tokens of the first admit replication, those of the second do not. Therefore, we can never map members of a picture system one-to-one onto those of a descriptional system and, if natural languages are descriptional systems, and propositions are paradigmatically expressed by language, it also follows that we cannot one-to-one map "pictorial content" onto propositional content. Furthermore, if the cognitive value of an expression is individuated by its character and the character of an expression by its type (and we extend characters to pictures), there always ought to be some cognitively significant difference between the characters of a picture and of a linguistic description, some loss (or gain) of information in any correlation of pictures with descriptions. If it is indeterminate to exactly which of indefinitely many types a given picture token belongs—because any of its indefinite number of features counts toward individuating its type—when we put the picture into words we ipso facto classify it arbitrarily under exactly one type, thereby disregarding certain of its aspects as irrelevant for its individuation, as "don't matters." Whether or not one thinks that its analog "character" makes a depiction richer than a description, it is clear that any such "translation" would impoverish the number of features relevant to identifying its type.[41]

A similar explanation applies to the pictorialness of metaphors. The cognitive significance of a metaphor at the level of its character in part depends on the perspective individuated by the schema to which the vehicle belongs. But the least difference between two expressions (tokens), even if both of them are interpreted metaphorically, can affect their schematic relations. Certainly any difference between their respective characters will affect their schematic association, but, as we said, even slight unpredictable differences in context, or in the context set of presuppositions, can change the constitution of the schema of a metaphor, the other metaphors to which it is related, and hence affect its characteristic, schema-relative cognitive significance. Indeed not only features of the type of the metaphor but even of its tokening may bear on its schematic membership. It is in this respect that a metaphor behaves as if it were a picture, image, or nondiscursive representation, that is, as if it were a member of a replete dense, or analog, system of representations that does not admit of replication, for which we possess no procedures that produce absolutely perfect replicas. The slightest difference between two metaphors can make a difference.

Let me emphasize that, when I say that the least difference can result in a difference of schema, I am allowing that even the formal notion of character may not always be individuated finely enough to capture all relevant identity conditions for two metaphors to bear the same cognitive significance, insofar as that depends on their respective schemata. Consider 'Tully' and 'Cicero' used metaphorically. These two co-referring proper names have the same content and (because their respective characters are constant) also the same character. But in some contexts one can be used metaphorically to express a property that the other would not. In the seventeenth century, for example (when even non-Quine-reading-philosophers knew that 'Tully' and 'Cicero' were the same Roman, namely, Marcus Tullius Cicero), one would have used 'x is a Cicero' to say metaphorically that someone is an outstanding orator but 'x is a (or my) Tully' to say that he is a defender of liberty, or to refer to him as the author, with affection.[42] For proper names like these, it would appear that only the fact that they are lexically different—the fact that they are different names—can mark the different schemata to which they belong. Character *simpliciter* will not do the job.[43]

For the same reason, synonymy (even defined as identity of character) is not sufficient to preserve schematic association and hence the cognitive significance that is a function of the schema to which a given metaphor belongs. 'Sweat' and 'perspiration' are about as close synonyms as any two words (differing only in their Fregean coloring), but we clearly cannot preserve the metaphorical interpretation of

(11) Tonya Harding is the bead of raw sweat in a field of dainty perspirers. (*Time Magazine*, Jan. 24, 1994, 51)

if we substitute the synonyms:

*(12) Tonya Harding is the bead of raw perspiration in a field of dainty
sweaters (sweating people).

*(13) Tonya Harding is the bead of raw perspiration in a field of dainty
perspirers.

or

*(14) Tonya Harding is the bead of raw sweat in a field of dainty
sweaters (sweating people).

Just as its density makes it impossible to "put a picture into words," so
the fact that no feature—linguistic or extralinguistic—of the utterance of
a metaphor can be discounted in determining its respective schema makes
it near impossible to express the knowledge conveyed by the character of
a metaphor except with that very metaphor. It is in this respect that (linguistic) metaphors are like syntactically not finitely differentiated—and
thus irreplicable—pictures.[44]

On this understanding of the pictorial character of a metaphor, we can
also now make semantic sense of the idea that metaphorical interpretation
is, even within a context, "nonfinite" or "endless." The point is not that
we can go on interpreting a metaphor without end, but that we lack
knowledge of definite—fixed, finitistic—conditions for individuating the
appropriate notion of a type for a metaphor that would exactly demarcate
the knowledge conveyed by its schema-dependent perspective. That is, we
lack knowledge of the means to express that knowledge in a finitely differentiated symbol scheme—one that is propositional. And perhaps this,
as Cavell wrote, is "the whole truth in the view that metaphors are
unparaphrasable, that their meaning is bound up in the very words they
employ."[45]

We can now appreciate what is right about Davidson's claim that what
a metaphor makes us notice is nonpropositional. Insofar as the notion of
propositional content is the idea of something that admits alternative
expressions in language, the schema-dependent cognitive significance
individuated at the level of the character of the metaphor does not fit the
bill of propositional content.[46] But what Davidson fails to mention is that
this is true *only* of the knowledge *by* metaphor individuated at the level of
its character. It is not true of what the metaphor expresses in its content
(in a context). Nor, contra Davidson, does the fact that a metaphor carries this increment of cognitive significance at the level of its character
count against its *having* propositional content.[47]

X   Belief in Metaphor: Marie Again

Let's now return to Marie. What light does our account of the cognitive
significance of metaphorical character throw on the behavior of metaphors in beliefs and belief-reports? To answer this, I shall first turn back
to indexicals and then draw a moral for metaphor.

We attribute beliefs and desires—on the received view: attitudes toward
propositions—among other reasons, to explain and predict the behavior
of agents. But when we attribute beliefs using sentences that contain
demonstratives and indexicals, what plays an explanatory role is not
merely their content but also their character and, in particular, the characters of their indexical and demonstrative elements. John Perry gives an
especially vivid example of this type of explanatory significance that
attaches to demonstratives and indexicals.

I once followed a trail of sugar on a supermarket floor, pushing my cart down the
aisle on one side of the counter and back the other side, seeking the shopper with
the torn sack to tell him of the mess. But with each trip around the counter, the
trail became thicker and I seemed unable to catch up. Finally, it dawned on me: I
was the shopper I was trying to catch. (1979/1988, 83)

And at that point, Perry stopped and cleaned up his mess. Now, what led
him to change his course of action? Presumably a new belief he had
acquired. But what belief was that? Well, the belief he would have
expressed by saying to himself: "I am the one making the mess." But
what belief is *that*? That is, if belief is prima facie a relation to a proposition, what *proposition* is expressed by the indexical sentence "I am the one
making the mess" that would also *explain* Perry's action? Surely he didn't
learn the proposition that the shopper with the torn sack was making a
mess; he knew that from the start. Was it, then, the proposition that *John
Perry* was making the mess? No—unless we add an additional but elliptic
premise that he would have, in turn, expressed to himself as '*I* am John
Perry'. For simply coming to believe the proposition that *John Perry* was
making a mess would not be enough to make *him* stop unless he also
believed that he himself *was* John Perry. And once we add the belief
expressed as '*I* am John Perry', we are back to a belief expressed by a
sentence that contains an indexical. Similar considerations hold for all
other candidate representations of the required belief. Unless we build
into our representation of Perry's belief that he believed that *he himself*
is the individual making the mess, we cannot explain why *he* acted as
he did. Hence, in Perry's belief, the first person indexical 'I' occurs

essentially; it is impossible to eliminate the indexical, or the indexical character by which he represents his belief to himself, if his belief is to explain his behavior.

To get a better sense of the power of indexicals to explain action, consider another example offered by both Kaplan (1989a) and John Perry (1977). Suppose you (Max) and I (JS) are walking toward each other down a dimly lit street and I see a mugger steal up behind you. I yell out in warning:

(15) You are about to be mugged

and, given that belief, run for help. You, stunned by what is about to happen, yell out (perhaps echoing me):

(16) I am about to be mugged

and, doing what one does with *that* kind of belief, mobilize yourself and turn to face your attacker while assuming a martial arts position.

Now, both (15) and (16) express the same singular proposition:

(17) ⟨Max, *About to be mugged*⟩.

Our different actions (I run for help, you defend yourself) cannot, then, be explained by the *contents* of our utterances. And if our respective utterances correctly express the contents of our respective beliefs, it follows that our different actions also cannot be explained by the contents of our beliefs, namely, (17). Instead, the actions seem to correlate with the *characters* of the sentences we uttered. Indeed, if I had the same martial arts training, I would act the same way you did if *I* were the one about to be mugged, and you (presumably) would act the same way I did were *you* the warner—though the content of my utterance of (16) and your utterance of (15) would not be (17) but (18):

(18) ⟨JS, *About to be mugged*⟩.

Same content, different characters, different actions; different contents, same characters, same actions.

Perry and Kaplan conclude from examples like this that belief cannot simply be a two-place relation between a believer and proposition(-al content)—be it singular (as in the New theory) or fully conceptualized (as in the Old theory). Instead we need a three-place relation between believers, propositional contents, and "ways of thinking" of contents. Perry and Kaplan differ in their specific formulations for this third element, but for both of them there is an additional kind of cognitive element that is individuated semantically, either by the characters or sentence types of action-explaining beliefs containing indexicals.

It would be helpful to distinguish two separate claims in the conclusion of this argument. The first is that it is necessary to acknowledge "ways of thinking" of the contents of beliefs in addition to the contents themselves. The second thesis is that *arbitrary* "ways of thinking" can be individuated by indexical characters or, more generally, by the sentence-types of the utterances accepted by the speaker. I shall grant the first, but the second is more problematic. What complicates matters is that a believer may have more than one way of thinking of a given content, even given one sentence-type or given one character by means of which he expresses the content.[48] This is obvious, as we mentioned earlier, with expressions like proper names whose characters are constant. But, even with nonconstant characters like that of 'I', we don't have to make ourselves into Dr. Jekylls and Mr. Hydes to acknowledge that most of us have substantially different ways of thinking of ourselves on different occasions—given our other beliefs, moods, purposes, and so on—and that different individuals can have different ways of thinking of themselves even though we all use the first-person indexical 'I'. But if there can be this kind of variation from context to context among our ways of thinking of things, we cannot *in general* systematically individuate ways of thinking by characters or linguistic types of arbitrary expressions or sentences.[49]

A similar story can be told for metaphors in belief. The metaphorical characters by which beliefs are expressed, and not merely their propositional contents, may play an analogous essential role in the explanation of their agents' behavior. Recall Marie's utterance (repeated here):

(19) I won't swallow that [referring to her mother's interdiction].

Its content in its context of utterance is expressed by (20) (repeated here):

(20) Marie won't obey her mother's interdiction.

But that expression of its content does not enable us to explain Marie's anorexic behavior. Now, the character of the sentence she in fact uttered is not, precisely speaking, that of (19) but that of (21):

(21) I won't Mthat['swallow'] that [referring to her mother's interdiction],

which contains a metaphorical expression whose character, in turn, determines the corresponding propositional content, expressed by (20), in its context. Moreover, (21) contains the information that *is* relevant to explaining Marie's behavior: the information conveyed by the character of the metaphorical expression Mthat['swallow'] by which she represents its content (in that context) to herself. Therefore, were we to report what Marie believes in order to explain her eating disorder, we must report the content of her utterance *under its metaphorical character*. This is to say two things. First, this character-istic information is information that is not *part* of the propositional content (in any particular context) of the sentence whose character it is, and, for that reason, it will not be expressed in any statement of that content. Second, it does not follow from the first point *alone* that this character-istic information is *necessarily* information of a "different kind" from that carried by content, information that *could not* be propositionally expressed (say, as the content of some other sentence). However, it *may* be of a different kind. As we just saw in the case of indexicals, it may not be possible to individuate all ways of thinking relevant to the explanation of action that are expressed by a metaphor by its character. The perspective conveyed by a metaphorical character is relative to the schema to which its vehicle belongs—and that perspective, as argued in the previous section, lends a pictorial dimension to the metaphor. So, to the extent to which its perspective enters into the explanatory role of the metaphor, one character may be associated with different action-explanatory "ways of thinking" for one metaphorical expression on different occasions, and, furthermore, those ways of thinking may contain nonpropositional pictorial elements.

Nonetheless, like Perry's example of an "essential" indexical, the case of Marie is an example of an "essential metaphor." It is the metaphorical character of the expression she used (or the character of the metaphorical expression), her way of thinking of the information contained in the content of the metaphor *rather than the content itself*, that is essential to explaining her action. Much more, of course, remains to be said about the role of metaphors in belief and other attitudinal reports and in indirect discourse. In particular, I am not claiming that it is never sufficient to report the content of a subject's utterance of a metaphor without preserving its metaphorical character. For it is often the case that belief ascriptions are vehicles for reporting *only* the contents of a subject's beliefs rather than the manner in which he holds them or how he thinks about their content, and belief reports based on utterances containing metaphors are no different. However, our discussion does show that a general account of metaphor in belief reports should take into account not only their propositional contents but also ways of thinking of those contents, both individuals and properties. Insofar as we acknowledge that the character of an indexical possesses its own explanatory role and cognitive significance that must be incorporated in a complete theory of belief, we should do no less for metaphorical character.

XI The Moral of the Story

We are now in a better position to understand both the problem of knowledge *by* metaphor and the errors in some of its traditional and more recent diagnoses. Decoration theorists failed to recognize, and therefore disregarded, what is cognitively significant about metaphorical character. In the same way, those recent philosophers who attempt to focus the question of metaphorical interpretation *solely* on propositional content fail to do justice to what is specific to metaphor by relegating it to vacuous explanatory factors like "the special ways that metaphorical utterances have of calling other things to mind."[50] Autonomy theorists, on the other hand, have recognized what is cognitively significant about metaphorical character but, lumping it together with propositional content, have taken it all to be sui generis and mysterious. Philosophers like Davidson, who could be said to focus *entirely* on the significance specific to metaphorical character, are thereby (mis)led to deny that metaphors have any proposi-tional content. I have tried to steer a middle course between the omissions of the decoration theorists and the excesses of the autonomy theorists. By identifying the cognitive significance specific to a metaphor with its character and distinguishing it from its propositional content, we can acknowledge that there *is* a genuine semantic and cognitive difference between the metaphorical and the literal without making it occult. What distinguishes metaphors is their context-sensitive character-istic perspec-tive. By subsuming metaphors within the general category of expressions of nonconstant character, including demonstratives and indexicals, we can both recognize what makes them different and begin to understand it.

Chapter 8

From the Metaphorical to the Literal

In closing, I want to take up two questions raised by my account that touch on the boundaries of metaphorical interpretation: the range of symbols that can be interpreted metaphorically and the range of interpretations that are not metaphorical. Is metaphorical interpretation limited to natural language? And what is a nonmetaphorical, or literal, interpretation of language? I'll touch on the first question briefly; the second will occupy most of the chapter although I shall not answer it conclusively. Nevertheless, having come this far, we are in a much better position to articulate both questions. That alone is a small step of progress.

I Nonlinguistic Metaphors

We often hear it said that a picture (say, of Napoleon in a Roman toga) is metaphorical, or that a dance gesture is a metaphor for an emotion. Pablo Picasso called his sculptures "visual metaphors." Anthropologists tell us that various social interactions and religious rituals should be explained as metaphors. George Lakoff suggests that a depiction of smoke or steam coming out of a cartoon character's ears is a metaphorical depiction of anger, and a character falling on his face, a pictorial metaphor for social clumsiness.[1] A video blurb for Goddard's movie "Weekend" describes "a weekend trip from Paris to Normandy as a shattering metaphor for the decline of the West."

How should we understand these claims of metaphoricity? Are nonlinguistic symbols, objects, and events the sorts of things that can be interpreted or used metaphorically (or, for that matter, literally)? I have argued that an essential element of metaphorical competence is semantic, the same semantic competence that underlies speakers' abilities to interpret demonstratives and indexicals. But the semantic competence underlying the ability to use demonstratives and indexicals is arguably task-specific to language. Of course, in addition to semantic knowledge, there is also an extralinguistic factor in the interpretation of demonstratives and indexicals: the contribution made, for indexicals, by their contextual parameters and, for demonstratives, by their completing demonstrations, either presentations or pointings. Likewise, we have acknowledged the essential role of its extralinguistic contextual parameter, the context set of presuppositions, in metaphorical interpretation. Nonetheless, if a necessary component of metaphorical interpretation is task-specific linguistic, or semantic, knowledge, it should follow that only objects of language can themselves be metaphors. And if that is the case, all these nonlinguistic symbols would be at best metaphorically, but not literally, metaphorical. Or our description of these nonlinguistic symbols, or symbolic interpretations, as metaphor would be parasitic on our talk of linguistic metaphors; that is, without a linguistic gloss on these symbols, they would not admit metaphorical interpretation.

The issue is not terminological, and it also cannot be answered (simply) by appeal to ordinary language. The question concerns the *mechanism* that is essential to and distinctive of metaphor. Are metaphors distinguished by the *sources* of the contextual presuppositions on which their interpretations depend—the extralinguistic skills employed in the recognition of similarities, exemplification relations, or salience of other kinds (including the prominence attached to stereotypical features or normal notions)? Likewise, maybe it is their extralinguistic demonstrations that distinguish demonstratives. Or are metaphors (or the class of M-figures) and demonstratives really distinguished by their respective kinds of semantic context-dependence involving specific constraints on their possible interpretations?

My approach has emphasized the specifically semantic, hence linguistic knowledge employed in metaphorical interpretation. This focus should be contrasted with Nelson Goodman's, for whom there is a set of symbolic skills that cuts across all symbol systems (natural languages, pictures, musical notation, sketches, etc.) and modalities (the visual, auditory, etc.), one mode of which is metaphor.[2] Although Goodman, like myself, argues that it is not enough to look at the function or effect of a metaphor, that there must be some mechanism specific to metaphor that accounts for its effects, we differ over whether that mechanism is language-specific or not. Elsewhere, in Stern (1997), I have argued that Goodman's own proposed mechanism—transfer—will not work for pictures and other symbols that do not admit replication of tokens of one type. But in part our different views depend on different pretheoretical notions of what is essential or distinctive to metaphor and our accounts of the nonmetaphorical or literal. Since a full answer to the first question therefore rests on a better understanding of the literal, let me turn now to the boundary between the metaphorical and literal.

II Historical and Contemporary Notions of the Literal

How, in light of my account, should we demarcate, within natural language, the literal and metaphorical? In chapter 1, I proposed, as a working hypothesis, that the literal meaning of simple expressions should be whatever our best semantic theory decides is their semantic interpretation and, for complex expressions and sentences, the rule-by-rule composition of the literal meanings of their constituents. In constructing my theory of metaphor I have also tried to avoid loading more weight on the literal than can be reasonably borne by the semantic. Still, a nagging problem that repeatedly surfaces in discussions of metaphor is its relation to the literal. Some (including deconstructionists and lit crit theorists) deny that there is a distinction to be drawn between the two, period. Others (e.g., George Lakoff and his school) acknowledge a distinction but claim that, despite the "scientific philosopher's" prejudice for a purely literal language, all or the most important part of natural language is metaphorical. Still others (such as Davidson) claim that all there is is the literal, at least if we are talking about meaning; the metaphorical is just a class of effects that could equally well be effects of other kinds of causal antecedents. And still others (such as Ted Cohen 1997) insist that the distinction is so self-evident that it needs no defense. As I said back in chapter 1, I assume that there is a distinction, if only because it is close to an analytic truth about metaphor that it "depends" on the literal. Whatever that turns out to mean at the end of the day, dependence requires a distinction.

The question concerns the difference in *what* the interpreter knows when she knows the literal and metaphorical interpretations of an expression or sentence. I am not concerned with *how* she processes this knowledge or the psychology of language comprehension or production. Many psychologists in recent years have argued that there is no difference in length of time or speed of processing in speaker-hearers' production or comprehension of literal and metaphorical language. Be that as it may, the fact that speakers process literal and metaphorical interpretations in the same way or at the same speed is compatible with the existence of two different kinds of interpretation corresponding to the literal and metaphorical.[3]

Unlike metaphor, the literal has received relatively little sustained study of its own. Let me begin by bracketing a number of different uses of the words "literal" and "literally" that are irrelevant for our theoretical purposes.

1. When we talk about what a sentence "literally" means, sometimes we intend what it *precisely* or *univocally* or *specifically* means. But the literal need be no more precise, univocal, or specific than the metaphorical. When Romeo calls Juliet 'the sun' (in his respective context), that is precisely, specifically, and univocally what he means; I cannot imagine a more precise, specific, or univocal way of describing Juliet than that.

2. At one or another time in history, philosophers have used the "literal" to refer to the empirical or factual. This use reflects a particular theory of meaning, verificationist or empiricist, that many of us no longer share. In any case, our use of the term nowadays does not and need not carry that baggage.

3. Some writers take "literally" to mean "actually," and then use this assumption to argue that metaphors, not being literally true, are also not (indeed cannot be) actually true. And because the truth with which we are typically concerned is the actual truth of our utterances, they also conclude that metaphors, not being actually true, are not true, period. Therefore, metaphors cannot be asserted; for assertions are uses of sentences in which the speaker represents himself as intending to speak a truth.[4] This understanding of "literal" as "actual" rests on a confusion. What is "actually" true is simply a proposition that is true in the actual world, namely, the circumstances of the context in which the utterance is performed. Contraries of the actual are the merely possible and the contrafactual.[5] The distinction between the metaphorical and the literal, on the other hand, is a distinction between two kinds of interpretations or uses of language, not between kinds of truth, or between the circumstances in which what is said is true or false. Metaphors no less than literal utterances of sentences can therefore be actually true—just in case their interpretation, or what they are used to say, is true in the circumstances in which they are uttered.[6] In any case, actual is not what we mean by "literal."[7]

4. What is often said to *be* literal is not to be *interpreted* literally. As Vincent Canby once wrote:

How many movies have you seen that literally froze your blood, or literally left you breathless, or literally drove you up the wall? If you can name one, you are dead or have a serious medical problem, or can defy gravity. (*New York Times*, Jan. 14, 1979; 17)

A word about the history of the notion of literal meaning may throw some light on our problem. The origins of the "literal"—"of or pertaining to the letter" (O.E.D.)—are obscure, but the dominant original context for the use of literal meaning—*sensus literalus*—was medieval (Christian) scriptural interpretation.[8] In *On Christian Doctrine* (1958), Augustine distinguishes two classes of signifying entities: words and extralinguistic things (persons, events, objects, actions, places, positions, times). That is, apart from linguistic signs, there are "natural signs," (extralinguistic) things that by their nature signify, much as smoke is a sign of fire. Among these, all the things signified by the words of Scripture are, in turn, signs of a "higher" or "deeper" spiritual order. And among these latter signi- fications, three kinds are usually distinguished: the moral (something sig- nified about how one ought to act), the allegorical (something signified about the Church), and the anagogical (something signified concerning God, the saints, angels, and other heavenly beings). These kinds of signi- fications of things are akin to the property or concept *exemplified*, or re- ferred to, by an object, as I argued in chapter 5. None of these is directly, however, a meaning of a word.

Among the meanings of words, the medievals sometimes distinguish the proper or analogical (of which a word can have more than one, in which case it is ambiguous) and the improper. Among the latter, a leading kind is metaphor. On other occasions, they first classify the meanings of words into three functions—history, fable, and argument—and then, as part of the text's historical role according to which its words set out things as they actually happened, they distinguish the various analogical, or proper, "modes" of signification from the metaphorical mode. In either case, metaphors (e.g., 'the lion of Judah' referring to Christ) are understood as comparisons between the subject and the thing signified by the predicate ('lion'); hence they are meanings or significations of words rather than of things. On the other hand, in addition to their proper and metaphorical meanings, which words possess directly and by which they signify things, indirectly the words also inherit the meanings or significances of the things they signify. So the meaning of the word is never the whole of its "mean- ing" or significance; indeed it is often the least important signification.

Now the term "literal" is sometimes used in this medieval literature interchangeably with the meaning of a word, as opposed to a meaning of a thing. In that sense the literal "includes" the metaphorical. Sometimes it is used interchangeably with "historical," in which use it signifies a spe- cific function of the meanings of words: to set down what actually oc- curred. Here too the literal or historical use of language can work either properly or metaphorically, subsuming both. And sometimes the "literal"

means specifically the "proper" use of a word as opposed to a metaphorical or metonymic use, which is "improper." What makes a use "proper"?
During the earlier Middle Ages, we often find the literal identified with
the historical because it is at that level that the text tells a story. However,
in the first half of the twelfth century, it has been argued (e.g., by Evans
[1984], 68), a sharper distinction begins to emerge between the historical,
which is concerned with narrative, and the literal, whose concern is the
relation between words and the things they signify. A literal (use of a)
word is now said to be a (use of the) word that signifies what it does "in
the first place" (*primo loco*). This seems to be one sense in which a meaning is proper—which, in turn, is contrasted with figurative meanings,
which are transferred and thus not in their first place.[9] But there may
also be a second sense of "proper" at work here. The Latin term *propria*
for "proper" also has the sense of "usual" or "regular," that is, according
to a rule, not in a normative sense but in the sense of conforming to a
regularity.[10] Thus the literal would simply be common usage of the word.

I have recounted this rough story about the history of the literal in
order to give a sense of the many pieces of baggage the term carries. The
literal is the meaning of words as opposed to things; it is the meaning
whose primary function is descriptive—to tell a narrative; it is a primary
as opposed to derived, or transferred, meaning; and it has the primacy of
the proper, the rule-governed or perhaps just the regularly used. These
features do not combine into one neat package, and insofar as the term is
used sometimes with one, sometimes with another trace of its history in
mind, we should not expect sharp uniformity of usage or meaning. But
with this background, I now want to turn to some implications of my
account for our current understanding of the notion of the literal. Let me
begin with three consequences of my approach for any analysis.

To begin with, my theory rules out certain standard ways of drawing
the literal/nonliteral-metaphorical distinction. Since I take metaphorical
competence, that is, the speaker's knowledge of the metaphorical character of expressions (or the characters of metaphorical expressions), to be
semantic, we obviously cannot distinguish the metaphorical from the literal by saying that the latter is the object of semantic competence whereas
the former is not (but is instead pragmatic). Likewise, we cannot subsume
the literal/metaphorical distinction under the distinction between sentence
and speaker's (or utterance) meaning.

By the same token, we cannot distinguish the literal from the metaphorical meaning of a *sentence* (or of any other complex expression) by
means of compositionality. On that characterization, a literal sentential

meaning would be one that is uniquely composed from, or functionally determined by, the meanings of its constituent expressions and their syntax, whereas a metaphorical interpretation would be achieved non-compositionally, top-down rather than bottom-up, subject to all sorts of noncompositional contextual contributions. The difficulty with this view of the distinction has to do primarily with its statement of the principle of compositionality. Unless we are told more about the kinds of meanings, the syntax, and the sense in which the whole is a "function" of its parts, the principle is tautologous or empty.[11] On the one hand, it *is* true that the *content* of a sentence at least one constituent of which is interpreted metaphorically is not compositional, but that is equally true of the content of (utterances of) sentences containing indexicals and demonstratives, utterances of sentences like 'I am happy'. What follows from that observation is *not* that (an utterance of) such a sentence is not meant literally, but that, if compositionality is a criterion of the literal, it is not a principle that applies (only) at the level of content. On the other hand, if it is the *character* of a sentence to which the principle of compositionality applies, then sentences containing metaphors might also be compositional. Metaphorical expressions, like dthat-descriptions, are (at least lexically) compositional. To be sure, there remains the problem of individuating the characters of eternal co-intensional expressions, but that, again, is a problem for both the metaphorical and the literal. In either case, compositionality will not distinguish the literal and metaphorical.

A second consequence of my account is that, strictly speaking, there are no literal or metaphorical *expressions* per se (except as terms of art); there are only literal and metaphorical *interpretations* of expressions. The same holds, as we'll see in a minute, for the distinction between dead and live metaphors: It is their interpretations rather than the metaphorically interpreted expressions themselves that are dead or alive. Thus consider the many cases where a dead metaphor is brought back to life by verbal resuscitation: where 'hot as hell' gets new life as 'hot as the hinges as hell', and 'full of wind' becomes, in a poem of Yeats, 'an old bellows full of angry wind'. We can also sometimes witness a metaphorical reincarnation take place by reuniting a lost, isolated metaphor with its family: by placing a given expression, with an interpretation that we may have learned to assign to it primitively, and not metaphorically, in the context of the family or network of metaphors to which it historically belonged. (I would suggest this as an explanation of the powerful impact on us of many of Lakoff and Johnson's examples of systems of "conventional metaphors.") By recovering the network from which an expression acquired its present, even if no longer metaphorical, interpretation, we can bring its metaphoricity back to life.

The third implication follows from my characterization of metaphor as a special kind of context-dependent expression, an expression whose character is sensitive to its context set of presuppositions. This might be taken to suggest that the literal should be characterized as context-*in*dependent interpretation. And I shall argue in section IV that this is indeed one dimension of the literal. However, it might also be objected, as John Searle (1983) has, that all sentences, including the literal, are really context-dependent; that sentences with the same literal meaning determine different truth-conditions in different contexts. In my terminology, that would be to say that one literal meaning determines different truth-conditions relative to different sets of presuppositions or beliefs; in Searle's terminology, it means relative to different Backgrounds (where a Background is a nonrepresentational mental state, to avoid what he thinks would otherwise be an infinite regress). Searle's argument for this claim does not work, however. Let me explain.

Searle (1983) begins by asserting that "it seems clear to" him (145ff.) that the word 'open' has the same literal meaning in all of the following sentences.

(1a) John opened the door.

(b) Mary opened her eyes.

(c) John opened his book to p. 37.

(d) The surgeon opened the wound.

But Searle does not tell us what he means by "literal meaning" or how he individuates literal meanings, the kinds of considerations that would justify his unqualified, confident assertion that all of these sentences have the same literal meaning. His only argument is that, if we allow that these tokens of 'open' have different literal meanings, "we would soon be forced to the conclusion that the word 'open' is indefinitely or perhaps even infinitely ambiguous since we can continue these examples; and indefinite ambiguity seems an absurd result" (146). I agree: indefinite or infinite ambiguity would be an absurd result. However, it is also absurd to jump from four- or five-way ambiguity to indefinite or infinite ambiguity. Searle has given us no reason to think that if this expression has a fixed even if multiple number of different senses that it has an indefinite, let alone infinite, number. Furthermore, Searle's claim that each of these sentences has different semantic-conditions, that is, truth-conditions, is, given the absence in them of explicit context-dependent expressions (e.g., indexicals or demonstratives), as strong evidence as there could be that they do have different *meanings*. What would instead have been a good argument for the context-dependence of literal meaning in an objectionable sense would have been evidence that any *one* of those sentences, with its literal meaning held constant, has different semantic or truth-conditions in different *actual* contexts. But Searle cites no evidence of that kind.[12]

What Searle's examples do illustrate nicely is (in the terminology introduced in ch. 2) the *presemantic* context-dependence of all, including literal, language. It is only given all kinds of background that we assign a particular type, with its meaning (or character), to a particular token. But that leaves open the possibility of characterizing the literal as a kind of *semantic* context-*in*dependence.[13] Yet that conclusion also cannot be the whole story if only because of the semantic context-dependence of indexicals and demonstratives. But it is a step in the right direction.

To move further in this last direction, I want to take a closer look at the way metaphors *become* semantically context-independent and thereby literal. This process is how metaphors have standardly been said to die— keeping in mind that dead metaphors are also often claimed to be the stuff from which the literal grows. If we can understand this organic process better, we may also be able to get a better grip on the literal.

III Dead Metaphors

The title "dead metaphor," as it is used in the literature, covers a variety of examples. First I'll bracket two of these, after which I'll turn to three kinds of genuinely metaphorical dead metaphors.

First, there are expressions whose (once) *literal* interpretation is now dead and long forgotten; only their (once) metaphorical interpretation survives, although at present it is not even recognized that it is (or was) metaphorical. For example: 'plastron' now refers to the lower shell of a turtle but originally denoted the breastplate of a suit of armor. Apparently the metaphorical interpretation drew on a perceived (functional) analogy between the turtle-shell and breastplate. Likewise, 'cosmos' originally referred to a woman's headdress, was later metaphorically applied to the ranks of an army, and only finally to the order of the universe.[14] Thus the *original* application of 'plastron' to the turtle-shell or 'cosmos' to the universe was metaphorical, although *our* use of the predicates *now* depends on no presuppositions about, say, armor or headpieces, applications that would now be archaic. In short, the present character of interpretation of these predicates has nothing metaphorical about it. To call them "metaphors" is only to recall their historical genesis, and to call them "dead metaphors" is just to comment on their ancestry.

A second group of dead metaphors that are only debatedly metaphors are so-called double-function terms (physical or sensory terms like 'hard', 'deep', and 'bright' that are applied to psychological states) and synaesthetic adjectives (predicates taken from one sensory modality that express features applicable to a second sensory modality). These "metaphors" follow relatively regular paths of development both in individuals' acquisition of language and in the growth of languages. But there is an important disanalogy between the phylogenetic and ontogenetic cases. In the phylogenetic case, there is clear "transfer" from one sensory domain to another and, as Williams (1976) shows, even apparent directions to the paths of transfer. Ontogenetically it is a different story. Although the child may first acquire the physical/sensory meaning of the expression (or its application to a home sensory domain) and the psychological (or second sensory domain) meaning later, the latter may be acquired *independently* of the former. Despite the prima facie hypothesis that the term is *extended* on the basis of a similarity between the two extensions, in fact similarity—or any other relation that might provide a "common core" meaning—seems to play little role in the child's process of acquisition.[15] Initially these double-function or synaesthetic predicates are homonyms for the child; hence ontogenetically it would be more plausible to count each meaning as primitive rather than derived. Only at a considerably later stage does she discover their phylogenetic or diachronic relation— that at some previous time in the history of the language one was literal, the other metaphorical. But what she then discovers is something about the history of the language, rather than a fact about her own interpretations. Of course, the discovery might have the *effect* of enriching her subsequent interpretations, bringing her presuppositions back into the process of interpretation and at that later stage making it metaphorical. But it is necessary to distinguish the individual's acquisition of the expression and its emergence in the growth of language. Perhaps we should distinguish whether an expression is a (dead) metaphor *in the language* from its status *for the individual*. Here, in short, ontogeny does not recapitulate phylogeny.[16]

The two kinds of dead metaphors I have just discussed are arguably not metaphors. What, then, are examples of genuine dead metaphors, that is, interpretations that are clearly metaphorical but dead or dying? Again, the easy part is saying what they are *not*. Dead metaphors should not be confused with metaphors that are merely trite, clichéd, or tired. The deadness of a metaphor is also not to be measured by its frequency of utterance. Some metaphors are as alive and as novel on their hundredth utterance as they were on their first; witness 'Juliet is the sun'. But if not by being repeated to death, how does a metaphor die? And how does the content of an expression, once determined metaphorically, become its (or a literal) meaning? Before making a first stab at an answer, let me emphasize a point I made earlier: I am not asking the diachronic question, How in the development and growth of a language did expressions that were metaphorical become literal? My question is synchronic and individualistic: What determines whether the interpretation of an expression (uttered by a speaker in a community at a time) is metaphorical, even dead metaphorical, or literal?

A first stab at an account of dead metaphor might be in terms of how the metaphorical interpretation is learned, acquired, or assigned. One idea in the literature is that a metaphorical interpretation of an expression Φ is dead just in case its acquisition does not "depend" on the literal meaning of Φ, or if (and perhaps only if) it is learned "independently" of its literal meaning.[17] But the difficulty with this proposal is that we cannot sever the connection between the metaphorical and the literal except at the cost of rendering the interpretation not just dead but non-metaphorical. Instead of characterizing metaphorical-literal dependence as a relation that either does or does not hold, let's distinguish both degrees of dependence on (contextual presuppositions related to) the literal (vehicle) and the degree to which the metaphorical interpretation depends on presuppositions *specific* to its actual context of utterance. I propose that a metaphorical interpretation of an expression Φ in a context c is alive to the degree to which that interpretation in c depends on presuppositions associated with Φ specific to c. As the interpretation of the metaphor ceases to be sensitive to or dependent on presuppositions *specific* to its *actual* context of utterance, the metaphor dies. And as the interpretation ceases to be context dependent at all, it becomes literal.

There are at least three kinds of examples of metaphors that don't meet (to different degrees) these conditions for metaphorical aliveness; their interpretation is metaphorical yet dead or dying. They also suffer from different causes of death. If we can better understand what makes each of them a dead metaphor, we can get a better grasp on the various elements in our pretheoretical notion of the literal.

1. *Routinized* metaphorical interpretations: Some expressions Φ interpreted metaphorically always *turn out* to have the same interpretation, no

matter what their specific context of utterance. Examples of these interpretations include the "default" interpretations of metaphors that exploit the normal notion or stereotypical features associated with Φ. The interpretation is not (uniquely) determined by the linguistic meaning of Φ. The interpreter computes extralinguistic presuppositions about features associated with Φ to yield a content for Φ in the context. But—and here is the distinguishing mark—the interpreter brings the *same* presuppositions to bear on the interpretation of Φ in each context, thereby yielding a constant content as its metaphorical interpretation. Or perhaps, although she knows that P is a metaphorical interpretation of Φ rather than its literal meaning, the interpreter nonetheless routinely assigns P as the metaphorical interpretation without actually "computing" it as the value of Mthat[Φ] in c. These metaphors, as it were, carry their context on their sleeve. Since the metaphor has the same interpretation (or we might say: to the degree to which the metaphor has the same interpretation) whenever it is uttered, drawing on the same set of presuppositions, its interpretation is not dependent on presuppositions that are specific to its actual context of utterance. It is (on its way to becoming) de facto dead. De jure, however, it is alive. Were we asked, for example, to justify the interpretation assigned to the expression, we would reconstruct the content as the value of a nonconstant metaphorical character applied to a context set of presuppositions.[18]

2. *Root-inized* metaphorical interpretations:[19] Think of a metaphor found in either a foreign or ancient literary text, something whose context of origin (utterance, literary production) is far removed from the interpreter's actual context—where the relevant contextual feature is, of course, the context set of presuppositions. Suppose we know as interpreters that the expression was intended by its author to be interpreted metaphorically. Suppose we can give an acceptable interpretation to the inscription only by typing it as a metaphor. But suppose, too, that it is *only* by recovering the particular presuppositions that obtained in its context of origin that we can give the metaphor an acceptable interpretation (on whatever criteria of acceptability we choose). That is, suppose there is absolutely no other set of presuppositions of our own—in our actual context—by which we can acceptably interpret the metaphor. We say to ourselves: "Unless we go along with the beliefs and presuppositions of its authors—their idiosyncratic beliefs—there is no making sense of this metaphor." We can, to be sure, "recover" the original presuppositions, and it is by applying the metaphorical character of the expression to those presuppositions that we yield its content. Hence there is no question

that the expression can be interpreted metaphorically. However, because of the particular dependence of the metaphor on those specific presuppositions, its acceptable interpretation is "rooted" in a particular context, here its context of origin. To interpret the metaphor, what we do is attempt to "re-create" or, for the sake of interpretation, put ourselves into that original context. But to the degree to which the expression, notwithstanding its acceptable interpretation according to those nonactual presuppositions, resists alternative interpretations—to the degree to which we find it *impossible* to assign any acceptable interpretation (by whatever standards) to the metaphor according to *our* presuppositions (or the presuppositions of any other counterfactual context)—to that extent the metaphor is dead. Even apart from the fact that the alternative interpretation would not be, we know, what its original author intended, a live metaphor is one that has the *potential* for different interpretations in different contexts. Metaphors (metaphorical expression types) that don't admit that power of interpretation—because there aren't available alternative sets of presuppositions given the choice of metaphor—can be *uprooted* from their original context only at the risk of thereby being killed as metaphors. Relative to their present context of interpretation, these metaphors are dead.

There is also a second feature to the deadness of root-inized metaphors. As I noted in chapter 3, one essential feature of indexicals and demonstratives is that their interpretation, that is, their content, is always fixed by their character relative to their actual context of utterance. There are no operators on character, operators that shift their context of interpretation—the context in which their content is generated—from their context of actual utterance to a counterfactual context. In chapter 6, I argued that a similar principle holds for metaphors. Their interpretation always clings to the context set of presuppositions in their actual context of utterance. To the extent to which root-inized metaphors violate this principle, they are also, then, not quite metaphors. Their character is more constant than that of live metaphors. Instead the role of the presuppositions in which their content is "rooted" is more like the presemantic status of the presuppositions that determine the contents of proper names. Dead metaphors of this root-inized type are on the way to becoming name-like.

In sum, routinized metaphors have lost their aliveness because, with the same presuppositions in each of their contexts of utterance, they have a de facto constant content in all contexts. Root-inized metaphors have lost their aliveness because, rooted in one counterfactual context, they have lost the potential for alternative interpretations in alternative (including the actual) contexts of utterance; their character has lost, you might say, its soul. The third, and last, class of metaphors I wish to discuss are not dead metaphors in either of these two ways, and it is also not clear that they correspond to any of our pretheoretical ideas of dead metaphors. However, they count as dead, or at least as not fully alive, on my criterion—and for a reason that is common to many metaphors in some form or to some degree. I'll call them *acquired* as opposed to *introduced* metaphors.

3. *Acquired metaphors.* Suppose that a speaker, Jack, hears another, Jill, say that Max is a Turing machine (no insult intended). Jill presupposes that Turing machines are very basic, rather unexciting rule-governed computational devices, some of whose operations are even hard-wired in, and she intends her use of the metaphor to express properties like being unexciting but reliable, steady and even predictable, solid, methodical, disciplined to act according to step-by-step rules to the point of boredom. Jack, on the other hand, knows that Turing machines are computers but nothing more than that. But Jack does know, and knows that Jill knows and knows that she knows that he knows, that Max is extremely orderly and methodical, that he is great at solving problems step-by-step, that he never misses a step, that he is not especially interesting as a personality, in fact that he is a real bore, but that he is utterly reliable, someone you can count on. Jack also believes that Jill is using the predicate 'is a Turing machine' metaphorically, and he assumes that Jill is familiar (more than he is) with Turing machines and intends to express certain properties true of Max by her utterance in accordance with her presuppositions about Turing machines and about Max. Now, although Jack does not himself share Jill's presuppositions about Turing machines, he observes Jill's use of the metaphor (possibly applied over time to others besides Max, this being one of Jill's favorite metaphors) and gradually becomes able to apply the metaphor himself. One day, let's suppose, he even exclaims in exasperation: "Max is a Turing machine." Let's say that in these circumstances Jack has *acquired* the metaphor 'is a Turing machine'.

We can characterize an acquired metaphor in these terms. Jack does not himself possess m-associated presuppositions for the expression 'is a Turing machine'; strictly speaking, then, the predicate has no metaphorical interpretation with respect to his individual context set of presuppositions c_j; that is, it does not express in c_j a set of properties, or a complex property, that would determine, for any individual i, that i is or is not a Turing machine, where the predicate is interpreted metaphorically. Jack himself could not *introduce* the metaphor. However, Jack is able to apply the expression 'is a Turing machine' (correctly, most of the time) as it *would* be applied if it *were* interpreted metaphorically. Indeed a third person, observing Jack's use of the expression, might *project* onto him a grasp of its metaphorical interpretation (much as adults sometimes project onto children their own grasp of a certain application of an expression as a metaphor). This and more: If Jack acquired 'is a Turing machine' from Jill with the intention of using it with the meaning (character) she (or the person from whom Jill learned the expression) gave it— that is, with its metaphorical character—and he believes that she was using it metaphorically, then not only is Jack able to use 'is a Turing machine' as it *would* be used metaphorically; one might argue that he has acquired it *as a metaphor*. Because he intends to use the predicate in accordance with the intentions of whoever introduced it, and he assumes it was introduced as a metaphor, his own utterances—despite the fact that they lack metaphorical interpretations in his own context—are metaphorical or, more precisely, metaphorically acquired.

Acquired metaphors are meant to illustrate the fact that some of our uses of metaphor are socially determined in ways that have not been sufficiently well appreciated in the literature, that we often piggy-back on others' presuppositions when we knowingly use metaphors. The way in which Jack's acquisition of the metaphor depends on Jill's presuppositions is reminiscent of Hilary Putnam's (1975) idea of the linguistic division of labor: that many ordinary speakers' uses of natural kind terms depend on or are parasitic on an expert's knowledge of full satisfaction-conditions for the kind-term. We use such terms with our own incomplete knowledge by deferring to experts. It is not clear that there are "experts" on metaphors, but the same principle of deference holds with respect to introducers and acquirers. And the more the interpretation depends on socially accessible contextual presuppositions, the more presemantic becomes the role of context and the less metaphorically alive.

The three kinds of dead, or dead-like, metaphors I have discussed—routinized, root-inized, and acquired—are examples of three dimensions of the literal: context-invariance of content, the presemantic status of its context, and its social character. None of these conditions is itself a sufficient condition for being literal, nor do I want to claim that they are jointly sufficient or individually necessary. But each condition corresponds to a criterion, or perhaps symptom, we associate with the literal in our pretheoretical conception.

The difference between being metaphorical and being literal is not, or not simply, a matter of standing at opposite poles on a linear continuum in which metaphors of different degrees of vitality and moribundity bridge the two extremes.[20] For one thing, it is never made clear by proponents of this view what the continuum measures or that what it measures can be quantified as the picture assumes. Furthermore, the continuum picture seems to rest on a confusion between the recognition and interpretation questions. Instead of addressing the question of what makes a metaphorical interpretation dead or alive, the picture addresses the question: How do we identify whether a given token of a metaphor is dead or alive? We don't (yet) have a good answer to the recognition question. But it ought to be clear that we do not perform the recognition task either by feel (e.g., degree of Humean vivacity) or by "looking" at the concrete surface expression or at the product of the interpretation without assessing its structure. Nor do we introspect the process we happened to employ to arrive at the interpretation. In any case, it is not necessary in order to say what makes an interpretation metaphorically dead that we explain how we identify one, nor should we look to an account of its identification for an explanation of the character of its interpretation.

But if the continuum picture is not right, what is the relation between the metaphorical and literal? Some think of literal meaning as the afterlife of a dead metaphor. But that cannot be the whole story: No one ever claimed that literal meaning *only* comes from dead metaphorical interpretations. I proposed earlier that as a metaphorical interpretation ceases to be dependent on presuppositions specific to its *actual* context of utterance, the metaphorical interpretation dies, and as the interpretation ceases to be context-dependent at all, it becomes literal. A full depiction of the literal would be another book. But with a glance back at our discussion of *de re* metaphors in chapter 5, let me sketch a different picture.

IV Literal Interpretations as Context-independent Interpretations

Metaphors move in families. I have emphasized the degree to which the interpretation, that is, content, of a metaphor in a context is sensitive to the networks to which its vehicle is presupposed to belong (in that context). Its exemplification-schema determines what the vehicle of the metaphor is presupposed to exemplify and its inductive network is essential to determining the implications by means of which we typically explicate the metaphor—and manifest our understanding of it—by metaphorically elaborating and extending it. In all these ways the content of a metaphor in a context is highly dependent on and sensitive to the other elements in the various complexes in which it figures. I have also argued that the exemplification-network to which a given metaphor (vehicle) belongs furnishes it with a cognitive perspective on its content, by which it conveys information or significance specific to its character in addition to its content. Similarly, I have tried to explain the pictorial dimension of a metaphor by the fact that its relevant network is sensitive to the slightest difference in features of the vehicle. Even the tightest synonymy relation does not preserve its network associations. Like a picture, no feature of the vehicle can be discounted as irrelevant to the individuation of its metaphorical type. For these kinds of considerations, I suggested, in chapter 5, section III, that on occasion we individuate a metaphor, not only in terms of its character and content (in a context), but also by reference to its contextual schema. On that criterion, two metaphors are the same if and only if their content (in the context), character, *and* context set of presuppositions (including ones about schema) are identical. Thus the network to which a given metaphor belongs and indeed the context in which it occurs are essential to its identity.

A literal (or one notion of a literal) interpretation is an interpretation, I now want to propose, that can be assigned to a word relatively independently of its context and, in particular, independently of networks to which the word belongs. When a metaphorical interpretation of an expression becomes a literal meaning of the word, it becomes the meaning *of the word*—that is, an interpretation that can be assigned to the word independently of its contextually presupposed networks. Its content becomes a feature *of*—possessed by—the word (type)—regardless of its containing schemas. This is the sense in which that content is *literal—of the letter*: of the word in isolation from its containing schema or context. Literal meaning is atomistic, unlike metaphorical interpretation, which, if not holistic, always depends on its containing context. Hence, once it becomes literal meaning, a content is assignable by type, the same content for all replicas of the type (except where the type is indexical or demonstrative).

In rejecting the continuum picture, I have implied that the literal is not simply a dead metaphor of the highest degree of moribundity (an interpretation than which there is none that is deader). From the point of view of my theory, a literal expression is always formally different in kind, not just degree, from a metaphorical expression: Even if the content of 'Mthat[Φ]' in c is identical with the content of a literal expression Ψ in c, 'Mthat[Φ]' and Ψ are obviously of different types.[21] Unlike routinized metaphors that have a context-invariant content, that is, the same content in all contexts, a literal expression has the same content *regardless* of the context in which it occurs, independently of—apart from—any context. We don't have to work through the contextual presuppositions associated with the expression to determine its content on that occasion. When a metaphorical interpretation of an expression Φ becomes the literal meaning of an expression Ψ (even where Φ and Ψ are homonyms), the content is "liberated" from context. Or, more precisely, the content is liberated from the semantic context. It remains, or perhaps becomes, presemantically context-dependent.

Parallel to this contextual liberation movement, there is an epistemological transformation that transpires as the metaphorical interpretation becomes a literal meaning. I argued in chapter 5 that the context-dependence of, say, exemplification-metaphors enables them to express contents, or properties, that the speaker-interpreter cannot express literally, for which he does not have the requisite conceptual resources at the time to express in a context-transcendent manner. The deficiency is epistemological: What the interpreter lacks is not just a word but the kind of understanding that is necessary for fully conceptualized, or *de dicto*, interpretation. A literal interpretation of an expression, in contrast, *is* a fully conceptualized (*de dicto*) interpretation: If such an interpretation is a propositional content, then a literal interpretation of a sentence is a content that contains no bare individuals, no bare properties, but exclusively their conceptual representations. Thus, as a speaker better understands a property or set of properties expressed by a metaphor by exploiting its contextual relations, as the metaphor is integrated into the interpreter's conceptual repertoire, she acquires the ability to express it apart from particular objects that exemplify it. The interpreter knows under what conditions it does and does not apply, apart from the conditions of a particular context in which it is the property exemplified by a particular thing.

Talk of the literal as purely conceptualized content may seem at odds with our talk of literal *meaning*, meaning rather than content. But a literal meaning is a meaning that in any context determines the same purely conceptualized content for an expression. Such a meaning is not merely context-invariant, or eternal, expressing the same content in every context. It is context-transcendent; the word has its literal meaning not simply in every context but out of context.[22] Of course, this is not to say that the metaphorical and the literal refer to different kinds of content or that they constitute different kinds of thinking.[23] The epistemological difference between the metaphorical and literal is not a difference in *what* we think but in *how* we represent to ourselves the contents of our thought.

At different points in this book I have offered suggestions as to how to understand the formula that the metaphorical depends on the literal. One interpretation I have not pursued is that the relevant dependence requires that the literal temporally precede the metaphorical. Indeed the opposite idea—which on the face of it seems absurd—was once proposed by no less than Jean-Jacques Rousseau. In his essay *On the Origin of Language*, Rousseau writes that the "First Language had to be figurative."[24] Perhaps we can now make sense of his thesis in the terms of my proposed account. Suppose that the context-oriented character of a metaphor enables us to express and represent to ourselves contents that are less than fully understood and fully conceptualized, and suppose that complete understanding—the fully conceptualized kind that is expressed literally— follows incomplete knowledge. In that case Rousseau might have been right after all. "Figurative language was the first to be born. Proper meaning was discovered last. One calls things by their true name only when one sees them in their true form."[25]

Notes

Preface

1. Johnson (1981), ix; cf. Lakoff and Johnson (1980), ix–x.

2. Compare the exchange between Hesse (1987) and Rorty (1987) on Davidson.

3. Still other authors such as Kittay (1987) supplement classical semantics with other purported semantic theories, such as semantic field theory; see ch. 6, sec. IX on the semantic status of such theories. In any case, these attempts shift the brunt of their explanation of metaphor away from classical semantics.

Chapter 1

1. The choice of example is not intended to raise special questions connected to the interpretation of metaphors in fiction; for related discussion, see below, ch. 6, sec. III.

2. The propositional information of a subsentential expression Φ is the content, or factor, Φ contributes to the information of any sentence to which it belongs.

3. I shall sometimes use this awkward phrase *speaker-hearer* and sometimes just one or the other of the hyphenated terms; unless explicitly noted, I do not intend to be exploiting a particular "perspective."

4. The classic exposition of this view is Beardsley (1962), although the position was very widely shared. For references and critical discussion, see Stern (1983). Some advocates of the deviance condition also tried to use it to explain the interpretation of a metaphor, e.g., by way of transfer, selective weighting, and elimination of the deviance-producing lexical features contained in the entries for the constituent words. See, e.g., Beardsley (1978), Levin (1977), Matthews (1971). The features responsible both for the recognition and interpretation of the metaphor would, then, be sentence-internal. For critical discussion of this model of interpretation, see below, ch. 6, sec. IX.

5. The phrase "twice-true" was coined by Cohen (1975), (1976). Other critics of the grammatical deviance condition at that time included Reddy (1969) and Binkley (1976). Diehard defenders of various versions of the deviance condition include Beardsley (1978) and Kittay (1987); for further discussion, see Stern (1983) and below, ch. 6, sec. IX.

6. Thanks to Mohammed-Ali Khalidi for the reference.

7. One might object to this example that it is so obviously true (taken literally) as to render it deviant on that ground. This may be true, but unless one assumes a strong analytic-synthetic distinction, it is not clear why this should be theoretically more problematic for this kind of example than for the earlier examples that are also true.

8. It is worth noting that in the psychoanalytic literature on metaphor, we are often warned that utterances by, say, schizophrenics, which *we* would take to be metaphorical in other contexts (if, for example, they were found in poetry), should not be interpreted metaphorically but literally.

9. See Récanati (1995), Glucksberg and Keysar (1993), Gibbs (1984), (1989), and Rumelhart (1993). Although many psychologists have challenged the serial literal-first model on the grounds that the processing time for metaphorical sentences is no longer than that for literal sentences, Récanati (1995) and Winner (1988) challenge this evidence, taking into account the possibility of masking effects. However, for independent reasons they favor a parallel-processing model, and in ch. 4, sec. IV I shall also sketch a model of metaphorical interpretation that supports this approach to metaphorical recognition.

10. Culler (1981), 19–20. Culler cites the example to illustrate the problem of interpretation, although he does not distinguish recognition from interpretation. He also proposes that the example supports a Davidsonian approach, yet notes that it presupposes a structure of interpretation that would be difficult to incorporate into Davidson's framework.

11. Nonetheless much of the literature on metaphor persists in conflating the recognition and interpretation questions; see, e.g., Black (1962), 25; Black (1993), 33–35; Beardsley (1958), 161; Ortony (1993b), 5; Sadock (1993), 478; and Grice (1975), 71. In ch. 2 I shall classify this role of the context as presemantic insofar as it enters into assignment of a metaphorical type to an utterance.

12. There are many steps in this argument at which one might balk; see below, ch. 7. I mention the argument here only to motivate the structure of the book.

13. I use *feature*, which is intended to be a neutral term, rather than, say, *property*, in order not to beg the question whether what is conveyed by a metaphor is proposition-like or a propositional constituent.

14. Among the dissenting minority are Matthews (1971), Cohen and Margalit (1972), L. J. Cohen (1993), Kittay (1987), Bergmann (1979), (1982), Berg (1988), and Leezenberg (1995). On the first four theories and how they differ from my account, see below, ch. 6, sec. IX. The last three views are those most similar to mine in the literature.

15. Rorty (1987), 285–286. Here Rorty claims to be offering an explication of Davidson's position; on differences between their views, see ch. 2, sec. III. For a similar conception of the role of context in metaphorical interpretation, see Scheffler (1979); Elgin and Scheffler (1987); and Stern (1988).

16. Davidson (1984), 245.

17. See Margalit and Goldblum (1994).

18. According to a variant text, the saying reads "Before [the priest] Eli's sun had set, the sun of [the prophet] Samuel had risen" (BT *Qedushin* 72b); for our purposes, the interpretation is more or less the same.

19. Examples (5) and (6) (slightly modified) originated with Avishai Margalit.

20. Carey (1981), 11. I am indebted to Arthur Danto for bringing these examples to my attention.

21. Cf. Sadock (1993), 44.

22. It is in terms of this close conceptual and formal parallel I wish to draw between metaphors and demonstratives that my account most differs from other contextualist semantic theories like Bergmann (1979), (1982).

23. Here I use *non-/constant character* where Kaplan uses *non-/stable character* to express the identical notion. I have departed from Kaplan's own terminology to avoid a potential misunderstanding that might result from the term "nonstable" that could be taken to mean that the *character* assigned to the expression itself changes from context to context. What is nonstable about a character for Kaplan (and nonconstant for me) is the fact that the *content* it determines can change or differ from context to context.

24. Cf. White (1996), 88.

25. On the other hand, in his original (1962) paper Black sometimes takes the metaphor to be the constituent word and in yet other passages talks as if it is not the individual word but "the system of associated commonplaces" that is metaphorical.

26. Original credit for the fundamental insight that it is always a whole schema or family of expressions that is interpreted (or transferred) metaphorically, never an individual expression, should, however, be given to Goodman (1976); on this theme, see below, chs. 5 and 7.

27. Black may also be concerned to capture the idea that, although the other constituents in the sentence (the so-called frame) are not metaphorical in "the same way as the metaphorical expression" (or focus) that undergoes, say, a change of extension, nonetheless they *also* undergo *some* change of interpretation. Hence in some sense the whole sentence is metaphorical. In reply I would argue: (1) insofar as we are concerned with propositional content, any changes, however significant, that are only emotive or attitudinal lie outside the scope of our story; and (2) if indeed there are changes in the propositional interpretation of other expressions in the sentence, there is no reason not to take each such expression to be metaphorical (in which case the sentence will simply contain multiple metaphors).

28. White (1996), 202. All the cases I describe in the previous three sentences in the text are raised by White as problems for a word-focused theory of metaphor and, in particular, for theories like Black's that (White claims) are limited to taking a metaphor to be a unique, simple (one-word) *focus* in a sentence. Although White may be right that Black's focus/frame apparatus is inadequate to describe, let alone explain, these more complex phenomena of metaphor, I shall try to show in chs. 5 and 6 how my semantic theory can capture them. I would add that

White's presentation of Black is not as black and white as he suggests: If one takes into account Black's own emphasis on the system (of associated commonplaces) relative character of metaphorical interpretation, his theory need not be interpreted as exclusively one-word-based as White alleges.

29. To anticipate a potential misunderstanding: We can either treat "metaphorical expressions" such as 'Mthat[Φ]' in the technical sense of ch. 4 as lexically complex expressions or treat the metaphorical interpretation of the expression Φ as the literal interpretation of the metaphorical expression 'Mthat[Φ]'.

30. Kronfeld (1980/81); cf. also Sweetser (1992).

31. See, e.g., Beardsley (1976).

32. See Kronfeld (1980/81) and, now, White (1996) for a sustained philosophical critique of this kind.

33. See Lakoff and Johnson (1980), Lakoff and Turner (1989), and Lakoff (1993).

34. For complementary thoughts about the evidence for linguistic theories in general, see Hornstein (1984), 10–12.

35. Plimpton (1976), 120–121.

36. Margalit (1978).

37. I owe these examples to Lakoff and Johnson (1980), 4.

38. It is especially risky to speculate on the basis of surface "appearance" whether a given expression is a *dead* metaphor. Kronfeld cites Alston's use of 'fork in the road' as a nice example of fallacious armchair theorizing. Although Alston tells a prima facie plausible story of how the phrase came to be metaphorical, in actual fact it did not historically originate as a metaphor but rather as a literal application of 'fork' meaning 'that which branches or divides'. Likewise, Brooks (1965a) cites, as an example of a dead metaphor brought back to life, the following line (quoted by Dorothy Sayers) from a nineteenth-century Oxford poem on the Israelites crossing the River Jordan dry-shod. When the bearers of the Ark stepped into the river, the waters suddenly rolled back, "And left the astounded river's bottom bare." This *is* a good live metaphor, but the expression 'bottom of the river', as it is generally used, is not a dead metaphor but a straightforward literal use. Hence this is also not an example of a resuscitated dead metaphor.

39. Cf. the entry for "Metaphor" in Preminger (1965), 136–141. However, an exception to this rule are White's (1996) arguments, building on his rich knowledge of poetry and literature, against philosophers' simplistic, single-word examples of metaphors. Yet, as I indicated earlier, I think many of his philosophical objections can be answered.

40. Aristotle does not reveal what he means by "genius" but one gloss might be the Kantian conception of genius, as the capacity to produce things that are inexplicable by rules, yet make sense. Cf. Cohen (1975), 671, who explains that metaphors are products of genius meaning that they are "not accomplished in terms of statable rules"—rules of the kind presumed to underlie linguistic competence.

41. Such a view is held by Isenberg (1963).

42. In denying these distinctions, I do not, of course, mean to deny that there remain significant differences between the metaphors of poetry and of ordinary speech. But these differences are not a function of different underlying competencies. Instead they are a function of different uses of a common competence to create different effects and products, a difference like that between the literal language used to write a shopping list and that used to write the *Gettysburg Address* or *Critique of Pure Reason*. I would argue that as competent speakers, we all have a mastery of metaphor, but that only some of us are masters of metaphor.

43. Langer (1942), 112.

44. Otto Neurath (commenting, incidentally, on the early Wittgenstein), cited by Carnap (1963), 29. This view, which begins with metaphor and eventually encompasses all language, probably originates with various medieval theological conceptions of language; for one prehistory, see Stern (2000). On the naturalistic study of language and its humanistic critique, see also Higginbotham (1982), 156–157.

45. To the extent to which they require explicit learning, peripheral metaphors are similar to dead metaphors whose interpretations are not grasped via general rules of context-oriented metaphorical interpretation (rules that require no learning) and must also be explicitly learned. However, interpretations of dead metaphors are learned one by one, whereas it is additional *rules* of interpretation that are learned in the case of peripheral metaphors. Thus core living metaphors are surrounded on the one side by dead metaphors and on the other by living but peripheral metaphors. Both differ from the core with respect to the kind of learning involved in their interpretation.

46. For examples and discussion of some of these additional skills and techniques, see Hrushovski (1984).

Chapter 2

1. Davidson (1978/1984), 247. All references to this paper will be to the 1984 reprint and will be cited in the text as WMM.

2. Other members of Davidson's camp include Cooper (1986); Blackburn (1984), 171–179; and Rorty (1987).

3. To anticipate a potential misunderstanding: In light of my own account in ch. 4, it will turn out that Davidson's claim (1a) is compatible with my own view, that "metaphorical expressions" of the form 'Mthat[Φ]' composed out of individual (simple) words Φ have metaphorical meanings. The reason is that although metaphorical expressions lexically represent metaphorical *interpretations* of individual simple words, they are themselves complex expressions.

4. Davidson (1986), 433–446. All in-text references to this paper will be cited as NDE.

5. Davidson (1984), 279; see also ibid., xix.

6. Searle (1993); Grice (1975).

7. Grice (1975), 71.

8. Grice assumes a linear literal-first model of interpretation (of the type I questioned in ch.1), and, more important, he also seems to suppose that we always at least attempt to interpret an utterance that cannot be taken literally first as an irony and, only when that fails, as a metaphor. At the same time, he allows for combination metaphorical/ironic interpretations, in which the content of the utterance interpreted metaphorically is also meant ironically.

9. A similar criticism applies to Martinich (1984) whose use of salience fares no better as a candidate for meaning than Grice's use of resemblance. Likewise, his introduction of the maxim "Be relevant," though relevant, is hardly sufficient to do all the work he wants it to do.

10. Compare Davidson's objection to positing a figurative meaning for similes: "The point of the concept of linguistic meaning is to explain what can be done with words. But the supposed figurative meaning of a simile explains nothing; it is not a feature of the word that the word has prior to and independent of the context of use, and it rests upon no linguistic customs except those that govern ordinary meaning" (WMM 255).

11. For a more detailed discussion of these Davidsonian themes, see Stern (1991).

12. Davidson (1984), 273–274.

13. On the connection between communication, literal meaning, and truth-conditions, see Davidson (1984), 45. Note that Davidson takes a *single* type of semantic interpretation, e.g., truth-conditions, to correspond to the required kind of understanding, or interpretation, thus leaving no allowance for partial degrees of understanding. This may have the advantage of simplicity but it is also a potential source of problems.

14. More specifically, I's theory is of what he expects S intends to say with his (S's) particular words on this occasion, given I's prior knowledge of S and of the first meanings S has previously attached to his (S's) words. S's theory, on the other hand, consists of his intentions that particular words of his will be interpreted by I as saying such-and-such, given his beliefs and his expectations about I's ability to interpret him (S) as saying those things with those words. So, if S believes that I will not be able to interpret him as saying such-and-such with certain words, he will not intend for those words to be interpreted in that way.

15. On this provocative claim, and some philosophers' reactions to it, see Hacking (1986) and Stern (1991).

16. Here I gloss over a number of Davidson's unsupported, and potentially problematic, claims about the means-ends ordering of intentions.

17. Despite its initial characterization as a "preliminary stab," there is nothing preliminary about Davidson's continued use of the notion of first meaning throughout NDE as the explication of literal meaning; see, e.g., NDE 442.

18. There may be exceptions to this rule. Knowledge of the secondary intention of an utterance (e.g., knowing that it is a promise or threat) may affect which first meaning is assigned to a constituent word; in this way, assignment of first meaning may also be sensitive to postsemantic contextual features that bear on the utterance's secondary intention.

19. Cf. Davidson's principle of the *autonomy of linguistic meaning*, in Davidson (1984), 164; cf. also 274. These notions of autonomy of meaning should, however, be distinguished from the notion I discuss in section V.

20. Davidson's argument should be distinguished from another argument in the literature, which treats metaphor as a distinctive kind of force or illocutionary act that runs on a line parallel to but different from assertion, questioning, lying, promising, criticizing, and so on. Just as assertion is a use of language in which one represents oneself as intending to say what is true; lying, a use representing oneself as believing what one does not; and promising, a use with the purpose of representing oneself as undertaking an obligation to perform some act; so metaphor would be a use of language in which one represents oneself as calling attention to certain similarities or other features. This is not simply to say that (many) metaphors in fact do direct our attention to similarities; that much is indisputable. The claim is that metaphors constitutively perform a distinctive illocutionary act, an act these writers roughly describe as "calling our attention to a certain likeness," or "inviting" us to "appreciate" a resemblance, or "inspiring" a certain vision, or "proposing" that things be viewed a certain way. These "proposals" or "invitations" or "attention-calling" acts may be apt or distorting, heuristically valuable or misleading, suggestive or confusing, but—and this is the crux of the claim—they are neither true nor false. Hence, if assertions are either true or false, *the* defining function of a metaphor *excludes* assertion. On these non-assertional functional characterizations of metaphor, see Loewenberg (1975), 174ff; Black (repr. 1981), 75 (who describes metaphor as "organizing our view" of the subject); and even more explicitly, Black (1993), 40–41. On the other hand, Fogelin (1988) allows for both information-giving and attention-calling uses for metaphor.

Undoubtedly some metaphors—in poetry and scientific contexts—are uttered with and *only* with such a non-assertional heuristic force. But metaphors occur in utterances whose sentences express all the grammatical moods, e.g.,

The Declarative: Juliet is the sun.

The Interrogative: Is Juliet really the sun?

The Imperative: For God's sake, Juliet, act (like) the sun!

The Optative: Would the sun kindly enter.

Indeed, we can use a metaphor to perform a speech act or utterance with *any* force—either the direct force corresponding to the mood of the sentence or some other indirect force—*in addition to* the act of drawing our attention to the resemblance (or other feature) that enters into the content of the metaphor. The fact that metaphors call likenesses to our attention does not exclude the possibility that they *also* make assertions.

Furthermore, one might argue that in order to explain why metaphors call (only) *specific* resemblances, analogies, or features to our attention, and not others, we must appeal to assertion (or some other act presupposing assertion). The idea would be that we assert propositions not simply that we believe are true but also that we believe are not *already* common knowledge or shared pre-suppositions in the context. Hence we survey the background or context for the kind of property or resemblance that would make Romeo's assertion informative as well as true. This additional requirement for assertion serves, then, to eliminate or filter out those resemblances or aspects that fail to serve the additional assertoric purpose of the utterance, thus explaining why only some and not other resemblances or features are expressed by a metaphor.

Finally, one might object to this argument that, for this purpose, *truth*-values or *truth*-conditions are not necessary as the constraints on metaphorical interpretation; weaker conditions like warranted assertability or acceptability, or even something weaker like "making sense," would also do the job. I am sympathetic to this objection, but it applies to one's theory of meaning as a whole. If we were to turn our general theory into a theory of, say, warranted assertability, analogous revisions could (and would) be made for metaphor.

21. This, despite Davidson's tendency to conflate, or interchange, "literal meaning" and "literal truth-conditions"; see, e.g., WMM, 247.

22. On the comparison to jokes (and riddles), see Aristotle (1984), *Rhetoric* $1412^{a}18–1412^{b}32$; Cohen (1978), (1983); and below, ch. 7, sec. V.

23. Davidson's use of multiple expressions in WMM to refer to the relation between the utterance of the metaphor and its "effect"—e.g., "makes us see," "alerts," "inspires," "leads us to notice," "prompts," "draws our attention to," "provokes"—may make one wonder whether there is a single relation at work, but in any case his "causal" account is epistemic. It should therefore be distinguished from Max Black's notorious claim that metaphors "create" similarities (1962, 37) by which he means, as he insists (in Black 1993, 35–38), not only reveal but also constitute or bring into existence. For yet another sense of how a metaphor may "make" (us recognize or notice) a similarity, see below, ch. 5, sec. II.

24. To support his reply, Davidson would, to be sure, appeal to Quine's rejection of the analytic-synthetic distinction. But the persistent objector might, in turn, reply that what is unacceptable about the analytic-synthetic distinction is its epistemological use to ground an a priori/a posteriori distinction, which is *not* a burden the distinction is made to shoulder here. For different and extended discussion of replies to the objection, see Margalit and Goldblum (1994), 235–237, and White (1996), 204–226.

25. For this reason, White's claim that "to apprehend a metaphor *as* a metaphor involves ignoring whatever literal sense [the sentence] may have" (1996, 226) may be too strong if that involves also ignoring its syntax; in any case, I have not been able to identify a specific argument for this particular conclusion in White's subtle examination of examples.

26. I am not raising the general question of the relation between truth-conditions and meaning, either to criticize or defend Davidson's program. For discussion, see Davidson (1984), especially essays 2, 4, 9, and 12, and Davidson's postscripts and references therein.

27. See Danto (1981), 179–189, who concludes from the argument (of the previous paragraph) establishing the non-extensionality of metaphorical contexts that they are indeed intensional contexts. For an *extensionalistic* explanation of the work done by intensions or meanings to account for the failure of substitutivity, see Elgin and Scheffler (1987) and, for critical discussion, Stern (1988). For further discussion of Goodman's theory of metaphor, see also Stern (1997).

28. *Time*, Feb. 28, 1985. On cross-cultural differences of metaphorical interpretation, see Asch (1961).

29. On the role of context more generally in metaphorical interpretation, see Scheffler (1979).

30. Rorty (1987), 284; cf. also 296. For the position Rorty is contrasting with Davidson's, see, e.g., Hesse (1987). Davidson emphasizes that his noncognitivist view does not mean (as it did for many earlier positivists) that metaphor is "confusing, merely emotive, unsuited to serious, scientific, or philosophic discourse" (WMM, 246), but his praise of metaphor never reaches the exalted heights of Rorty's; at best Davidson thinks "metaphor is a *legitimate* device not only in literature but in science, philosophy, and the law" (ibid., my italics).

31. See Davidson (1967/1980), 149–162.

32. However, see Davidson's most recent statements on this issue: "It is clear that there may be no clue to the character of an appropriate law in the concepts used on some occasion to characterize an event. What may be the case is that if a singular causal statement is to be *explanatory* in some desired sense, it must put its hearer in mind of at least the general nature of a relevant law" (1995, 265).

33. A number of brief comments: (1) In the quoted passage Davidson makes the same claim for irony as for metaphor, and indeed I think his analogy works better for irony. However, in ch. 6 I'll argue that the two figures ought to be explained differently; so I shall simply ignore irony here. (2) Both Davidson's exposition of Donnellan's idea of a referential definite description and his characterization of malapropism as a change of meaning are not beyond challenge; e.g., his focus on referential descriptions that do not semantically designate the intended referent is misleading, albeit admittedly inspired by some of Donnellan's original examples. Nonetheless for the sake of argument I shall grant him his way of presenting these two subjects. (3) As Roger White has pointed out (pers. comm.), Davidson's remark in the quotation that the speaker says "something true" (with the false literal sentence) apparently conflicts with his well-known thesis that metaphors do not convey "a definite cognitive content" or propositional content and, therefore, ought not to be either true or false. What to make of this slip is not clear. (4) In the quotation Davidson does not elaborate on the analogy between metaphor and referential descriptions. It might be argued in his defense that he did not mean anything stronger than to note a similarity in passing and, in particular, that he did not mean to propose the referential definite description as a model by which to understand metaphorical use and its dependence on the literal. In reply I would rejoin that throughout NDE Davidson emphasizes the distinction between literal/first meaning and speaker's meaning, illustrating each (with malapropisms, referential descriptions, etc.) and leading his reader to think that he intends his claims to be generalizable. It is in that spirit that I suggest this second Davidsonian model of metaphorical/literal dependence.

34. I owe the example to Sidney Morgenbesser. One might object that the example is not a malapropism but a semantic error; on Davidson's characterization, however, it counts as a malapropism. On distinguishing malapropism from other kinds of semantic speech errors, see Fay and Cutler (1977).

35. I am indebted throughout this paragraph to discussion with Lauren Tilling-hast.

36. Here I assume, as I'll argue in ch. 3, that demonstratives are directly referential terms; i.e., their propositional content (in a context) or truth-conditional factor is the individual to which they refer rather than a Fregean sense, concept, or intensional entity.

37. See Davidson's comments in (1984), essays 2, 3, 4, and 9; and Weinstein (1974). Davidson introduces the relativization to time to account for tense, even apart from occurrences of the indexical 'now'.

38. Because Davidson's own apparently preferred treatment of demonstratives relativizes the truth-predicate for sentences to contextual parameters, his strategy makes him vulnerable to some of the same objections that Kaplan raises against other relativized-truth accounts, like the index-theories of R. Montague and D. Lewis: see Kaplan (1989a), 507–510. An alternative treatment of demonstratives within absolute truth-theory, proposed by Weinstein (1974); Burge (1974); Taylor (1980); Higginbotham (1988), (forthcoming); and Larson and Segal (1995), takes utterances rather than sentences as the truth-vehicles, but conditions the T-sentence on an antecedent clause that specifies the relations that must hold between the contextual values and sentence in order for the utterance to have truth-conditions. This strategy avoids Kaplan's criticisms but raises large issues for our understanding of the notion of truth.

39. For the line of argument in this paragraph I am indebted to Roger White.

40. Note that this notion of autonomy of meaning is entirely different from Davidson's principle of the same name (see note 19 above).

41. A full explanation of how we should technically capture this dependence of the metaphorical interpretation of an expression Φ on its literal meaning will, however, have to wait until ch. 6.

42. See Higginbotham (1989), 159–165.

43. Cf. Higginbotham (1989), 162.

44. There is also the question of how conditions like (A) or (I) could even be learned on accounts like Davidson's. Because the conditions in question primarily exclude interpretations the sentence does not and never could have, and these excluded interpretations are presumably never part of the linguistic data to which speakers are exposed, the conditions cannot be inductively learned from confirming instances. On the rationalist consequences of these facts—the "absence of negative evidence" as it is known in the psycholinguistics literature—see Higginbotham (1989), 162ff. and Hornstein (1984), 4–7.

45. The contrapositive reasoning I have just rehearsed is meant to be reminiscent of one of Chomsky's (1980) arguments for the so-called competence-performance distinction and his related argument that a theory of linguistic competence proper will explicate only what the speaker *knows* about *specifically linguistic* properties that contribute to his complex ability that issues in acceptable *speech*; see also Chomsky (1968), (1988). For yet another notion of meaning as "partial" understanding, see Spolsky (1987/88).

46. On the latter, see Hills (1997).

47. To anticipate a possible objection: An empirical distinction between knowledge of, or competence in, language and extra- or nonlinguistic abilities and knowledge need not entangle us in the epistemological quandaries of the analytic-synthetic distinction. On this issue, see also Chomsky (1988) and Higginbotham (1989).

48. Here I follow Williams's (1977) analysis of verb phrase anaphora involving an interpretive (or copying) rule of Discourse Grammar rather than a deletion rule of Sentence Grammar; cf. also Chomsky (1968), 33–35; and Kempson (1977), 128–132.

49. According to my semantic theory, as I'll argue in ch. 6, the violations in (14) and (15) are formally different. In (14) the antecedent, which is literal, and the anaphor, which is metaphorical, will be formally assigned different characters:

(14a) *The largest blob of gases in the solar system *is the sun*, and Juliet/Achilles *Mthat['is the sun']*.

In (15), however, the antecedent and anaphor, both metaphors (indeed both sharing the same metaphorical expression type), will have the same character.

(15a) *Juliet Mthat['is the sun'], and Achilles Mthat['is the sun'].

In (14) the violation on copying is at the level of character; in (15) at the level of content. In fact, there is some evidence that the difference in "level" at which the copying constraint is violated affects our intuitions of unacceptability. It is possible to cancel the implication of univocality at the level of content, as in (15), but not at the level of character, as in (14). (Thanks to Malka Rapaport for these examples.) Contrast (14b) and (15b):

(14b) *The largest blob of gases in the solar system is the sun, and Juliet/
Achilles is, too—but not in the same sense/way.

(15b*) Juliet is the sun, and Achilles is, too—but not in the same sense/way.

To avoid a possible confusion, note also that

(15c) *Juliet is the sun and Achilles is the sun

whose underlying interpretation is also (15a) will be unacceptable for the same reason (and more or less to the same degree) as (15). Although both occurrences of 'is the sun' are metaphorical and therefore share the same character, in order for (15c) to be acceptable (and, say, true), one of the following three alternatives would have to obtain: either (i) both occurrences would have to have the same content, given the same context (as we shall argue in ch. 4: the same set of contextual presuppositions); or (ii) each conjunct would have to have a (possibly different) content (under which it is true) but be determined relative to the same (set of) context(-ual presuppositions); or (iii) each conjunct would have to have an acceptable (and true) content relative to a possibly different set of contextual presuppositions. Alternative (i) cannot be presumed without special pleading, given our common knowledge of Juliet and Achilles, common knowledge that will be part of the context. Alternative (iii) would require that the context change during the utterance of the single sentence, a possibility that also needs special pleading. Alternative (ii) is ruled out for the same reason either as (i) or (iii). I shall return to discuss this example in ch. 6, sec. IV, but for now I would emphasize, in order to motivate the need for metaphorical meaning, that what matters is the impossibility of literal/metaphorical crossover of interpretation. (Thanks also to Jay Atlas for discussion of these matters.)

50. It should be observed that on Davidson's account *both* Romeo's and Paris's utterances are absurdly false according to what they literally mean—which is *all* they mean according to Davidson. And insofar as they have the same truth-value, it is not clear how he can even *describe* Romeo's and Paris's disagreement.

51. Note that my argument is *not* that metaphorical interpretations are (literally) infinite in number, hence that there is no finitistic base on which to rest compositionality for a language containing metaphors. Although some have taken that line, there is no evidence that any expression, no matter how many interpretations or meanings it has, has an *infinite*, or truly unbounded, or even indefinitely or incommensurately large, number of *simple* interpretations. For discussion, see Ross (1981), Lycan (1987), and Grandy (1990).

52. I owe these examples to Cynthia Welsh. The two meanings of 'ear' seem to be entirely unrelated historically: The hearing organ ear derives from Indo-European 'ous-', which refers to the bodily part; 'ear [of corn]' derives from Indo-European 'ak', which refers to a sharp side or point. The case of 'corn' is slightly different: The two meanings of 'corn' seem to have roots with similar meanings ('greno', meaning grain, and 'ker', meaning to grow), although they are entirely unrelated nowadays.

53. Cf. Chomsky (1977), 67–69.

Chapter 3

1. See Kaplan (1989a,b), selections of which are now reprinted in various collections, e.g., Ludlow (1997); see also Kaplan (1973), (1979), and (1990) for ancestors and descendants of the main monograph. For reasons of space, I have limited this chapter to the two main themes that bear on my application to metaphor; I take up additional topics in later chapters as they apply to metaphor. I also use the notes, more in this chapter than in others, to indicate complications, qualifications, and problems I could not address in the streamlined exposition in the text. Readers unfamiliar with Kaplan's monograph are strongly urged to study the wonderfully clear original to get a sense of the theory as a whole.

2. Where there is no explicit verbalized linguistic modifier for the pure demonstrative, I would argue that one is tacitly supplied in context. As a consequence, *all* complete demonstratives of surface form 'That[Δ]' where Δ stands for a non-linguistic demonstration have as their underlying semantic form: 'That $F[\Delta]$' where 'F' is a placeholder for some predicate.

3. The theory that was criticized was only questionably held by Frege or by any other historical figure. But one positive by-product of the critique was that it stimulated a renaissance in Frege studies, among them and especially relevant to my account, Burge (1977), (1979a). My aim here is not to set the record straight or to argue for one or another theory, but simply to provide necessary background.

4. See Kripke (1980), Donnellan (1966), Putnam (1975), Kaplan (1989a), and Perry (1977).

5. On rigid designation, see Kripke (1980) whose analysis of naming in terms of rigid designation was subsequently criticized by Kaplan (1989a), 492–497; (1989b), 568–576; and Almog (1986).

6. See Burge (1977), 354–362; Perry (1977); Evans (1981), (1982). A classic alternative to perspectivalism would be Russell's (1956) notion of direct acquaintance.

7. For criticism of this strain in the New theory, see Wettstein (1986); Taschek (1987).

8. Which is not to say that each purely conceptual, qualitative representation will necessarily be expressible verbally, say, by an eternal complete definite description.

9. For possible difficulties with this formalization, see Braun (1995).

10. On my choice of terminology "nonconstant" instead of Kaplan's own term "nonstable" see ch. 1, n. 23. Note also that in assigning characters to all expressions across the board, we encounter a major difficulty for Kaplan's theory, as he already notes at the end of (1989a), 558–563. In the case of proper names, and indeed *all* eternal directly referential expressions, "all three kinds of meaning—referent, content, and character—collapse"; hence "proper names do not seem to fit into the whole semantical and epistemological scheme" based on the character-content distinction (562). For different solutions for this problem, see White (1982) and Almog (1984).

11. For this terminology, see Almog (1986).

12. In addition to the differences between direct reference and rigid designation noted in the text, it has also been argued that rigid designation is primarily a metaphysical notion and direct reference, semantic; see Kaplan (1989a); Almog (1986); and, for criticism, Breen (1993).

13. On logical constants, see Salmon (1990); on ordinary proper names, see Kaplan (1989a), 558–563, and Almog (1984).

14. Kaplan (1989a), 494–497 originally proposed this "metaphysical" notion of a singular proposition as a "more vivid" alternative to the possible worlds conception, which he nonetheless continued to employ in the formal Logic of Demonstratives. For subsequent criticism that renders the metaphysical conception inevitable, see Salmon (1990); Soames (1988); and Kaplan's (1989b) own reflections, 579, n. 28.

15. On natural kind and substance terms, see Kripke (1980); Putnam (1975). On the syntax of predicate demonstratives, see Jackendoff (1990), 48–51, and Hankamer and Sag (1976).

16. One might object that the predicate demonstrative should really be analyzed as 'the shape of that' since we demonstrate the given shape by pointing at an object whose shape it is; here the singular demonstrative would be rigid. But this fails to give the correct content for 'is that shape'. Even if the demonstrative 'that' is rigid, its demonstratum might have different shapes in different circumstances.

But the propositional constituent of 'is that shape' is the *actual* shape of the demonstratum. So, 'is that shape' at best could be analyzed as 'is the actual shape of that' or, more explicitly, as 'has the shape S such that it is actually the case that S is the shape of t' where t is the direct referent of the occurrence of 'that' in the context. But even so, it is the shape that is the content of the phrase, and since its extension may vary over circumstances, the predicate is nonrigid, hence not directly referential.

17. I have not, to be sure, said what a property is, but by the same token, I also have not said what an individual is. For now I defer these metaphysical questions.

18. One might also argue that, on pain of regress, there *must* be some predicates that are directly referential, i.e., do not fix their extension or reference by way of satisfaction of a descriptive condition. In the text, however, I focus on the epistemological character of direct vs. indirect reference because this will be the pertinent issue for metaphor in chs. 5 and 6.

19. Despite the difference I shall point out between indexicals and dthat-descriptions, knowledge of the character of the latter is also something its speaker knows solely in virtue of his knowledge of language. However, this is not the case for complete demonstratives whose characters are a function of the characters of their accompanying extralinguistic demonstrations, e.g., visual presentations. Furthermore, if we think of the appearance that constitutes a presentation as something like a picture (as does Kaplan 1989a, 526–527), then the mode by which it "presents" the demonstratum differs sharply from the mode by which a linguistic expression refers to its referent. For some of these differences, see my Goodman-inspired discussion in ch. 7, sec. IX and in Stern (1997). In any case, this is one respect in which complete demonstratives differ from both indexicals and dthat-descriptions.

20. For good surveys of the alternative strategies, see Soames (1986) and Récanati (1996).

21. See Kaplan (1989a), 522–523, 541–553; Kaplan (1989b), 591–598; and the exchange between Crimmins (1992b) and Richard (1993a).

22. I gloss over the fact that only 'I' and 'here' are treated in Kaplan's Logic of Demonstratives as directly referential constants, while 'now' and 'actually' are treated as sentential operators; cf. Kaplan (1989b), 580, n. 30.

23. Optional parameters can be added beyond these four that constitute a minimal (semantic) context, e.g., an addressee for 'you' or temporal indexicals such as 'today' and 'yesterday'.

24. For discussion, see Stern (ms.).

25. For reasons of space I cannot address the question for complete demonstratives in this book, although what I say about dthat-descriptions has definite implications for nonlinguistic demonstrations. In his (1989b), 579–582, Kaplan distinguishes two possible relations of the pure demonstrative 'that' to its "completing" demonstration. (1) 'That' is a functor or operator for which the demonstration is an argument or operand; the demonstration syntactically completes, or saturates, the otherwise empty argument-place in the demonstrative functor.

(Compare, however, Kaplan's second thoughts about his "unfortunate" decision to treat 'Dthat' in "Logic of Demonstratives" as an operator whose argument is a definite description [ibid., 579, n. 29].) (2) From the point of view of semantics, 'That' is an autonomous, well-formed, lexically complete, singular term (like a constant) but in need of a pragmatic interpretation on each of its occurrences. The demonstration, like a stage direction, plays this pragmatic role, facilitating the assignment and thereby completing the interpretation. I shall not pursue the issue here, but related questions will arise for dthat-descriptions below.

26. Kaplan (1989a), 490; on Husserl and demonstratives, see Smith (1981), (1982).

27. Although I have found some variation among speakers' intuitions, many find sentences like (5) and (7), interpreted as occurring in one context, to be not simply false but ungrammatical. For discussion of this alternative applied to demonstratives, see Braun (1996) and below. Note also that cross-contextual statements can be informative regardless of whether the characters of their indexical elements are the same or different. (4) is uninformative and trivial, as we originally observed, only when the whole sentence occurs in one context (as one naturally assumes). However, split between two contexts, especially ones that are remotely separated over time, (4) might be as informative as (5).

28. Much more would obviously have to be said in defense of this as a general strategy to explain the informativeness of utterances containing (exclusively) proper indexicals; I offer one such defense in Stern (ms.).

29. See David Braun (1996), who proposes a second argument for positing representational differences in the characters of complete demonstratives that turns simply on the truth-value, and not cognitive significance, of demonstrative sentences. Consider an utterance of (*) 'That is larger than that', where the speaker demonstrates in a single context one object for the first occurrence of the demonstrative and a different thing for the second occurrence. Since the two occurrences of 'that' have the same linguistic meaning, if linguistic meaning determines character, they must also have the same character. But one character in the same context determines the same content. How, then, can (*) ever be true?

30. Note that Kaplan distinguishes the "Fregean Theory of Demonstra*tions*" from the "Fregean Theory of Demonstra*tives*."

31. Although the typical token, or performance, of a presentation is by a particular agent at a particular time and place, I also assume that the identities of the agent, time, and place (or indeed that the presentation has an agent, time, and place) do not enter into individuation of its type. Kaplan himself argues (1989a, 524ff.) that a presentation does not require an agent and that no particular perspective is essential to it, but he does think that the appearance of each presentation type must be presented *from some perspective*. Hence he takes the standard form for a presentation (P), cited in the text below, to be "The individual that has appearance *A from here now*," adding the last two indexicals. My own view is that it is true that every appearance is seen from some perspective (and that every picture depicts from some perspective), but the representation of that appearance (type) need not include a representation *of* the perspective from which it is seen, or

of the fact that it is seen from a perspective. Hence there is no need to explicitly mention the time and place from which the presentatum is presented, using the indexicals 'here' and 'now'. Furthermore, inclusion of the indexicals 'here' and 'now' in the character of a presentation-type creates a technical problem for Kaplan's solution to Frege's puzzle for demonstratives. Specifically, it can be shown in the Logic of Demonstratives that, where (and only where) they contain indexical or demonstrative constituents, there exist models in which two demonstrations ∂ and β have different characters while their respective complete demonstratives have the *same* character. For details of this argument, see Stern (1979), ch. 4.

32. The superscript Ps in (9) are presentation-quotes: The quotation-name names the presentation described by the enclosed definite description.

33. To be more precise, this is true of the Fregean position as reconstructed in a possible worlds, or points of evaluation, framework like Kaplan's Logic of Demonstratives. The reconstruction is not, however, unproblematic. As Gilead Bar-Elli (pers. comm.) has noted to me, the Kaplanian reformulation analyzes sense (content) as an intension, or function from possible worlds to extensions; for Frege, however, functions belong to the realm of referents, not senses. Thus the reformulation obscures a fundamental Fregean distinction. For further difficulties with the analysis of content and character in terms of functions on points of evaluation, see Braun (1995).

34. This supposition is not without problems. If, as Kaplan suggests in the quotation, we think of an appearance as picture-like, pictures are both syntactically and semantically distinct from descriptions. For discussion of these differences, see, e.g., Goodman (1976) and below, ch. 7, sec. IX. Kaplan alludes to the fact that he is aware of these differences and of the consequent impossibility of "translating" a picture into a description when he says that we "try"—at most try, I would add—to put the picture into words.

35. A similar strategy can be used to solve Braun's problem, raised above in n. 29, posed by multiple occurrences of a simple demonstrative as in 'that is larger than that'.

36. This treatment is not without its problems, e.g., those mentioned in n. 31 and n. 34. On other disanalogies between presentations and descriptions, see Stern (ms.). Nonetheless the Fregean theory of demonstrations is on the right track in its approach to the problem of cognitive significance for complete demonstratives, and it is superior to other accounts, such as Kaplan's indexical theory of demonstrations.

37. Where Φ is already rigid or directly referential, this effect of 'Dthat' will be redundant.

38. See Kaplan's own statements in his (1989b), 581–582 that testify to the pressures pulling him in opposite directions.

39. Two other arguments offered by Kaplan for the simplicity of dthat-descriptions bear mention. First, he argues that "'dthat' was intended to be a surrogate for a true demonstrative, and the description which completes it was intended to be a surrogate for the completing demonstration," to which he adds

parenthetically: "a 'pointing,' being extralinguistic, could hardly be a part of syntax" (1989b, 581). But even if one is skeptical about the possibility of incorporating pointings and gestures into syntax, the relevant notion of demonstration is not the gesture but the presentation, and, on the Fregean theory of demonstrations, presentations can be assigned a syntax. Second, although Kaplan's main reason for denying that 'Dthat' is an operator is to avoid the conclusion that the Dthat-description is *propositionally* or *content*-wise complex, once we distinguish character from content, it is not obvious why syntax should mirror content rather than character. Differences in character, as much as in content, can make a difference in "semantical form"—so long as the latter is not identified with *propositional* form. Indeed, given Kaplan's own identification of characters with the bearers of cognitive significance and logical truth—in contrast to content, which is the bearer of metaphysical properties like necessity and contingency—one would expect syntax to display the semantic structure of character and not that of content.

40. Further support that the characters of dthat-descriptions are syntactically structured is to be found by comparison with complex demonstratives of the form 'that F'. For discussion of similarities and differences between the two classes of expressions, see Neale (1993); Richard (1993b); Higginbotham (1988); Davies (1982b); Taylor (1980); and Braun (1994).

41. The dilemma has its origins, perhaps, in Kaplan's original invention of 'Dthat' in his (1989b) as an attempt to capture the semantically significant features of Donnellan's idea of the referential use of a definite description. One way out of the dilemma would be to treat the dthat-description as lexically complex but syntactically simple. (Cf. Richard 1986.) Let the lexicon contain a rule for generating expressions—e.g., if Φ is a primitive expression in L, then 'Dthat[Φ]' is also—each of which would count as a primitive for purposes of syntax and semantics, i.e., as an expression whose semantic value is not a function of the values of its parts and their mode of construction. But there are a number of difficulties with this solution. (1) It is implausible to deny that dthat-descriptions have constituent syntactic structure. Co-referential (and co-extensive) terms can be intersubstituted within their scope preserving the reference (extension) of the whole, and transparency is the very mark of constituent syntactic structure. (Note that the extensionality of dthat-descriptions follows from the fact that their direct referent is always the individual *actually* denoted by the constituent description. Despite their extensionality, different factors legislate against the possibility of quantifying into dthat-descriptions.) (2) The possible worlds semantics framework makes it difficult if not impossible to mark this distinction, given the provable equivalence of the characters of 'Dthat[Φ]' and 'The x: AN[Φx]'—and the undeniable fact that the latter is syntactically complex. One might try to gloss this second problem by conceding the limitations of the formal system. And in fact these conflicting elements are the result of an attempt to construct a *lexical representation* to express a *use* of language, thereby creating new representational structure not already present in the expression whose *use* is being modeled. However, glossing the difficulty does not solve it.

42. I am indebted here to Mark McCullagh for this analogy and its moral.

Chapter 4

1. On nominative metaphors, which I argue are derived from predicative metaphors, see below, ch. 6, sec. VI. As with predicate demonstratives (see ch. 3, sec. III), I also want to extend the idea of direct reference from singular terms interpreted metaphorically to general terms interpreted metaphorically. On the idea that metaphors may "directly" refer to or express properties (just as singular demonstratives directly refer to individuals), see below, ch. 5, sec. VI.

2. See Black's comment that such an interpretation would "produce an effect of paradox and provoke a demand for justification" (1962, 40)—i.e., bafflement or incomprehension. Black also notes the community-relative status of associated commonplaces, and hence of metaphorical interpretations. However, his example—"men who take wolves to be reincarnations of dead humans will give the statement 'man is a wolf'" (ibid.) a different interpretation—is not clear. Does he mean that, with such a belief, 'man is a wolf' would metaphorically mean that (each?) wolf is a reincarnated human?

3. Searle (1993), 105; on the role of "stereotypes" in meaning, see Putnam (1975).

4. See Crimmins (1992a), 94–96. Crimmins refers to normal notions and ideas, rather than features, where notions and ideas are mental particulars; my use of his term is not meant to bear his metaphysical commitments. Indeed I am not carefully distinguishing features as attributes of things and as notions or ideas of those attributes. In any case, the normal/idiosyncratic distinction is sociological, not metaphysical: Both kinds of features are publicly shareable, accessible to more than one individual to entertain, and mind-independent. Nor is there one reason or explanation for the "normalcy" of all ideas.

5. Rubinstein (1972), 90–91. The article is rich in many such examples.

6. As Black (1962) already noted; the properties, he writes, "may, in suitable cases, consist of deviant implications established *ad hoc* by the writer" (78).

7. See White (1996), 175–177, to whom I owe both the example and its explication.

8. D'Avanzo (1967), 15; cited in White (1996), 305, n. 9. D'Avanzo is commenting on a letter from Keats to Reynolds of February 19, 1818.

9. For a suggestive survey of types of examples and their respective theories, see Thompson and Thompson (1987).

10. See Stalnaker (1972); (1973), 450; (1974); (1978). Strictly speaking, Stalnaker defines the context set as the set of possible worlds in which the presuppositions are true, not as the presuppositions themselves. For our purposes, we need not commit ourselves to a stand on his particular formal representation of presuppositions; nor need we commit ourselves to Stalnaker's possible worlds analysis of propositions. Cf. also Soames (1982), Kartunnen (1974), and Gazdar (1979), 315–332.

11. Strictly speaking, presupposition is a relation between an agent and a proposition. Here I speak as if the contextual parameter consists of presupposed *properties* rather than propositions. More precisely, what is presupposed is the proposition that certain properties are m-associated with the literal vehicle for the metaphor, the expression Φ that is interpreted metaphorically. We can, however,

define property-presupposition in terms of the primary notion of presupposition whose object is a proposition: If P is a property and Q a proposition, then for any P, any speaker S, and any individual x, P is presupposed by S of x iff there is some Q containing ... Px ... such that Q is presupposed by S. Note that this is not intended as a characterization specifically of metaphorically relevant property-presupposition; i.e., presuppositions involving specifically properties presupposed to be m-associated with the expression under interpretation. For discussion of this condition, see Leezenberg (1995), 169.

12. On the semantic notion, see Strawson (1952), 175ff.; van Fraassen (1978). The semantic conception of presupposition was troubled by a number of problems that led to the rise of the pragmatic notion: e.g., the unclear relation between presupposition and entailment, the difficulty distinguishing conventionally and conversationally induced presuppositions, and the projection problem. Although the pragmatic notion rejects logical entailment as the defining source of presuppositions, it retains the insight of the semantic notion that presupposition is a function of the expressions used on the occasion.

13. The pragmatic and semantic notions are not, then, incompatible. That a presupposition is semantically required may be one reason it is pragmatically required for the appropriateness of the utterance, although not all pragmatically necessary presuppositions are semantically necessary.

14. See Stalnaker (1974), 201–202 on barbershop small talk where the participants pretend not to know the obvious, or so represent themselves, simply in order "to be civil, and to pass the time."

15. Turbayne (1970), 13. See also Hunter (1973), 519: "A metaphor pretends that one thing is something else, thus making an implicit comparison between two things." It is also possible that these views assume the flawed literal deviance thesis.

16. See Stalnaker (1978).

17. Soames (1982), 430–431.

18. Stalnaker (1978), 322–323. This is also an example of the process by which an assertion can change a context, which Lewis (1979) refers to as *accommodation*.

19. Black (1993), 36–41; cf. Goodman (1976), 78–79; (1984), 68.

20. Manns (1977), 174.

21. Contrast this sense of 'making us see or notice' with Davidson's causal account of metaphorical effects in WMM, as discussed earlier in ch. 2, sec. III.

22. In this case, we might say that the speaker did not use his metaphor "teleologically," i.e., as directed to express that particular content. At the other extreme, one might imagine a purely "attributive" (or blind) use of a metaphor to express the content, whatever it might be, that is determined in its context by the character of the metaphor. Most cases of metaphor are, I would think, mixed. The speaker has a content in mind that he uses the metaphor to express, but he is also willing to allow that he will have expressed, or that he will be committed to, whatever additional properties are presented and generated by the same metaphorical character. I return to these issues in chs. 5 and 7.

23. Stalnaker (1973), 449.

24. Cf. Caton (1981).

25. Cf. Soames (1982) on "taking p for granted."

26. Stalnaker (1973), 451. Stalnaker explicates the relation between the utterance and presupposition (and the force of "would") in part by arguing that presupposition is a linguistic or speech disposition. Because of independent worries about the explanatory power of dispositional accounts of language or speech, and the lack of an underlying mechanism for the disposition, I instead focus on the nomic (or conventionally law-like) character of the relation. Both the dispositional and nomic analyses support counterfactual or subjunctive conditional claims about the relation between the utterance and its presuppositions.

27. Here is another way of making the point. The pragmatic notion of presupposition characterizes it both as a propositional attitude and as that which is required for the appropriateness of an utterance. Prima facie we'd say, as does (P2), that p is a presupposition of an utterance u of a sentence s in its context c *because u* would be inappropriate in c unless its respective speaker S actually believed, or represented himself as believing, that p. Instead the claim is that its respective individual speaker S presupposes that p whenever he utters s (which requires p to be appropriate) *because p* is a presupposition of s (which is the case, in turn, because *any normal* speaker of s would presuppose that p). This reverses the order of explanation.

28. See Stalnaker (1973), 451.

29. Strictly speaking (8) is a simile but, as I shall argue in ch. 6, secs. VII–VIII, similes should be analyzed on the same model as metaphors. Hence the difference makes no difference for our purposes.

30. This is one of various kinds of mixed metaphor; for discussion of others, see ch. 5. It should be noted that not all mixed metaphors are inappropriate. A true master of metaphor is able to exploit the prima facie inappropriateness of a mixed metaphor to yield a powerful combination. For some examples, see White (1996), 137–144.

31. In addition, it may not be clear what it means to say that the state is a car. In terms of the notion of exemplification, which I'll develop in ch. 5, it is not obvious that cars (unlike ships) exemplify any property attributable to states or governments.

32. This is another example of Lewis's (1979) idea of contextual accommodation.

33. Of course, the claim is not that *all* metaphorical statements, without exception, have determinate truth-conditions. Like some literal statements, some metaphorical statements also do not have determinate content—and for the same variety of possible reasons: vagueness, incompleteness, ambiguity, and so on. For my view, it is strictly speaking sufficient if there is at least one metaphor with a determinate content.

34. In a Chomskian grammar (circa GB), character roughly corresponds to the semantic level of "logical form (LF)," i.e., those aspects of its meaning that are determined by sentence-grammar. Strictly speaking, LF is narrower and more

finely individuated than character since two co-intensional expressions of constant character have the same character but possibly not the same LF. In any case, LFs, like characters, do not by themselves determine content, truth-conditions, or "semantic representations" (SRs), in Chomsky's terminology. They do, however, in combination with contextual features or the products of other "cognitive faculties." See Chomsky (1977), 163ff.

35. On this example, see White's (1996), 45–49, excellent discussion. White describes such cases as "ambiguity of construal." In a similar vein, he discusses Davidson's example: 'Tolstoy was a great moralizing infant', which he correctly points out admits multiple interpretations. With the apparatus of my theory, we can distinguish the different interpretations by the different scopes of the Mthat-operator, e.g.,

(a) Tolstoy Mthat['was a great moralizing infant']

(b) Tolstoy Mthat['was a']$_i$ great moralizing Mthat['infant']$_i$.

(b) might be equivalently stated as

(b*) Tolstoy Mthat['was an infant'] and a great moralizer

(c) Tolstoy Mthat['was a great']$_i$ moralizing Mthat['infant']$_i$.

(c) might be equivalently stated as

(c*) Tolstoy Mthat['was a great infant'] and a moralizer.

In (b) and (c) I have used subscripts to "link" the superficially separate constituents of the metaphor whose interpretations are dependent on each other. It is an open question whether all such *possible* interpretations can in fact be realized or whether there are constraints that mark one reading and exclude others. On the issue of individuation of metaphors, see ch. 5, sec. III.

36. On this model of metaphor recognition, see ch. 1, sec. I. The sense in which all the alternative characters are made *simultaneously* available is that there is no fixed ordering among them, according to which one character in the metaphor set (such as (14a), the so-called literal character) must be initially entertained and then excluded prior to entertaining alternatives. So, since we can ignore all such ordering, for all theoretical purposes we can think of the alternatives as simultaneously available.

37. Austin (1962), 142–147. For an Austin-inspired approach to semantics, compatible with my argument, see Récanati (1996). I am also indebted to Dan Sperber for raising some of these issues in conversation. However, the difference between the second and third stages is grounds not to assimilate metaphor simply to "loose talk," as Sperber and Wilson (1985/86) propose.

38. Note that in both the literal and metaphorical cases, it would be a mistake to argue that *simply* because the sentence uttered in one context is called "true" and in another context "false," we should assign different contents, or truth-conditions, to the utterances.

39. I am not claiming, I should add, that the truth-predicate is itself relativized. The context-dependent "roughness" of an absolute truth-predicate will be mirrored by a parallel context-dependent "roughness" in the right-hand clause of the Tarskian biconditional that gives its truth-condition.

40. See Evans (1984), Maimonides (1963), Strauss (1952), and ch. 8 below.

41. For a helpful description in similar terms of this process of interpretation, see also White (1996), 80–84.

42. On exemplification, see below, ch. 5, secs. II–III.

43. I emphasize assertion, not because it is the only or the most important use of metaphor, but because it is presently the best understood of the many uses of language. However, it should be emphasized that the very same principles that apply elsewhere in explaining language use apply here; there is no need to appeal to any rules specific to metaphor. Cf. Sperber and Wilson (1995), 237, for a similar moral drawn from their not entirely different explanation of metaphor in terms of relevance.

44. On "Quinean," see Fodor (1983), 107ff. Of course, even with the difference highlighted in this paragraph, the p- and f-presuppositions are far from the kind of input employed by an informationally encapsulated module. If nothing less than the latter is required for semantics, it is not clear that any stage of metaphorical interpretation will pass the test.

45. Very few predicates in the language are this straightforward, with an explicit one- or two-criterion "definition." The predicate may also have other contents or meanings, but I assume that this is uncontroversially one of them.

Chapter 5

1. For examples of metaphor that cannot be neatly forced into the mold of similarity, see Miller (1993) and, in reply, Fogelin (1988).

2. Here I take the terms of similarity to be the referent of the literal vehicle of the metaphor, (namely, the sun) and the referent of the subject term of the sentence (namely, Juliet). See, however, Black (1962, 35) who seems to hold (confusingly) that the relation holds between the metaphorical expression M and its "literal equivalent" L.

3. This clarification disposes of Searle's argument that, since similarity statements entail that each of the terms of the similarity relation possess the shared property, the comparison theory cannot account for metaphors that express properties that are true of the subject of the statement but only *believed* to be true of the referent of the vehicle of the metaphor (or, even worse, are known to be false of the referent, though they are part of the stereotype of the term). Searle charges that the similarity theory should (contrary to fact) count all such metaphors false. For a different reply, see Fogelin (1988), 43–45. On my view that different metaphors may indeed have different grounds, the ground of these "stereotypical" metaphors is not similarity at all but features in the stereotypical characterization. Hence these counterexamples do not necessarily count against the similarity thesis as a ground for *some* (but not all) metaphors.

4. On the primacy of metaphorical predications, see below, ch. 6, sec. VI. Some authors recognize the distinction between similarity as a ground of metaphor and the logical form of metaphors but have no way of articulating it; see, e.g., Skulsky (1986). Most psychologists of metaphor fail to attend to the distinction at all, although, in all fairness, they are more concerned with *how* we understand or

comprehend metaphors—i.e., the *processes* we use—than with *what* is being processed, the nature of the knowledge or competence, be it content or character, the so-called *task*.

5. For replies to many objections to similarity theories of metaphor, see Fogelin (1988), 33–68.

6. The author of the example is R. P. Blackmur, cited by Beardsley (1962/1981), 110.

7. Fogelin (1988), 62, who calls this widely cited objection the "reversibility argument," credits it originally to Monroe Beardsley; for a recent statement of the objection, see Moran (1989), 93, who states (erroneously, as I shall argue next): "resemblance and similarity are both symmetrical relations: If *A* resembles *B*, then *B* resembles *A*. Hence, if metaphor were some kind of assertion of resemblance, we should be able to reverse any of the parts without loss or change of meaning." As Beardsley (1962/1981) originally formulated the objection, it was aimed against the claim that metaphors *are* (elliptic) statements of similarity or comparison (or elliptic similes). However, the objection applies even apart from that additional assumption. It should also be noted that Beardsley's formulation of the "reversal" is not true to form: The "reversal" of 'this man is a lion' is not 'this lion is a man' but 'a lion is this man', just as the reversal of 'this man is like a lion' would be 'a lion is like this man'. The whole noun phrase, not just its head, must be reversed. The same confusion over reversibility runs through the literature; see, e.g., Glucksberg and Keysar (1990).

8. The asymmetry of similarity statements was, interestingly, already noted by the rabbis of the Talmud. The fifth-century Babylonian sage Rava argues that a day of rain is "greater than the day of the Mosaic revelation" based on the scriptural prooftext "My discourse [i.e., the Mosaic revelation] shall come down like the rain" (Deut. 32, 2). Rava explains: in a similarity statement, one term is "dependent on" or subordinate to the other: The small one (i.e., the less important, more peripheral case) is dependent on the great one (i.e., the prototype or central case). Here, then, rain, which occupies the predicative position, must be more central, important, or prototypical than the Mosaic revelation, which is in the subject position, thus subordinate to what fills the predicative position. See BT *Ta'anit* 7a.

9. Similarity is a special case of a "matching function" that measures the degree to which two objects, represented as sets of features, match each other depending on measures of their common and distinctive features, weighted according to their relative salience and according to their relative importance. Formally, the matching function f for the similarity of a and b [$s(a,b)$] can be stated as

(MF) $s(a,b) = f(A \cap B, A-B, B-A)$

or, more specifically, as the linear combination, or contrast,

(CFM) $s(a,b) = \Phi f(A \cap B) - \partial f(A-B) - \beta f(B-A)$

where the function f is a measure of the salience of the features in A and B; Φ, ∂, and β are parameters marking the relative importance of the shared and distinctive features; $A \cap B$ are the features shared by A and B; and $(X-Y)$ are the features distinctive of X.

10. See Fogelin (1988). For an instructive, and perhaps the earliest, attempt to apply Tversky's work to metaphor, see Kittay (1982).

11. Formally: $s(a, b) = \Phi f^B(A \cap B) - \partial f^A(A-B) - \beta f^B(B-A)$. Where the feature has either high salience in *both* A and B (in which case, it will be judged that a and b are literally similar) or low salience in *both* (in which case, the two will be judged not similar), Tversky's and Ortony's similarity equations make the same predictions.

12. A second criterion of metaphoricity for Ortony is *attribute inequality*, the fact that in many metaphors or nonliteral similarity statements the A and B features are drawn from different domains. It cannot, then, be (literally) the *same* or the *identical* attribute that is common to the subject and referent; at best *similar* attributes are shared or matched. Attribute inequality, Ortony suggests, either enhances the salience imbalance or sometimes contributes to judgments of metaphoricity in place of increased salience of the B features (Ortony 1979, 168–169).

13. In emphasizing the direct role of salience in their account, I am not disagreeing with G&K's own stress on the structure of metaphors as class-inclusion statements. With that claim I entirely agree, although I take it to be a matter of the logical form of metaphors rather than the nature of the ground—and that is my concern here. For the most recent version of their account, see now Glucksberg (in press).

14. G&K (1990) do not refer, as I do, to inference to mark the difference. They write that the one can be "paraphrased" as the other or that the metaphorical predication is "available" (7) for metaphorical but not literal comparisons. I would argue that, for truth-relevant purposes, the two are equivalent and that the function of 'like' is sometimes presuppositional or aspectual. For reasons of space, I cannot pursue this here. However the disanalogy is described, the difference is significant.

15. See Peirce (1955), 102 and Goodman (1976), 52. For a not unrelated idea, see also Henle (1958) and Alston (1964), (1980).

16. A few comments: (1) As indicated in the text, I depart from Goodman whose nominalism forces him to take exemplification to be reference to labels rather than properties. For discussion of difficulties with his nominalism in this connection, see Stern (1988); I assume that properties, if not unproblematic, are unavoidable. (2) Goodman introduces exemplification to account specifically (though not exclusively) for the symbolic and referential properties of works of art; my use of the notion is not meant to imply that all metaphors are works of art. (3) Although Goodman discusses both exemplification and metaphor, it has been only recently that he has attempted to put them together; see his (1984), 61–65.

17. See also Goodman's refusal to supply "general instructions how to determine what a work exemplifies" (Goodman 1978, 172).

18. On the significance for metaphor of the display involved in exemplification, see below, ch. 7.

19. Note that this is *not* to deny an underlying resemblance relation. Insofar as the metaphor is true and all things possess the properties they exemplify, Juliet

and the sun will resemble each other in having P. However, this similarity is a consequence rather than a ground of the metaphorical interpretation.

20. It goes without saying that this analysis of the passage is meant merely to illustrate how our account applies to an actual example; more sensitive and better-informed readers are invited to offer better explications of the text.

21. Goodman (1984), 83.

22. For yet another sun-metaphor, see the example from *Antony and Cleopatra,* discussed earlier in ch. 5, sec. I and in White (1996), 175–177.

23. See Brooke-Rose (1958), 209.

24. Wittgenstein (1980), 15.

25. One difference between the two is that for exemplification metaphors the exemplified properties must be true of the exemplifying object; not so for features in normal notions, some of which (e.g., stereotypical features) may be false of the literal referent.

26. Goodman (1976), 71–72. Although my idea of exemplification/sampling is adopted from Goodman, he did not, at least initially, connect his idea of family-transfer with the schema-relativity of sampling. For later thoughts associating the two, see Goodman (1984), 63–69.

27. Cf. White (1996), 80–83 on this example.

28. See ch. 1, sec. III (i); ch. 4, n. 35.

29. See White (1996), 43ff. on this example. Note that 'great' is an attributive adjective; hence it cannot be interpreted, even metaphorically, independently of a (explicit or implied) noun it modifies.

30. On this example, see again White (1996), 58f.

31. For further discussion of this metaphor see ch. 7 below. Although it is not obviously based on exemplification, it is an extended metaphor; for further discussion, see section IV below. The question-marks prefacing the two metaphorical expressions in 1–12 mark my uncertainty whether these should be identified as metaphors.

32. One might consider this passage a mixed metaphor but, again, with the proviso that not all mixed metaphors are awkward or unacceptable. Here there is no interpretive difficulty moving from one to the other metaphor, in part because they are interpretively independent.

33. See Grandy (1987) and Kittay and Lehrer (1981).

34. See Kittay and Lehrer (1981), 31–63 (reprinted as ch. 7, 1 of Kittay 1987); Tirrell (1989), Lakoff and Johnson (1980), Lakoff and Turner (1989), Sweetser (1990), and White (1996), among others.

35. The other main determinant of the meaning of a word in semantic field theory is its set of paradigmatic relations: its relations to other words, either like or unlike in meaning, with which it can co-occur in the same linguistic context, hence that belong to its same grammatical category; e.g., synonyms, antonyms, hyponyms, converses, parts and wholes, and contraries. Exemplification-schemas consisting

of contraries are one example of paradigmatically related words, although our schemas can vary with context more than the standard cases of paradigmatically related words. In any case, the description of paradigmatic relations, and the fields they partition, as "semantic" is not straightforward. Even where the paradigmatic relations are relatively stable across utterances, and where knowledge of the partitioned lexical groups is shared within the linguistic community, knowledge of this is not specific to the language faculty, unlike syntax and semantic character. Therefore, without drawing a sharp analytic-synthetic distinction, it is not clear how to distinguish such knowledge from other community-wide empirical background knowledge or presuppositions. For this reason, I treat this knowledge as contextual but utterance-invariant. Metaphorical interpretations based on utterance-invariant contextual knowledge also remain relatively constant across utterances; their speakers "carry" their knowledge of these lexical fields with them from utterance to utterance, furnishing them with ready-made schemas to interpret certain metaphors exemplificationally. On these "routinized" metaphors, see below, ch. 8, sec. III.

36. In *Aspects*-style transformational grammar, thematic relations were expressed by the subcategorization rules of the base; see Chomsky (1965), 90–106. On the connection between Kittay's syntagmatic relations and thematic roles, see also Ludlow (1991).

37. There has been relatively little specific discussion of verbs interpreted metaphorically, but see Torreano (1997), who follows Glucksberg and Keysar's (1990) model of metaphorical comprehension. She does not, however, discuss the role of thematic roles in metaphorical interpretation.

38. The verb might also take an instrument, and indeed it is not impossible that in (10) the prepositional phrase is instrumental rather than locational. This difference does not, however, affect my argument.

39. I owe some of these examples to Margalit and Goldblum (1995). See also White's (1996, 90–92) critical presentation of Beardsley's (1962, 295) criticisms of John Crowe Ransom, who, following I. A. Richards's terminology, had proposed that the underlying vehicle in Shakespeare's metaphor 'Mark how the blood of Caesar follow'd it/ As rushing out of doors ...' (*Julius Caesar* III, ii, 178) is a page rushing out of doors, shifting away from the blood, which is (in Richards's sense) the tenor. Beardsley attacks Crowe (and Richards) for their "idiosyncratic" choice, or invention, of a page who is obviously not to be found in the actual lines of the poem. White uses this discussion to motivate his own idea that metaphorical interpretations are underdetermined by the meanings of their words; that is to say, in our terminology, that the characters of the expressions interpreted metaphorically, or metaphorical expressions, do not, independently of their extralinguistic context (i.e., presuppositions) determine their content (in a context). I would add that both Crowe and Beardsley seem to be right in part. Crowe correctly sees that the metaphor 'rushing out of doors' requires an Agent as thematic role, hence some person, such as a page. Beardsley correctly sees that this requirement does not uniquely determine a single (kind of) person (or noun phrase referring to a person) to discharge the thematic role. To that degree, 'page' as opposed to 'householder' is undetermined and, if you will, idiosyncratic. But

Beardsley fails to mention that *some* person (or noun phrase) is necessary. Insofar as 'page' is sufficient to play the role and the role must be discharged, the choice is not idiosyncratic.

40. Kenner (1959), 87; cited by Brooke-Rose (1958), 206. Note also Brooke-Rose's comment that the verb metaphor "only changes a noun implicitly. As Professor Kenner says, 'we aren't calling a ship a plough'" (ibid., 207). On the contrary, this is precisely how the verb metaphor determines its thematic argument. Cf. also White (1996), 272, n. 31 and Nowottny (1962), 56–57 for similar readings.

41. Cf. Jackendoff (1983).

42. See Lakoff and Johnson (1980), Lakoff (1987), Lakoff and Turner (1989), Turner (1987), Sweetser (1990), and Lakoff (1993).

43. For some brief comments, see Stern (1982) and, for a judicious critical review, M. S. McGlone's chapter in Glucksberg (in press).

44. See Jackendoff and Aaron (1991), 324.

45. I am glossing over many differences between our accounts concerning the semantic status of metaphorical interpretation. Rather than say that we substantively disagree, it would be more correct to say that we address different kinds of phenomena involving metaphor. Terminology aside, their concern is with issues I regard as pragmatic: issues that bear on the presuppositions that ground particular metaphors in context. Unlike Lakoff, I see no incompatibility between the role of networks in the interpretation of metaphors and classical semantic theory (within which I include my theory).

46. My own "metaphorical expressions" (of the form 'Mthat[Φ]') are, of course, terms of art.

47. G&K use "prototype" or "prototypical" where I use "exemplar." In the psychological literature, the former refers to feature-representations relevant to the evaluation of typicality judgments about categories, the latter to perceived individuals that are members of categories. To avoid theoretical complications with the former, and to emphasize the parallel to exemplification where the exemplifying object is an individual, I have shifted to the latter term. Note also that when G&K write, e.g., that "to refer to someone as a Demjanjuk *alludes* to the original war criminal, *and also* makes metaphorical use of his name" (1993, 410) or that "metaphor vehicles can have two referents simultaneously" (ibid., 412), they are unsuccessfully attempting, for lack of theoretical vocabulary, to distinguish the two kinds of reference involved in exemplification. Similarly, their failure to distinguish the question of the logical form of metaphors from the question of the role of similarity and exemplification in the generation of metaphorical properties leaves it very unclear how they would analyze, say, verbs used metaphorically. In order to recast them in the class-inclusion form, they would run into the same kinds of problems that face comparison theorists. For a brief discussion, see now Glucksberg (in press), ch. 3. However, if we distinguish logical form from grounds like exemplification, we can claim, on the one hand, that verb-metaphors also exemplify or sample certain actions or events (types) and, on the other, that their (one-place) predicative logical form is an independent matter.

48. See Lakoff (1993), 231; cf. Lakoff and Turner (1989).

49. So "exemplification" is the answer to Lakoff's question: "How is it possible for one kind of thing (a general situation) to be metaphorically categorized in terms of a fundamentally spatial notion like 'confining' " (1993, 236)?

50. A similar sort of loose generalization of the term "metaphor" to include all mappings is to be found in Lakoff's use of the ACTIONS ARE SELF-PROPELLED MOVEMENTS metaphor in step 3. The metaphorical force of this mapping emerges only when one takes into account the destination (thematic) argument of "movements" that metaphorically expresses the purpose of an action (e.g., making progress toward one's end is moving forward). Once one drops this element of the thematic relation, it is not clear that much that is metaphorical remains in the mapping.

51. By the same token, G&K do not always sufficiently acknowledge the role of systematic networks (like those described by Lakoff). For example, they admit that 'has a crumbling foundation' in the sentence 'the theory's foundation is crumbling' does not itself refer to a superordinate category; it only "implicitly acknowledges" that theories belong to the superordinate categories of structures (G&K 1990, 420). But without something like networks, the question arises of how one identifies relevant or appropriate but only implied superordinate categories.

52. Lakoff may assume that the SPECIFIC is physical (rather than psychological) because of his narrow conception of the nonmetaphorical or literal: namely, "those concepts that are not comprehended via conceptual metaphor" (1993, 205) and instead are understood directly by way of our "physical experiences," our sensorimotor experience of space, body and orientation, social relations, and our "culture" (a notion Lakoff never explains; see Lakoff and Johnson 1980, 56ff.; Lakoff 1993, 78ff.) Again, he writes: "As soon as one gets away from concrete physical experience and starts talking about abstractions or emotions, metaphorical understanding is the norm," suggesting that the metaphorical/nonmetaphorical distinction is to be drawn along the lines of these different subject-matters or domains and, in particular, that the subject matter of the literal is the physical or sensory. If metaphorical mappings are at bottom mappings from the non-metaphorical, that may also be why Lakoff assumes that something physical (or known by sensorimotor abilities and skills) is necessarily meant by 'jail' in its literal meaning. For reasons of space, I shall not discuss Lakoff's conception of the literal. For some discussion of its empiricist and associationist orientation, see Jackendoff (1983) and Jackendoff and Aaron (1991). Indeed the deepest difference between Lakoff's and Jackendoff's respective approaches to these issues lies in the difference between the kinds of cognitive mechanisms (empiricist vs. rationalist) that they take to be employed in metaphorical interpretation.

53. Cf. also Keysar and Glucksberg (1992), 652ff.; Gibbs (1992b).

54. See Keysar and Glucksberg (1992), 651–653; Gibbs (1994); and Glucksberg (in press), especially ch. 5 by M. S. McGlone.

55. Here I use the word "catachresis" as does Black (1962), 33, n. 8, without its negative connotations of misuse.

56. For discussion of this use of metaphor in science, see Boyd (1993).

57. Compare G&K's statement that in ordinary languages that have names for superordinate categories, the category referred to by a metaphor, e.g., 'a jail' in 'my job is a jail' "can be described by a list of distinguishing features but it is difficult to enumerate these features exhaustively" (1990, 410). The point is not just that it is "difficult" to enumerate its membership conditions, but that we lack sufficient *understanding* to do so.

58. Two other prima facie analogous problems of applied metaphor might be mentioned here. One is the use of metaphors to describe the expressive properties of works of art. It is widely acknowledged that its metaphorical character is essential to artistic expression; Goodman indeed makes metaphorical exemplification a necessary condition of expression. On the other hand, it is also assumed that expression-claims, e.g., 'the painting is sad [expresses sadness]', are truth-valued; hence that they have propositional content, and so what they say ought to be equally expressible in literal language. Although this problem appears similar to the case of theological metaphors, I am not convinced they ought to be treated the same way. Unfortunately, I do not yet have an explanation for this problem. A second case is the use of metaphors to describe phenomenologically charac-terized psychological states, especially in literature; on this topic, see Denham (1998).

59. Alston (1980), 139. The argument presented here is more or less Alston's although I have made no attempt to be faithful to all details of his exposition.

60. For a similar kind of argument, see my discussion of Max Black's cognitive autonomy theory of metaphor in ch. 7. There I argue that it is possible to capture the distinctive metaphorical information by character-istic information. Depend-ing on one's theology, that may also be possible for theological metaphors.

61. Strictly speaking, no creature or created thing could exemplify these prop-erties, since exemplification implies possession. The "pointing" must be less direct.

62. On the individuation of properties expressed by metaphors, see ch. 6, sec. III.

63. Pascal (1966), 112 (no. 270); cf. also 105 (no. 255), and 205 (no. 302).

Chapter 6

1. The qualification is not vacuous; for an argument that there are grammatical constraints on metaphorical interpretation, see Stern (1983).

2. For simplicity, where Φ consists of the copula 'is' followed by a definite de-scription (e.g., 'is the sun'), I treat it as a one-place predicate. I also assume that names in predicative position function like predicates rather than singular terms. Therefore, in 'Quayle is no Kennedy', I take the proper name to be predicative, as in 'is a Kennedy', and to express a property as its propositional content. I shall return below to proper names in nominative position where the story is different.

3. I owe the phrase to Cohen (1990). My four kinds of incompetence are not exhaustive; Cohen assures me that there are always 613 ways to get things wrong.

4. Kaplan (1979), 402–403. The first approach is usually attributed to Montague-Scott, the second to Frege.

5. I am indebted to Michael Byrd, many years ago, for the example, and to Charles Parsons, also many years ago, for discussion of the subject of these paragraphs. On metaphors and counterfactuals, see also Tormey (1983) and Margalit and Goldblum (1995).

6. See Stalnaker (1968), (1976); and for a different but related account (to which I owe the idea of contraction) Levi (1977). Nothing in my solution depends on a particular theoretical account of counterfactuals.

7. There has been virtually no discussion of the behavior of metaphors in indirect discourse or the attitudes. One exception is L. J. Cohen (1993) who argues that, because metaphorical interpretation is "preserved" from oratio recta to oratio obliqua, a metaphor cannot be a speech act ("metaphorizing") and it cannot be explained by speech act theory. He does not, however, discuss the problems discussed below that arise in moving from direct to indirect discourse. For criticism of Cohen, see Lamarque (1982), Martinich (1984), and also White (1996), 188–189. Although I agree with White's desideratum that the content of the metaphor in the belief- or indirect-discourse report must be the same as its content when it occurs in its original (reported) assertive utterance, I see no reason to conclude that all such reports are "decidedly peculiar, or jokey" or "highly perverse" (188).

8. See Kaplan (1989a), 555, n. 71 on the *pseudo de re*.

9. I ignore for now whether a report *in other words* (than those of the original utterance), with a different character, but that nonetheless expresses the same content, suffices for a true report. I'll assume that the same general position, whatever it turns out to be, that applies to the question of how far a literal report can deviate from the reported utterance will apply to metaphor.

10. See Kaplan (1989a), 510–512, on "monsters," operators whose operands are characters and shift the context to which the characters apply. Cf. also Richard (1982) and Salmon (1986), 27–44, for examples of tense operators where it does appear that some interpretations must be relativized to contexts other than the speaker's; and Récanati (1996, 1997) for extended discussion of the problem of context-shifting. Despite Récanati's qualifications of Kaplan's theory, none of his counterexamples violates the general principle because of which Kaplan bans monsters.

11. Where the speaker already has similar enough, if not the same, presuppositions as the subject of his report, their interpretations of the metaphor will, of course, ipso facto be the same or close enough. This is not infrequently the case, and not only with more or less dead metaphors. See my discussion in ch. 8 of "routinized metaphors" that have live, productive characters that apply to their contexts to yield their respective contents, but that "carry" their contexts along with them from utterance to utterance.

12. The idea of insulated presuppositions is analogous to Barwise and Cooper's (1981) notion of nonpersistence. A nonpersistent statement is a statement that holds in a situation s but possibly not in a larger situation s' extending s. A set of presuppositions c_s is insulated iff there is some assertion s that is interpretable in c_s but not in a larger set of presuppositions $c_{s'}$ that contains c_s as a proper part.

13. Ibid. Here Fogelin assumes that metaphors are figurative comparisons or likenesses; hence his reference to likeness claims.

14. On the semantics of 'good' and similar adjectives, with special attention to their context-dependence, see Kamp (1975) and Bartsch (1987).

15. See Fogelin (1988), 91, n. 9. Fogelin ignores the fact that where the truth-values of utterances of the same sentence differ, so must their truth-conditions or propositional contents. He (correctly) wishes to sever shift of reference from shift of meaning, but does not allow for the possibility of shift of propositional content.

16. The literal and metaphorical contents of the expression (under its respective interpretations) are different properties, but they are not different *kinds* of content. Nor are the two kinds of truth—metaphorical truth (the truth of an utterance under its metaphorical interpretation) and literal truth (the truth of an utterance under its literal interpretation)—different *kinds* of truth (whatever that would mean).

17. See Washington (1992) and Carpintero (1994). If the value is not identical to the displayed token, it may be the type of that token.

18. Jakobson (1960).

19. Searle (1993); cf. Fogelin (1988), 38ff.

20. Throughout this section I am indebted to conversation with Patti Nogales, who first pointed out to me Fogelin's problematic passage. See her discussion of the argument in Nogales (1999), 183–185.

21. On metaphorical reference, see Berg (ms.).

22. See Kaplan (1973) on blind and directed pointings.

23. For a different view of the relation, see White (1996), 234–245.

24. Fogelin (1988), 28, proposes that "Aristotle seems to be using the term 'metaphor' in a broad generic sense as a way of indicating that similes are also figures of speech," i.e., that "metaphor" here refers to the whole class of figures. I know of no other passage in Aristotle where he unequivocally uses "metaphor" in this broad sense, and, other than the fact that this reading supports Fogelin's own view, it is also far from the best interpretation of the passage in question. Therefore, I'll stick with the narrow meaning of "metaphor" and what Aristotle seems to be literally, and insightfully, arguing.

25. For classic expressions of this view, see Cicero (1942) 3.38.156–39.157 and Quintilian (1922) Bk. VIII, vi, 8–9, who explicitly say that metaphors are "shorter" similes. Among recent authors, the best defense of the (sophisticated) position is Fogelin (1988).

26. For reasons that will immediately become clear, this claim is not identical to the stated claim in ch. 5, although it captures the correct idea behind the formulation.

27. Like any assertion, that of a metaphor "makes" presuppositions, among them, those necessary for its interpretability in its context including the

comparison-judgment through which the property that is metaphorically expressed is determined. In this sense, we might say that metaphorical utterances 'make' comparisons, not that those comparisons are either a causal effect of the utterances or their contents, what they assert.

28. On Fogelin's use of "elliptic," see also his explanation (1988), 45; clearly it is not syntactic or linguistic ellipsis. On "like" as a hedge, see Lakoff (1973).

29. See Goodman (1976) and Fogelin (1988), who both assume that there is one class of figures. Note that the figures or tropes do not exhaust the forms of non-literal interpretation, such as ellipsis, e.g., Dylan Thomas's 'a grief ago' that should probably be interpreted as elliptical for 'a period of grief ago', or 'the sun is very hot today' (pers. comm., James McCawley) that should be interpreted as 'the air heated by the sun is hot today'.

30. Cohen (1975), 670.

31. Grice (1975), 71. My italics.

32. Searle (1993), 108–109. My italics.

33. Fogelin (1988), 9–10.

34. On complex figurative statements, see Berg (1988), who does not develop the following argument but to whose imaginative examples I am indebted for suggesting the argument to me.

35. Further evidence that irony is postsemantic is the strong effect of intonation and tone on irony. Irony is also often taken to be an expression of feeling, attitude, or evaluation—unlike metaphor that is not associated with a specific feeling or attitude. On the difference between irony and metaphor, see also Winner (1988), 32–34; Winner and Gardner (1993); Gibbs (1993); and Sperber and Wilson (1981).

36. Following my practice throughout this book, I do not include under the heading "semantic" the pragmatic, use, or speech act theories of Searle, Fogelin, Grice, Cooper, Ted Cohen, and others. Because of our very different conceptions of semantics, I also don't attempt to do justice to the older generation of theories like those of Black, Beardsley, Henle, or Richards. No one, of course, has a monopoly on the term "semantics" but the issue is the character of the explanatory theory, and I assume that this difference will be acknowledged even by those who insist that the aforementioned theories ought to be called "semantic."

37. Matthews (1971); Levin (1977); and to some extent Beardsley's later versions of his theory in (1976), (1978).

38. See Beardsley (1978); also Katz (1977), 13–22; Levin (1977); Mack (1975); Matthews (1971).

39. Cohen and Margalit (1972), 735; see also Cohen (1993) for a later version of the same idea.

40. On the virtues of "the method of cancellation" as opposed to "the method of multiplication" in semantic theory more generally, see Cohen (1993), 61–64.

41. Cohen (1993) claims that "lexical entries for a natural language can draw no clear distinction between features that are supposed to be 'purely linguistic' and features that are supposed to represent common knowledge or commonly

accepted beliefs" (75); as evidence, he cites the lexicographical practices of the *Concise Oxford Dictionary*. Although I am sympathetic to worries about a sharp analytic-synthetic distinction, it is not obvious that it parallels the dictionary-encyclopedia distinction or that dictionary entries should be taken as authoritative evidence of the mental lexicon insofar as it is part of linguistic competence.

42. I am indebted here to Judy Feldmann for raising this issue.

43. Kittay (1987); all in-text parenthetic page references for the remainder of this section are to this work. For an introduction to semantic field theory, see Lehrer (1974) and Grandy (1987).

44. See Kittay's repeated statements that her semantic features include empirical and pragmatic considerations, e.g., 50, 56–57, 81–82, 91, 140. On the semantic status of semantic field theory in general, see Grandy (1987).

45. At the end of her account, Kittay herself seems to acknowledge that not all metaphors in fact do involve some kind of incongruity, even pragmatic incongruity. To account for the non-incongruous examples, she proposes another principle (or principles, the "general" and "specific independence of applicability conditions" principles) according to which an utterance is ambiguous, or polysemous, with its literal and metaphorical interpretations. It remains unclear to me why, having made this explicit concession, Kittay continues to assert that incongruity is a necessary condition for being a metaphor.

46. The example originates in Reddy (1969); see also Beardsley (1978) and, for criticisms of Beardsley similar to those I level against Kittay, Stern (1983).

47. It should be noted that linguistic, or semantic, anaphora is entirely intra-sentential or sentence-internal. Although there is a rich literature on the linguistic constraints on anaphoric relations, especially on disjoint anaphoric reference, we have relatively little theoretical understanding of how cross-sentential anaphora works. The two should not be assimilated to one model.

48. Two further problems with Kittay's analysis should be mentioned. (1) Even though she claims that literal incongruity is a necessary condition for recognition and interpretation of a metaphor, Kittay acknowledges that it is not sufficient. What, then, would be sufficient (given incongruity) on her account? Kittay proposes the following "alternative conditions": "if the utterance was *intended* to be understood metaphorically or if it is *possible to attribute* a metaphorical interpretation—appropriate to the context—to the utterance" (148). It is difficult to see how these criteria do not beg the question. (3) In cases of truly novel metaphor, Kittay supposes that the topic domain may be unarticulated, at least conceptually; instead of conceptual units, the terms for the constituents in the topic domain must represent "relatively discrete experiential phenomena"(170). Exactly how the Expressibility Principle can make these nonconceptual phenomena verbally explicit requires considerably more explanation that Kittay offers. Apart from the question of how one can *map* one semantic field onto a second if it is non-conceptualized, it is also hard to see how there can be incongruity or contradiction between two fields, one of which is unarticulated and nonconceptual.

49. See Grandy (1987) and Kittay (1987), 230–257.

50. Cf. Kittay (1987), 171, 175–176, 233ff.

51. In some passages Kittay seems to suggest that the point of her project is not, as I have been assuming, to show how it is possible to *supplement* our received conception of semantics with semantic field theory in order to construct a theory of metaphor, but to jettison the received conception. In reply to Davidson, she counters: "Second order discourse [which includes metaphor] also has a deep structure ... which will not submit to the logical form of first order discourse," and "truth-theoretic semantics ... will give the logical form or deep structure only of sentences interpreted in their first-order meaning" (141–142). These remarks suggest that a theory of second-order meaning like metaphor must reject, or replace, truth-theoretic semantics (at least for that purpose).

52. Of course, the fact that Kittay can *formalize* the function (see 144–145, 172–175) does not itself show that the function is semantic, nor does the formalization per se explain it.

53. I am indebted here to Jesse Prinz for discussion.

54. On this, see below, ch. 7, sec. III.

55. Cf. Bergmann (1982).

56. On this recurring theme in theoretical linguistics, see Chomsky (1965), (1980), and Higginbotham (1982).

57. Of course, there is the obvious difference that knowledge of the contextual parameters for the indexicals (the time, place, speaker, etc.) is generally shared and accessible to all ordinary speakers, whereas knowledge of the presuppositions necessary for metaphorical interpretation may, as Aristotle noted, sometimes require "genius." Likewise, there are obvious differences between individuals' capacities to produce metaphors and their capacities to comprehend them. But all this is a matter of knowledge of context rather than knowledge of metaphorical character.

58. I am indebted here, and throughout this reply, to extremely helpful comments by Roger White.

Chapter 7

1. The example originates with Merleau-Ponty, but I learned of it from Danto (1978). Alternative accounts that do not take 'swallow' to be metaphorical might exploit the causal powers of the sound or phonetic properties of the word, or take it as a pun or clang-word in Freud's terminology. In stipulating that (1) is a metaphor, I do not wish to dismiss but merely to bracket the identification question.

2. A similar example, reported in Rubenstein (1972), 92, concerns a writer "who gave ample evidence of the presence of intense unconscious castration anxiety." After submitting an article to a prestigious magazine, he was asked by the editor to cut his article, a request to which the writer reacted with inordinate rage. Rubinstein hypothesizes that the writer "read the letter [of the editor] as request-ing him not to cut (i.e., shorten) the article but to cut (i.e., to cut off) the ARTICLE (i.e., his penis and/or testicles)." Thus his violent reaction was in per-fect accord with his fear.

3. For a different but not incompatible interpretation of this passage, see T. Cohen (1997).

4. Cf. also Wayne Booth's "catchfish" example in Booth (1978).

5. Ibn Ezra (1975); cited in Septimus (ms.). The English translation is Septimus'. On Ibn Ezra's theory of metaphor, see now Fenton (1997).

6. Houseman (1933), quoted and criticized in Brooks (1965b).

7. Vickers (1988), 743.

8. See Hobbes (n.d.) I, 5; Locke (1975), III, X, 34.

9. For a similar argument, see Davidson (1984), 261.

10. The phrase "cognitive autonomy" was coined, I believe, by Margalit (1970). Proponents include Richards (1936), Brooks (1965b), and Black (1962).

11. Another argument against literal paraphrasability as a requirement on all metaphors would focus on the *de re* metaphors we discussed in ch. 5, sec. VI.

12. Cf. Bergmann (1982).

13. On this motif, see Burge (1979b), (1989).

14. Cavell (1967), 79–80, where he also quotes Empson.

15. I owe the phrase to Margalit and Goldblum (1994).

16. I do not mean to suggest that there do not remain serious problems as to how to individuate contexts and contents. If we identify the context of a metaphor with a set of presuppositions, strictly speaking two contexts are the same if and only if they contain the very same presuppositions; yet one context can be an extension of another and, in practice, certain differences are frequently ignored. Similar problems infect the idea of "one interpretation." Thus when literary theorists cite examples of poetic metaphors that have admitted, or borne, repeatedly new "interpretations" over time as evidence for the claim that a (good?) metaphor is inexhaustible—that each time we read it, we find something new in it—it is not absolutely clear that these cases should be described as ones in which the metaphor has *one,* always extendible, or endless, interpretation in one context or different, though related, interpretations, each of which is finite, relative to different contexts of interpretation. For a further obscurity, see my later discussion in section V of the problems in distinguishing the presemantic presuppositions that determine the schema to which a metaphor belongs from the semantically relevant presuppositions about the features sorted by the schema.

17. I borrow the term "directions" from Strawson (1950); cf. White (1996), 40–41.

18. Cf. Boyd (1993) and White (1996), 180, 307–308 (to whom I also owe the term "embryonic" meaning).

19. As Jim Higginbotham once observed to me (pers. corr.), if it were true that, for each paraphrase of a metaphor, we could always *explicitly* identify yet another feature not part of the paraphrase, then why not just tack that feature onto the paraphrase? And if we can't make it explicit, why think that the paraphrase as it stands is not complete?

20. For an example of how the Gricean conversational maxims that govern assertion accomplish this, see above, ch. 4, sec. IV.

21. Cf. White (1996), 40–41.

22. Or so it was reported in *Time Magazine*, February 18, 1985.

23. For this example, I am indebted to Ted Cohen who assures me that he only mentions but never uses it. Both the Nigerian 'bedbug' and American (or W. C. Fieldsian) English 'chickadee' are, I assume, partly dead metaphors although I also assume that they are both still recognized as metaphors, i.e., their interpretations are context-dependent and "computed" from metaphorically relevant, culturally fixed presuppositions. It is also worth observing, along the lines of our remarks in ch. 1, sec. III (iv), that, for our present purposes, namely, to illustrate a fixed, fairly determinate content, such partly dead metaphors are preferable to completely "live" ones whose interpretation would require a great deal of contextual stage-setting in order to fix their content determinately.

24. Chomsky (1959).

25. See Scheffler (1991); the terminology is his.

26. See, however, Scheffler (1991), 12, n. 23. Note also that, if one insists on conflict, the prior beliefs or expectations (e.g., the belief that [literally] Juliet is not the sun) will also generally be tacit.

27. What of so-called twice-true metaphors that involve no anomaly? For an example like Ted Cohen's 'no man is an island', one might argue that its interpretation proceeds by negating what we would understand by the metaphorical interpretation of an utterance of 'a man is an island'. The surprise would then be linked to the simple atomic statement rather than its negation, along the lines suggested in the text. For utterances like the tautologous 'men are men', possibly it is also the antecedent *unlikelihood* that we could ever say something true *and* informative about the content of the one expression using the other that makes the metaphorical interpretation surprising—if it is. In either case, whatever the exact explanation, it seems clear that it must revolve around the character of the metaphor.

28. It is not certain that this network is based on presuppositions involving a symbolic relation like exemplification; it may be historically linked to the not-much-earlier invention of printing and the growing power and elitism based on literacy.

29. On this passage, see also Tirrell (1989) and Thompson and Thompson (1987), 169f. On the book-metaphor elsewhere in Shakespeare, see also White (1996), 65ff. and above, ch. 5, sec. III.

30. Cf. Tirrell (1989) on the "expressive commitment" of a metaphor: a "commitment to the viability and value of a particular way of talking about something" (22), and Moran (1989) on "framing."

31. Cf. also Ricoeur (1978), 144.

32. Likewise, Davidson (1986) denies that there is an answer to the question "How many facts or propositions are conveyed by [say] a photograph?" because this is a "bad question. A picture is not worth a thousand words, or any other

number. Words are the wrong currency to exchange for a picture"—or, for the same reason, for a metaphor (263).

33. Moran (1989), 94–101; it is not clear whether Moran himself endorses the conclusion of the argument or simply formulates it to motivate Davidson's move. Davidson hints at the argument when he denies, for example, that the aspects and resemblances that a metaphor makes us see are "definite cognitive content that its author wishes to convey and that the interpreter must grasp if he is to get the message" (1986, 262). The term "irresistible" is borrowed from Wayne Booth (1978), 54.

34. Moran's target is more specific than my presentation indicates. He takes the irresistibility of metaphor to be a problem specifically for those who *both* think of metaphor paradigmatically as successful metaphor, where the success involves "framing" together the terms of the metaphor, *and* also hold that metaphors make assertions.

35. The fact that metaphors and pictures "bring" an indefinite, even potentially infinite, number of things "to our attention" should count no more against their possession of content or meaning than the fact that the most literal of utterances can likewise bring such an unbounded number of things to our attention counts against *their* having a meaning or content. Nor is it clear why the fact that even the simplest of pictures typically has multiple truth-conditions—i.e., the fact that its "truth-conditions" do not correspond one-to-one to the truth-condition of a single atomic sentence—should count against its *having* truth-conditions or propositional content, as Davidson seems to suggest. For a similar, and similarly obscure, argument in a different context, see Fodor (1975), 180.

36. See Thompson and Thompson (1987), 163–165.

37. Davidson (1986), 253, my italics. Cf. also the critical remarks on this passage by Thompson and Thompson (1987), 175–176.

38. Indeed there is some evidence that metaphors that play exclusively on purely visual appearances, e.g., 'the moon is a sickle', are those that are least connected to a family. So, to the extent to which a metaphor is based just on a visual property, the less pictorial it is in our sense, where the pictorialness of the metaphor is due to its place in a network.

39. Goodman (1976), 130–232; Haugeland (1981); see also Peacocke (1986), (1989) and, for a thorough overview, Rollins (1989).

40. For further discussion, see Stern (1997). Throughout the last four paragraphs, I am indebted to discussion and correspondence with David Hills. As I noted in ch. 3, n. 34, this difference between pictures and discursive symbols or descriptions has significant implications for Kaplan's use of descriptions as a model for non-linguistic presentations (which he thinks of as something like pictures), hence for his attempt to use dthat-descriptions as a model for complete demonstratives. For further discussion, see Stern (forthcoming). It is this difference that possibly lies behind Kaplan's (1989a) comment that we can only "*try* to put the appearance into words" (526). The same difference, I should note, legislates against certain analyses of pictorial metaphors, such as Goodman (1976), that require replication for transfer; on this, see below, ch. 8, sec. I and Stern (1997).

41. One should not conclude that pictures are necessarily more "finely" individuated than descriptions. "Fineness" may vary along different dimensions. For an argument that the characters of two co-denoting descriptions (in a digital schema) might differ while visual presentations (that would belong to an analog/pictorial schema) of the co-referent would not, see Peacocke (1989), 306–312.

42. I am indebted for this bit of scholarship to W. R. Johnson and Christopher Bobonich. Another, more contemporary, example would employ 'Superman' and 'Clark Kent' as metaphors (ignoring problems of reference of fictional names).

43. These limitations of the notion of character clearly reflect the same general limitations of the notion of character for the semantics of proper names; see above, ch. 3. Furthermore, to the extent that intuitive, philosophical differences like this are not expressed by our formal apparatus, this is a sample of the limitations of formalization in semantics; on this theme, see Kaplan (1989a,b).

44. See also our third criterion for the individuation of metaphors in ch. 5, sec. III, according to which a metaphor is individuated by its character, content, and context (including network). Although the linguistic type of the metaphor is presumably individuated by its character, to capture its full cognitive significance a finer criterion like the third is necessary.

45. Cavell (1967), 79. For a similar suggestion, see also Moran (1989), 112. I should add that, as with complete demonstratives that can have richer and poorer presentational contents, there is a continuum of differences of degree to which metaphors are sensitive to their respective schemas and, correspondingly, a continuum of differences in their respective character-dependent cognitive significances.

46. This is the qualifying complication to which I alluded earlier in section IX. Furthermore, in Stern (forthcoming), I argue that a similar situation obtains for the complete demonstrative whose character is a function of the character of its presentation component, which is also pictorial, i.e., dense, analog, or nondiscursive. Hence our knowledge of neither the character of a complete demonstrative nor that of a metaphorical expression is knowledge only of descriptional, propositional language. But if we are willing to grant complete demonstratives a kind of knowledge or cognitive value associated with their character, metaphors deserve equal treatment.

47. Note that, despite his official hard line, Davidson (1978) himself admits in his unguarded moments that "of course [what we notice or see by a metaphor] *may* be [propositional] and, when it is, it usually may be stated in fairly plain words" (263, his italics). See also White's (1996) discussion of Davidson's claim (194–203). I agree with White that the propositional content of the metaphor in its context— roughly, what he suggests would be captured by the "School Comprehension Test"—does not "capture the creative significance of the use of metaphor" (201), but I would argue that we can begin to capture it by taking into account the perspective carried by its metaphorical character (relative to its networks) and that such additional significance in no way excludes the propositionality of metaphorical content. I am indebted here, too, to correspondence with White.

48. Cf. Crimmins (1992a), 44ff., and Richard (1990). Note that Crimmins's counterexamples are of different "ways of thinking" associated with proper names. Since the characters and contents of co-directly referring proper names (and other simple eternal expressions) are equivalent, it is not surprising that there is no systematic individuation of ways of thinking by their characters or linguistic types. Indeed Crimmins's counterexamples are really no more than a good illustration of the inadequacy of Kaplan's character/content-based semantic theory to account for proper names or other simple eternal expressions.

49. Although it is not possible to individuate *arbitrary* ways of thinking by characters or linguistic types, it may be possible to do so for specific kinds. For example, it may be possible to appeal to Crimmins's (1992a) idea of *normal notions* associated with, or individuated by, the characters of some expressions, relative to linguistic communities, to account for the special role of the indexicals in explaining human actions. Associated with the first-person indexical 'I' would be a normal notion of an agent that consists (among other things) of a set of dispositions to act in certain ways in certain circumstances; associated with 'now' would be a normal notion that consists of a set of dispositions to perform actions that their agents believe should be performed at certain times at those same times (or at times believed to be the same as those times). Note that if it is a normal notion that is associated with, and individuated by, the character of the indexical that does the explanatory work, the indexical will be just as essential as it would be if it were its character proper doing the explanation. Of course, individual speakers may associate their own idiosyncratic notions with individual tokens or occurrences of the indexicals in addition to the normal notion.

50. Searle (1993), 102.

Chapter 8

1. Lakoff (1993), 241.

2. See especially Goodman (1984), 55–70.

3. See Gibbs (1984), (1989); Dascal (1987), (1989); Récanati (1995).

4. See Johnson (1981), 171–177.

5. By the "merely possible" I mean the nonactual possible since, on most theories of possibility, the actual (and necessary) is also possible. Depending on one's theory, the fictional may belong here as well. I take "actual" and "real" to be synonymous (as well as "actually," "really," and "in fact") and the present to be the temporal analogue of the actual.

6. Here I treat "actual" as an indexical; see Lewis (1978); and Kaplan (1989a). On the actual truth of metaphors, see also Goodman (1976), 68–80.

7. This argument, and understanding of the literal, also rests on another confusion that assimilates literal language to the language of empirical descriptions, histories, and scientific theories, and metaphors to the language of fictions, myths, and other imaginative texts. See, e.g., Cassirer (1946), 83–99. For a more sophisticated account of metaphor as a kind of "fictional language," see Walton (1993).

Works of the former kind are in turn assumed to be, in some clearly recognized but hard-to-make-precise sense, "about" reality, the real world, actuality, or what is true in fact. Fictions, myths, and other products of the imagination are not "about" reality or actuality in the same way, and those who mistakenly interpret them as if they were descriptions of the actual or real world should, in turn, be criticized for taking them literally or "at face value" (Margalit and Halbertal 1992, 84). This division is confused. Metaphors are not themselves works like myths, fictions, or imaginative texts, although those works may employ metaphors. But they may also (and obviously do) employ literal language, and they are no less mythic or fictional or imaginative if they are written in literal language from start to finish. On the other hand, scientific descriptions and explanations of the actual world, as well as histories, also make frequent use of metaphors, and they are no less truth-valued for their metaphorical mode of expression. In sum, the literal-metaphorical distinction cannot be collapsed onto distinctions between the scientific and the mythic/fictional or between the actual and imaginative.

8. We also find recognition of the literal meaning of a text among the Greeks, as well as differences between levels of meaning or interpretation, say, in Philo and among the Neo-Platonist exegetes. See Lamberton (1986) for references. Among Jewish exegetes, there is arguably no notion specifically of the literal, although the idea of *peshat* is sometimes presented as if it were literal meaning. However, a more accurate explication of the term would be "contextual meaning"; see Kamin (1986) and Halivni (1991) and references therein. Throughout this discussion I ignore many differences of detail among medieval authors. For more detailed discussion, see Evans (1984).

9. Evans (1984), 107, 110.

10. Evans (1984), 107.

11. See Margalit (1978); Partee (1984).

12. The qualifier "actual" is meant to rule out cases, like some examples Searle cites, in which the physical world is *imagined* to be different than it actually is. Since I do not believe that any of us have clear intuitions about what we would say or mean under those circumstances, I think it makes good methodological sense to limit ourselves to the actual.

13. Similar remarks apply to the various deconstructionist philosophers and literary theorists who deny the literal-nonliteral distinction on the grounds that all meaning is relative to a culture or various kinds of beliefs and presuppositions. True as this observation surely is, all it shows is that all meaning is presemantically context-dependent; the literal-nonliteral distinction, which hinges on semantic and postsemantic context-independence, is an entirely separate matter.

14. The examples are Henle's (1958), 186ff.

15. See Asch and Nerlove (1960); Winner and Gardner (1978).

16. Contrast the account of children's metaphors in Cohen and Margalit (1972), 723. Although I cannot discuss children's metaphors at length here, suffice it to say that the empirical facts are not unambiguous. One must distinguish both mistaken overgeneralizations from metaphorical uses and adult observers' projections

of their own metaphorical interpretations onto the children's uses from the children's uses themselves. On projections, see below.

17. See Alston (1964), 99.

18. Compare our earlier distinction in ch. 3, sec. VII between the *de facto* context-sensitivity of dthat-descriptions and the *de jure* context-sensitivity of indexicals.

19. I owe this phrase to Charles Parsons.

20. Alston (1964), 99–103; on the continuum picture, see also Lycan (1984), 200.

21. Compare Kaplan's (1989a), 560–562, idea of dubbing a new word in the language: We announce: "Let That[Δ] be A" where there is also a change of character.

22. This would be more in line with our conception of meaning as constraint—i.e., as character. However, the traditional notion of meaning did not distinguish character and content, and once we do distinguish them, it not evident that it must be character rather than content that is literal. Clearly ordinary language is no guide here.

23. See Cassirer (1946), 83–99 who argues that there is a distinct kind of metaphorical as opposed to literal perception. On this view, the metaphorical-literal distinction, like the a priori–a posteriori distinction, would mark a difference, say, in our modes of justification; for an apparently similar idea, see Black (1993).

24. Rousseau (1966), 12–13. Rousseau's own explanation of his claim rests on the assumption that the function of language is primarily to express "passions," and that ideas, in addition to words, are what are transferred.

25. Ibid., 12.

References

Almog, J. (1984), "Semantical Anthropology," in P. French, T. Uehling, and H. Wettstein, eds., *Midwest Studies in Philosophy* IX (Minneapolis, University of Minnesota Press): 479–489.

Almog, J. (1986), "Naming without Necessity," *Journal of Philosophy* 83: 210–242.

Alston, W. P. (1964), *Philosophy of Language* (Englewood Cliffs, N.J., Prentice Hall).

Alston, W. P. (1980), "Irreducible Metaphors in Theology," in E. T. Long, ed., *Experience, Reason, and God* (Washington D.C., The Catholic University of America Press): 129–148.

Aristotle (1984), *Poetics* and *Rhetoric*, in J. Barnes, ed., *The Complete Works of Aristotle*, 2 vols. (Princeton, N.J., Princeton University Press).

Asch, S. (1961), "The Metaphor: A Psychological Inquiry," in M. Henle, ed., *Documents of Gestalt Psychology* (Berkeley, University of California Press): 86–94.

Asch, S. and Nerlove, H. (1960), "The Development of Double Function Terms in Children: An Exploratory Study," in B. Kaplan and S. Wapner, eds., *Perspectives in Psychological Theory* (New York, International Universities Press): 47–60.

Augustine (1958), *On Christian Doctrine*, trans. D. Robertson (Indianapolis, Bobbs-Merrill Publishers).

Austin, J. L. (1962), *How to Do Things with Words* (Oxford, Clarendon Press).

Barsalou, L. W. (1983), "Ad Hoc Categories," *Memory and Cognition* 11: 211–227.

Bartsch, R. (1987), "Context-dependent Interpretations of Lexical Items," in J. Groenendijk, D. De Jongh, and M. Stokhof, eds., *Foundations of Pragmatics and Lexical Semantics* (Dordrecht, Foris Publications).

Barwise, J. and Cooper, R. (1981), "Generalized Quantifiers and Natural Language," *Linguistics and Philosophy* 4: 159–219.

Beardsley, M. (1958), *Aesthetics: Problems in the Philosophy of Criticism* (New York, Hartcourt, Brace).

Beardsley, M. (1962), "Metaphorical Twist," *Philosophy and Phenomenological Research* 22: 293–307; reprinted in Johnson (1981): 105–122.

Beardsley, M. (1976), "Metaphor and Falsity," *The Journal of Aesthetics and Art Criticism* 35: 218–222.

Beardsley, M. (1978), "Metaphorical Senses," *Nous* 12: 3–16.

Berg, J. (1988), "Metaphor, Meaning, and Interpretation," *Journal of Pragmatics* 12: 695–709.

Berg, J. (ms.), "Metaphorical Reference."

Bergmann, M. (1979), "Metaphor and Formal Semantics," *Poetics* 8: 213–230.

Bergmann, M. (1982), "Metaphorical Assertions," *Philosophical Review* 91: 229–242.

Binkley, T. (1976), "On the Truth and Probity of Metaphor," *Journal of Aesthetics and Art Criticism* 33: 171–180.

Black, M. (1962), "Metaphor," in *Models and Metaphors* (Ithaca, N.Y., Cornell University Press): 25–47; reprinted in Johnson (1981): 63–82.

Black, M. (1993), "More about Metaphor," in Ortony (1993a): 19–41.

Blackburn, S. (1984), *Spreading the Word: Groundings in the Philosophy of Language* (Oxford, Oxford University Press).

Booth, W. (1978), "Metaphor as Rhetoric: The Problem of Evaluation," *Critical Inquiry* 5: 49–72.

Booth, W. (1988), *The Company We Keep* (Chicago, University of Chicago Press).

Boyd, R. (1993), "Metaphor and Theory Change: What is 'Metaphor' a Metaphor For?", in Ortony (1993a): 481–532.

Braun, D. (1994), "Structured Characters and Complex Demonstratives," *Philosophical Studies* 74: 193–219.

Braun, D. (1995), "What Is Character?" *Journal of Philosophical Logic* 24: 227–240.

Braun, D. (1996), "Demonstratives and Their Linguistic Meanings," *Nous* 30: 145–173.

Breen, D. (1993), *Rigidity, Essence, and Identity* (Ph.D. dissertation, University of Chicago).

Brooke-Rose, C. (1958), *A Grammar of Metaphor* (London, Secker and Warburg).

Brooks, C. (1947), *The Well-Wrought Urn* (New York, Harcourt Brace, and World).

Brooks, C. (1965a), "Metaphor, Paradox, and Stereotype," *British Journal of Aesthetics* 5: 315–328.

Brooks, C. (1965b), *Modern Poetry and the Tradition* (New York, Oxford University Press).

Burge, T. (1974), "Demonstrative Constructions, Reference, and Truth," *Journal of Philosophy* 71: 205–223.

Burge, T. (1977), "Belief De Re," *Journal of Philosophy* 74: 338–362.

Burge, T. (1979a), "Sinning against Frege," *Philosophical Review* 88: 398–432.

Burge, T. (1979b), "Individualism and the Mental," in P. French, T. Uehling, and H. Wettstein, eds., *Midwest Studies in Philosophy IV: Studies in Metaphysics* (Minneapolis, University of Minnesota Press): 73–121.

Burge, T. (1986), "Intellectual Norms and the Foundations of Mind," *Journal of Philosophy* 83: 697–720.

Burge, T. (1989), "Wherein Is Language Social?" in A. George, ed., *Reflections on Chomsky* (Oxford, Basil Blackwell Ltd.): 175–191.

Carey, J. (1981), *Donne: Life, Mind, and Art* (London and Boston, Faber and Faber).

Carnap, R. (1963), "Autobiography," in P. A. Schilpp, ed., *The Philosophy of Rudolph Carnap* (La Salle, Ill., Open Court): 3–84.

Carpintero, M. G. (1994), "Ostensive Signs: Against the Identity Theory of Quotation," *Journal of Philosophy* 91: 264–275.

Cassirer, E. (1946), *Language and Myth*, trans. S. K. Langer (New York, Dover).

Caton, C. E. (1981), "Stalnaker on Pragmatic Presuppositions," in P. Cole, ed., *Radical Pragmatics* (New York, Academic Press): 83–100.

Cavell, S. (1967), "Aesthetic Problems of Modern Philosophy," in M. Black, ed., *Philosophy in America* (Ithaca, Cornell University Press): 74–97.

Chomsky, N. (1959), Review of *Verbal Behavior*, by B. F. Skinner, *Language* 35: 26–58.

Chomsky, N. (1965), *Aspects of the Theory of Syntax* (Cambridge, Mass., MIT Press).

Chomsky, N. (1968), *Language and Mind*, Enlarged Edition (New York, Harcourt Brace Jovanovitch).

Chomsky, N. (1977), *Essays in Form and Interpretation* (New York, North-Holland).

Chomsky, N. (1980), *Rules and Representations* (New York, Columbia University Press).

Chomsky, N. (1988), *Language and Problems of Knowledge: the Managua Lectures* (Cambridge, Mass., MIT Press).

Cicero (1942), *De Oratore*, vol. 2, trans. H. Racham (Cambridge, Harvard University Press).

Cohen, G. A. (1995), *Self-Ownership, Freedom, and Equality* (Cambridge, Cambridge University Press).

Cohen, L. J. (1985), "A Problem about Ambiguity in Truth-Theoretic Semantics," *Analysis* 45: 129–135.

Cohen, L. J. (1993), "The Semantics of Metaphor," in Ortony (1993a): 58–70.

Cohen, L. J. and Margalit, A. (1972), "The Role of Inductive Reasoning in the Interpretation of Metaphor," in D. Davidson and G. Harman, eds., *Semantics of Natural Language* (Dordrecht, Reidel): 721–762.

Cohen, T. (1975), "Figurative Language and Figurative Acts," *Journal of Philosophy* 72: 669–690; reprinted in Johnson (1981): 182–199.

Cohen, T. (1976), "Notes on Metaphor," *Journal of Aesthetics and Art Criticism* 34: 249–259.

Cohen, T. (1978), "Metaphor and the Cultivation of Intimacy," *Critical Inquiry* 5, 1: 3–12.

Cohen, T. (1983), "Jokes," in E. Schaper, ed., *Pleasure, Preference and Value* (Cambridge, Cambridge University Press).

Cohen, T. (1990), "Figurative Incompetence," *Raritan* 10, 2: 30–44.

Cohen, T. (1997), "Metaphor, Feeling, and Narrative," *Philosophy and Literature* 21: 223–244.

Cooper, D. (1986), *Metaphor* (Oxford, Oxford University Press).

Crimmins, M. (1992a), *Talk about Belief* (Cambridge, Mass., MIT Press).

Crimmins, M. (1992b), "Context in the Attitudes," *Linguistics and Philosophy* 15: 185–198.

Culler, J. (1981), "The Problem of Metaphor," in T. E. Hope et al., eds., *Language, Meaning, and Style: Essays in Memory of Stephen Ullmann* (Leeds, Leeds University Press): 5–20.

Danto, A. (1978), "Freudian Explanations and the Language of the Unconscious," in Joseph H. Smith, ed., *Psychoanalysis and Language* (New Haven, Yale University Press): 325–353.

Danto, A. (1981), *The Transfiguration of the Commonplace* (Cambridge, Mass., Harvard University Press).

Dascal, M. (1987), "Defending Literal Meaning," *Cognitive Science* 11: 259–281.

Dascal, M. (1989), "On the Roles of Context and Literal Meaning in Understanding," *Cognitive Science* 13: 253–257.

D'Avanzo, M. L. (1967), *Keats' Metaphors for the Poetic Imagination* (Durham, N.C., Duke University Press).

Davidson, D. (1967), "Causal Relations," *Journal of Philosophy* 64: 691–704; reprinted in D. Davidson (1980), *Essays on Actions and Events* (Oxford, Oxford University Press): 149–162.

Davidson, D. (1975), "Thought and Talk," in S. Guttenplan, ed., *Mind and Language* (Oxford, Oxford University Press); reprinted in Davidson (1984): 155–170.

Davidson, D. (1978), "What Metaphors Mean," *Critical Inquiry* 5: 31–47; reprinted (in revised form) in Davidson (1984): 245–264.

Davidson, D. (1984), *Inquiries into Truth and Interpretation* (Oxford, Oxford University Press).

Davidson, D. (1986), "A Nice Derangement of Epitaphs," in LePore (1986): 433–446.

Davidson, D. (1995), "Laws and cause," *Dialectica* 49: 263–279.

Davies, M. (1982a), "Idiom and Metaphor," *Proceedings of the Aristotelian Society* 83: 67–85.

Davies, M. (1982b), "Individuation and the Semantics of Demonstratives," *Journal of Philosophical Logic* 11: 287–310.

Davis, S. (1991), ed., *Pragmatics: A Reader* (Oxford, Oxford University Press).

Denham, A. (1998), "Metaphor and Judgments of Experience," in *European Review of Philosophy*, vol. 3, eds., R. Casati and C. Tappolet (Stanford, CSLI Publications): 225–253.

Donnellan, K. (1966), "Reference and Definite Descriptions," *Philosophical Review* 75: 281–304.

Elgin, C. Z. (1983), *From Reference to Reference* (Indianapolis, Hackett).

Elgin, C. Z. and Scheffler, I. (1987), "Mainsprings of Metaphor," *Journal of Philosophy* 84: 331–335.

Evans, G. (1981), "Understanding Demonstratives," in H. Parret and J. Bouveresse, eds., *Meaning and Understanding* (Berlin/New York, De Gruyter): 280–303.

Evans, G. (1982), *The Varieties of Reference* (Oxford/New York, Clarendon Press).

Evans, G. R. (1984), *The Language and Logic of the Bible* (Cambridge, Cambridge University Press).

Fay, D. and Cutler, A. (1977), "Malapropisms and the Structure of the Mental Lexicon," *Linguistic Inquiry* 8: 505–520.

Fenton, P. B. (1997), *Philosophie et Exégèse dans Le Jardin De La Métaphore de Moïse Ibn 'Ezra, Philosophe et Poète Andalou Du XII Siècle* (Leiden, Brill).

Fernandez, J. W. (1986), *Persuasions and Performances: The Play of Tropes in Culture* (Bloomington, Indiana, Indiana University Press).

Fernandez, J. W. (1991), ed., *Beyond Metaphor: The Theory of Tropes in Anthropology* (Stanford, Cal., Stanford University Press).

Fodor, J. (1975), *The Language of Thought* (New York, Thomas Y. Crowell Co.).

Fodor, J. (1983), *The Modularity of Mind* (Cambridge, Mass., MIT Press).

Fogelin, R. (1988), *Figuratively Speaking* (New Haven, Yale University Press).

Fogelin, R. (1994), "Metaphors, Similes, and Similarity," in Hintikka (1994): 23–39.

Frege, G. (1966), "On Sense and Meaning," in P. T. Geach and M. Black, trans. and eds., *Translations from the Philosophical Writings of Gottlob Frege* (Oxford, Basil Blackwell Ltd.).

Frege, G. (1984), "Thoughts," in B. McGuiness (1984), ed., *G. Frege, Collected Papers on Mathematics, Logic, and Philosophy* (Oxford, Basil Blackwell Ltd.); reprinted in Salmon and Soames (1988): 33–55.

Garfield, J. (1987), ed., *Modularity in Knowledge Representation and Natural Language Understanding* (Cambridge, Mass., MIT Press).

Gazdar, G. (1979), *Pragmatics: Implicature, Presupposition, and Logical Form* (New York, Academic Press).

Gibbs, R. W. (1984), "Literal Meaning and Psychological Theory," *Cognitive Science* 8: 274–304.

Gibbs, R. W. (1989), "Understanding and Literal Meaning," *Cognitive Science* 13: 243–251.

Gibbs, R. W. (1990), "Comprehending Figurative Referential Descriptions," *Journal of Experimental Psychology: Learning, Memory, and Cognition* 16: 56–66.

Gibbs, R. W. (1992a), "When is Metaphor? The Idea of Understanding in Theories of Metaphor," *Poetics Today* 13: 575–606.

Gibbs, R. W. (1992b), "Categorization and Metaphor Comprehension," *Psychological Review* 99: 572–577.

Gibbs, R. W. (1993), "Process and products in making sense of tropes," in Ortony (1993a): 252–276.

Gibbs, R. W. (1994), *The Poetics of Mind* (New York, Cambridge University Press).

Glucksberg, S. (in press), *Understanding Figurative Language: From Metaphors to Idioms* (Oxford, Oxford University Press).

Glucksberg, S. and Keysar, B. (1990), "Understanding Metaphorical Comparisons: Beyond Similarity," *Psychological Review* 97: 3–18.

Glucksberg, S. and Keysar, B. (1993), "How Metaphors Work," in Ortony (1993a): 401–424.

Glucksberg, S., Keysar, B., and McGlone, M. S. (1992), "Metaphorical Understanding and Accessing Conceptual Schema: Reply to Gibbs (1992)," *Psychological Review* 99: 578–581.

Glucksberg, S. and Manfredi, D. (forthcoming), "Metaphoric Comparisons," in C. Cacciari, ed., *Similarity: Proceedings of the Workshops of the International Center for Cognitive and Semiotic Studies* (Milano, Italy, Bompiani).

Goodman, N. (1972a), "Sense and Certainty," in *Problems and Projects* (Indianapolis, Hackett): 60–68.

Goodman, N. (1972b), "On Likeness of Meaning," in *Problems and Projects* (Indianapolis, Hackett): 221–230.

Goodman, N. (1976), *Languages of Art*, Second Edition (Indianapolis, Hackett).

Goodman, N. (1978), "Reply to Beardsley," *Erkenntnis* 12: 95–118; reprinted in Goodman (1984): 80–85.

Goodman, N. (1979), "Metaphor as Moonlighting," *Critical Inquiry* 6: 125–130; reprinted in Goodman (1984): 71–77.

Goodman, N. (1984), *Of Mind and Other Matters* (Cambridge, Mass., Harvard University Press).

Grandy, R. (1987), "In Defense of Semantic Fields," in E. LePore, ed., *New Directions in Semantics* (London, Academic Press): 259–280.

Grandy, R. (1990), "Understanding and the Principle of Compositionality," *Philosophical Perspectives* 4: 557–571.

Grice, H. P. (1975), "Logic and Conversation," in D. Davidson and G. Harman, eds., *The Logic of Grammar* (Encino, Cal., Dickenson): 64–75.

Gruber, J. S. (1965/1976), *Studies in Lexical Relations* (Ph.D. dissertation, Massachusetts Institute of Technology; distributed by Indiana University Linguistics Club, Bloomington, Indiana; reprinted as part of *Lexical Structures in Syntax and Semantics* (Amsterdam, North-Holland Publishers).

Hacking, I. (1986), "The Parody of Conversation," in LePore (1986): 447–458.

Halivni, D. W. (1991), *Peshat and Derash* (New York, Oxford University Press).

Hankamer, J. and Sag, I. (1976), "Deep and Surface Anaphora," *Linguistic Inquiry* 7: 391–428.

Haugeland, J. (1981), "Analog and Analog," *Philosophical Topics* 12: 213–225.

Henle, P. (1958), "Metaphor," in P. Henle, ed., *Language, Thought, and Culture* (Ann Arbor, Michigan, University of Michigan Press): 173–195; reprinted in Johnson (1981): 83–104.

Hesse, M. (1987), "Unfamiliar Noises II: Tropical Talk: The Myth of the Literal," *Proceedings of the Aristotelian Society*, supp. volume 61: 297–311.

Higginbotham, J. (1982), "Noam Chomsky's Linguistic Theory," *Social Research* 49, 1: 143–157.

Higginbotham, J. (1988), "Contexts, Models, and Meanings: A Note on the Data of Semantics," in R. M. Kempson, ed., *Mental Representations: The Interface between Language and Reality* (Cambridge, Cambridge University Press): 29–48.

Higginbotham, J. (1989), "Knowledge of Reference," in A. George, ed., *Reflections on Chomsky* (London, Basil Blackwell Ltd.): 159–165.

Higginbotham, J. (forthcoming), "Perspectives on Demonstratives."

Hills, D. (1997), "Aptness and Truth in Verbal Metaphor," *Philosophical Topics* 25, 1: 117–154.

Hintikka, J. (1994), ed., *Aspects of Metaphor* (Dordrecht, Kluwer).

Hintikka, J. and Sandu, G. (1994), "Metaphor and Other Kinds of Nonliteral Meaning," in Hintikka (1994): 151–188.

Hobbes, J. (n.d.) *Leviathan*, ed., M. Oakeshott (Oxford, Basil Blackwell Ltd.).

Hornstein, N. (1984), *Logic as Grammar* (Cambridge, Mass., MIT Press).

Hornstein, N. (1986), "Pragmatics and Grammatical Theory," *Proceedings of the Annual Meeting of the Chicago Linguistic Society* 22: 234–247.

Housman, A. E. (1933), *The Name and Nature of Poetry* (Cambridge, The University Press).

Hrushovski, B. (1984), "Poetic Metaphor and Frames of References, with examples from Eliot, Rilke, Mayakovsky, Mandelshtam, Pound, Creeley, Amichai, and the New Tork Times," *Poetics Today* 5: 5–43.

Hunter, J. P. (1973), ed., *The Norton Introduction to Literature: Poetry* (New York, Norton).

Ibn Ezra, M. (1975), *Kitab al-muhadara wa'l-mudhakara* (Heb: *Sefer ha-'Iyyunim veha-Diyyumim*), trans. and ed., A. Halkin (Jerusalem, n.p.).

Isenberg, A. (1963), "On Defining Metaphor," *Journal of Philosophy* 60: 609–622.

Jackendoff, R. (1983), *Semantics and Cognition* (Cambridge, Mass., MIT Press).

Jackendoff, R. (1990), *Semantic Structures* (Cambridge, Mass., MIT Press).

Jackendoff, R. and Aaron, D. (1991), Review of *More Than Cool Reason: A Field Guide to Poetic Metaphor*, by G. Lakoff and M. Taylor, *Language* 67: 320–338.

Jakobson, R. (1960), "Linguistics and Poetics," in T. Sebeok, ed., *Style in Language* (Cambridge, Mass., MIT Press): 350–377.

Johnson, M. (1981), ed., *Philosophical Perspectives on Metaphor* (Minneapolis, University of Minnesota Press).

Kamin, S. (1986), *Rashi's Exegetical Categorization in respect to the Distinction between Peshat and Derash* (in Heb.) (Jerusalem, Magnes Press).

Kamp, J. A. W. (1975), "Two Theories about Adjectives," in E. Keenan, ed., *Formal Semantics of Natural Language* (Cambridge, Cambridge University Press): 123–155.

Kaplan, D. (1973), "Bob and Carol and Ted and Alice," in J. Hintikka, J. Moravcsik, and P. Suppes, eds., *Approaches to Natural Language* (Dordrecht, Reidel): 490–518.

Kaplan, D. (1979), "Dthat," in P. French, T. Uehling, and H. Wettstein, eds., *Contemporary Perspectives in the Philosophy of Language* (Minneapolis, University of Minnesota Press): 383–400.

Kaplan, D. (1989a), "Demonstratives," in J. Almog, J. Perry, and H. Wettstein, eds., *Themes from Kaplan* (Oxford, Oxford University Press): 481–563.

Kaplan, D. (1989b), "Afterthoughts," in J. Almog, J. Perry, and H. Wettstein, eds., *Themes from Kaplan* (Oxford, Oxford University Press): 565–614.

Kaplan, D. (1990), "Words," *Proceedings of the Aristotelian Society*, suppl. vol. 64: 93–119.

Kartunnen, L. (1974), "Presupposition and Linguistic Context," *Theoretical Linguistics* 1: 181–194.

Katz, J. J. (1977), *Propositional Structure and Illocutionary Force: A Study of the Contribution of Sentence-Meanings to Speech-Acts* (New York, Thomas Y. Crowell Comp.).

Kempson, R. (1977), *Semantic Theory* (London, Cambridge University Press).

Kenner, H. (1959), *The Art of Poetry* (New York, Rinehart).

Keysar, B. and Glucksberg, S. (1992), "Metaphor and Communication," *Poetics Today* 13: 633–658.

Khatchadurian, H. (1968), "Metaphor," *British Journal of Aesthetics* 8: 227–243.

Kittay, E. F. (1982), "The Creation of Similarity: A Discussion of Metaphor in Light of Tversky's Theory of Similarity," *PSA* 1: 394–405.

Kittay, E. F. (1987), *Metaphor: Its Cognitive Force and Linguistic Structure* (Oxford, Oxford University Press).

Kittay, E. F. and Lehrer, A. (1981), "Semantic Fields and the Structure of Metaphor," *Studies in Language* 5: 31–63.

Kripke, S. (1980), *Naming and Necessity* (Cambridge, Mass., Harvard University Press).

Kronfeld, C. (1980/81), "Novel and Conventional Metaphors: A Matter of Methodology," *Poetics Today* 2: 13–24.

Lakoff, G. (1973), "Hedges: A Study of Meaning Criteria and the Logic of Fuzzy Concepts," *Journal of Philosophical Logic* 2: 458–508.

Lakoff, G. (1987), *Women, Fire, and Other Dangerous Things* (Chicago, University of Chicago Press).

Lakoff, G. (1993), "The Contemporary Theory of Metaphor," in Ortony (1993a): 202–251.

Lakoff, G. and Johnson, M. (1980), *Metaphors We Live By* (Chicago, University of Chicago Press).

Lakoff, G. and Turner, M. (1989), *More than Cool Reason: A Field Guide to Poetic Metaphor* (Chicago, University of Chicago Press).

Lamarque, P. (1982), "Metaphor and Reported Speech: In Defence of a Pragmatic Theory," *Journal of Literary Semantics* 11: 14–18.

Lamberton, R. (1986), *Homer the Theologian* (Berkeley, University of California Press).

Langer, S. K. (1942), *Philosophy in a New Key* (Cambridge, Mass., Harvard University Press).

Larson, R. and Segal, G. (1995), *Knowledge of Meaning: An Introduction to Semantic Theory* (Cambridge, Mass., MIT Press).

Leezenberg, M. (1995), *Contexts of Metaphor* (Ph.D. dissertation, Institute for Logic, Language, and Computation, University of Amsterdam, ILLC dissertation series).

Lehrer, A. (1974), *Semantic Fields and Lexical Structure* (Amsterdam, North-Holland).

LePore, E. (1986), ed., *Truth and Interpretation: Perspectives on the Philosophy of Donald Davidson* (Oxford, Basil Blackwell Ltd.).

Levi, I. (1977), "Subjunctives, Dispositions, and Chances," *Synthese* 34: 423–455.

Levin, S. (1977), *The Semantics of Metaphor* (Baltimore, The Johns Hopkins University Press).

Levin, S. (1993), "Language, Concepts, and Worlds: Three Domains of Metaphor," in Ortony (1993a): 124–135.

Levinas, E. (1990), *Difficult Freedom* (Baltimore, Maryland, Johns Hopkins Press).

Lewis, D. (1970), "General Semantics," *Synthese* 22: 18–67; reprinted in Lewis (1983), *Philosophical Papers*, vol. 1 (Oxford, Oxford University Press): 189–229.

Lewis, D. (1978), "Anselm and Actuality," *Nous* 4: 175–188; reprinted in Lewis (1983): 10–21.

Lewis, D. (1979), "Scorekeeping in a Language Game," *Journal of Philosophical Logic* 8: 339–359; reprinted in Lewis (1983): 233–249.

Locke, J. (1975), *An Essay Concerning Human Understanding*, ed. P. H. Nidditch (Oxford, Oxford University Press).

Loewenberg, I. (1975), "Identifying Metaphors," *Foundations of Language* 12: 315–338; reprinted in Johnson (1981): 154–181.

Ludlow, P. (1991), Review of *Metaphor: Its Cognitive Force and Linguistic Structure*, by E. F. Kittay, *Journal of Philosophy* 88: 324–330.

Ludlow, P. (1997), ed., *Readings in the Philosophy of Language* (Cambridge, Mass., MIT Press).

Lycan, W. (1984), *Logical Form in Natural Language* (Cambridge, Mass., MIT Press).

Lycan, W. (1987), Review of *Portraying Analogy*, by J. F. Ross, *Linguistics and Philosophy* 10: 1–18.

Mac Cormac, E. R. (1985), *A Cognitive Theory of Metaphor* (Cambridge, Mass., MIT Press).

Mack, D. (1975), "Metaphoring as Speech Act: Some Happiness Conditions for Implicit Similes and Simple Metaphors," *Poetics* 4: 221–256.

Maimonides, M. (1963), *The Guide of the Perplexed*, trans. S. Pines (Chicago, University of Chicago Press).

Manns, J. (1977), "Goodman on Metaphor," *The Personalist* 58: 173–178.

Margalit, A. (1970), "The Cognitive Status of Metaphors" (in Heb.), (Ph.D. dissertation, Hebrew University of Jerusalem).

Margalit, A. (1978), "The Platitude Principle in Semantics," *Erkenntnis* 13: 377–395.

Margalit A. and Goldblum, N. (1994), "Metaphors in an Open-Class Test," in Hintikka (1994): 219–241.

Margalit, A. and Goldblum, N. (1995), "A Metaphor Game," *Synthese* 104: 299–323.

Margalit, A. and Halbertal, M. (1992), *Idolatry* (Cambridge, Mass., Harvard University Press).

Martinich, A. P. (1984), "A Theory for Metaphor," *Journal of Literary Semantics* 13: 35–56.

Matthews, R. (1971), "Concerning a 'Linguistic Theory' of Metaphor," *Foundations of Language* 7: 413–425.

Miller, G. (1993), "Images and models, similes and metaphors," in Ortony (1993a): 357–400.

Moran, R. (1989), "Seeing and Believing: Metaphor, Image, and Force," *Critical Inquiry* 16, 1: 87–112.

Neale, S. (1993), "Term Limits," *Philosophical Perspectives* 7: 89–123.

Newport, E. L. and Bellugi, U. (1978), "Linguistic Expressions of Category Levels in a Visual-Gesture Language: A Flower is a Flower is a Flower," in E. Rosch and B. B. Lloyd, eds., *Cognition and Categorization* (Hillsdale, N.J., Erlbaum).

Nogales, P. (1999), *Metaphorically Speaking* (Stanford, Cal., CSLI/Cambridge University Press).

Nowottny, W. (1962), *The Language Poets Use* (London, Athlone Press).

Ortony, A. (1979), "Beyond Literal Similarity," *Psychological Review* 86: 161–180.

Ortony, A. (1993a), ed., *Metaphor and Thought,* second edition (Cambridge, Cambridge University Press).

Ortony, A. (1993b), "The role of similarity in similes and metaphors," in Ortony (1993a): 342–356.

Partee, B. (1984), "Compositionality," in F. Landman and F. Veltman, eds., *Varieties of Formal Semantics* (Dordrecht, Foris Publications): 281–311.

Pascal, B. (1966), *Pensées,* trans. A. J. Krailsheimer (New York, Penguin Books).

Peacocke, C. (1986), "Analogue Content," *Proceedings of the Aristotelian Society,* suppl. vol. 60: 1–17.

Peacocke, C. (1987), "Depiction," *Philosophical Review* 96: 383–410.

Peacocke, C. (1989), "Perceptual Content," in J. Almog, J. Perry, and H. Wettstein, eds., *Themes from Kaplan* (Oxford, Oxford University Press): 297–329.

Peirce, C. S. (1955), "Logic as Semiotic: The Theory of Signs," reprinted in *Philosophical Writings of Peirce,* ed., Justus Buchler (New York, Dover).

Perry, J. (1977), "Frege on Demonstratives," *Philosophical Review* 86: 474–497.

Perry, J. (1979), "The Problem of the Essential Indexical," *Nous* 13: 3–21; reprinted in N. Salmon and S. Soames (1988), eds., *Propositions and Attitudes* (Oxford, Oxford University Press): 83–101.

Plimpton, G. (1976), ed., *Writers at Work: The Paris Review Translations,* Fourth Series (New York, Viking).

Preminger, A. (1965), ed., *The Princeton Handbook of Poetic Terms* (Princeton, N.J., Princeton University Press).

Putnam, H. (1975), "The Meaning of 'Meaning'," in H. Putnam (1975), *Mind, Language, and Reality, Philosophical Papers,* vol. 2 (Cambridge, Cambridge University Press).

Pylyshyn, Z. W. (1993), "Metaphorical Imprecision and the "top-down" research strategy," in Ortony (1993): 543–559.

Quine, W. v. O. (1969), "Ontological Relativity," in *Ontological Relativity and Other Essays* (New York, Columbia University Press).

Quine, W. v. O. (1978), "A Postscript On Metaphor," *Critical Inquiry* 5: 161–162.

Quintilian (1922), *The Institutio Oratoria of Quintilian III*, trans. H. E. Butler (London, William Heinemann).

Récanati, F. (1995), "The Alleged Priority of Literal Interpretation," *Cognitive Science* 19: 207–232.

Récanati, F. (1996), "Domains of Discourse," *Linguistics and Philosophy* 19: 445–475.

Récanati, F. (1997), "Context-shifting in Metarepresentations" (Paris, C.R.E.A. Rapports et Documents, Rapport No. 9720, C.N.R.S.).

Reddy, M. (1969), "A Semantic Approach to Metaphor," *Papers from the Fifth Regional Meeting of the Chicago Linguistics Society* (Chicago, University of Chicago-Linguistics Dept.): 240–251.

Reddy, M. (1993), "The Conduit Metaphor: A Case of Frame Conflict in Our Language About Language," in Ortony (1993): 137–163.

Reinhart, T. (1970), "On Understanding Poetic Metaphor," *Poetics* 5: 383–402.

Reinhart, T. (1976), "Patterns, Intuitions, and the Sense of Nonsense," *PTL: A Journal for Descriptive Poetics and Theory of Literature* 1: 85–103.

Richard, M. (1982), "Tense, Propositions, and Meanings," *Philosophical Studies* 41: 337–351.

Richard, M. (1986), "Quotation, Grammar, and Opacity," *Linguistics and Philosophy* 9: 383–403.

Richard, M. (1988), "Direct Reference and Ascriptions of Belief," in Salmon and Soames (1988): 169–196.

Richard, M. (1990), *Propositional Attitudes: An Essay on Thoughts and How We Ascribe Them* (Cambridge, Cambridge University Press).

Richard, M. (1993a), "Attitudes in Context," *Linguistics and Philosophy* 16: 123–148.

Richard, M. (1993b), "Articulated Terms," *Philosophical Perspectives* 7: 207–230.

Richards, I. A. (1936), *The Philosophy of Rhetoric* (London, Oxford University Press).

Ricoeur, P. (1962), *The Rule of Metaphor: Multidisciplinary Studies in the Creation of Meaning in Language*, trans. R. Czerny (Toronto, University of Toronto Press).

Ricoeur, P. (1978), "The Metaphorical Process as Cognition, Imagination, and Feeling," *Critical Inquiry* 5: 143–159; reprinted in Johnson (1981): 228–247.

Rollins, M. (1989), *Mental Imagery: On the Limits of Cognitive Science* (New Haven, Yale University Press).

Rorty, R. (1987), "Unfamiliar Noises I: Hesse and Davidson on Metaphor," *Proceedings of the Aristotelian Society*, supp. volume 61: 283–296.

Rosch, E. (1973), "On the internal structure of perceptual and semantic categories," in T. E. Moore, ed., *Cognitive Development and the Acquisition of Language* (New York, Academic Press).

Ross, J. F. (1981), *Portraying Analogy* (Cambridge, Cambridge University Press).

Rousseau, J-J. (1966), *On the Origin of Language*, trans. J. H. Moran and A. Gode (New York, Frederick Unger).

Rubinstein, B. (1972), "On Metaphor and Related Phenomena," in R. Holt and E. Peterfreund, eds., *Psychoanalysis and Contemporary Science*, vol. 1 (New York, Macmillan): 70–108.

Rumelhart, D. E. (1993), "Some Problems with the Notion of Literal Meanings," in Ortony (1993): 71–82.

Russell, B. (1956), "Philosophy of Logical Atomism," in R. C. Marsh, ed., *Logic and Knowledge* (London, George Allen and Unwin Ltd.): 175–282.

Sadock, J. M. (1993), "Figurative speech and linguistics," in Ortony (1993): 42–57.

Salmon, N. (1986), *Frege's Puzzle* (Cambridge, Mass., MIT Press).

Salmon, N. (1988), "Reflexivity," in Salmon and Soames (1988): 240–274.

Salmon, N. (1990), "A Millian Heir Rejects the Wages of Sinn," in C. A. Anderson and J. Owens, eds., *Propositional Attitudes* (Stanford, Cal., C.S.L.I. Lecture Notes).

Salmon, N. and Soames, S. (1988), eds., *Propositions and Attitudes* (Oxford, Oxford University Press).

Scheffler, I. (1954), "An Inscriptional Approach to Indirect Quotation," *Analysis* 14: 83–90.

Scheffler, I. (1979), *Beyond the Letter* (London, Routledge and Kegan Paul).

Scheffler, I. (1991), "In Praise of the Cognitive Emotions," in *In Praise of the Cognitive Emotions* (New York, Routledge): 3–17.

Searle, J. (1978), "Literal Meaning," *Erkenntnis* 13: 207–224.

Searle, J. (1983), *Intentionality* (Cambridge, Cambridge University Press).

Searle, J. (1993), "Metaphor," in Ortony (1993): 83–111.

Septimus, B. (n.d.), *Maimonides on Language*.

Skulsky, H. (1986), "Metaphorese," *Nous* 20: 351–369; reprinted in J. Garfield and M. Kiteley (1991), eds., *Meaning and Truth* (New York, Paragon House): 582–598.

Smith, D. W. (1981), "Indexical Sense and Reference," *Synthese* 49: 101–127.

Smith, D. W. (1982), "What is the Meaning of 'This'?," *Nous* 16: 181–208.

Snyder, J. (1980), "Picturing Vision," *Critical Inquiry* 7, 4: 499–526.

Soames, S. (1982), "How Presuppositions Are Inherited: A Solution to the Projection Problem," *Linguistic Inquiry* 13: 483–545; reprinted in Davis (1991): 428–470.

Soames, S. (1986), "Incomplete Definite Descriptions," *Notre Dame Journal of Formal Logic* 27, 3: 349–375.

Soames, S. (1988), "Direct Reference, Propositional Attitudes, and Semantic Content," in Salmon and Soames (1988): 197–239.

Sperber, D. and Wilson, D. (1981), "Irony and the Use-Mention Distinction," in P. Cole, ed., *Radical Pragmatics* (New York, Academic Press).

Sperber, D. and Wilson, D. (1985/86), "Loose Talk," *Proceedings of the Aristotelian Society* 86: 153–171; reprinted in Davis (1991): 540–549.

Sperber, D. and Wilson, D. (1995), *Relevance: Communication and Cognition*, Second Edition (Oxford, Basil Blackwell).

Spolsky, E. (1987/88), "The Limits of Literal Meaning," *New Literary History* 19: 419–440.

Spurgeon, C. (1952), *Shakespeare's Imagery and What It Tells Us* (Cambridge, Cambridge University Press).

Stalnaker, R. (1968), "A Theory of Conditionals," in N. Rescher, ed., *Studies in Logical Theory* (Oxford, Blackwell Publishers): 98–112.

Stalnaker, R. (1972), "Pragmatics," in D. Davidson and G. Harman, eds., *Semantics of Natural Language* (Dordrecht, Reidel): 380–397.

Stalnaker, R. (1973), "Presuppositions," *Journal of Philosophical Logic* 2: 447–457.

Stalnaker, R. (1974), "Pragmatic Presuppositions," in M. Munitz and P. Unger, eds., *Semantics and Philosophy* (New York, New York University Press): 197–213.

Stalnaker, R. (1976), "Indicative Conditionals," in A. Kasher, ed., *Language in Focus* (Dordrecht, Reidel Publishing Company): 179–196.

Stalnaker, R. (1978), "Assertion," in P. Cole, ed., *Syntax and Semantics* 9: *Pragmatics* (New York, Academic Press): 315–332; reprinted in Davis (1991): 278–289.

Stern, J. (1979), *Metaphor as Demonstrative: A Formal Semantics for Demonstratives and Metaphors* (Ph.D. dissertation, Columbia University).

Stern, J. (1982), Review of *Contemporary Perspectives on Metaphor*, ed. by M. Johnson, *Journal of Aesthetics and Art Criticism* 40: 231–234.

Stern, J. (1983), "Metaphor and Grammatical Deviance," *Nous* 17: 577–599.

Stern, J. (1985), "Metaphor as Demonstrative," *Journal of Philosophy* 82: 677–710.

Stern, J. (1988), "Metaphor without Mainsprings: A Rejoinder to Elgin and Scheffler," *Journal of Philosophy* 85: 427–438.

Stern, J. (1991), "What Metaphors Do Not Mean," in P. French, T. Uehling, and H. Wettstein, eds., *Midwest Studies in Philosophy,* vol. XVI: *Philosophy and the Arts* (South Bend, Indiana, Notre Dame University Press): 13–52.

Stern, J. (1997), "Metaphors in Pictures," *Philosophical Topics* 25, 1: 255–294.

Stern, J. (1998), "Metaphor and Philosophy of Language," in M. Kelly, ed., *Oxford Encyclopedia of Aesthetics*, 4 vols. (Oxford, Oxford University Press), vol. 3: 212–215.

Stern, J. (2000), "Maimonides on Language and the Science of Language," in R. Cohen and H. Levine, eds., *Maimonides and the Sciences* [*Boston Studies in the History and Philosophy of Science*] (Dordrecht, Kluwer).

Stern, J. (ms.), "A Little of 'This' and a Little of 'That'."

Strauss, L. (1952), *Persecution and the Art of Writing* (Glencoe, Ill., The Free Press).

Strawson, P. F. (1950), "On Referring," *Mind*: 59: 320–344.

Strawson, P. F. (1952), *Introduction to Logical Theory* (London, Metheun).

Sweetser, E. (1990), *From Etymology to Pragmatics: Metaphorical and Cultural Aspects of Semantic Structure* (Cambridge, Cambridge University Press).

Sweetser, E. (1992), "English Metaphors for Language: Motivations, Conventions, and Creativity," *Poetics Today* 13: 705–736.

Swinburne, R. (1992), *Revelation: From Metaphor to Analogy* (Oxford, Oxford University Press).

Taschek, W. (1987), "Content, Character, and Cognitive Significance," *Philosophical Studies* 52: 161–189.

Taylor, B. (1980), "Truth Theory for Indexical Languages," in M. Platts, ed., *Reference, Truth, and Reality* (London, Routledge): 182–198.

Thompson, A. and Thompson, J. O. (1987), *Shakespeare, Meaning, and Metaphor* (Iowa City, University of Iowa Press).

Tirrell, L. (1989), "Extending: The Structure of Metaphor," *Nous* 23: 17–34.

Tirrell, L. (1991), "Reductive and Nonreductive Simile Theories of Metaphor," *Journal of Philosophy* 88: 337–358.

Tormey, A. (1983), "Metaphors and Counterfactuals," in J. Fisher, ed., *Essays on Aesthetics: Perspectives on the Work of Monroe C. Beardsley* (Philadelphia, Temple University Press): 235–246.

Torreano, L. A. (1997), *Understanding Metaphorical Use of Verbs* (Ph.D. dissertation, Princeton University).

Turbayne, C. (1970), *The Myth of Metaphor* (Columbia, S.C., University of South Carolina Press).

Turner, M. (1987), *Death Is the Mother of Beauty* (Chicago, University of Chicago Press).

Tversky, A. (1977), "Features of Similarity," *Psychological Review* 84: 322–352.

van Fraassen, B. (1978), "Presupposition, Implication, and Self-reference," *Journal of Philosophy* 65: 136–151.

Vickers, B. (1988), "Rhetoric and Poetics," in Quentin Skinner et al., eds., *Cambridge History of Renaissance Philosophy* (Cambridge, Cambridge University Press).

Walton, K. (1993), "Metaphor and Prop-Oriented Make-Belief," *European Journal of Philosophy* 1: 39–57.

Washington, C. (1992), "The Identity Theory of Quotation," *Journal of Philosophy* 89: 551–581.

Weinstein, S. (1974), "Truth and Demonstratives, " *Nous* 8: 179–184.

Wettstein, H. (1986), "Has Semantics Rested on a Mistake?" *Journal of Philosophy* 83: 185–209.

White, R. W. (1996), *The Structure of Metaphor: The Way the Language of Metaphor Works* (Oxford, Basil Blackwell).

White, S. (1982), "The Language of Thought," *Pacific Philosophical Quarterly* 63: 347–365.

Williams, E. S. (1977), "Discourse and Logical Form," *Linguistic Inquiry* 8: 101–139.

Williams, J. (1976), "Synaesthetic Adjectives: A Possible Law of Semantic Change," *Language* 52: 461–478.

Winner, E. (1988), *The Point of Words: Children's Understanding of Metaphor and Irony* (Cambridge, Mass., Harvard University Press).

Winner, E. and Gardner, H. (1978), "The Development of Metaphoric Competence: Implications for Humanistic Disciplines," *Critical Inquiry* 5: 123–141.

Winner, E. and Gardner, H. (1993), "Metaphor and Irony: Two Levels of Understanding," in Ortony (1993): 425–445.

Wittgenstein, L. (1980), *Culture and Value*, trans. P. Winch (Chicago, University of Chicago Press).

Wollheim, R. (1980), *Art and Its Objects*, second edition (Cambridge, Cambridge University Press).

Zangwill, N. (1991), "Metaphor and Realism in Aesthetics," *Journal of Aesthetics and Art Criticism* 49: 57–62.

Index